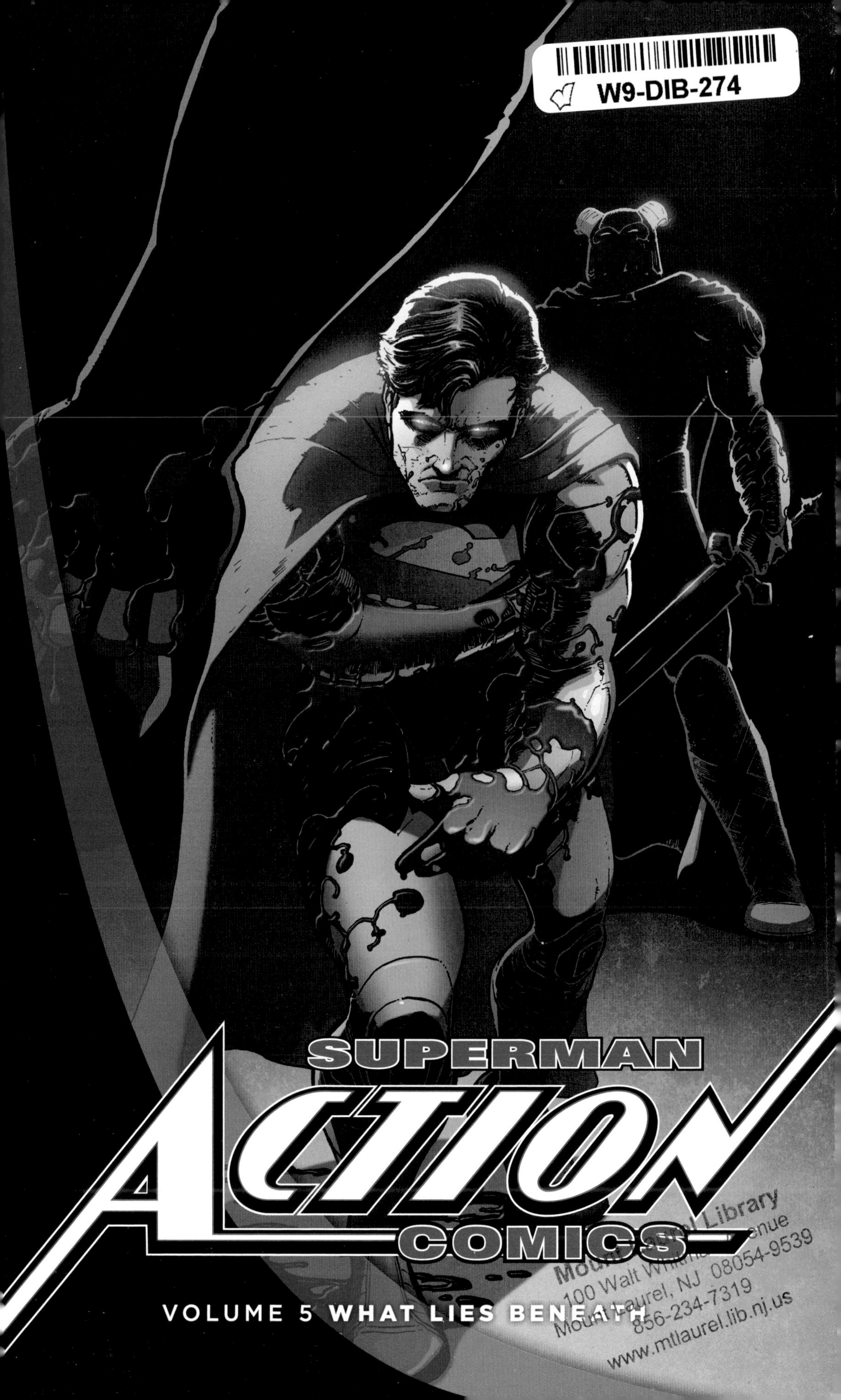

SUPERMAN ACTION COMICS

VOLUME 5 WHAT LIES BENEATH

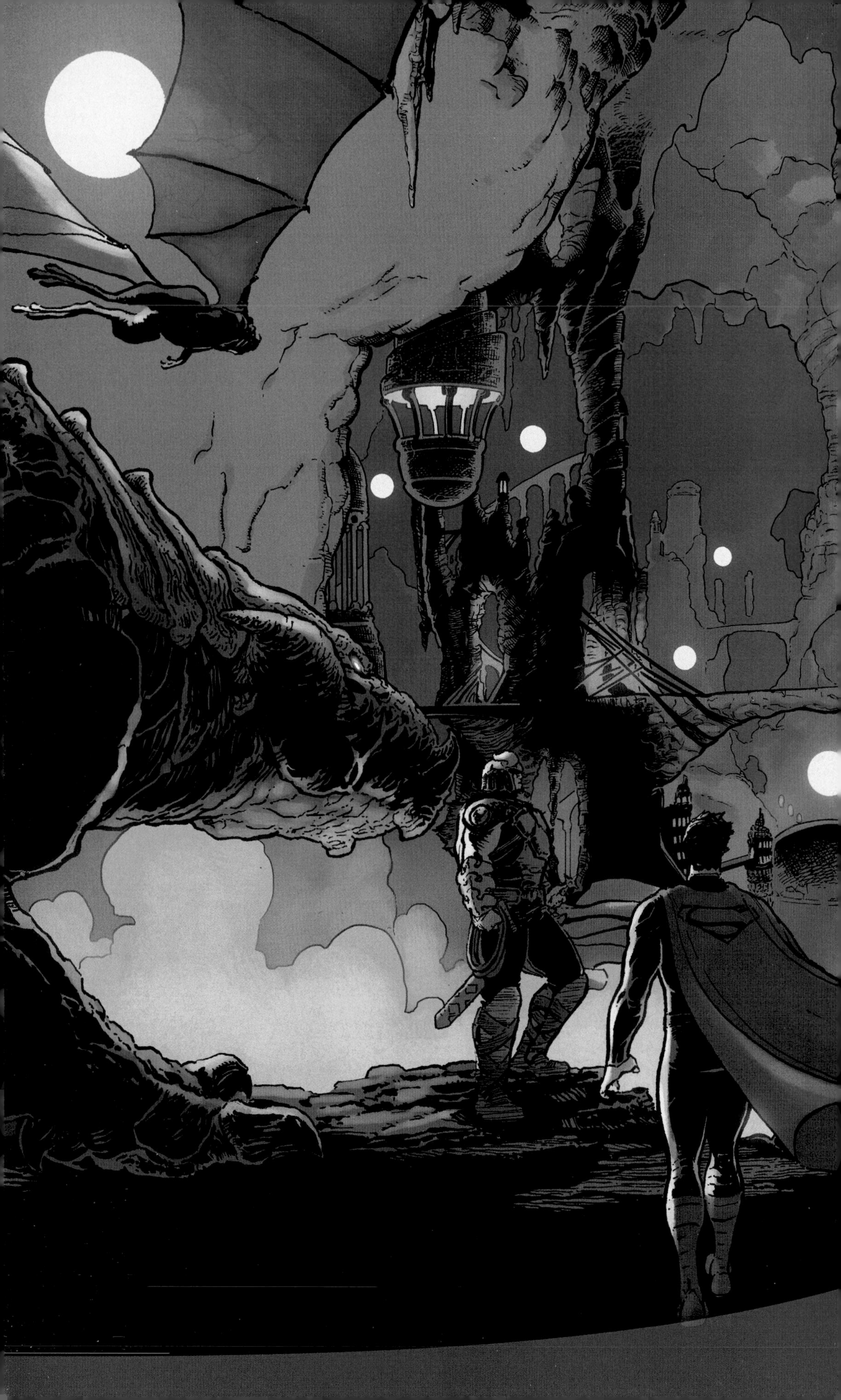

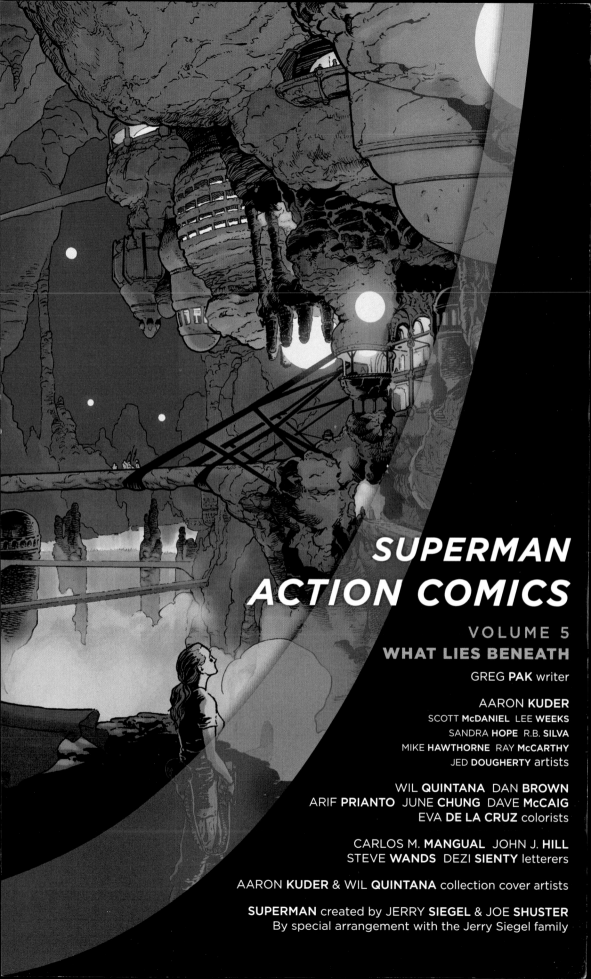

SUPERMAN
ACTION COMICS

VOLUME 5
WHAT LIES BENEATH

GREG **PAK** writer

AARON **KUDER**
SCOTT **McDANIEL** LEE **WEEKS**
SANDRA **HOPE** R.B. **SILVA**
MIKE **HAWTHORNE** RAY **McCARTHY**
JED **DOUGHERTY** artists

WIL **QUINTANA** DAN **BROWN**
ARIF **PRIANTO** JUNE **CHUNG** DAVE **McCAIG**
EVA **DE LA CRUZ** colorists

CARLOS M. **MANGUAL** JOHN J. **HILL**
STEVE **WANDS** DEZI **SIENTY** letterers

AARON **KUDER** & WIL **QUINTANA** collection cover artists

SUPERMAN created by JERRY **SIEGEL** & JOE **SHUSTER**
By special arrangement with the Jerry Siegel family

EDDIE BERGANZA MIKE COTTON Editors – Original Series RICKEY PURDIN Associate Editor – Original Series
ANTHONY MARQUES Assistant Editor – Original Series ROBIN WILDMAN Editor
ROBBIN BROSTERMAN Design Director – Books ROBBIE BIEDERMAN Publication Design

BOB HARRAS Senior VP – Editor-in-Chief, DC Comics

DIANE NELSON President DAN DIDIO and JIM LEE Co-Publishers GEOFF JOHNS Chief Creative Officer
AMIT DESAI Senior VP – Marketing and Franchise Management
AMY GENKINS Senior VP – Business and Legal Affairs NAIRI GARDINER Senior VP – Finance
JEFF BOISON VP – Publishing Planning MARK CHIARELLO VP – Art Direction and Design
JOHN CUNNINGHAM VP – Marketing TERRI CUNNINGHAM VP – Editorial Administration
LARRY GANEM VP – Talent Relations and Services ALISON GILL Senior VP – Manufacturing and Operations
HANK KANALZ Senior VP – Vertigo and Integrated Publishing
JAY KOGAN VP – Business and Legal Affairs, Publishing JACK MAHAN VP – Business Affairs, Talent
NICK NAPOLITANO VP – Manufacturing Administration SUE POHJA VP – Book Sales
FRED RUIZ VP – Manufacturing Operations COURTNEY SIMMONS Senior VP – Publicity BOB WAYNE Senior VP – Sales

SUPERMAN – ACTION COMICS VOLUME 5: WHAT LIES BENEATH

DC Comics, 4000 Warner Blvd., Burbank, CA 91522
A Warner Bros. Entertainment Company.
Printed by RR Donnelley, Owensville, MO. USA. 5/8/15. First Printing.
ISBN: 978-1-4012-5488-9

Library of Congress Cataloging-in-Publication Data

Pak, Greg, author.
Superman - Action Comics. Volume 5, What lies beneath / Greg Pak, writer ; Aaron Kuder, artist.
pages cm. — (The New 52!)
ISBN 978-1-4012-5488-9
1. Graphic novels. I. Kuder, Aaron, illustrator. II. Title. III. Title: What lies beneath.

PN6728.S9P35 2015
741.5'973—dc23

2014027375

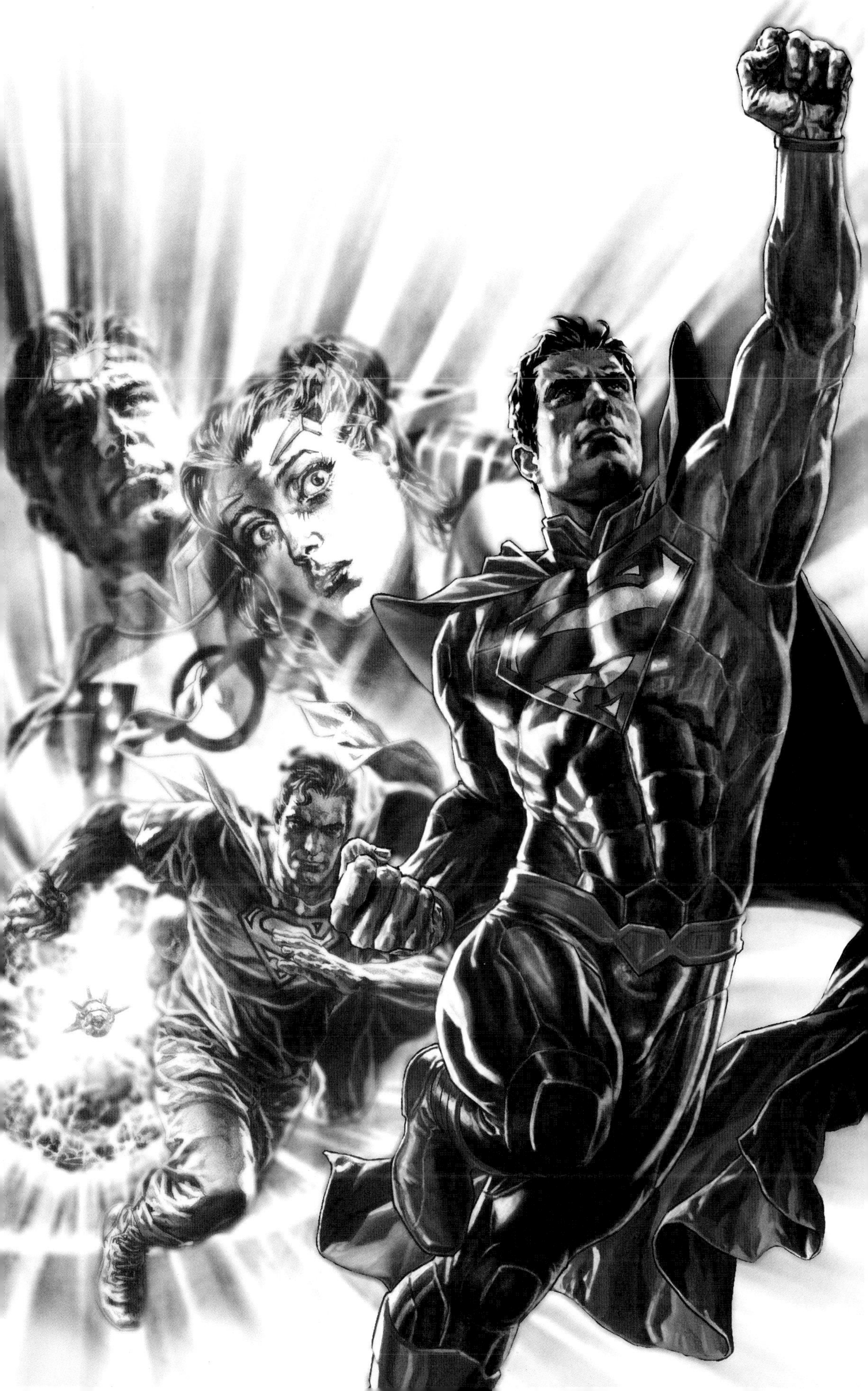

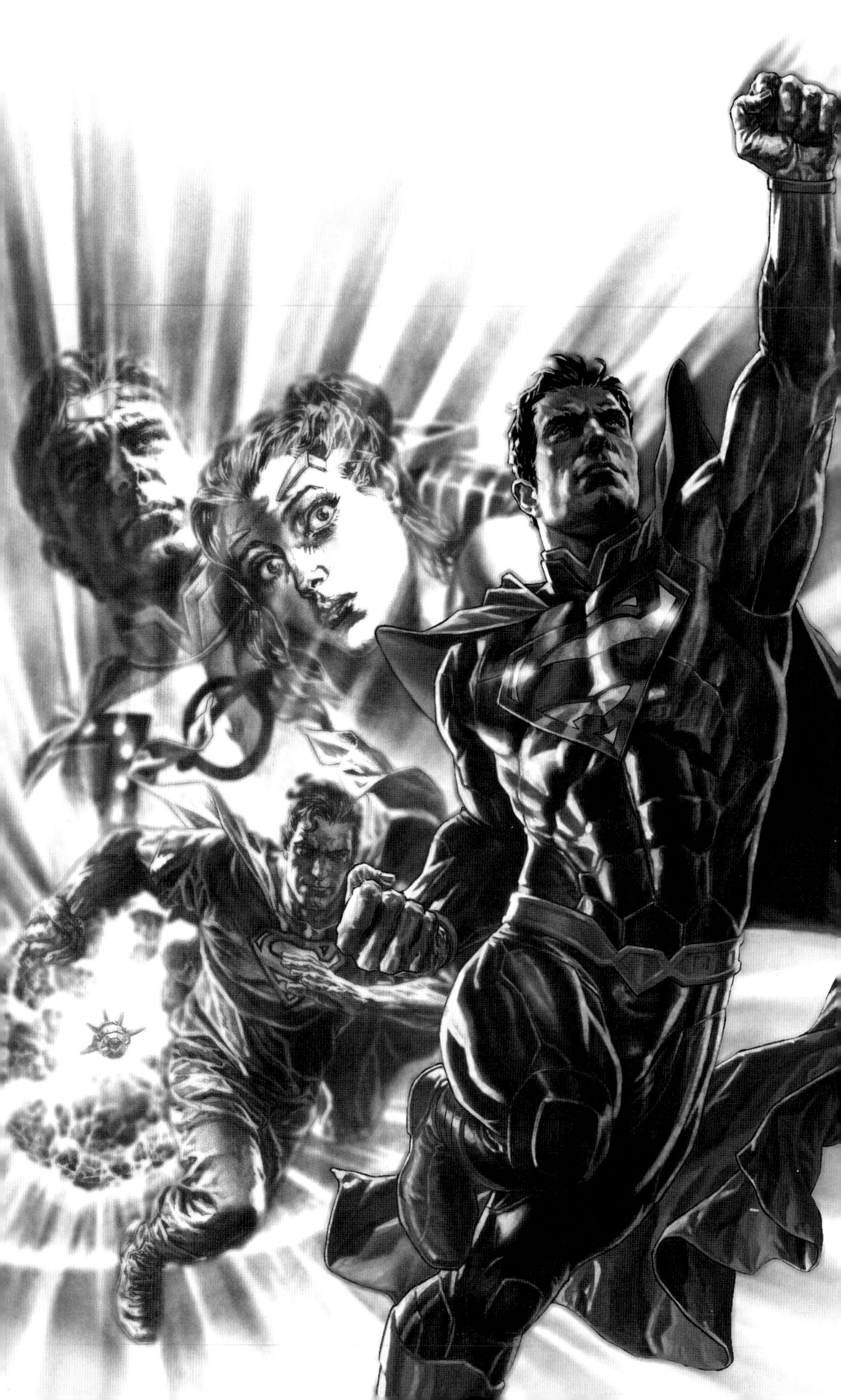

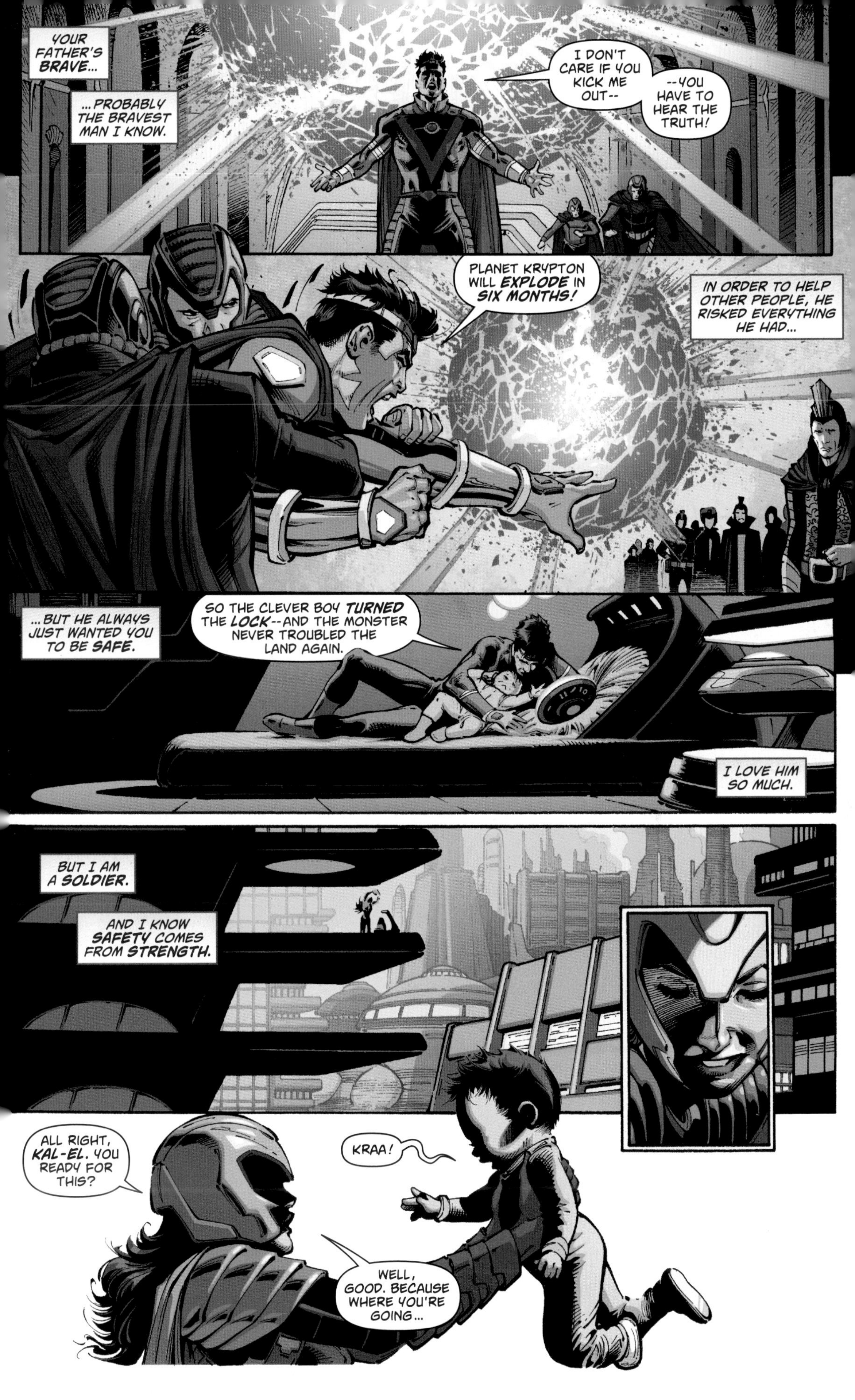

YOUR FATHER'S BRAVE...
...PROBABLY THE BRAVEST MAN I KNOW.
I DON'T CARE IF YOU KICK ME OUT--
--YOU HAVE TO HEAR THE TRUTH!
PLANET KRYPTON WILL EXPLODE IN SIX MONTHS!
IN ORDER TO HELP OTHER PEOPLE, HE RISKED EVERYTHING HE HAD...
...BUT HE ALWAYS JUST WANTED YOU TO BE SAFE.
SO THE CLEVER BOY TURNED THE LOCK--AND THE MONSTER NEVER TROUBLED THE LAND AGAIN.
I LOVE HIM SO MUCH.
BUT I AM A SOLDIER.
AND I KNOW SAFETY COMES FROM STRENGTH.
ALL RIGHT, KAL-EL. YOU READY FOR THIS?
KRAA!
WELL, GOOD. BECAUSE WHERE YOU'RE GOING...

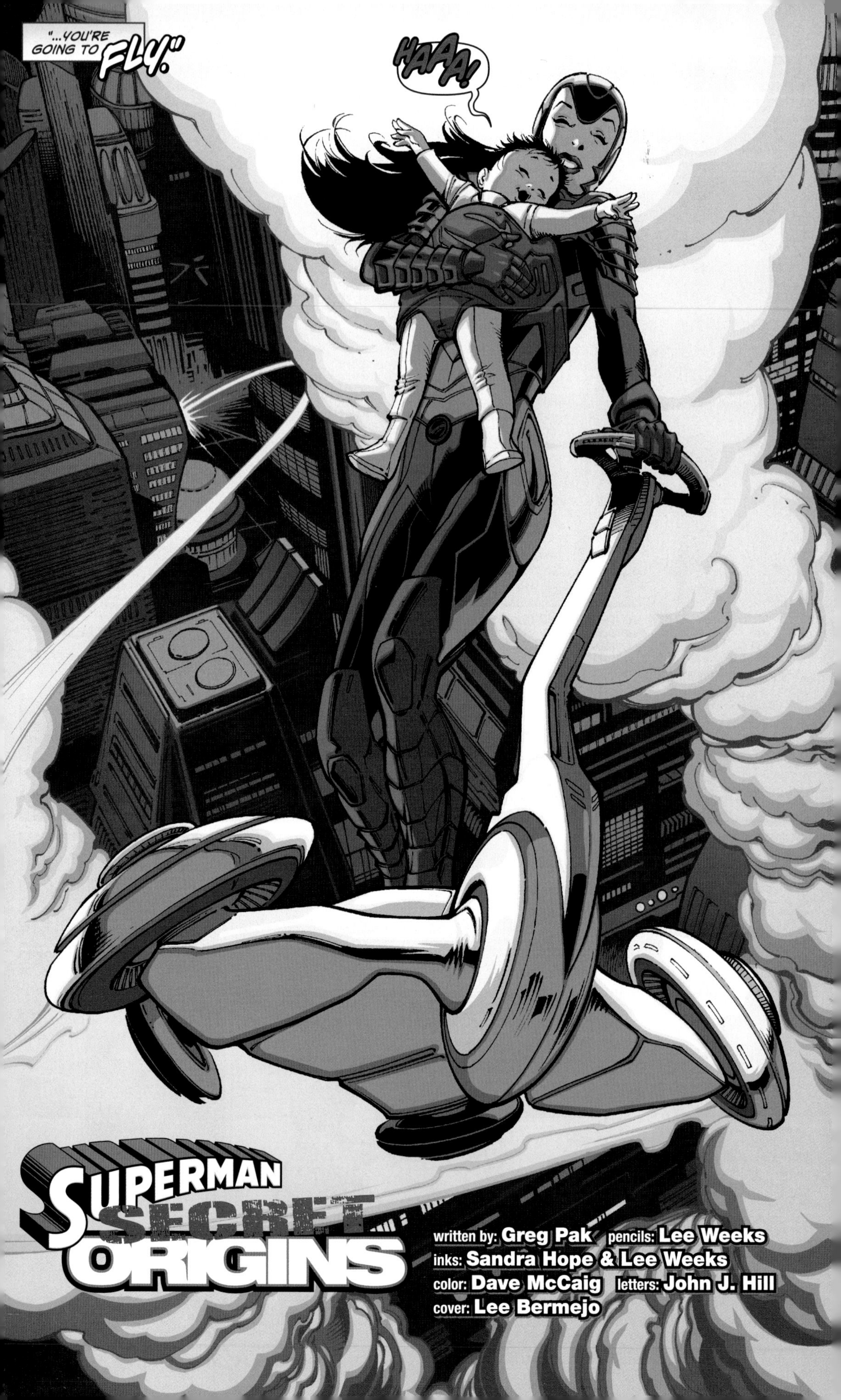

"...YOU'RE GOING TO FLY."
HAAAA!
SUPERMAN SECRET ORIGINS
written by: Greg Pak pencils: Lee Weeks
inks: Sandra Hope & Lee Weeks
color: Dave McCaig letters: John J. Hill
cover: Lee Bermejo

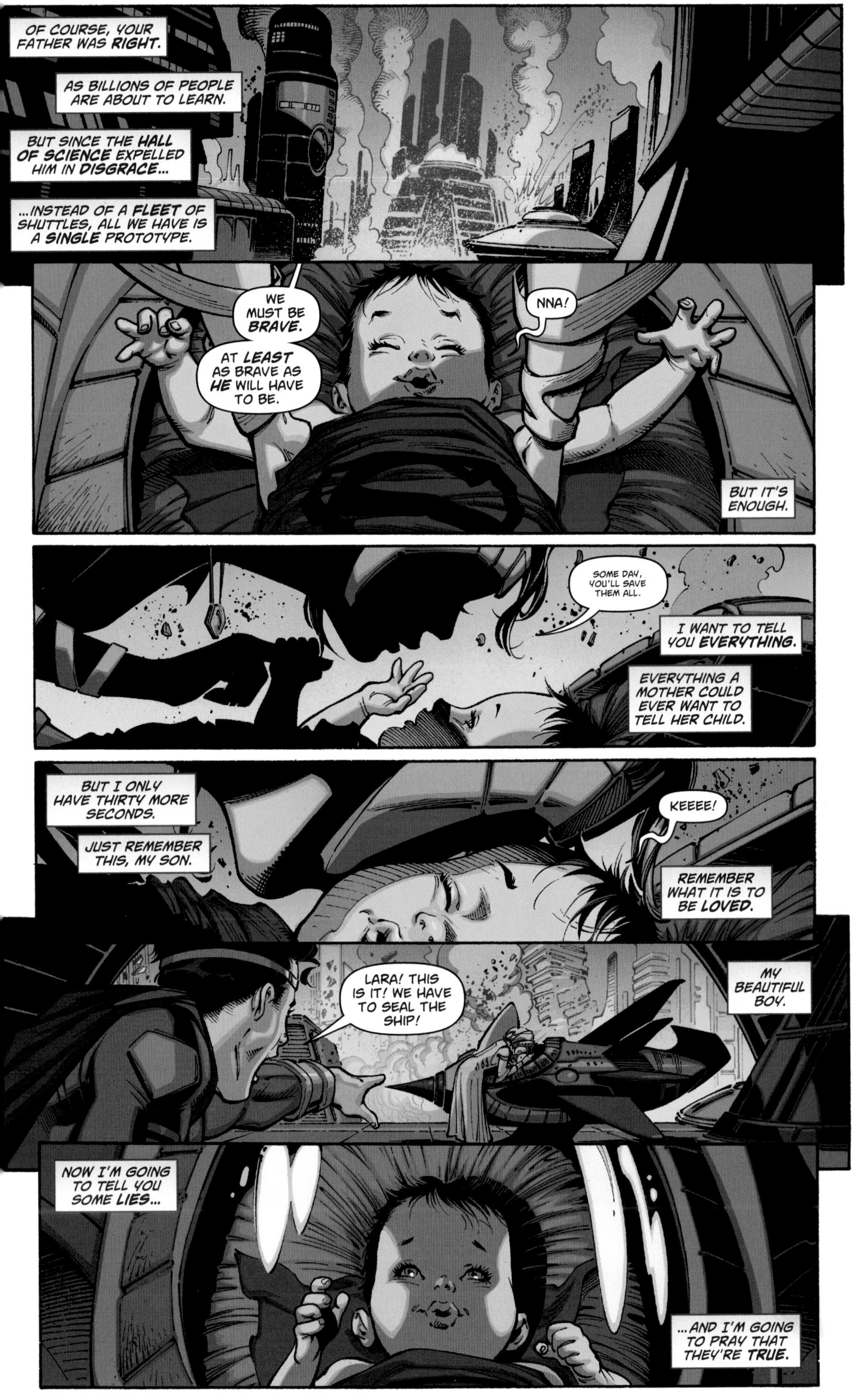
OF COURSE, YOUR FATHER WAS RIGHT.
AS BILLIONS OF PEOPLE ARE ABOUT TO LEARN.
BUT SINCE THE HALL OF SCIENCE EXPELLED HIM IN DISGRACE...
...INSTEAD OF A FLEET OF SHUTTLES, ALL WE HAVE IS A SINGLE PROTOTYPE.
WE MUST BE BRAVE.
AT LEAST AS BRAVE AS HE WILL HAVE TO BE.
NNA!
BUT IT'S ENOUGH.
SOME DAY, YOU'LL SAVE THEM ALL.
I WANT TO TELL YOU EVERYTHING.
EVERYTHING A MOTHER COULD EVER WANT TO TELL HER CHILD.
BUT I ONLY HAVE THIRTY MORE SECONDS.
JUST REMEMBER THIS, MY SON.
KEEEE!
REMEMBER WHAT IT IS TO BE LOVED.
LARA! THIS IS IT! WE HAVE TO SEAL THE SHIP!
MY BEAUTIFUL BOY.
NOW I'M GOING TO TELL YOU SOME LIES...
...AND I'M GOING TO PRAY THAT THEY'RE TRUE.

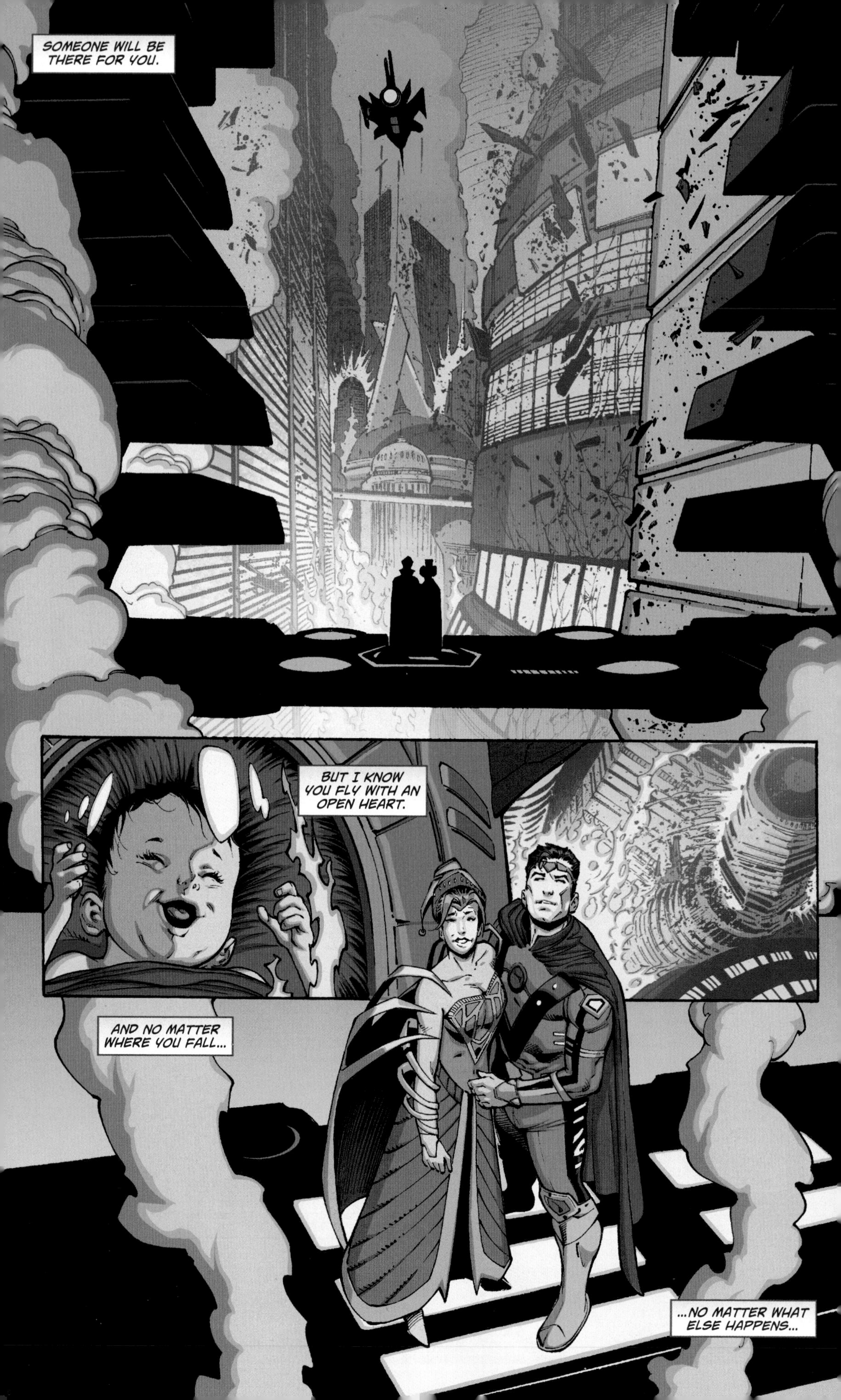
SOMEONE WILL BE THERE FOR YOU.
BUT I KNOW YOU FLY WITH AN OPEN HEART.
AND NO MATTER WHERE YOU FALL...
...NO MATTER WHAT ELSE HAPPENS...

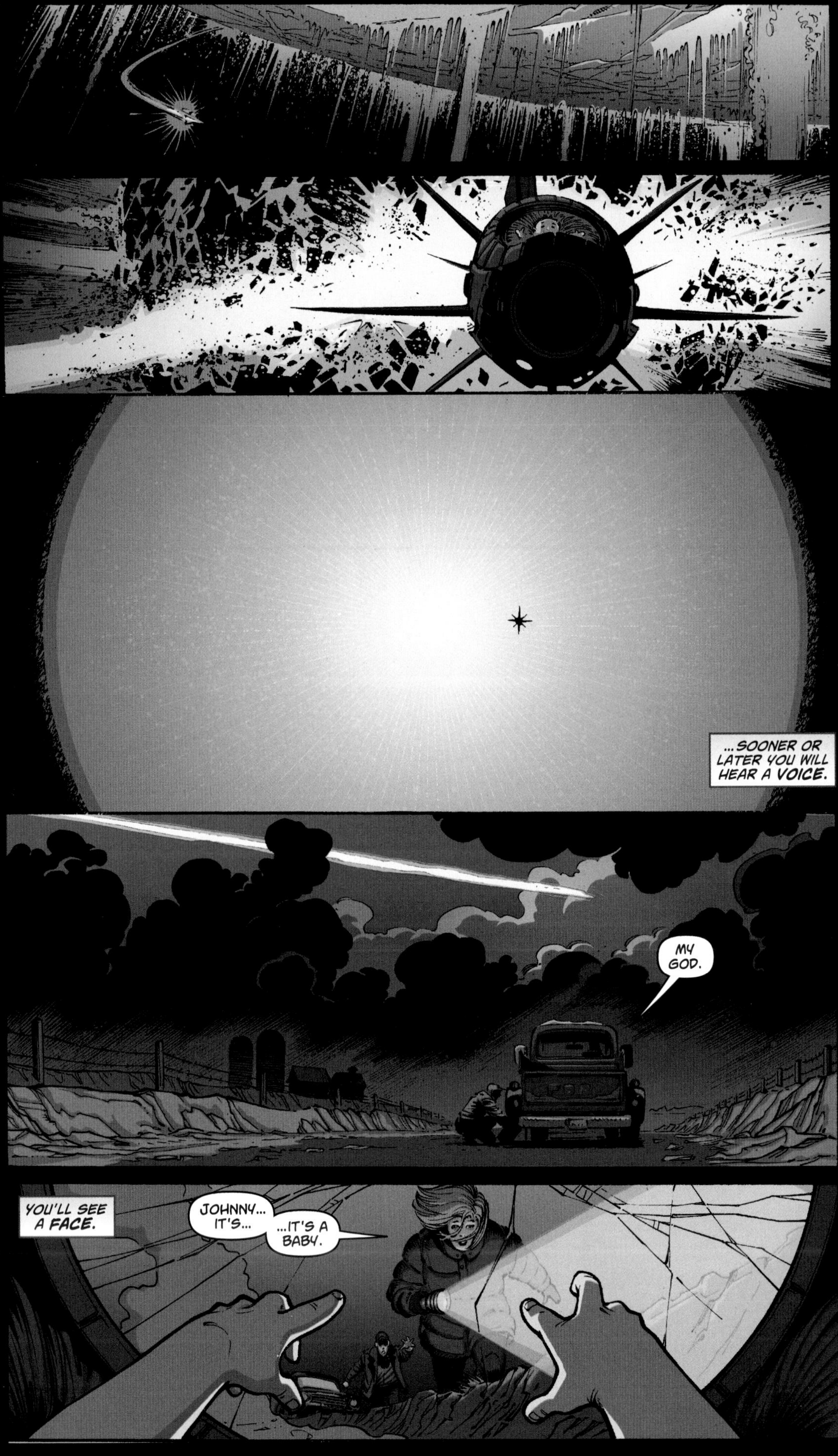
...SOONER OR LATER YOU WILL HEAR A VOICE.
MY GOD.
YOU'LL SEE A FACE.
JOHNNY... IT'S...
...IT'S A BABY.

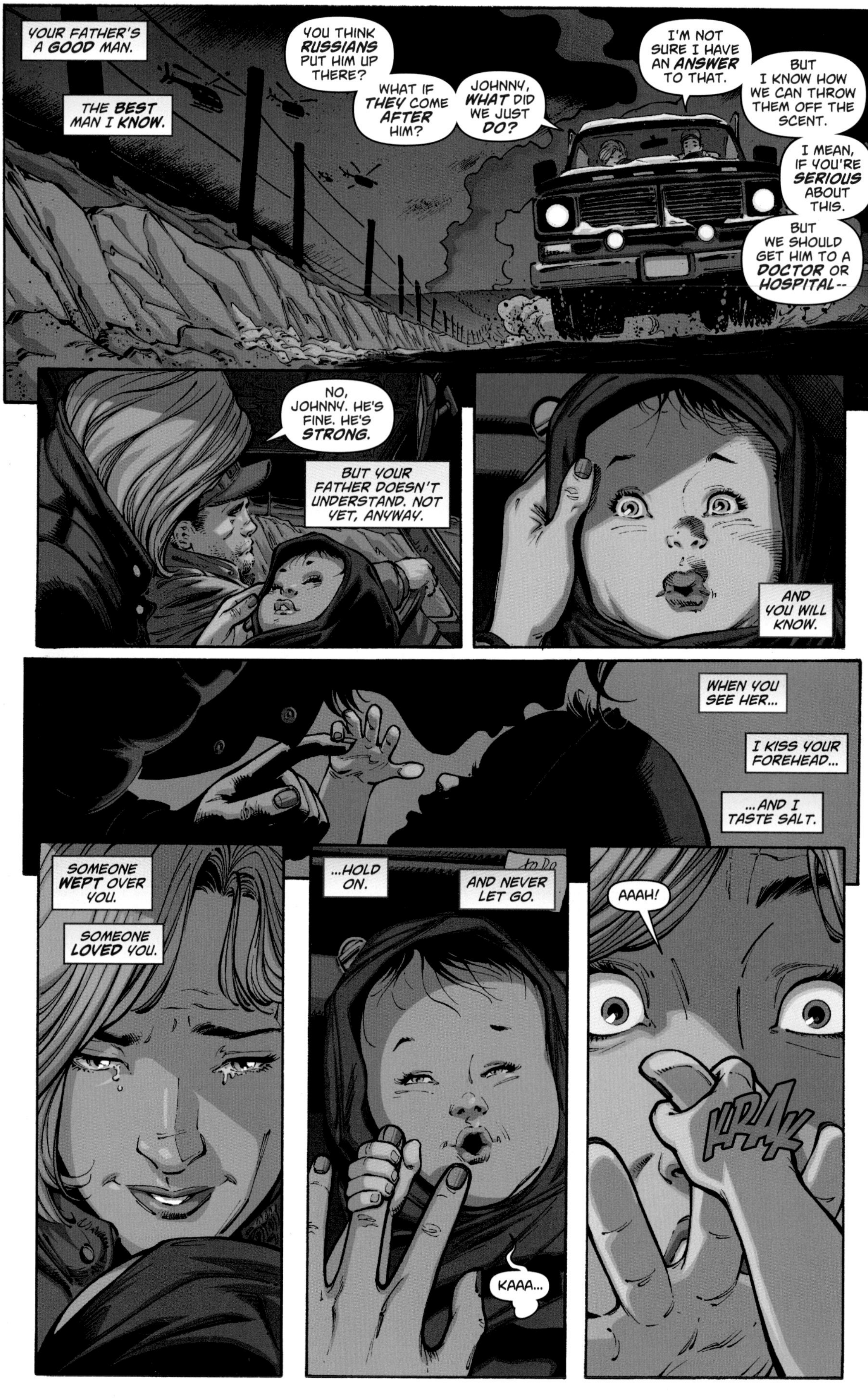
YOUR FATHER'S A GOOD MAN.
THE BEST MAN I KNOW.
YOU THINK RUSSIANS PUT HIM UP THERE?
WHAT IF THEY COME AFTER HIM?
JOHNNY, WHAT DID WE JUST DO?
I'M NOT SURE I HAVE AN ANSWER TO THAT.
BUT I KNOW HOW WE CAN THROW THEM OFF THE SCENT.
I MEAN, IF YOU'RE SERIOUS ABOUT THIS.
BUT WE SHOULD GET HIM TO A DOCTOR OR HOSPITAL--
NO, JOHNNY. HE'S FINE. HE'S STRONG.
BUT YOUR FATHER DOESN'T UNDERSTAND. NOT YET, ANYWAY.
AND YOU WILL KNOW.
WHEN YOU SEE HER...
I KISS YOUR FOREHEAD...
...AND I TASTE SALT.
SOMEONE WEPT OVER YOU.
SOMEONE LOVED YOU.
...HOLD ON.
AND NEVER LET GO.
KAAA...
AAAH!
KRAK

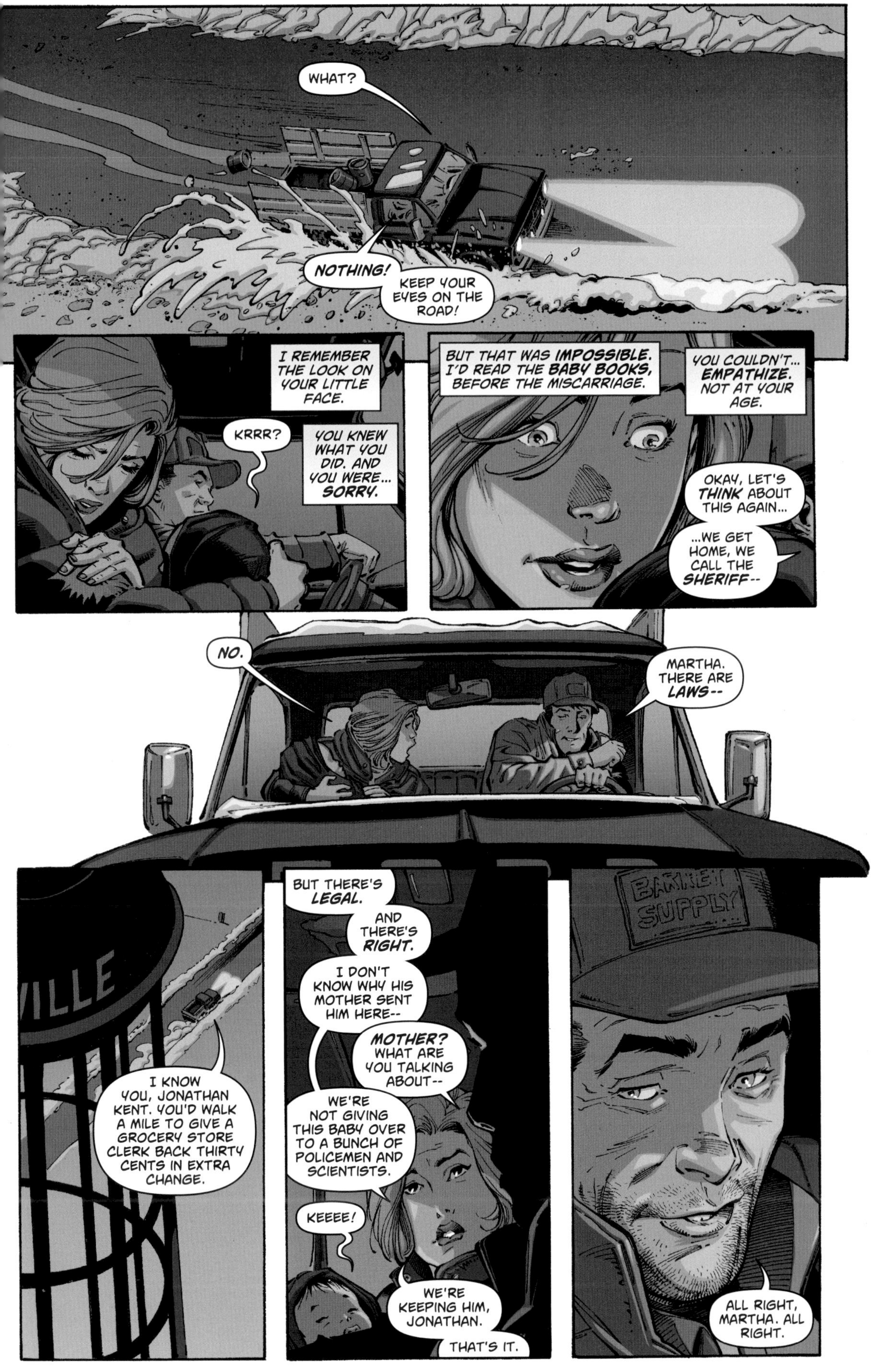
WHAT?
NOTHING!
KEEP YOUR EYES ON THE ROAD!
I REMEMBER THE LOOK ON YOUR LITTLE FACE.
KRRR?
YOU KNEW WHAT YOU DID. AND YOU WERE... SORRY.
BUT THAT WAS IMPOSSIBLE. I'D READ THE BABY BOOKS, BEFORE THE MISCARRIAGE.
YOU COULDN'T... EMPATHIZE. NOT AT YOUR AGE.
OKAY, LET'S THINK ABOUT THIS AGAIN...
...WE GET HOME, WE CALL THE SHERIFF--
NO.
MARTHA. THERE ARE LAWS--
BUT THERE'S LEGAL.
AND THERE'S RIGHT.
I DON'T KNOW WHY HIS MOTHER SENT HIM HERE--
MOTHER? WHAT ARE YOU TALKING ABOUT--
I KNOW YOU, JONATHAN KENT. YOU'D WALK A MILE TO GIVE A GROCERY STORE CLERK BACK THIRTY CENTS IN EXTRA CHANGE.
WE'RE NOT GIVING THIS BABY OVER TO A BUNCH OF POLICEMEN AND SCIENTISTS.
KEEEE!
WE'RE KEEPING HIM, JONATHAN.
THAT'S IT.
ALL RIGHT, MARTHA. ALL RIGHT.

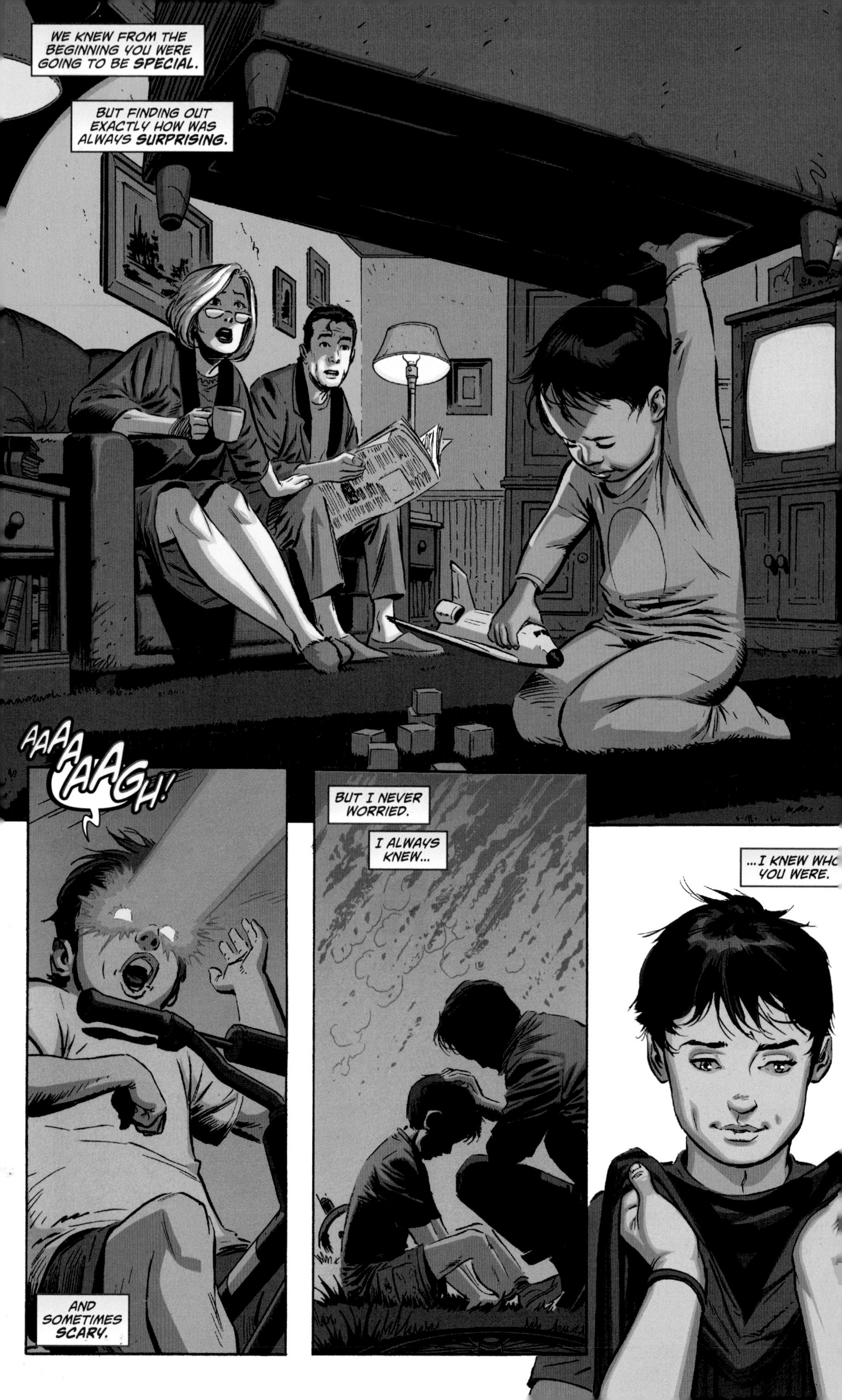
WE KNEW FROM THE BEGINNING YOU WERE GOING TO BE SPECIAL.
BUT FINDING OUT EXACTLY HOW WAS ALWAYS SURPRISING.
AAAAAAAGH!
AND SOMETIMES SCARY.
BUT I NEVER WORRIED.
I ALWAYS KNEW...
...I KNEW WHO YOU WERE.

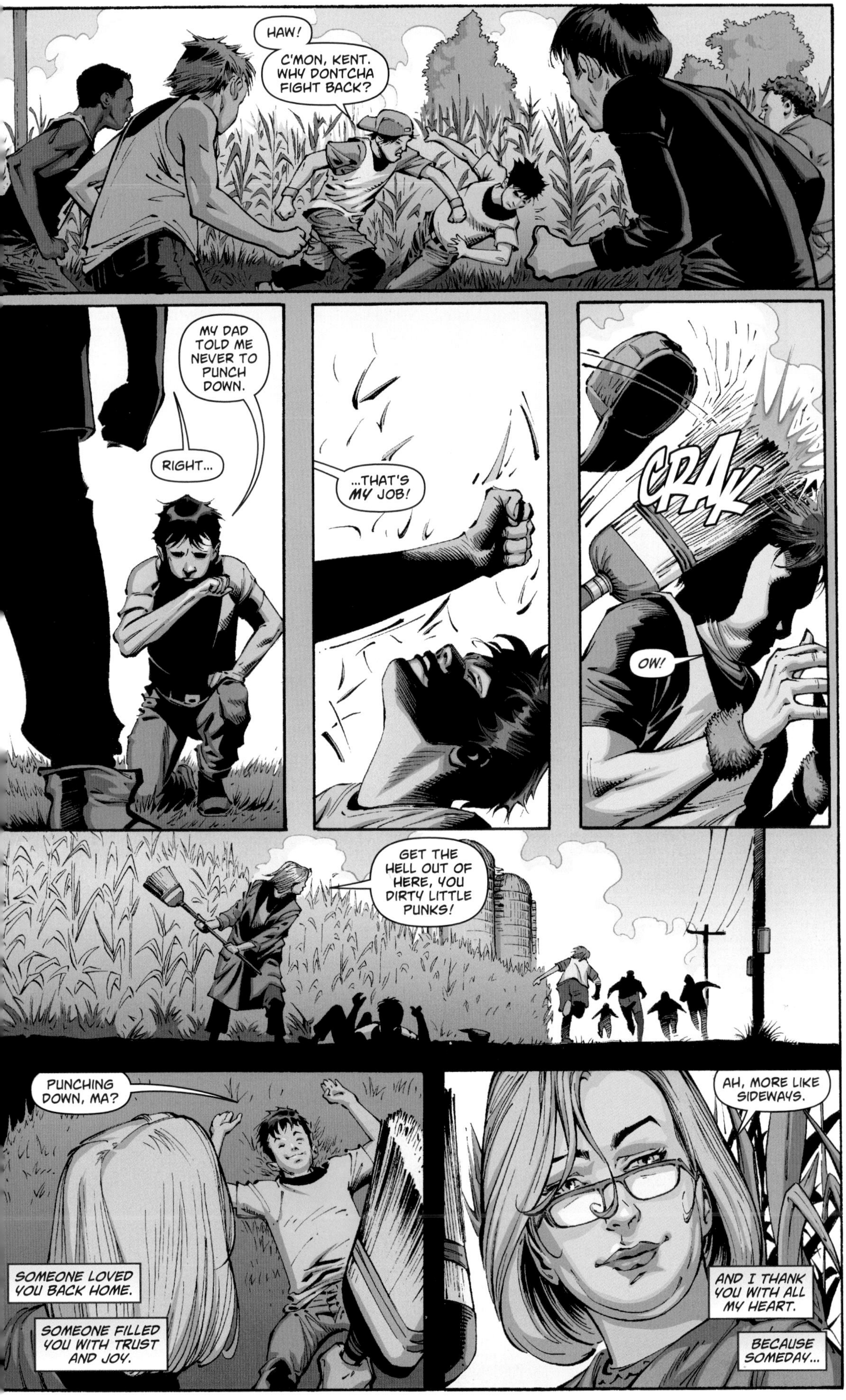
HAW!
C'MON, KENT. WHY DONTCHA FIGHT BACK?
MY DAD TOLD ME NEVER TO PUNCH DOWN.
RIGHT...
...THAT'S MY JOB!
CRAK
OW!
GET THE HELL OUT OF HERE, YOU DIRTY LITTLE PUNKS!
PUNCHING DOWN, MA?
SOMEONE LOVED YOU BACK HOME.
SOMEONE FILLED YOU WITH TRUST AND JOY.
AH, MORE LIKE SIDEWAYS.
AND I THANK YOU WITH ALL MY HEART.
BECAUSE SOMEDAY...

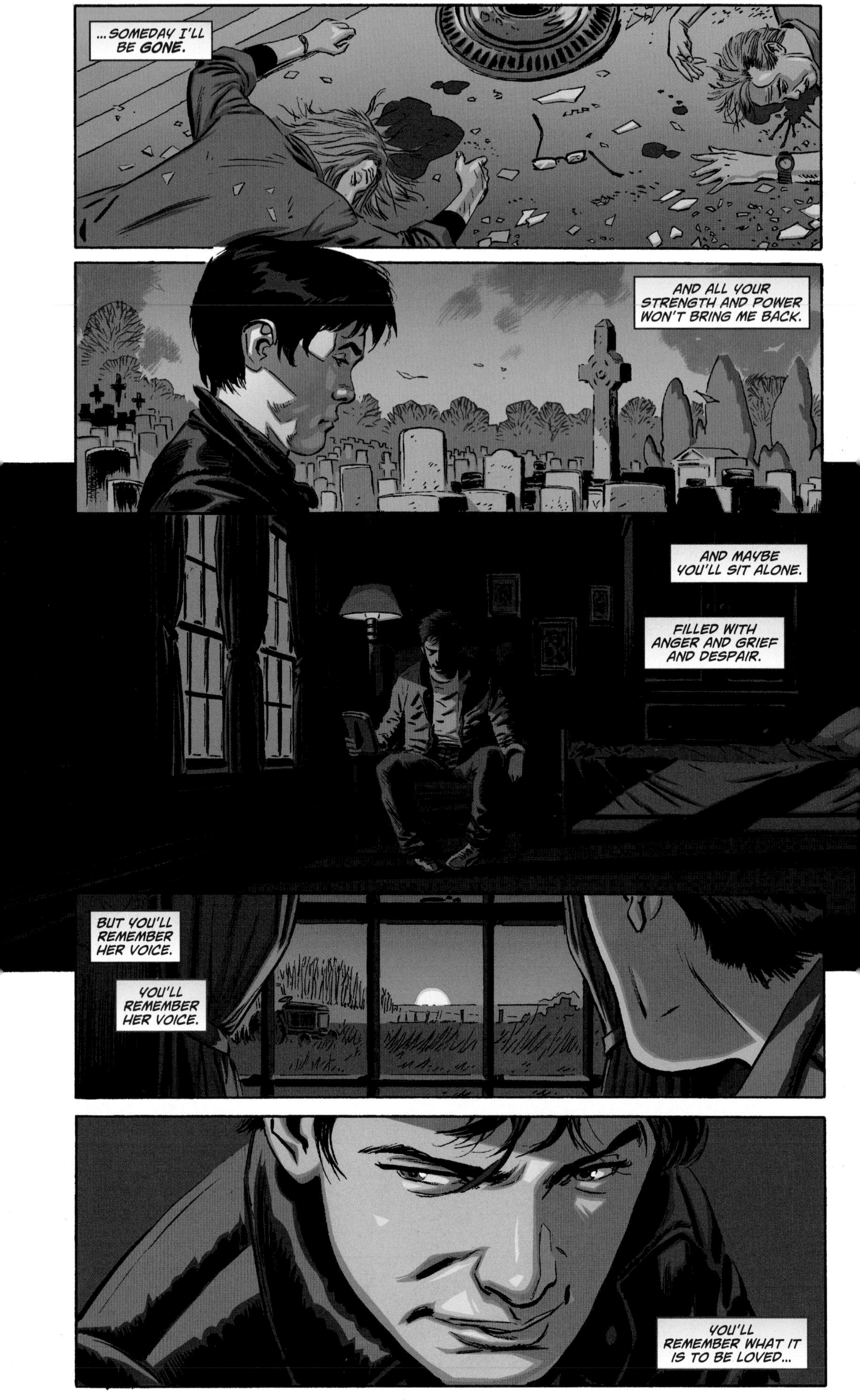
...SOMEDAY I'LL BE GONE.
AND ALL YOUR STRENGTH AND POWER WON'T BRING ME BACK.
AND MAYBE YOU'LL SIT ALONE.
FILLED WITH ANGER AND GRIEF AND DESPAIR.
BUT YOU'LL REMEMBER HER VOICE.
YOU'LL REMEMBER HER VOICE.
YOU'LL REMEMBER WHAT IT IS TO BE LOVED...

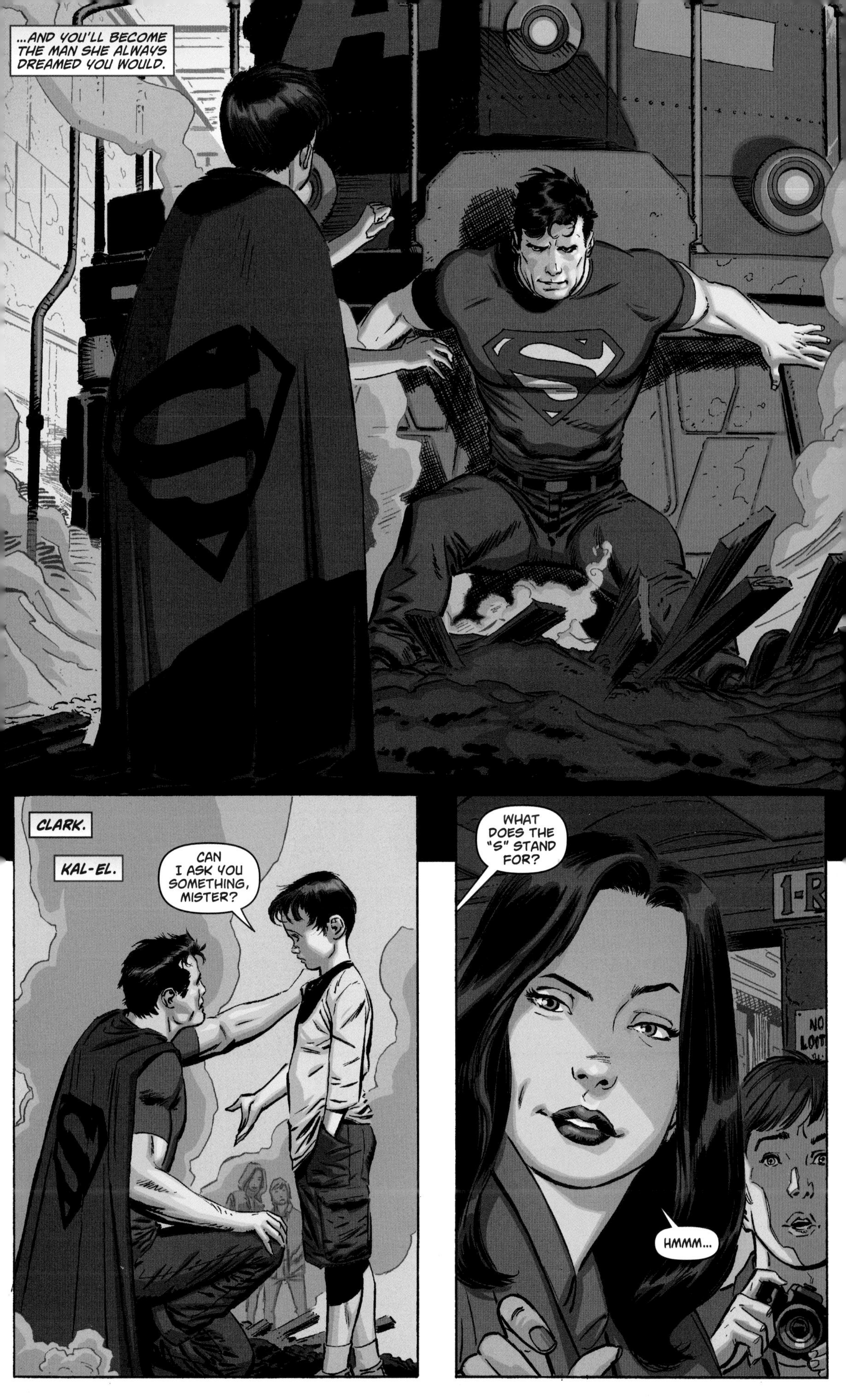
...AND YOU'LL BECOME THE MAN SHE ALWAYS DREAMED YOU WOULD.
CLARK.
KAL-EL.
CAN I ASK YOU SOMETHING, MISTER?
WHAT DOES THE "S" STAND FOR?
HMMM...

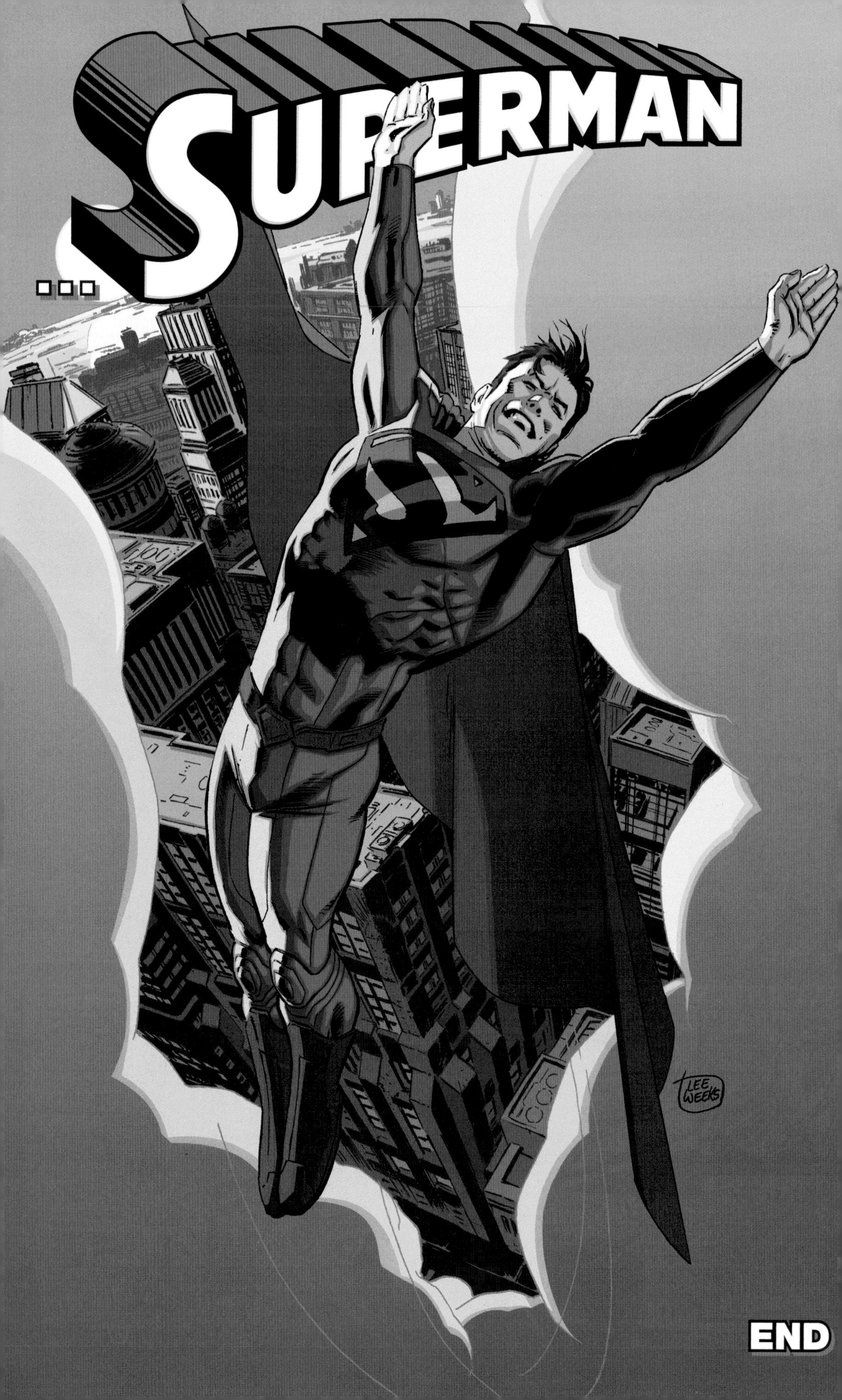
SUPERMAN
...
LEE WEEKS
END

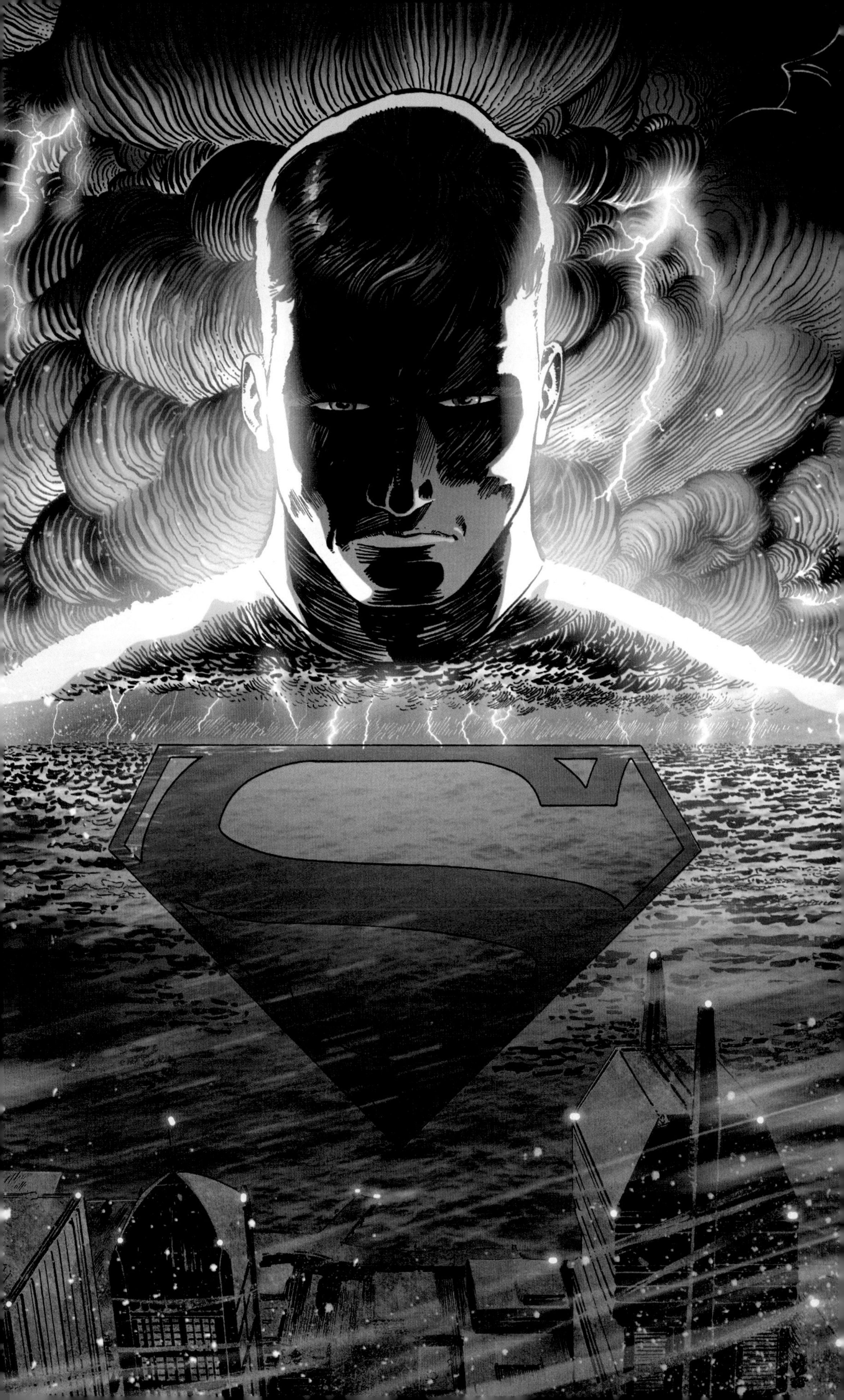

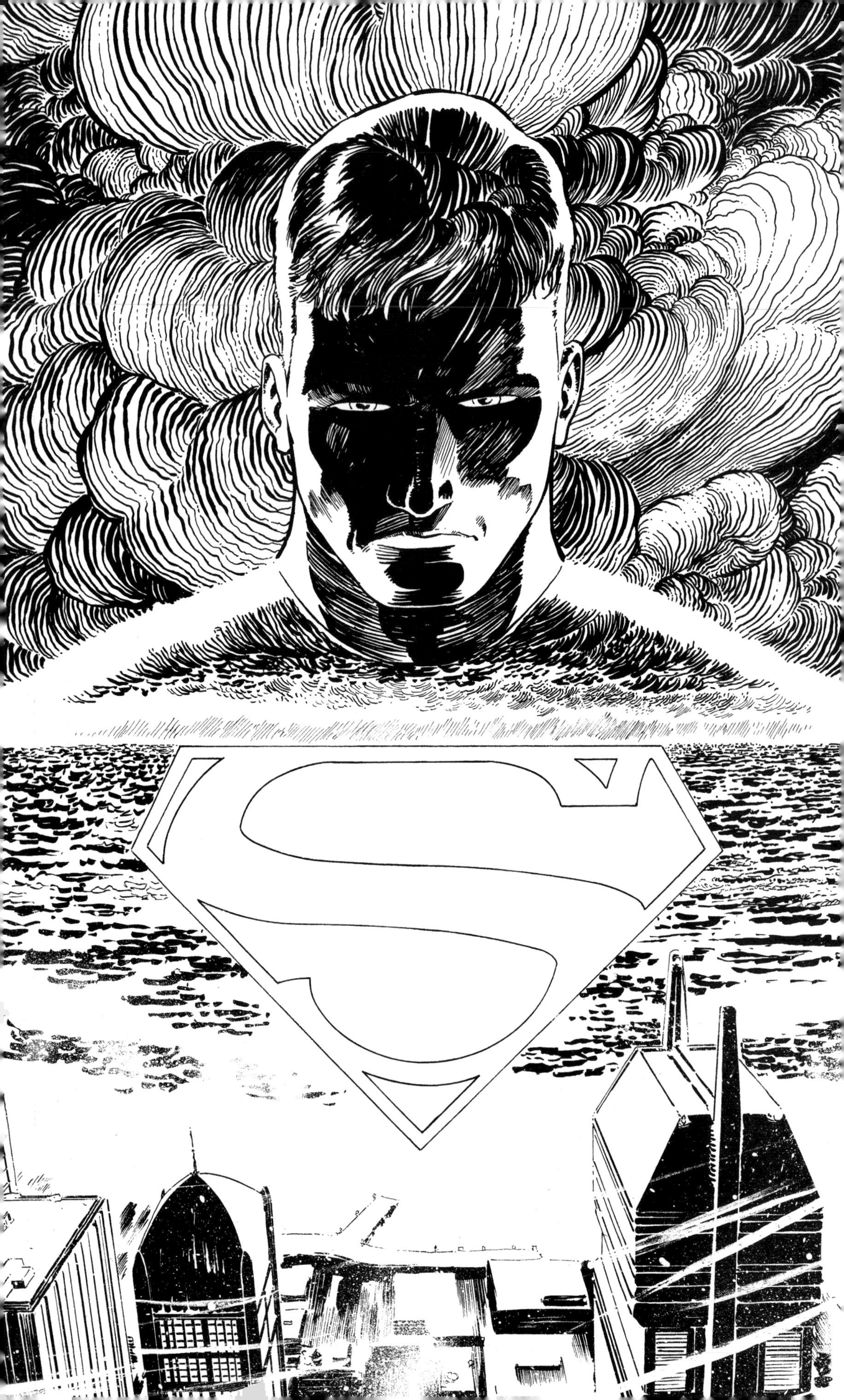

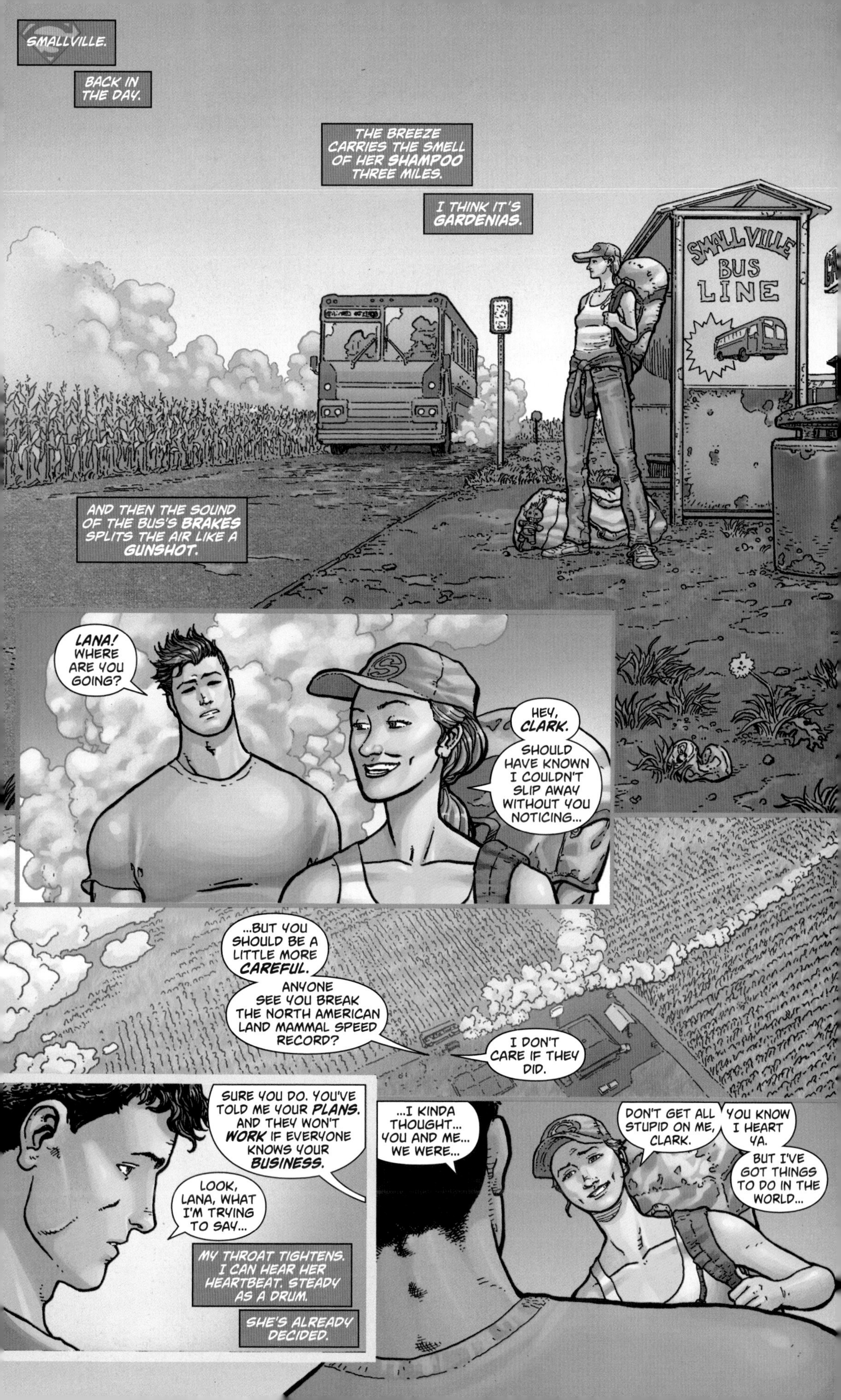
SMALLVILLE.
BACK IN THE DAY.
THE BREEZE CARRIES THE SMELL OF HER SHAMPOO THREE MILES.
I THINK IT'S GARDENIAS.
SMALLVILLE BUS LINE
AND THEN THE SOUND OF THE BUS'S BRAKES SPLITS THE AIR LIKE A GUNSHOT.
LANA! WHERE ARE YOU GOING?
HEY, CLARK.
SHOULD HAVE KNOWN I COULDN'T SLIP AWAY WITHOUT YOU NOTICING...
...BUT YOU SHOULD BE A LITTLE MORE CAREFUL.
ANYONE SEE YOU BREAK THE NORTH AMERICAN LAND MAMMAL SPEED RECORD?
I DON'T CARE IF THEY DID.
SURE YOU DO. YOU'VE TOLD ME YOUR PLANS. AND THEY WON'T WORK IF EVERYONE KNOWS YOUR BUSINESS.
LOOK, LANA, WHAT I'M TRYING TO SAY...
MY THROAT TIGHTENS. I CAN HEAR HER HEARTBEAT, STEADY AS A DRUM.
SHE'S ALREADY DECIDED.
...I KINDA THOUGHT... YOU AND ME... WE WERE...
DON'T GET ALL STUPID ON ME, CLARK.
YOU KNOW I HEART YA.
BUT I'VE GOT THINGS TO DO IN THE WORLD...

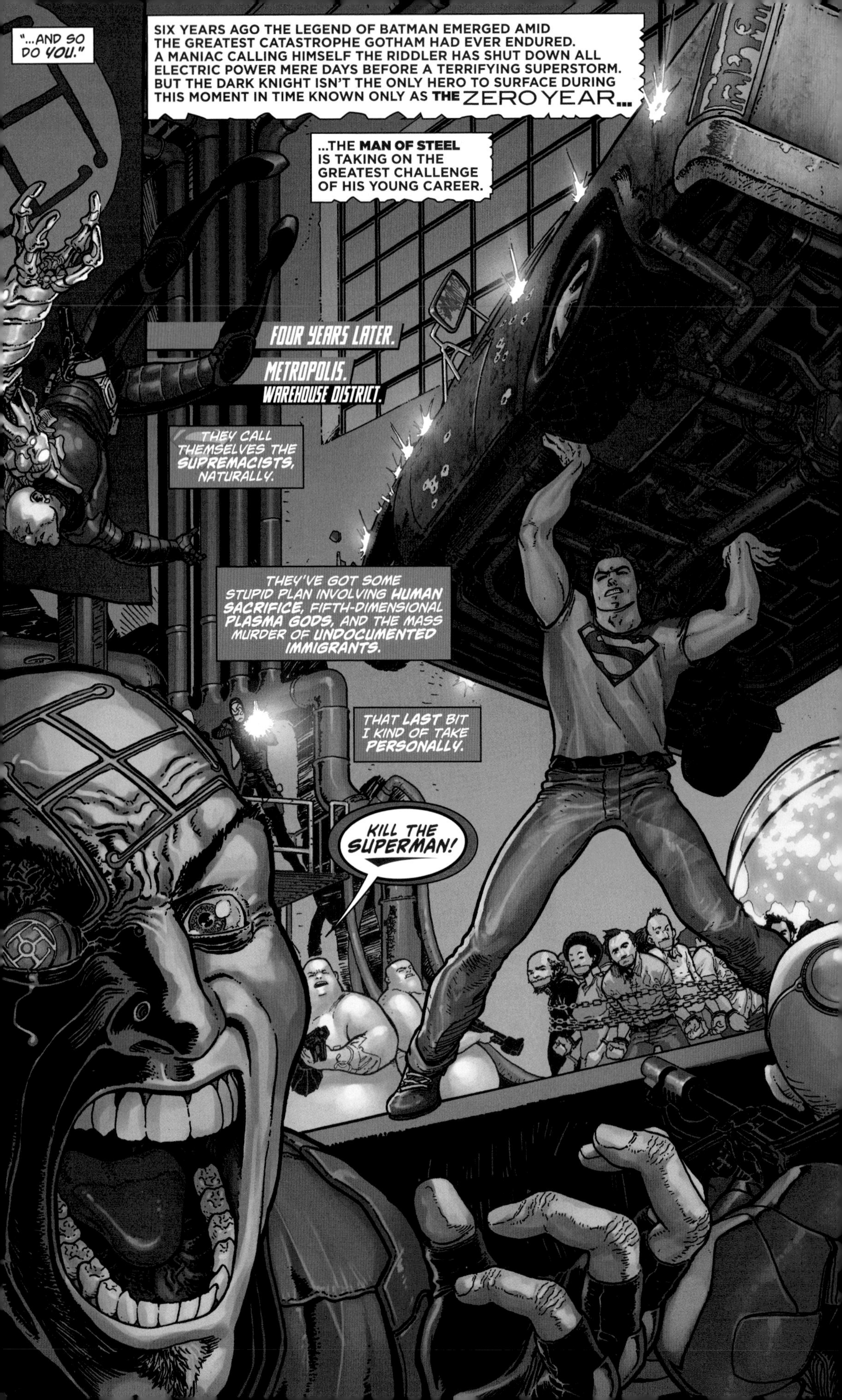
"...AND SO DO YOU."
SIX YEARS AGO THE LEGEND OF BATMAN EMERGED AMID THE GREATEST CATASTROPHE GOTHAM HAD EVER ENDURED. A MANIAC CALLING HIMSELF THE RIDDLER HAS SHUT DOWN ALL ELECTRIC POWER MERE DAYS BEFORE A TERRIFYING SUPERSTORM. BUT THE DARK KNIGHT ISN'T THE ONLY HERO TO SURFACE DURING THIS MOMENT IN TIME KNOWN ONLY AS THE ZERO YEAR...
...THE MAN OF STEEL IS TAKING ON THE GREATEST CHALLENGE OF HIS YOUNG CAREER.
FOUR YEARS LATER.
METROPOLIS.
WAREHOUSE DISTRICT.
THEY CALL THEMSELVES THE SUPREMACISTS, NATURALLY.
THEY'VE GOT SOME STUPID PLAN INVOLVING HUMAN SACRIFICE, FIFTH-DIMENSIONAL PLASMA GODS, AND THE MASS MURDER OF UNDOCUMENTED IMMIGRANTS.
THAT LAST BIT I KIND OF TAKE PERSONALLY.
KILL THE SUPERMAN!

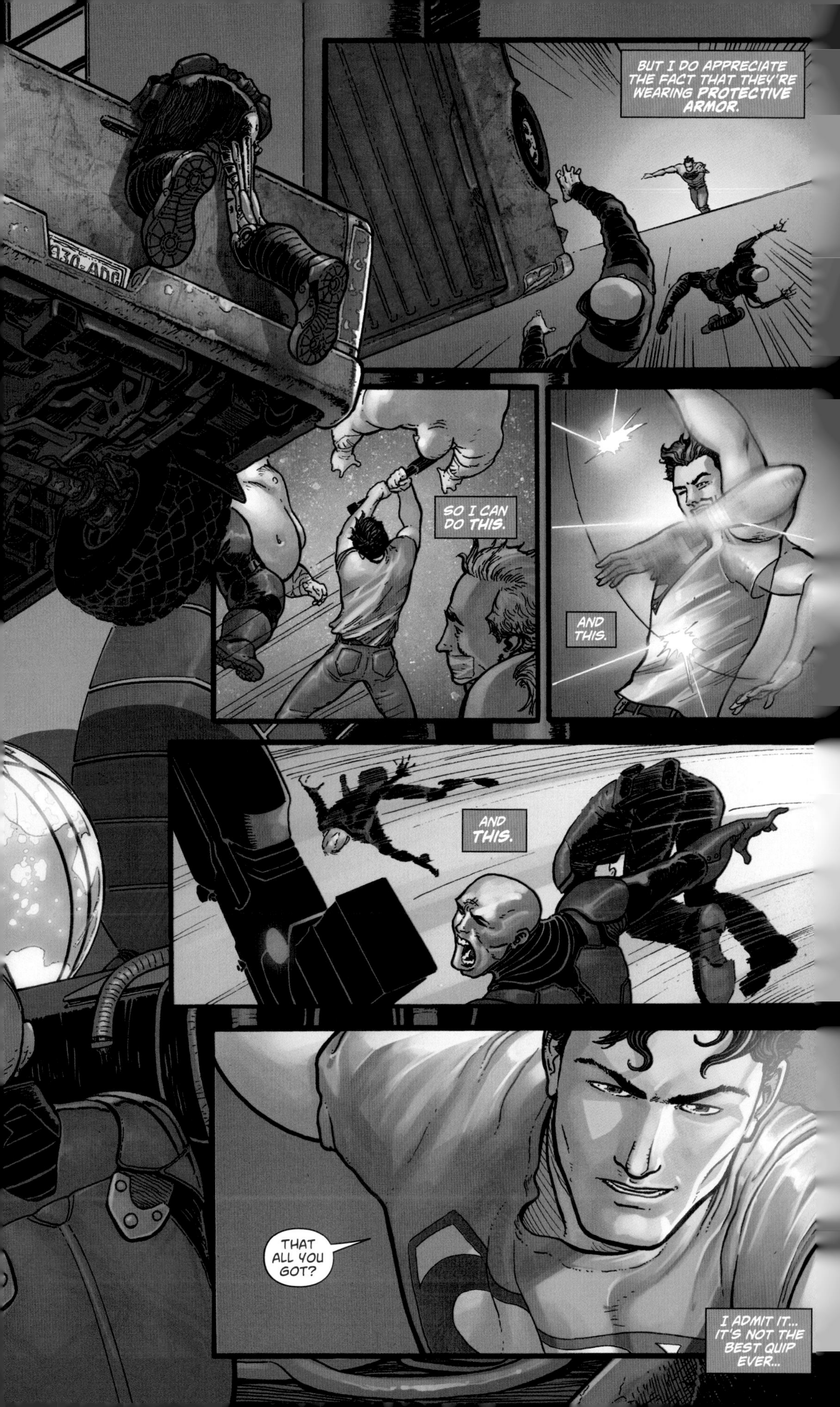

BUT I DO APPRECIATE THE FACT THAT THEY'RE WEARING PROTECTIVE ARMOR.
SO I CAN DO THIS.
AND THIS.
AND THIS.
THAT ALL YOU GOT?
I ADMIT IT... IT'S NOT THE BEST QUIP EVER...

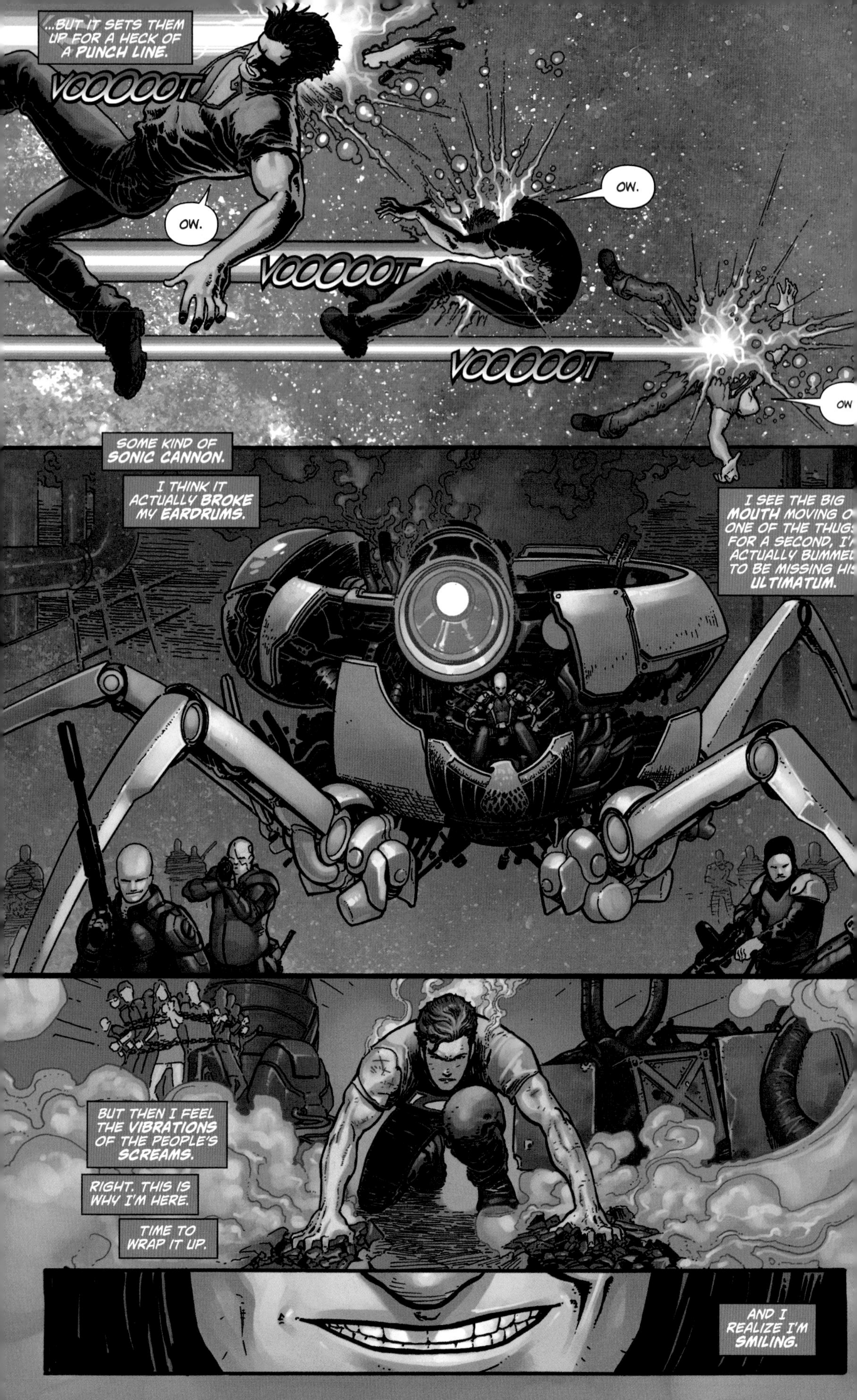
...BUT IT SETS THEM UP FOR A HECK OF A PUNCH LINE.
VOOOOOOT
OW.
OW.
VOOOOOT
VOOOOOT
OW
SOME KIND OF SONIC CANNON.
I THINK IT ACTUALLY BROKE MY EARDRUMS.
I SEE THE BIG MOUTH MOVING O ONE OF THE THUGS FOR A SECOND, I'M ACTUALLY BUMMED TO BE MISSING HIS ULTIMATUM.
BUT THEN I FEEL THE VIBRATIONS OF THE PEOPLE'S SCREAMS.
RIGHT. THIS IS WHY I'M HERE.
TIME TO WRAP IT UP.
AND I REALIZE I'M SMILING.

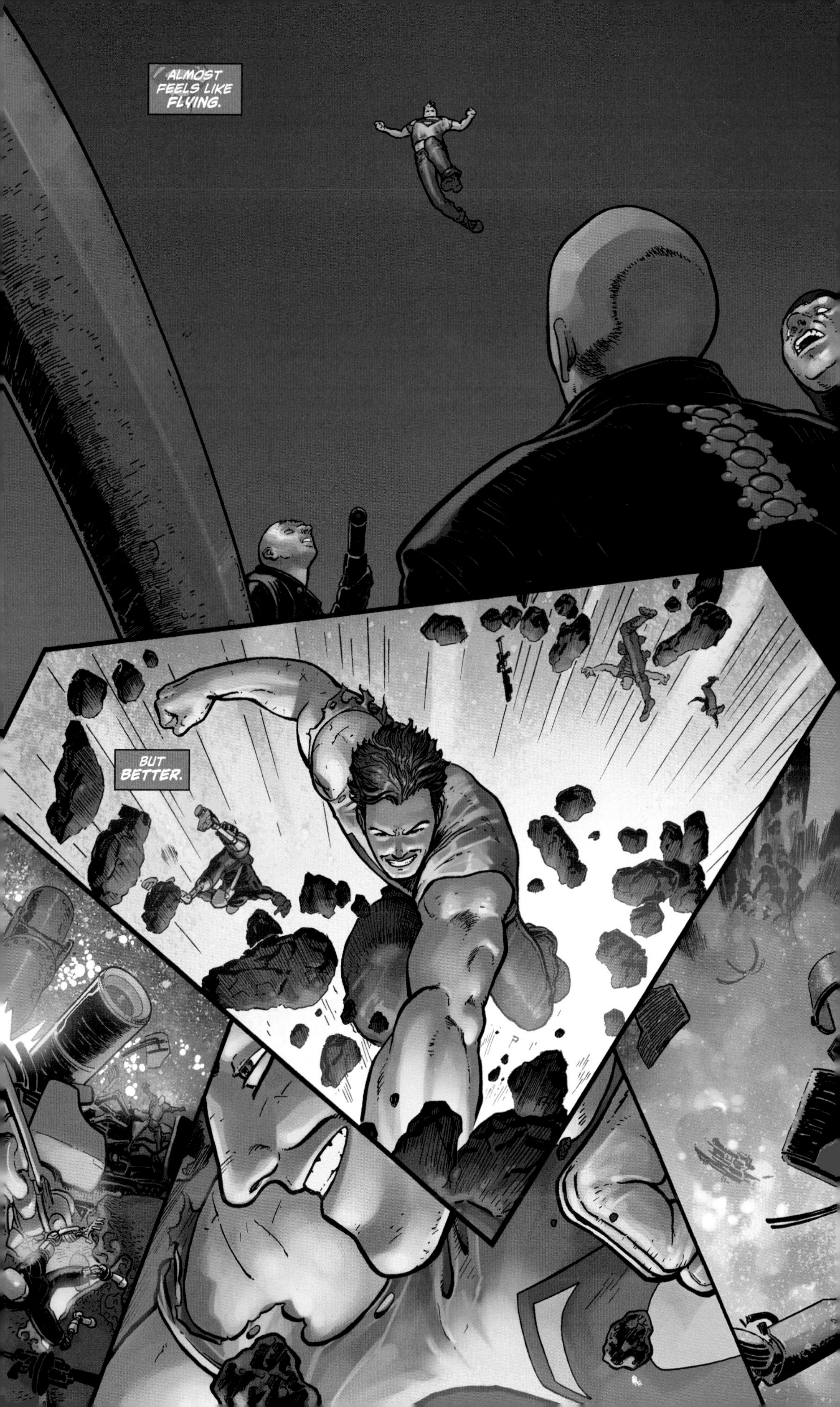
ALMOST FEELS LIKE FLYING.
BUT BETTER.

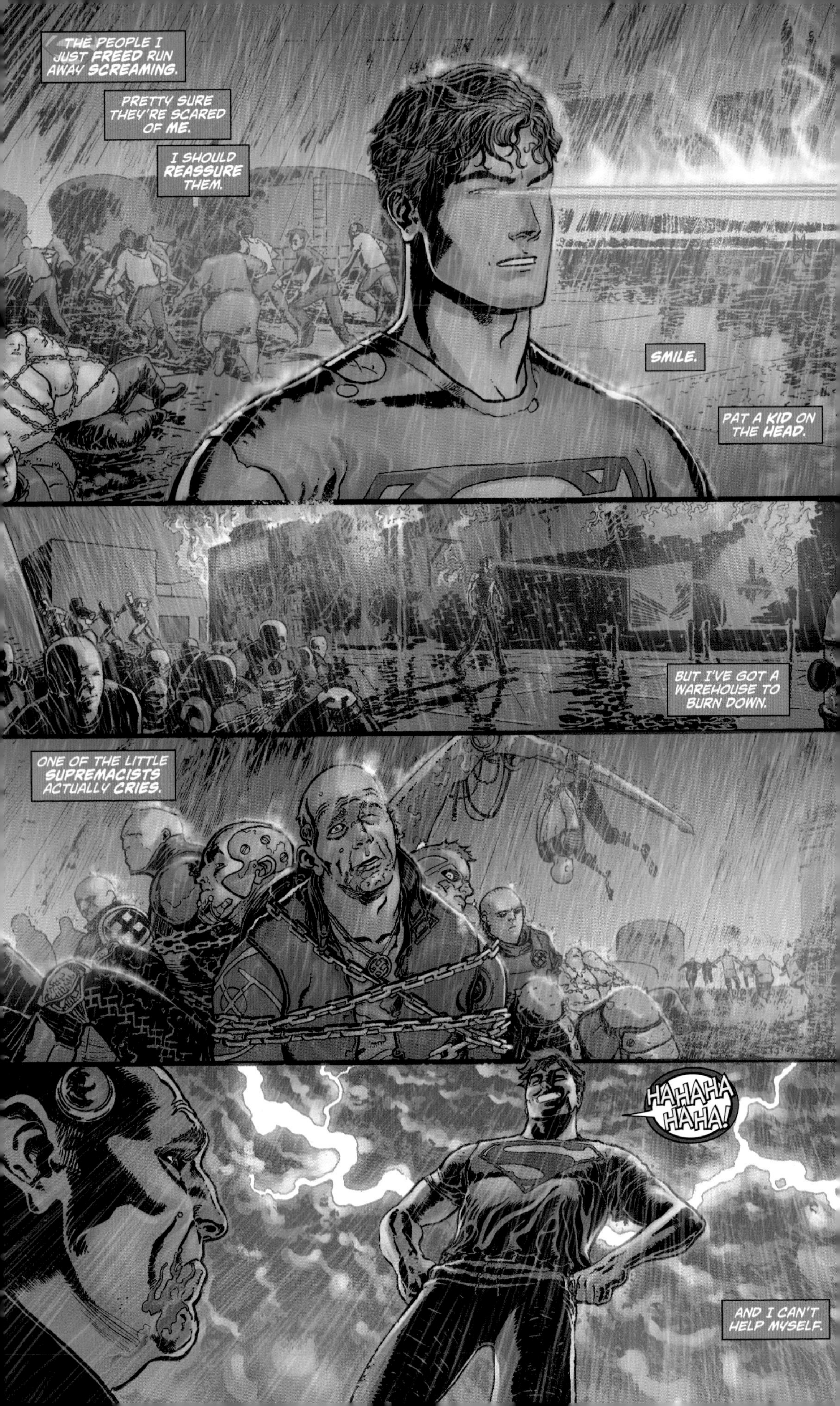
THE PEOPLE I JUST FREED RUN AWAY SCREAMING.
PRETTY SURE THEY'RE SCARED OF ME.
I SHOULD REASSURE THEM.
SMILE.
PAT A KID ON THE HEAD.
BUT I'VE GOT A WAREHOUSE TO BURN DOWN.
ONE OF THE LITTLE SUPREMACISTS ACTUALLY CRIES.
HAHAHA HAHA!
AND I CAN'T HELP MYSELF.

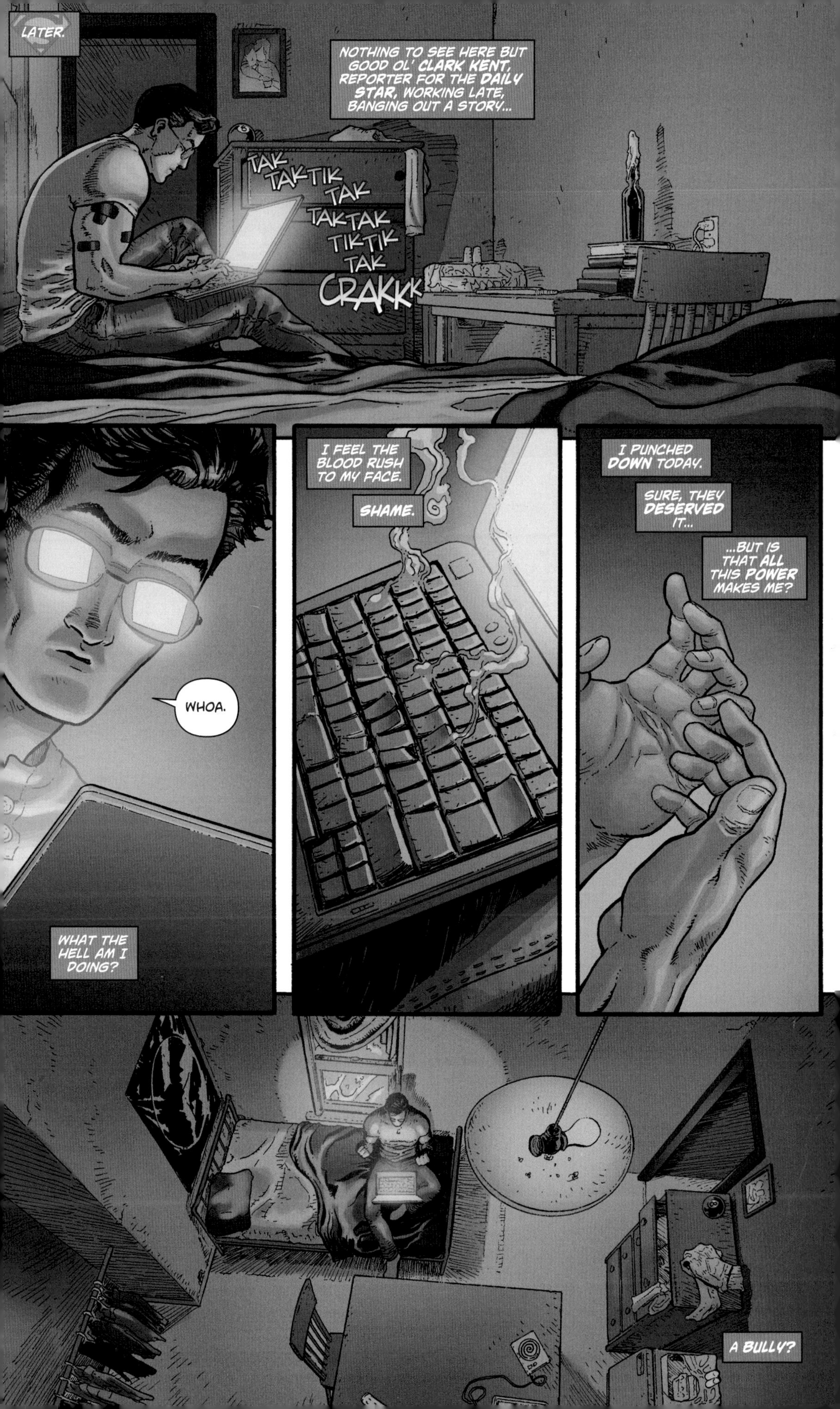
LATER.
NOTHING TO SEE HERE BUT GOOD OL' CLARK KENT, REPORTER FOR THE DAILY STAR, WORKING LATE, BANGING OUT A STORY...
TAK TAKTIK TAK TAKTAK TIKTIK TAK
CRAKKK
WHOA.
WHAT THE HELL AM I DOING?
I FEEL THE BLOOD RUSH TO MY FACE.
SHAME.
I PUNCHED DOWN TODAY.
SURE, THEY DESERVED IT...
...BUT IS THAT ALL THIS POWER MAKES ME?
A BULLY?

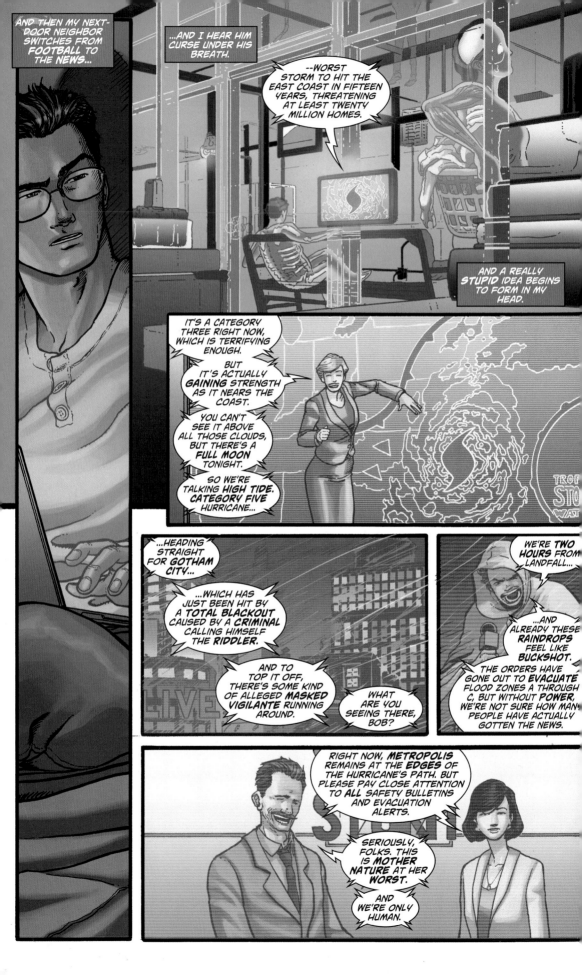

AND THEN MY NEXT-DOOR NEIGHBOR SWITCHES FROM *FOOTBALL* TO THE *NEWS*...

...AND I HEAR HIM *CURSE* UNDER HIS BREATH.

--WORST STORM TO HIT THE EAST COAST IN FIFTEEN YEARS, THREATENING AT LEAST TWENTY MILLION HOMES.

AND A REALLY *STUPID* IDEA BEGINS TO FORM IN MY HEAD.

IT'S A CATEGORY THREE RIGHT NOW, WHICH IS TERRIFYING ENOUGH.

BUT IT'S ACTUALLY *GAINING* STRENGTH AS IT NEARS THE COAST.

YOU CAN'T SEE IT ABOVE ALL THOSE CLOUDS, BUT THERE'S A *FULL MOON* TONIGHT.

SO WE'RE TALKING *HIGH TIDE*, *CATEGORY FIVE* HURRICANE...

...HEADING STRAIGHT FOR *GOTHAM CITY*...

...WHICH HAS JUST BEEN HIT BY A *TOTAL BLACKOUT* CAUSED BY A *CRIMINAL* CALLING HIMSELF THE *RIDDLER*.

AND TO *TOP* IT OFF, THERE'S SOME KIND OF ALLEGED *MASKED VIGILANTE* RUNNING AROUND.

WHAT ARE YOU SEEING THERE, BOB?

WE'RE *TWO HOURS* FROM LANDFALL...

...AND ALREADY THESE *RAINDROPS* FEEL LIKE *BUCKSHOT*.

THE ORDERS HAVE GONE OUT TO *EVACUATE* FLOOD ZONES A THROUGH C, BUT WITHOUT *POWER*, WE'RE NOT SURE HOW MANY PEOPLE HAVE ACTUALLY GOTTEN THE NEWS.

RIGHT NOW, *METROPOLIS* REMAINS AT THE *EDGES* OF THE HURRICANE'S PATH. BUT PLEASE PAY CLOSE ATTENTION TO *ALL* SAFETY BULLETINS AND EVACUATION ALERTS.

SERIOUSLY, FOLKS. THIS IS *MOTHER NATURE* AT HER *WORST*.

AND WE'RE ONLY HUMAN.

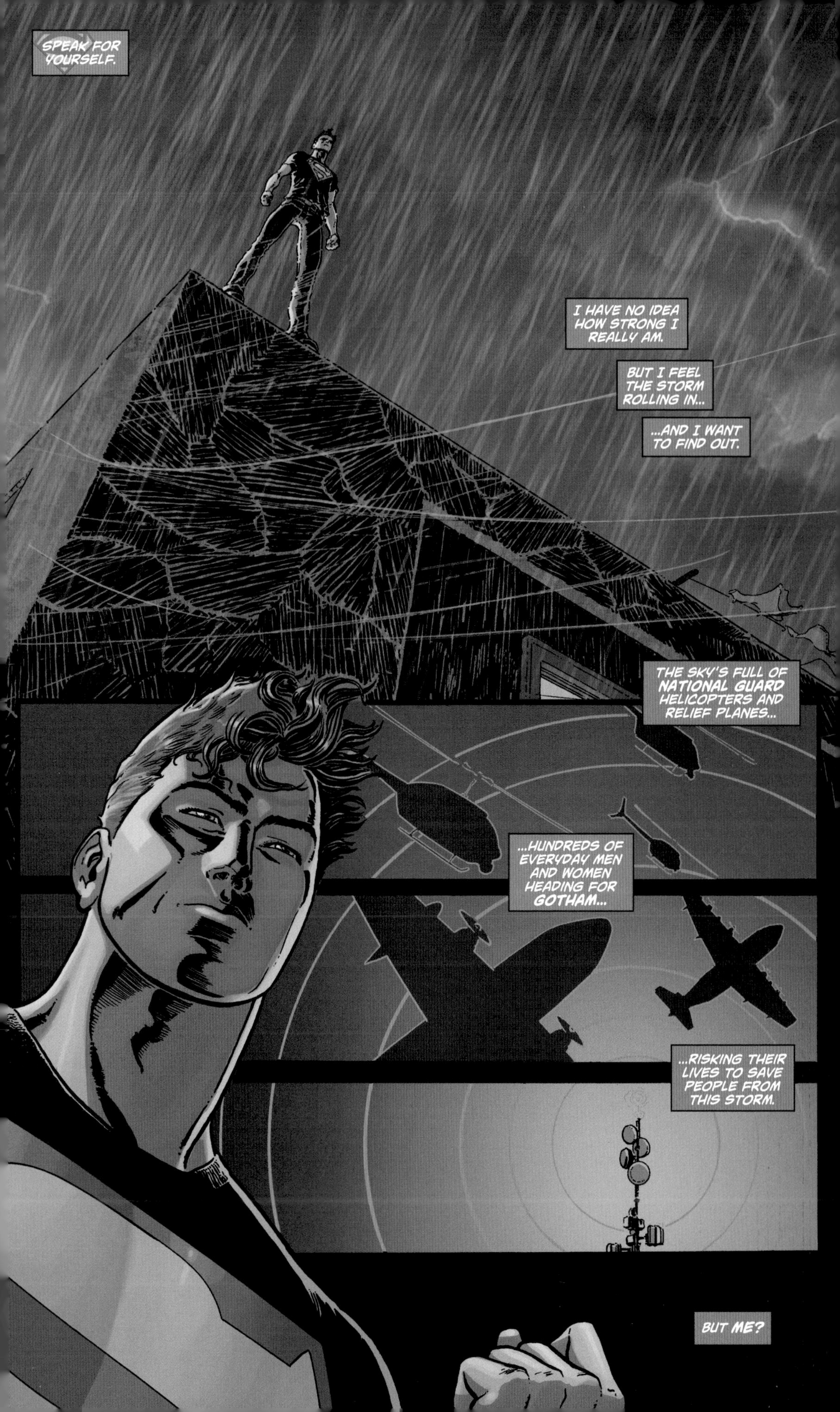
SPEAK FOR YOURSELF.
I HAVE NO IDEA HOW STRONG I REALLY AM.
BUT I FEEL THE STORM ROLLING IN...
...AND I WANT TO FIND OUT.
THE SKY'S FULL OF NATIONAL GUARD HELICOPTERS AND RELIEF PLANES...
...HUNDREDS OF EVERYDAY MEN AND WOMEN HEADING FOR GOTHAM...
...RISKING THEIR LIVES TO SAVE PEOPLE FROM THIS STORM.
BUT ME?

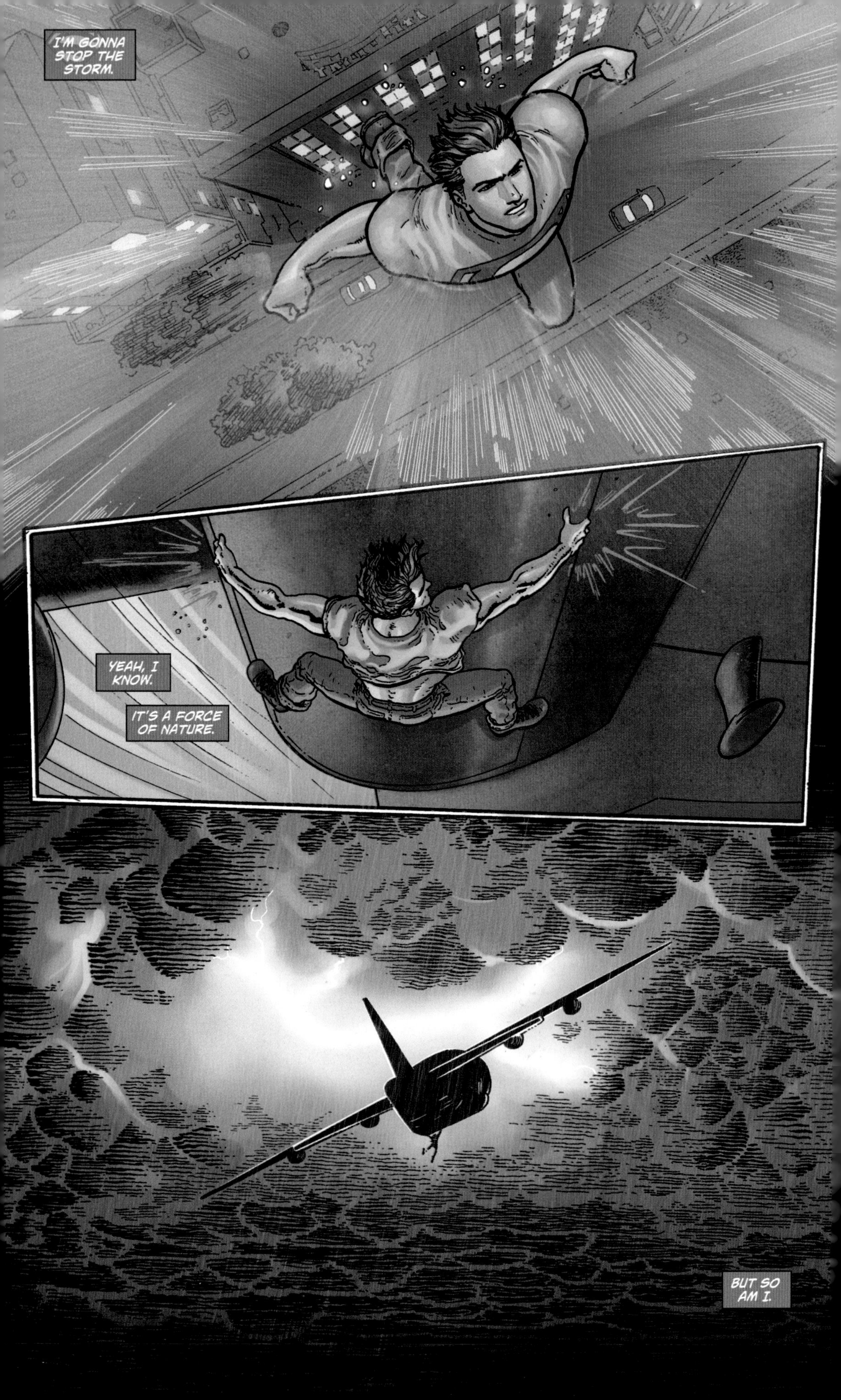
I'M GONNA STOP THE STORM.
YEAH, I KNOW.
IT'S A FORCE OF NATURE.
BUT SO AM I.

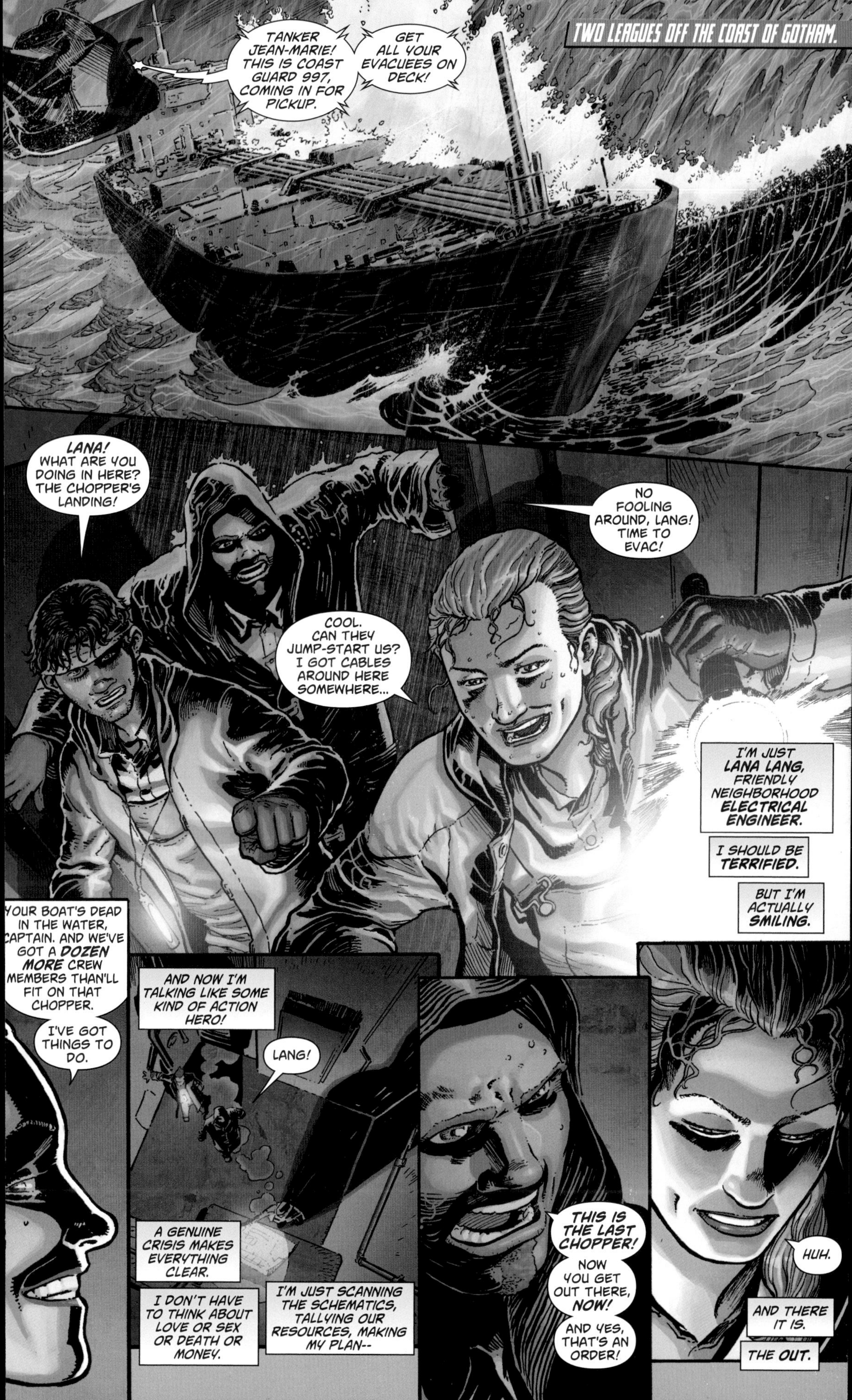
TWO LEAGUES OFF THE COAST OF GOTHAM.
TANKER JEAN-MARIE! THIS IS COAST GUARD 997, COMING IN FOR PICKUP.
GET ALL YOUR EVACUEES ON DECK!
LANA! WHAT ARE YOU DOING IN HERE? THE CHOPPER'S LANDING!
NO FOOLING AROUND, LANG! TIME TO EVAC!
COOL. CAN THEY JUMP-START US? I GOT CABLES AROUND HERE SOMEWHERE...
I'M JUST LANA LANG, FRIENDLY NEIGHBORHOOD ELECTRICAL ENGINEER.
I SHOULD BE TERRIFIED.
BUT I'M ACTUALLY SMILING.
YOUR BOAT'S DEAD IN THE WATER, CAPTAIN. AND WE'VE GOT A DOZEN MORE CREW MEMBERS THAN'LL FIT ON THAT CHOPPER.
I'VE GOT THINGS TO DO.
AND NOW I'M TALKING LIKE SOME KIND OF ACTION HERO!
LANG!
A GENUINE CRISIS MAKES EVERYTHING CLEAR.
I DON'T HAVE TO THINK ABOUT LOVE OR SEX OR DEATH OR MONEY.
I'M JUST SCANNING THE SCHEMATICS, TALLYING OUR RESOURCES, MAKING MY PLAN--
THIS IS THE LAST CHOPPER!
NOW YOU GET OUT THERE, NOW!
AND YES, THAT'S AN ORDER!
HUH.
AND THERE IT IS.
THE OUT.

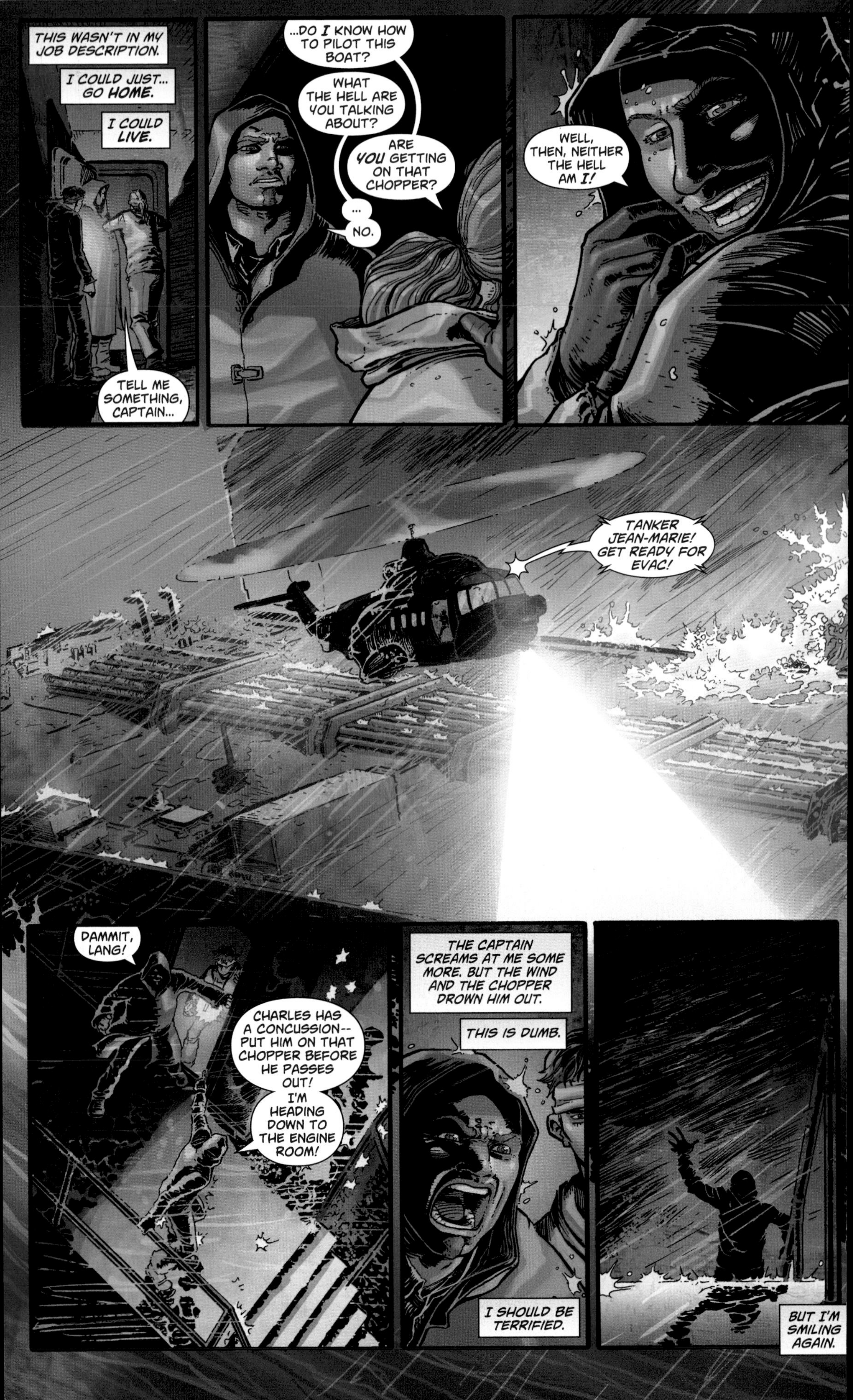
THIS WASN'T IN MY JOB DESCRIPTION.
I COULD JUST... GO HOME.
I COULD LIVE.
TELL ME SOMETHING, CAPTAIN...
...DO I KNOW HOW TO PILOT THIS BOAT?
WHAT THE HELL ARE YOU TALKING ABOUT?
ARE YOU GETTING ON THAT CHOPPER?
...
NO.
WELL, THEN, NEITHER THE HELL AM I!
TANKER JEAN-MARIE! GET READY FOR EVAC!
DAMMIT, LANG!
CHARLES HAS A CONCUSSION-- PUT HIM ON THAT CHOPPER BEFORE HE PASSES OUT!
I'M HEADING DOWN TO THE ENGINE ROOM!
THE CAPTAIN SCREAMS AT ME SOME MORE. BUT THE WIND AND THE CHOPPER DROWN HIM OUT.
THIS IS DUMB.
I SHOULD BE TERRIFIED.
BUT I'M SMILING AGAIN.

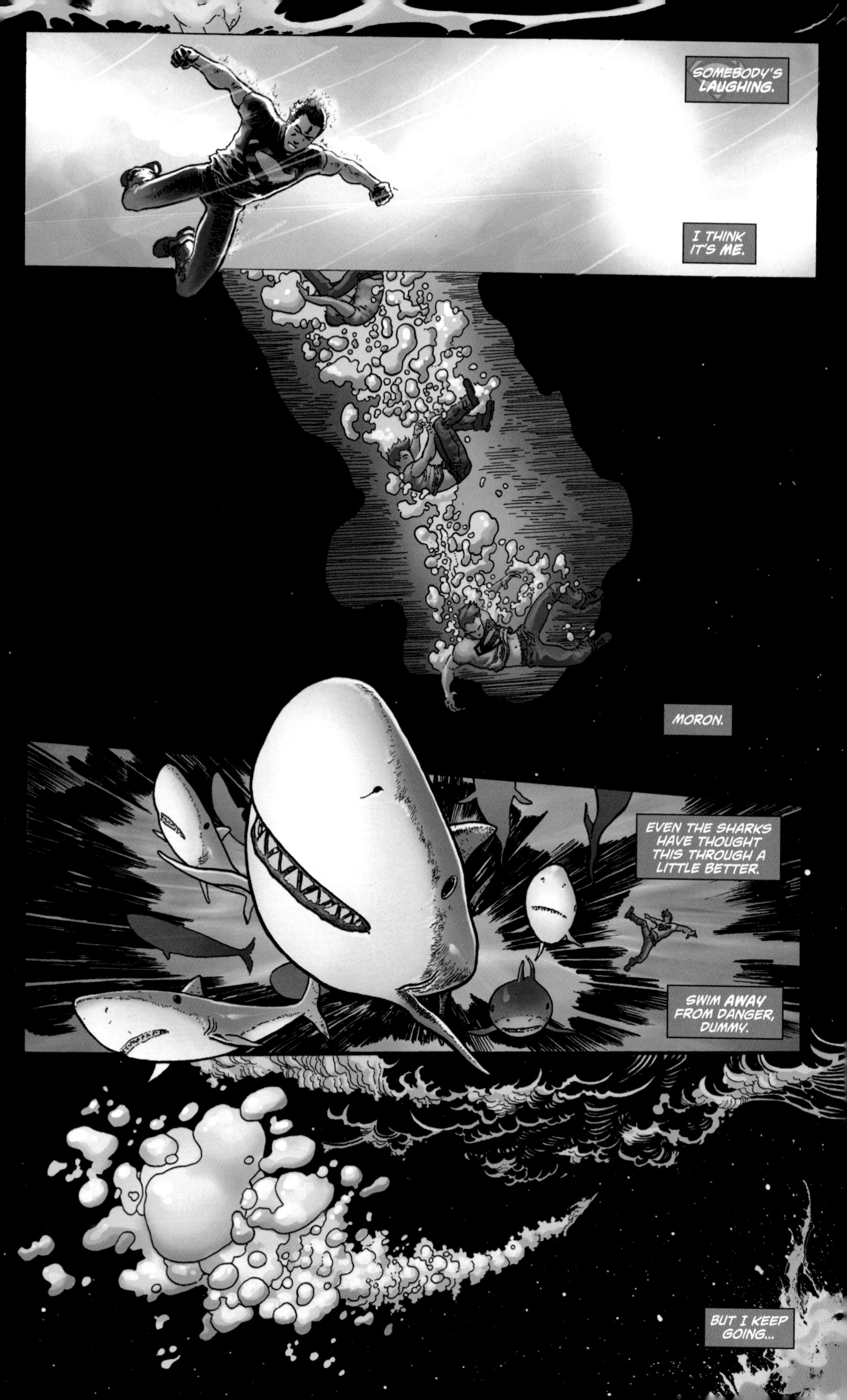
SOMEBODY'S LAUGHING.
I THINK IT'S ME.
MORON.
EVEN THE SHARKS HAVE THOUGHT THIS THROUGH A LITTLE BETTER.
SWIM AWAY FROM DANGER, DUMMY.
BUT I KEEP GOING...

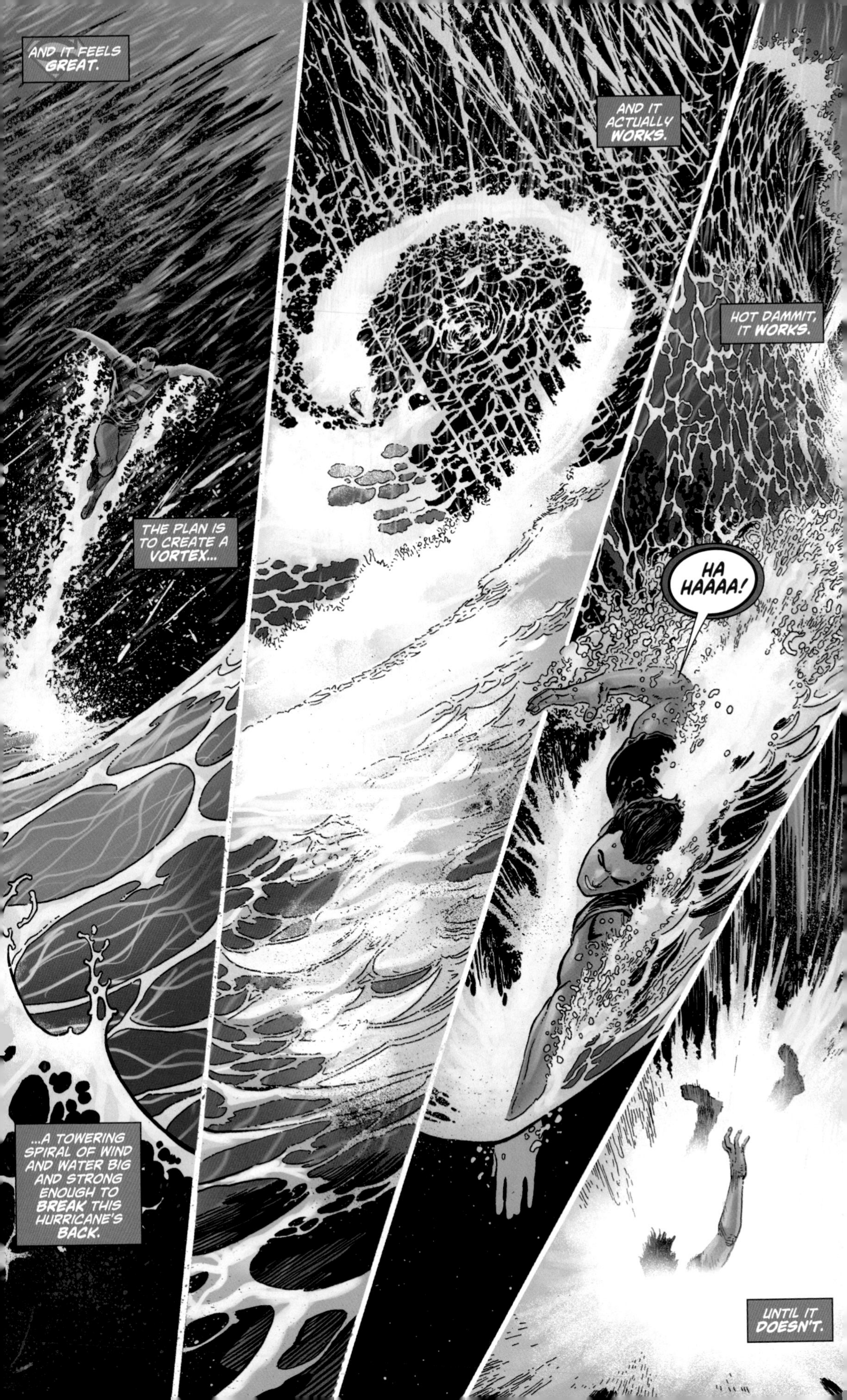
AND IT FEELS GREAT.
THE PLAN IS TO CREATE A VORTEX...
...A TOWERING SPIRAL OF WIND AND WATER BIG AND STRONG ENOUGH TO BREAK THIS HURRICANE'S BACK.
AND IT ACTUALLY WORKS.
HOT DAMMIT, IT WORKS.
HA HAAAA!
UNTIL IT DOESN'T.

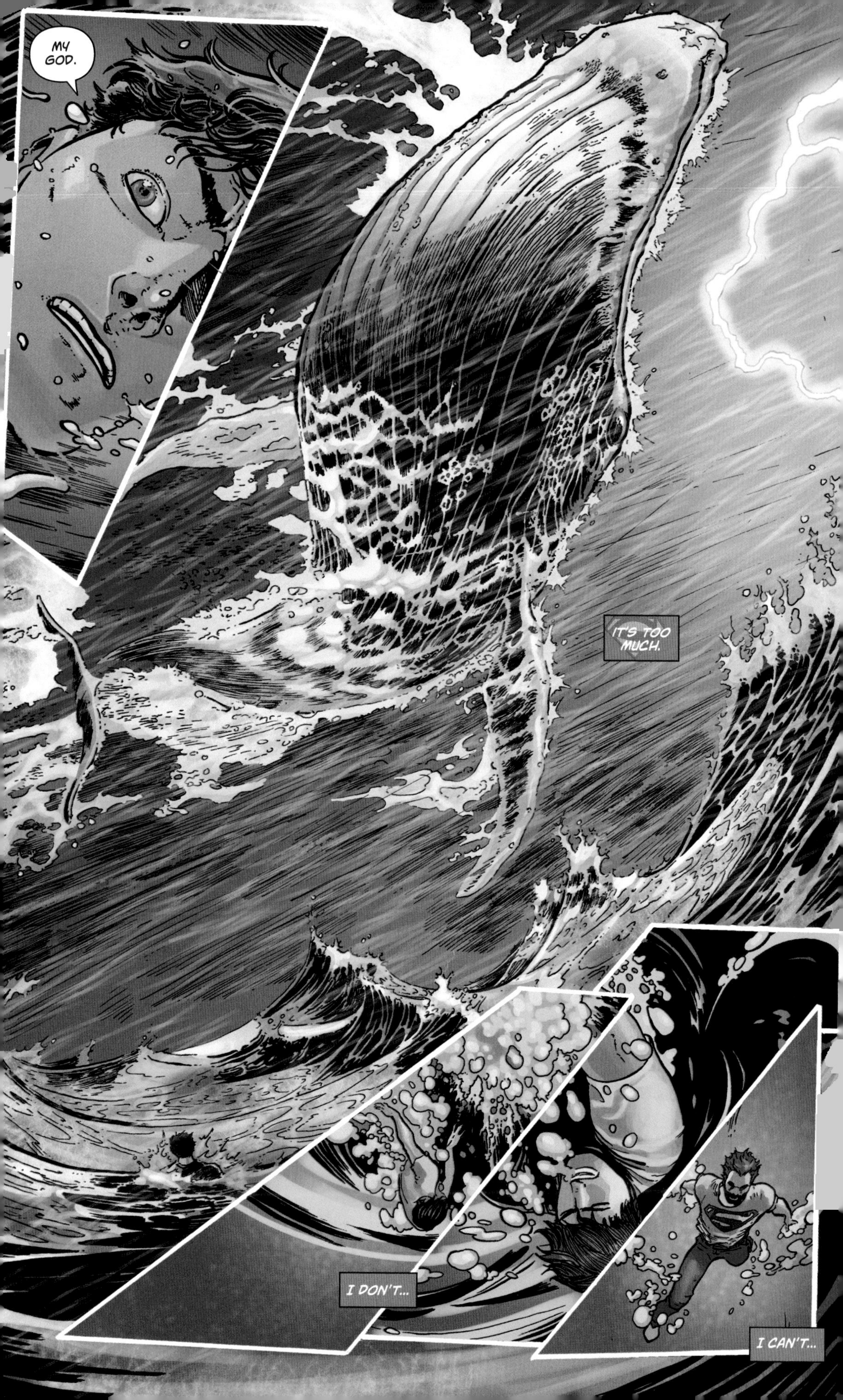
MY GOD.
IT'S TOO MUCH.
I DON'T...
I CAN'T...

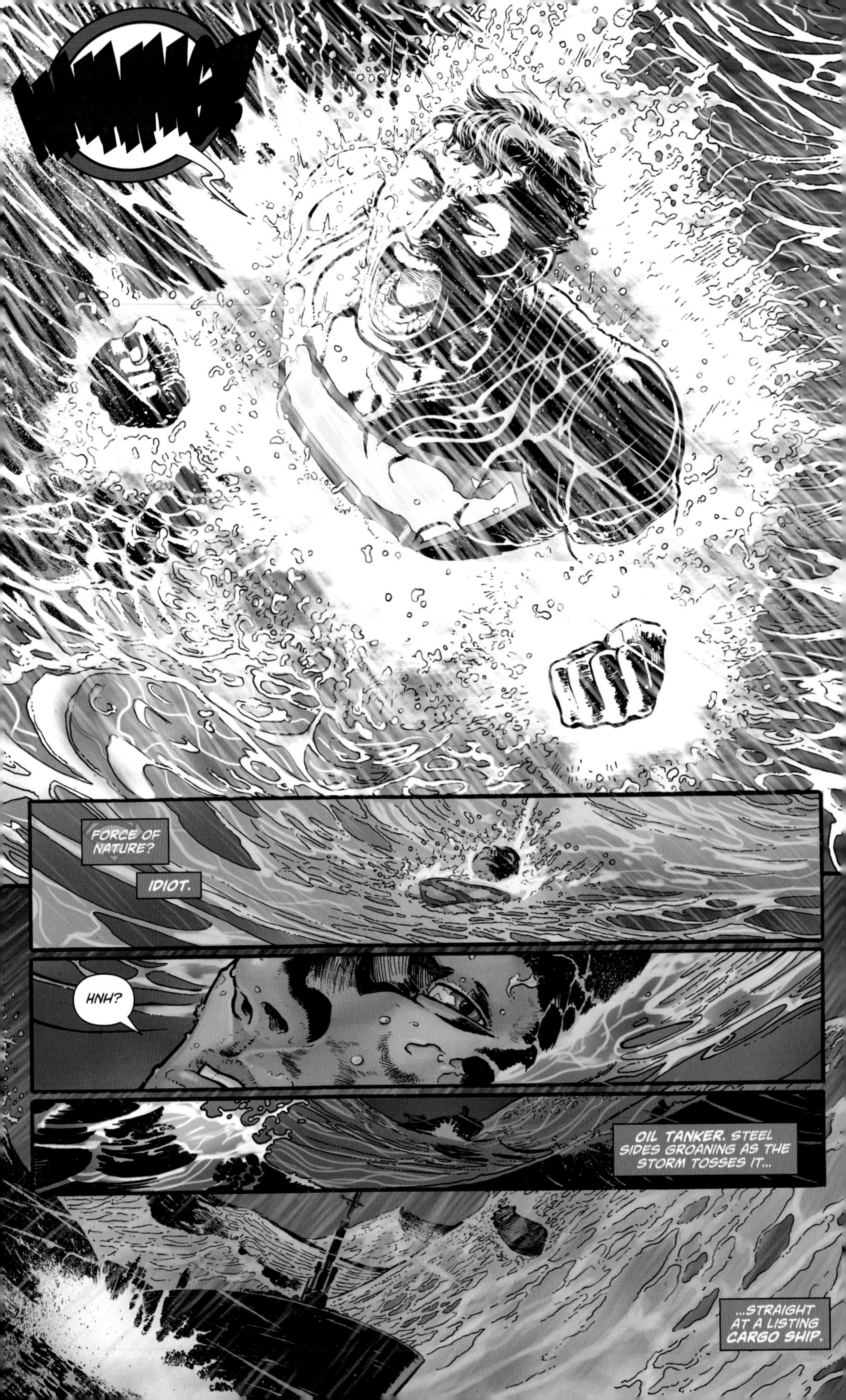
FORCE OF NATURE?
IDIOT.
HNH?
OIL TANKER. STEEL SIDES GROANING AS THE STORM TOSSES IT...
...STRAIGHT AT A LISTING CARGO SHIP.

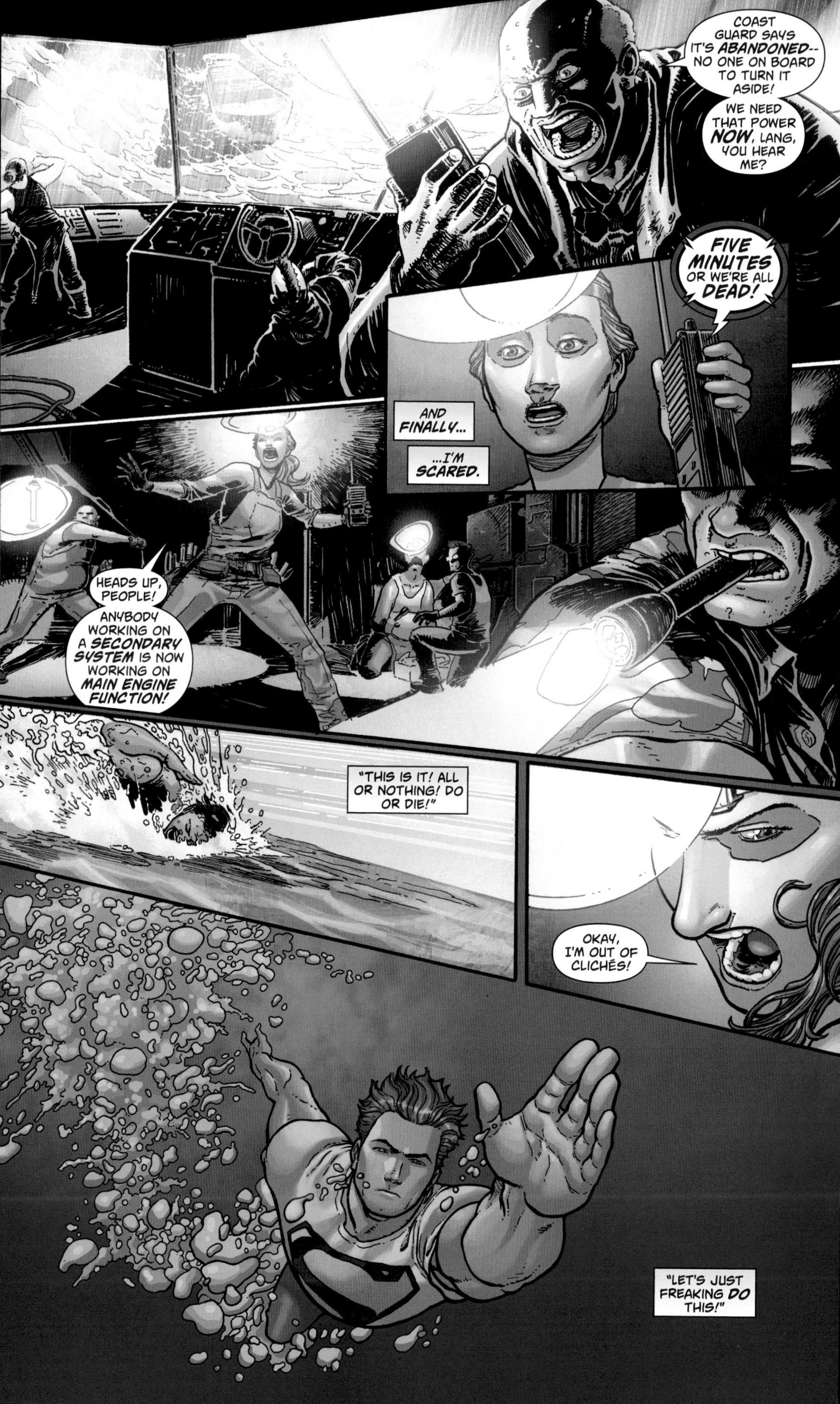
COAST GUARD SAYS IT'S ABANDONED-- NO ONE ON BOARD TO TURN IT ASIDE!
WE NEED THAT POWER NOW, LANG, YOU HEAR ME?
FIVE MINUTES OR WE'RE ALL DEAD!
AND FINALLY...
...I'M SCARED.
HEADS UP, PEOPLE!
ANYBODY WORKING ON A SECONDARY SYSTEM IS NOW WORKING ON MAIN ENGINE FUNCTION!
"THIS IS IT! ALL OR NOTHING! DO OR DIE!"
OKAY, I'M OUT OF CLICHÉS!
"LET'S JUST FREAKING DO THIS!"

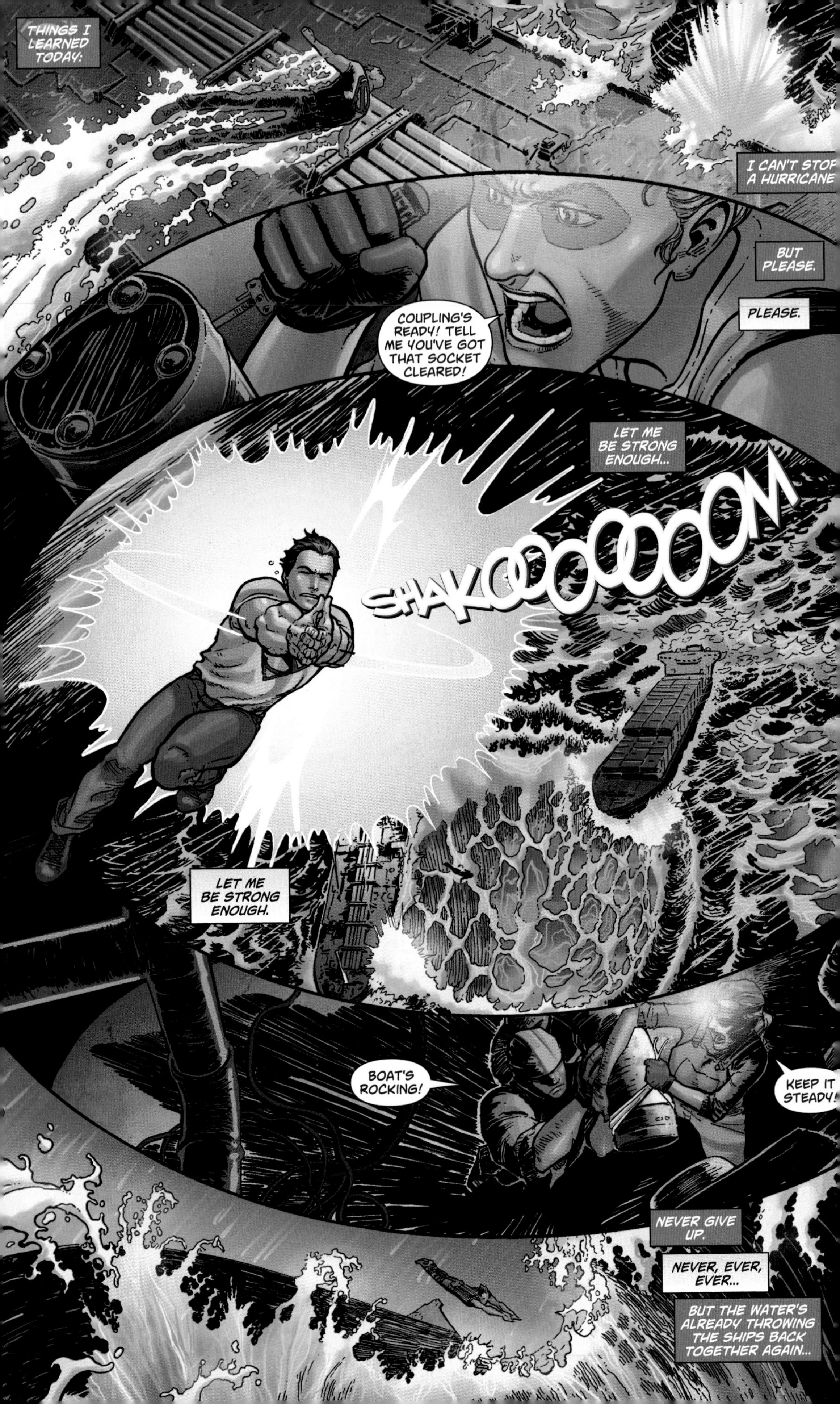

THINGS I LEARNED TODAY:
I CAN'T STOP A HURRICANE
BUT PLEASE.
PLEASE.
COUPLING'S READY! TELL ME YOU'VE GOT THAT SOCKET CLEARED!
LET ME BE STRONG ENOUGH...
SHAKOOOOOOOOM
LET ME BE STRONG ENOUGH.
BOAT'S ROCKING!
KEEP IT STEADY!
NEVER GIVE UP.
NEVER, EVER, EVER...
BUT THE WATER'S ALREADY THROWING THE SHIPS BACK TOGETHER AGAIN...

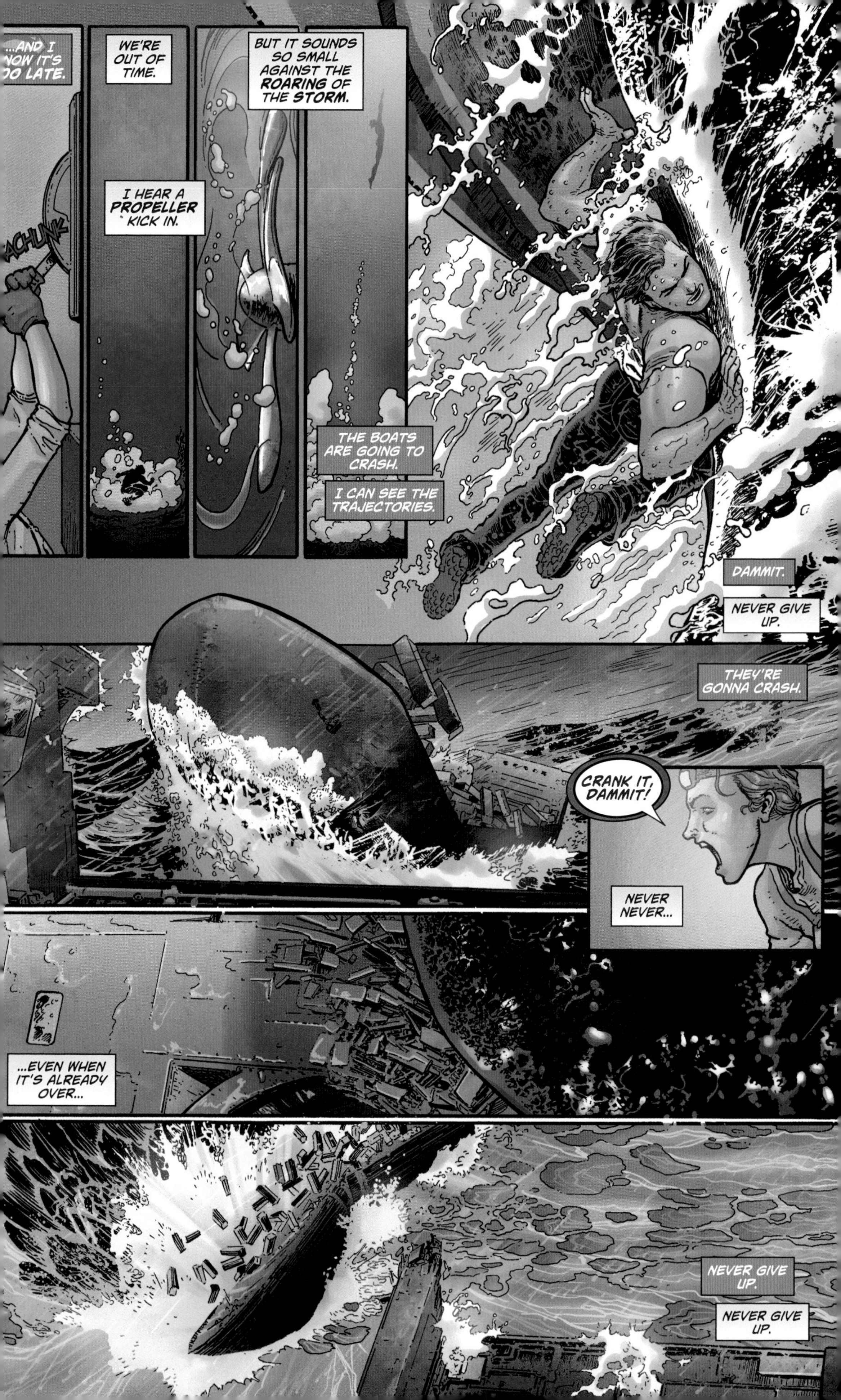
...AND I
NOW IT'S
OO LATE.
WE'RE OUT OF TIME.
BUT IT SOUNDS SO SMALL AGAINST THE ROARING OF THE STORM.
ACHUNK
I HEAR A PROPELLER KICK IN.
THE BOATS ARE GOING TO CRASH.
I CAN SEE THE TRAJECTORIES.
DAMMIT.
NEVER GIVE UP.
THEY'RE GONNA CRASH.
CRANK IT, DAMMIT!
NEVER NEVER...
...EVEN WHEN IT'S ALREADY OVER...
NEVER GIVE UP.
NEVER GIVE UP.

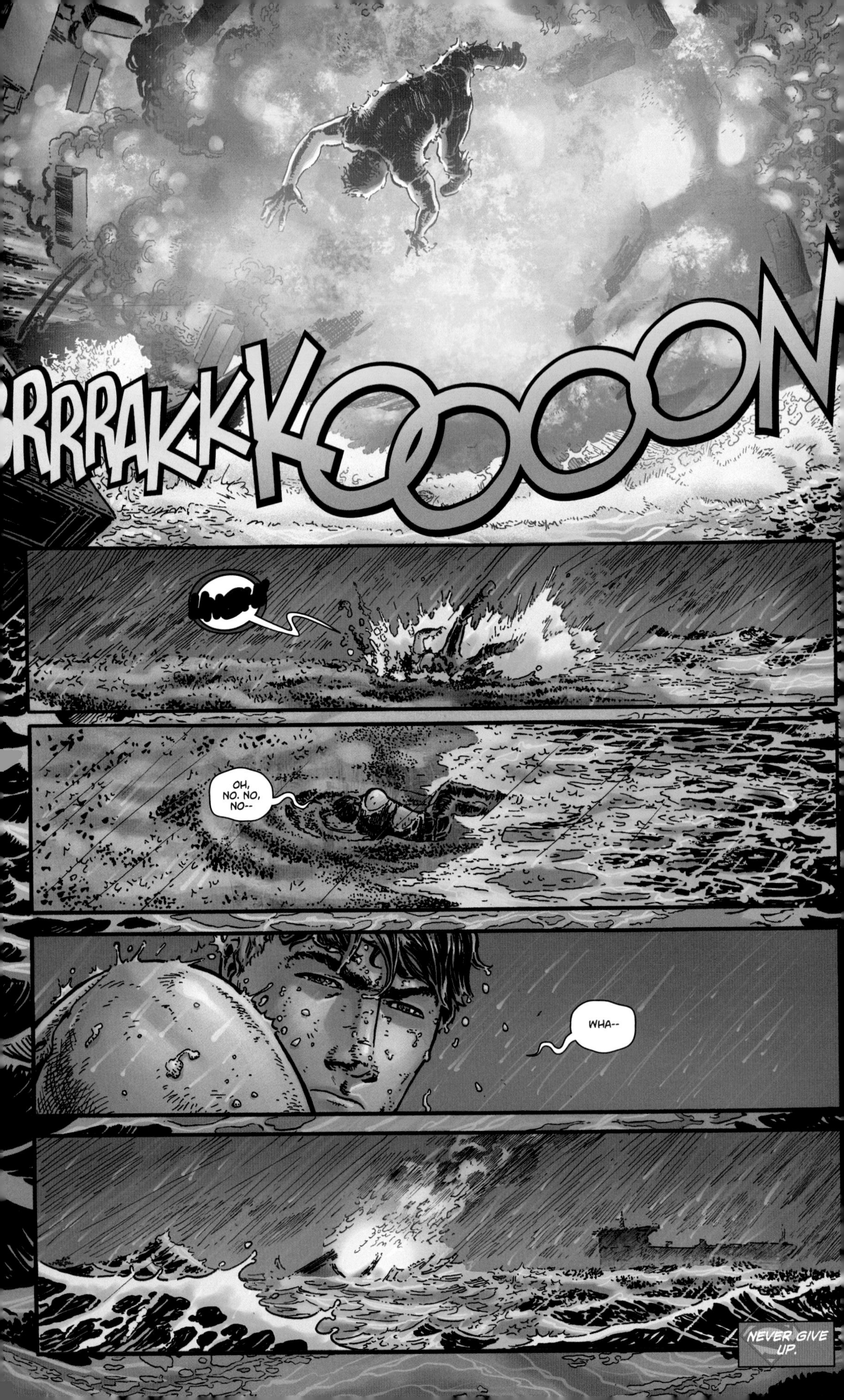
BRRRAKKKOOOOOM
OH, NO. NO, NO--
WHA--
NEVER GIVE UP.

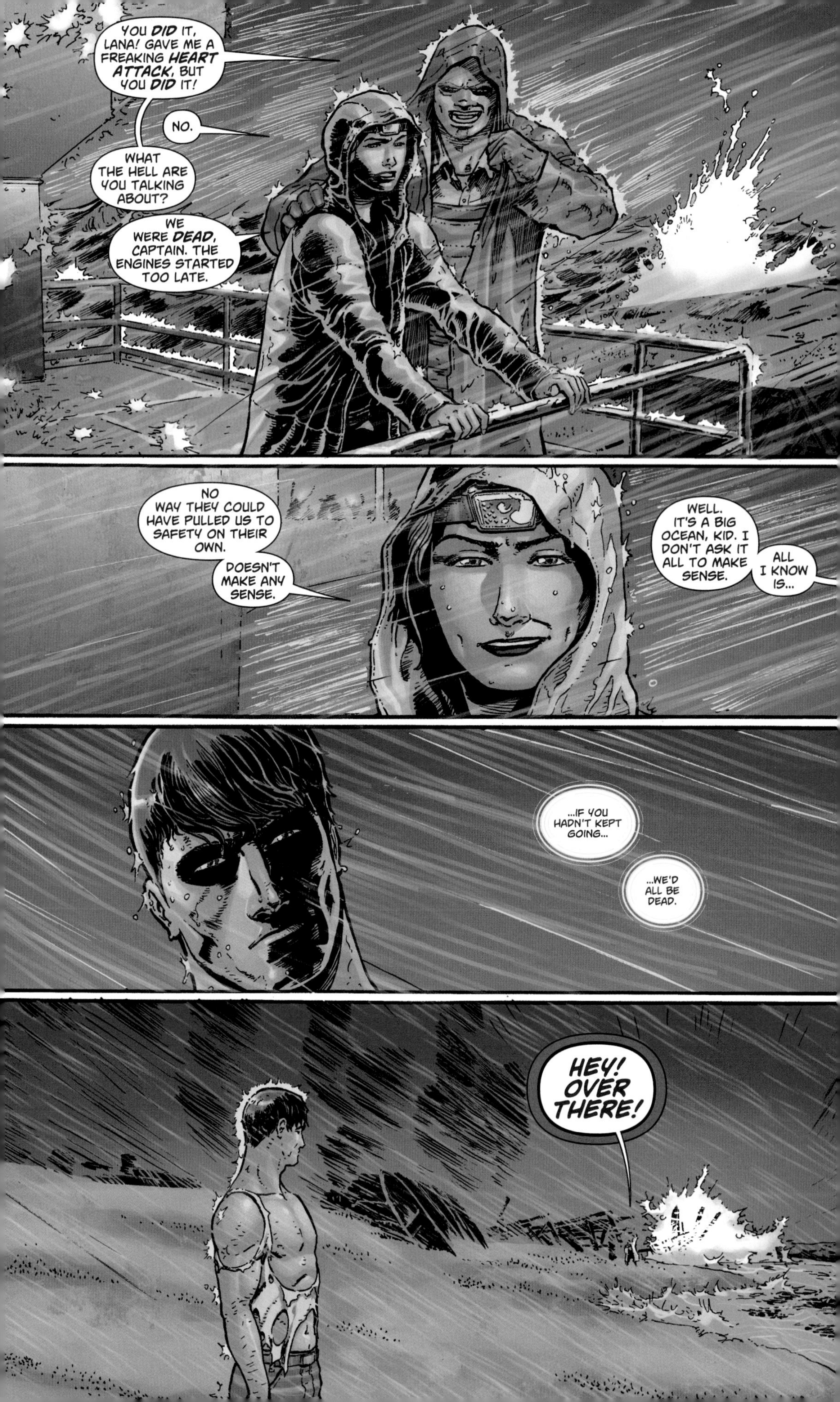

YOU DID IT, LANA! GAVE ME A FREAKING HEART ATTACK, BUT YOU DID IT!
NO.
WHAT THE HELL ARE YOU TALKING ABOUT?
WE WERE DEAD, CAPTAIN. THE ENGINES STARTED TOO LATE.
NO WAY THEY COULD HAVE PULLED US TO SAFETY ON THEIR OWN.
DOESN'T MAKE ANY SENSE.
WELL. IT'S A BIG OCEAN, KID. I DON'T ASK IT ALL TO MAKE SENSE.
ALL I KNOW IS...
...IF YOU HADN'T KEPT GOING...
...WE'D ALL BE DEAD.
HEY! OVER THERE!

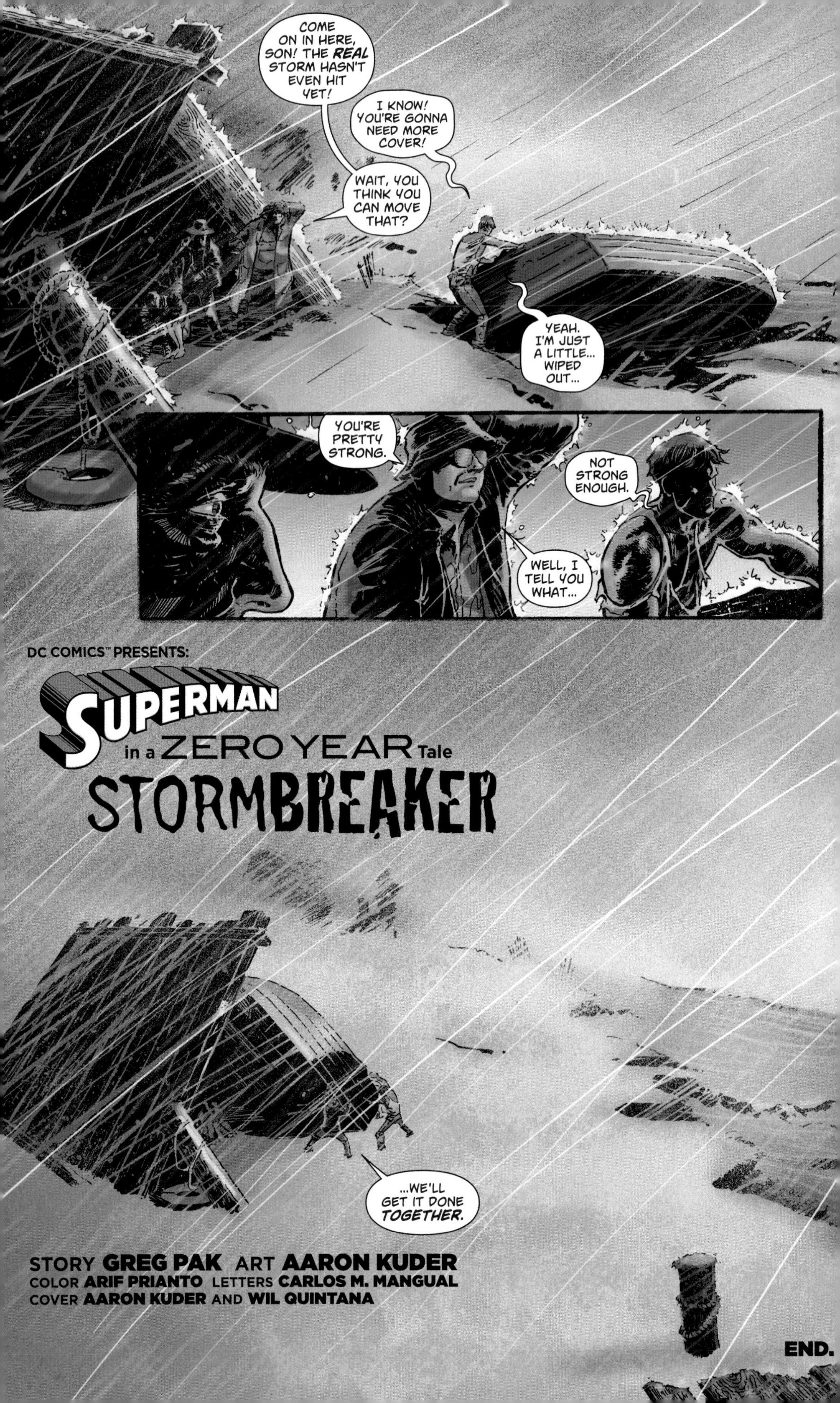

COME ON IN HERE, SON! THE REAL STORM HASN'T EVEN HIT YET!
I KNOW! YOU'RE GONNA NEED MORE COVER!
WAIT, YOU THINK YOU CAN MOVE THAT?
YEAH. I'M JUST A LITTLE... WIPED OUT...
YOU'RE PRETTY STRONG.
NOT STRONG ENOUGH.
WELL, I TELL YOU WHAT...
DC COMICS™ PRESENTS:
SUPERMAN
in a ZERO YEAR Tale
STORMBREAKER
...WE'LL GET IT DONE TOGETHER.
STORY GREG PAK ART AARON KUDER
COLOR ARIF PRIANTO LETTERS CARLOS M. MANGUAL
COVER AARON KUDER AND WIL QUINTANA
END.

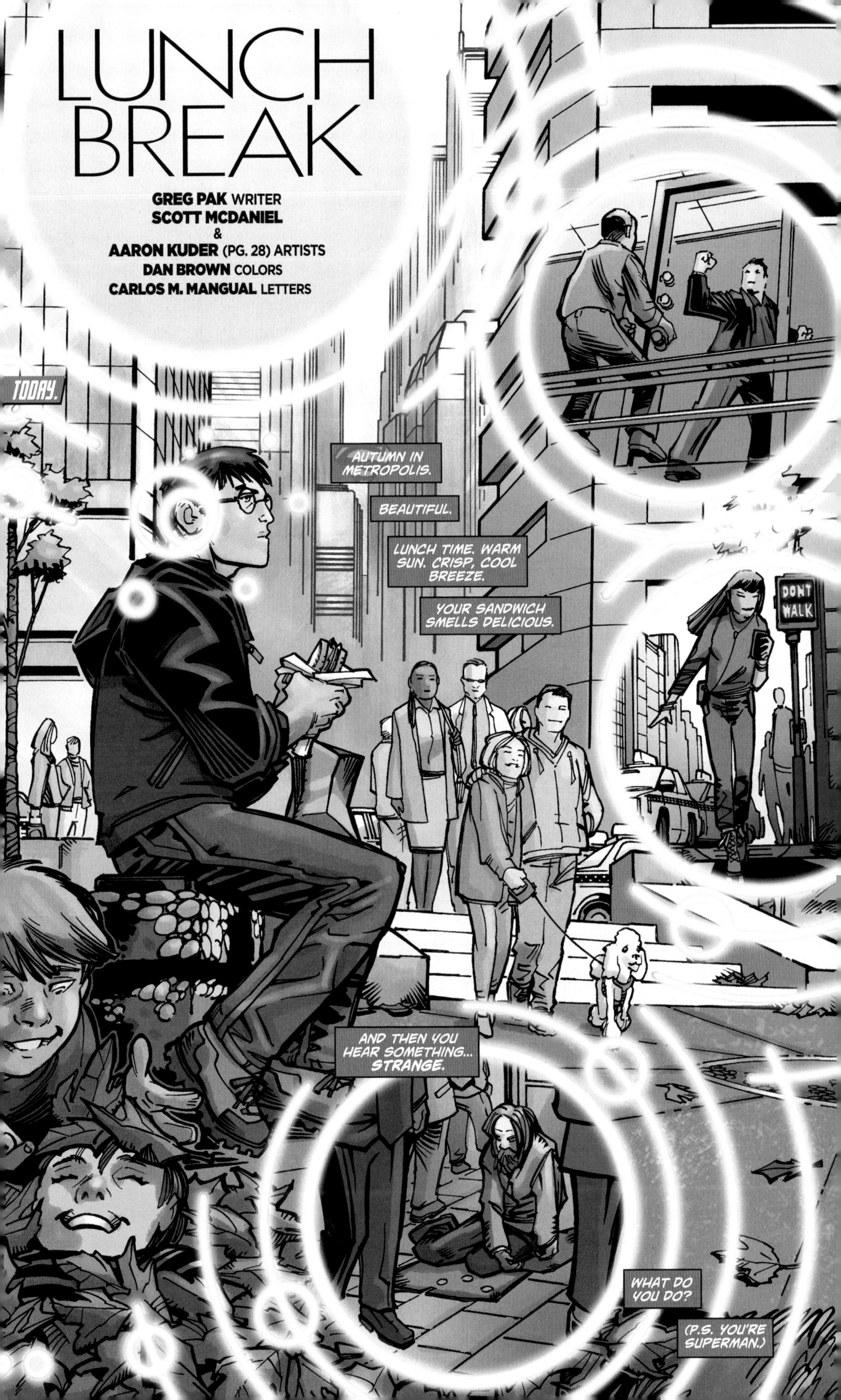
LUNCH BREAK
GREG PAK WRITER
SCOTT MCDANIEL
&
AARON KUDER (PG. 28) ARTISTS
DAN BROWN COLORS
CARLOS M. MANGUAL LETTERS
TODAY.
AUTUMN IN METROPOLIS.
BEAUTIFUL.
LUNCH TIME. WARM SUN. CRISP, COOL BREEZE.
YOUR SANDWICH SMELLS DELICIOUS.
DONT WALK
AND THEN YOU HEAR SOMETHING... STRANGE.
WHAT DO YOU DO?
(P.S. YOU'RE SUPERMAN.)

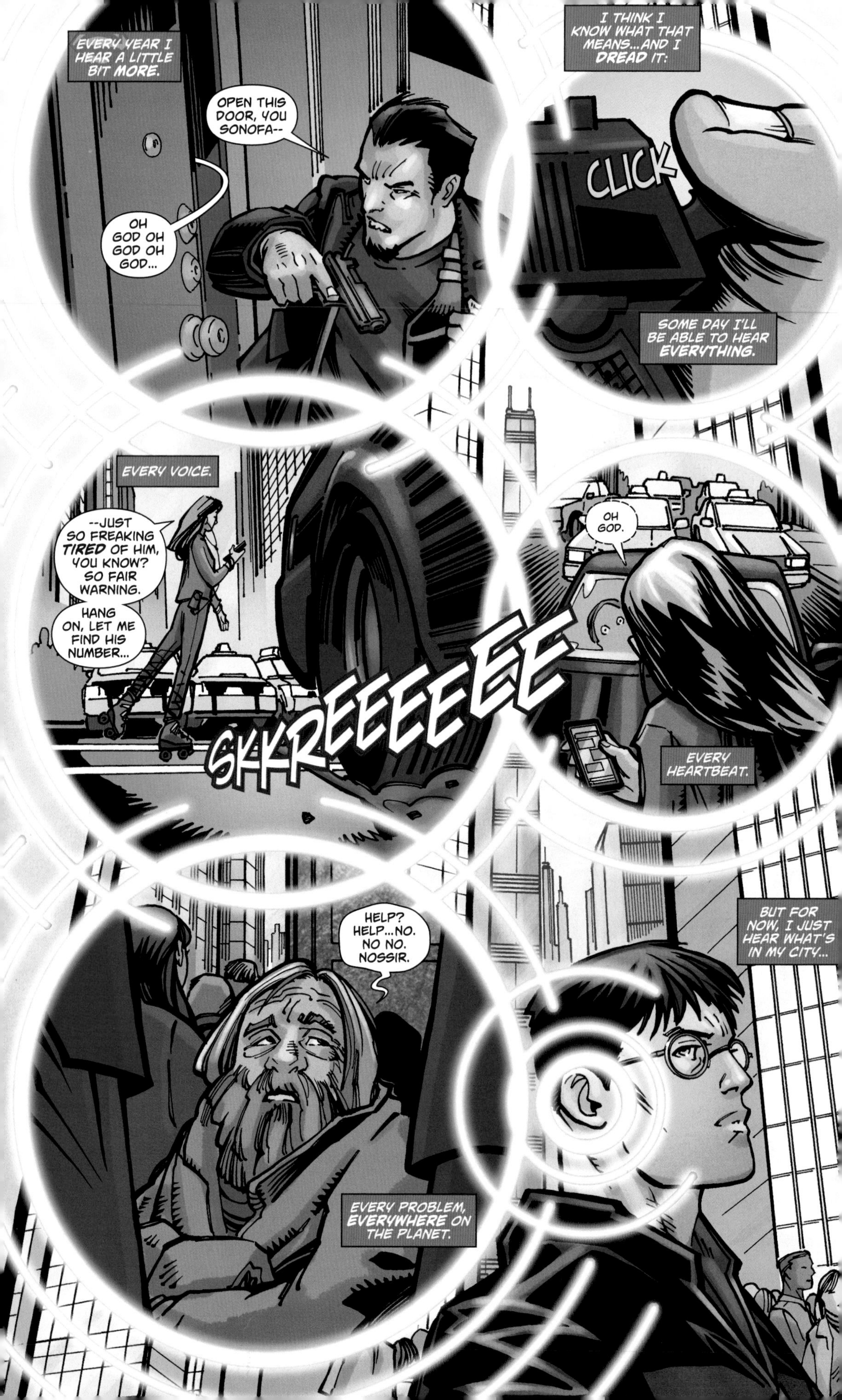
EVERY YEAR I HEAR A LITTLE BIT MORE.
OPEN THIS DOOR, YOU SONOFA--
OH GOD OH GOD OH GOD...
I THINK I KNOW WHAT THAT MEANS...AND I DREAD IT:
CLICK
SOME DAY I'LL BE ABLE TO HEAR EVERYTHING.
EVERY VOICE.
--JUST SO FREAKING TIRED OF HIM, YOU KNOW? SO FAIR WARNING.
HANG ON, LET ME FIND HIS NUMBER...
OH GOD.
SKKREEEEEEEE
EVERY HEARTBEAT.
HELP? HELP...NO. NO NO. NOSSIR.
EVERY PROBLEM, EVERYWHERE ON THE PLANET.
BUT FOR NOW, I JUST HEAR WHAT'S IN MY CITY...

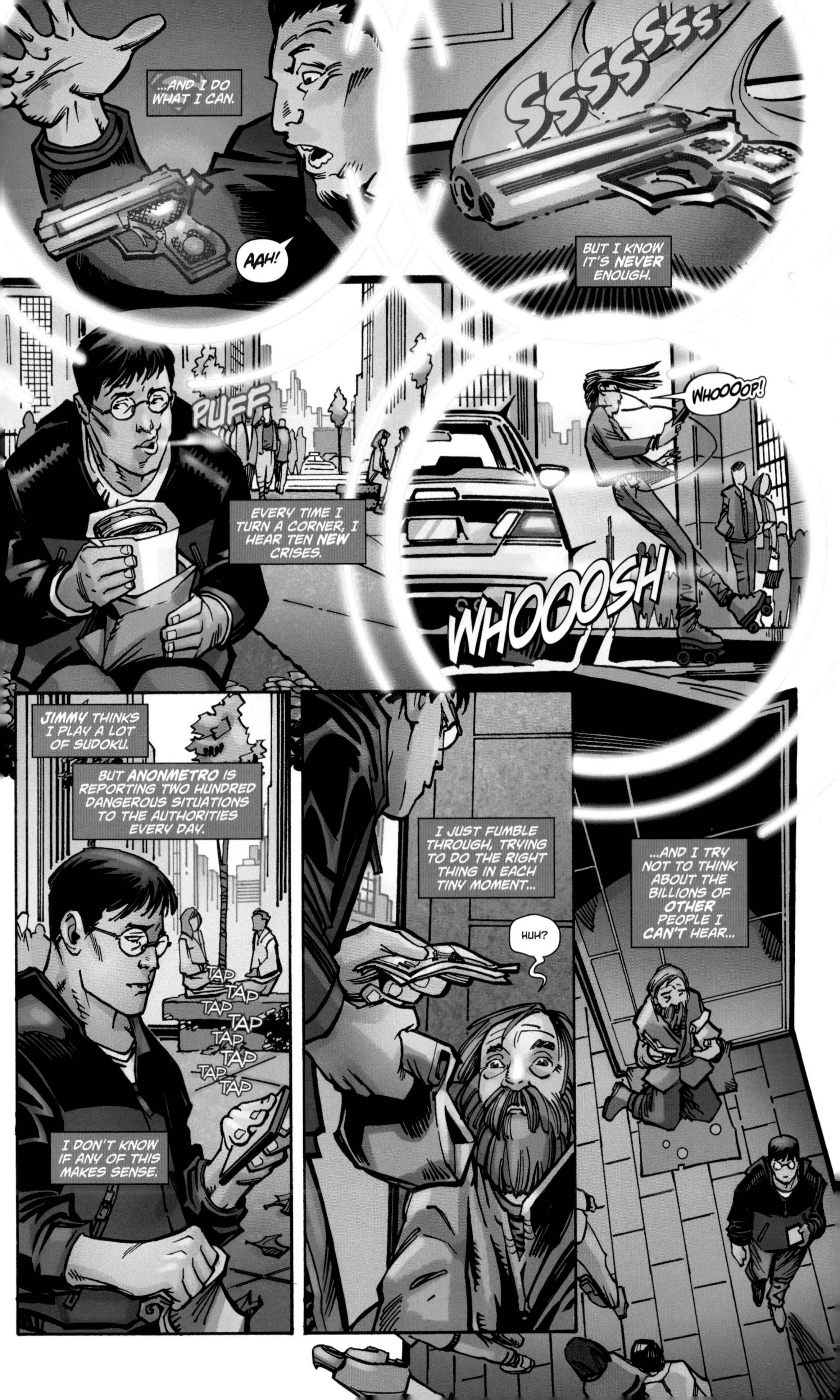
...AND I DO WHAT I CAN.
AAH!
SSSSSSS
BUT I KNOW IT'S NEVER ENOUGH.
PUFF
EVERY TIME I TURN A CORNER, I HEAR TEN NEW CRISES.
WHOOOOP!
WHOOOSH
JIMMY THINKS I PLAY A LOT OF SUDOKU.
BUT ANONMETRO IS REPORTING TWO HUNDRED DANGEROUS SITUATIONS TO THE AUTHORITIES EVERY DAY.
TAP TAP TAP TAP TAP TAP TAP TAP
I DON'T KNOW IF ANY OF THIS MAKES SENSE.
I JUST FUMBLE THROUGH, TRYING TO DO THE RIGHT THING IN EACH TINY MOMENT...
HUH?
...AND I TRY NOT TO THINK ABOUT THE BILLIONS OF OTHER PEOPLE I CAN'T HEAR...

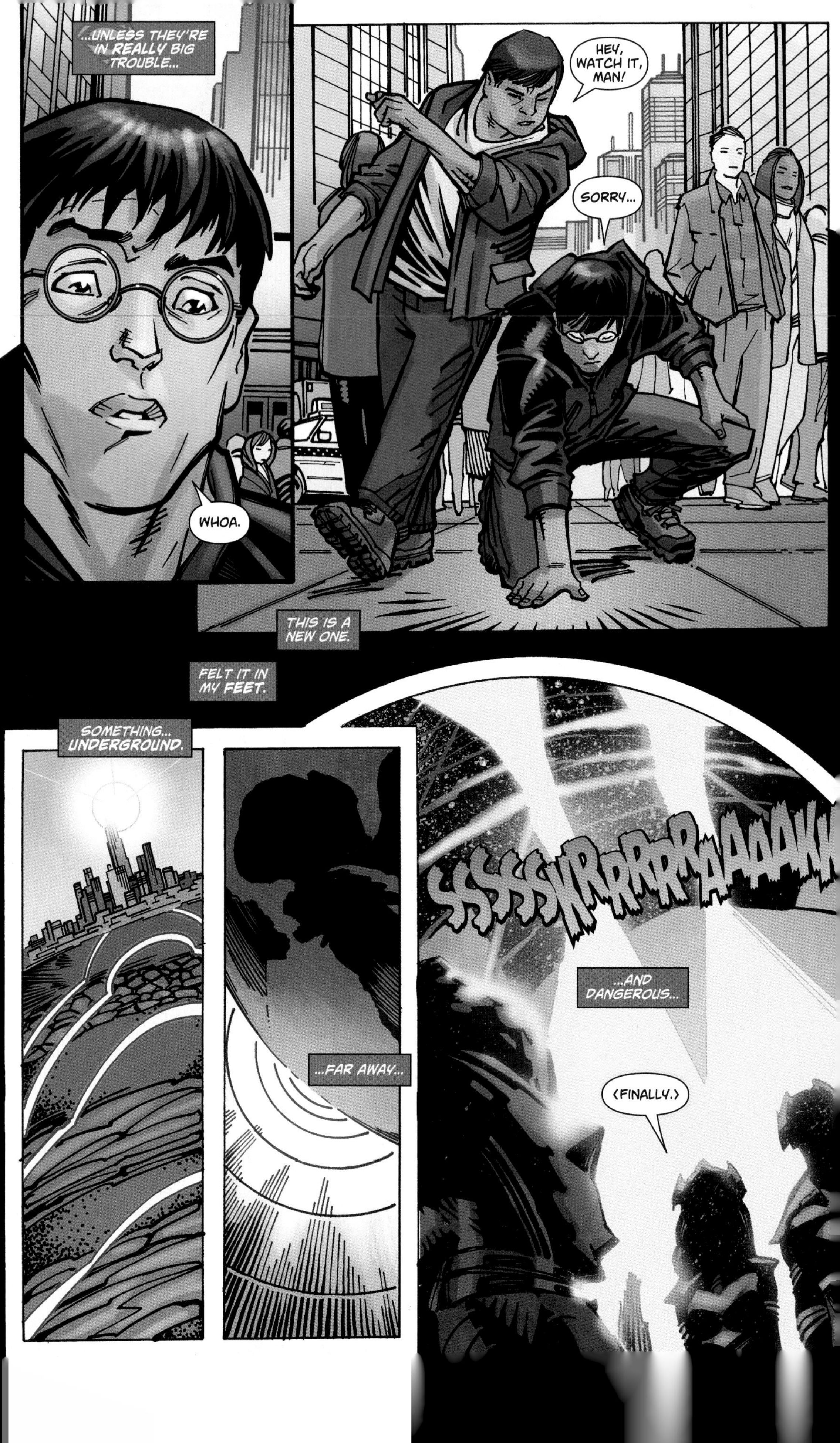

...UNLESS THEY'RE IN REALLY BIG TROUBLE...
WHOA.
HEY, WATCH IT, MAN!
SORRY...
THIS IS A NEW ONE.
FELT IT IN MY FEET.
SOMETHING... UNDERGROUND.
...FAR AWAY...
SSSSSKRRRRAAAAKK
...AND DANGEROUS...
‹FINALLY.›

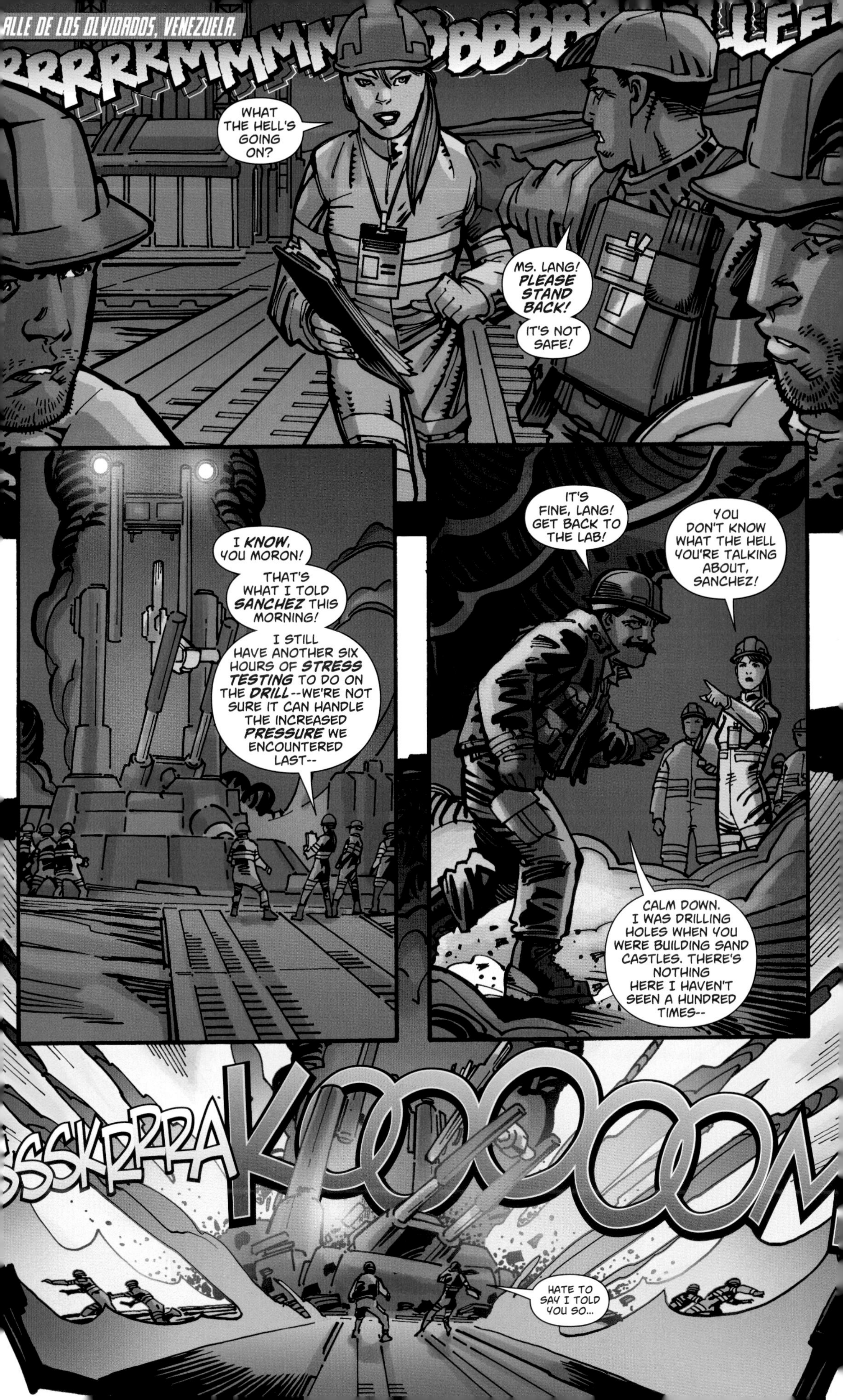
ALLE DE LOS OLVIDADOS, VENEZUELA.
RRRRRMMMMN BBBBR LEF
WHAT THE HELL'S GOING ON?
MS. LANG! PLEASE STAND BACK!
IT'S NOT SAFE!
I KNOW, YOU MORON!
THAT'S WHAT I TOLD SANCHEZ THIS MORNING!
I STILL HAVE ANOTHER SIX HOURS OF STRESS TESTING TO DO ON THE DRILL--WE'RE NOT SURE IT CAN HANDLE THE INCREASED PRESSURE WE ENCOUNTERED LAST--
IT'S FINE, LANG! GET BACK TO THE LAB!
YOU DON'T KNOW WHAT THE HELL YOU'RE TALKING ABOUT, SANCHEZ!
CALM DOWN. I WAS DRILLING HOLES WHEN YOU WERE BUILDING SAND CASTLES. THERE'S NOTHING HERE I HAVEN'T SEEN A HUNDRED TIMES--
SSKRRRAKOOOOOOM
HATE TO SAY I TOLD YOU SO...

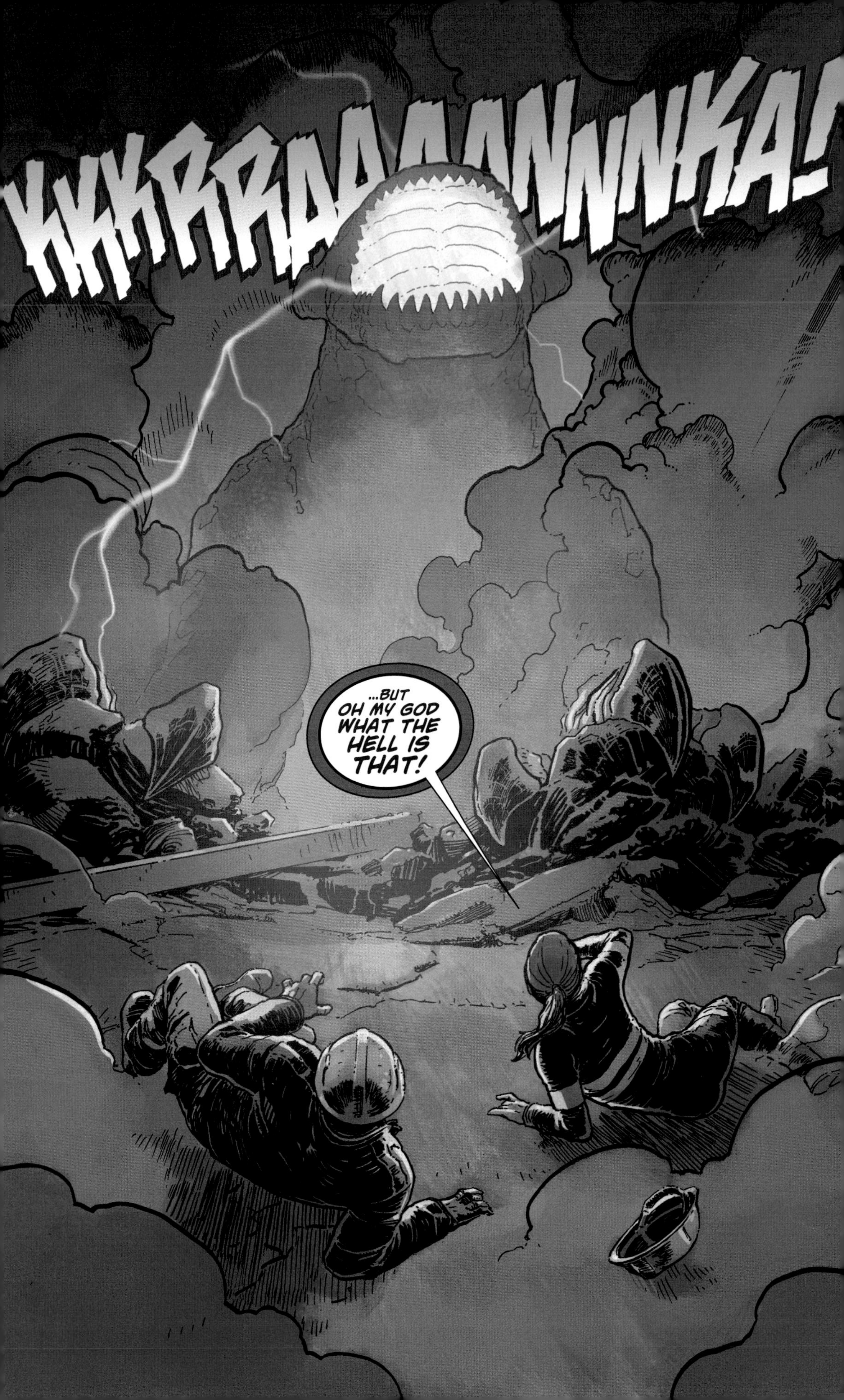
KKKRRAAAANNNKA!
...BUT OH MY GOD WHAT THE HELL IS THAT!

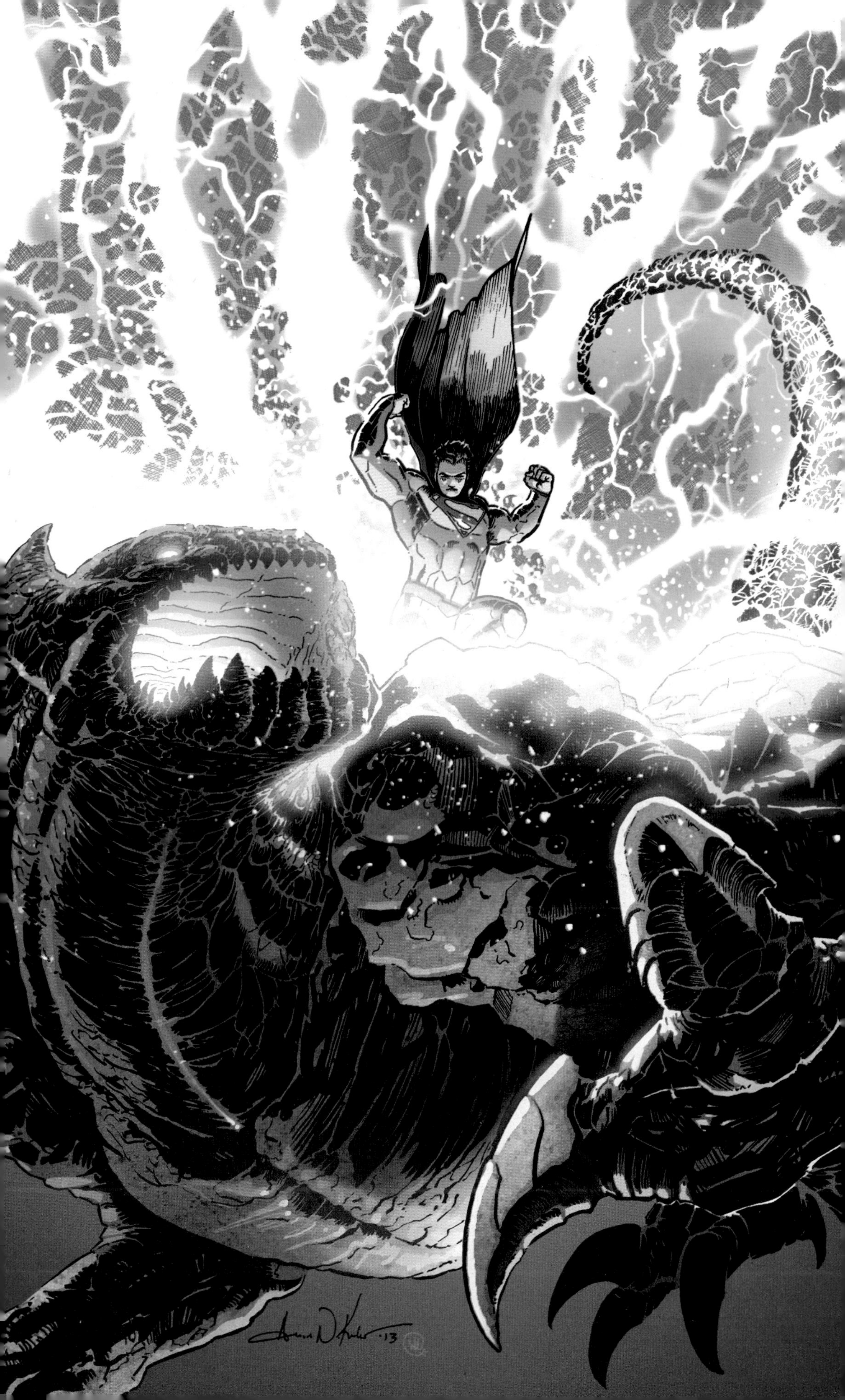

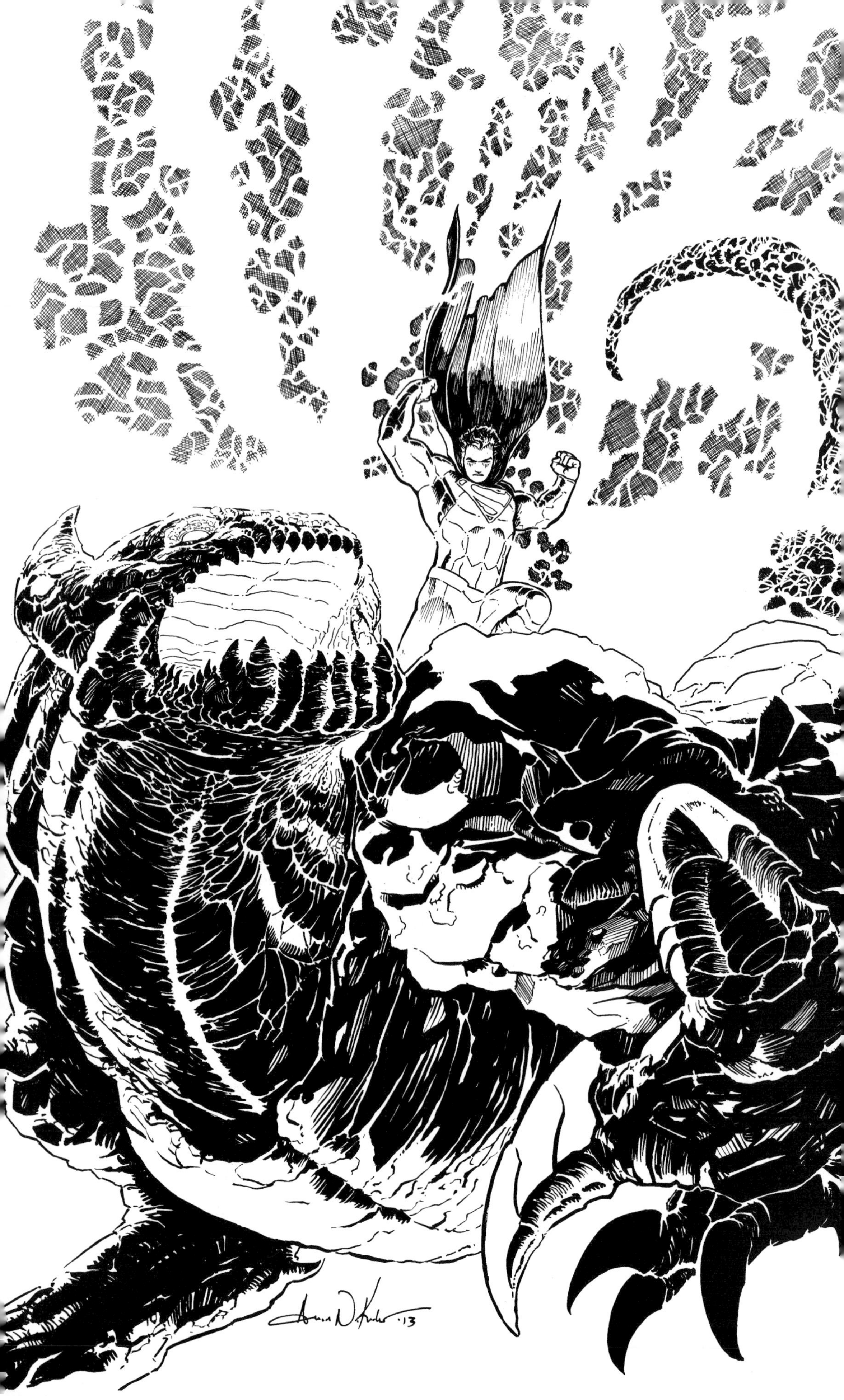

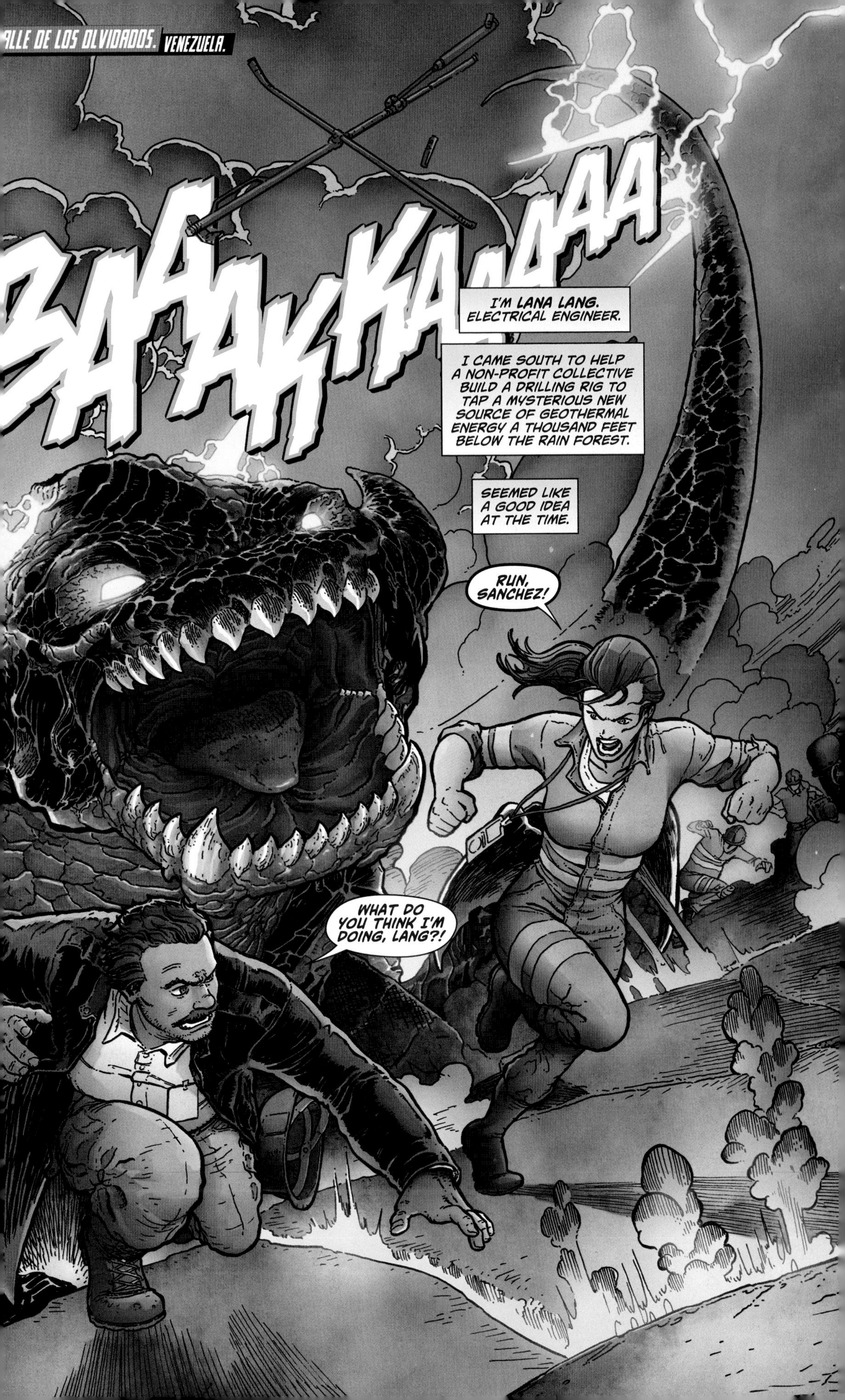
ALLE DE LOS OLVIDADOS. VENEZUELA.
BAAAKKAAAAA
I'M LANA LANG. ELECTRICAL ENGINEER.
I CAME SOUTH TO HELP A NON-PROFIT COLLECTIVE BUILD A DRILLING RIG TO TAP A MYSTERIOUS NEW SOURCE OF GEOTHERMAL ENERGY A THOUSAND FEET BELOW THE RAIN FOREST.
SEEMED LIKE A GOOD IDEA AT THE TIME.
RUN, SANCHEZ!
WHAT DO YOU THINK I'M DOING, LANG?!

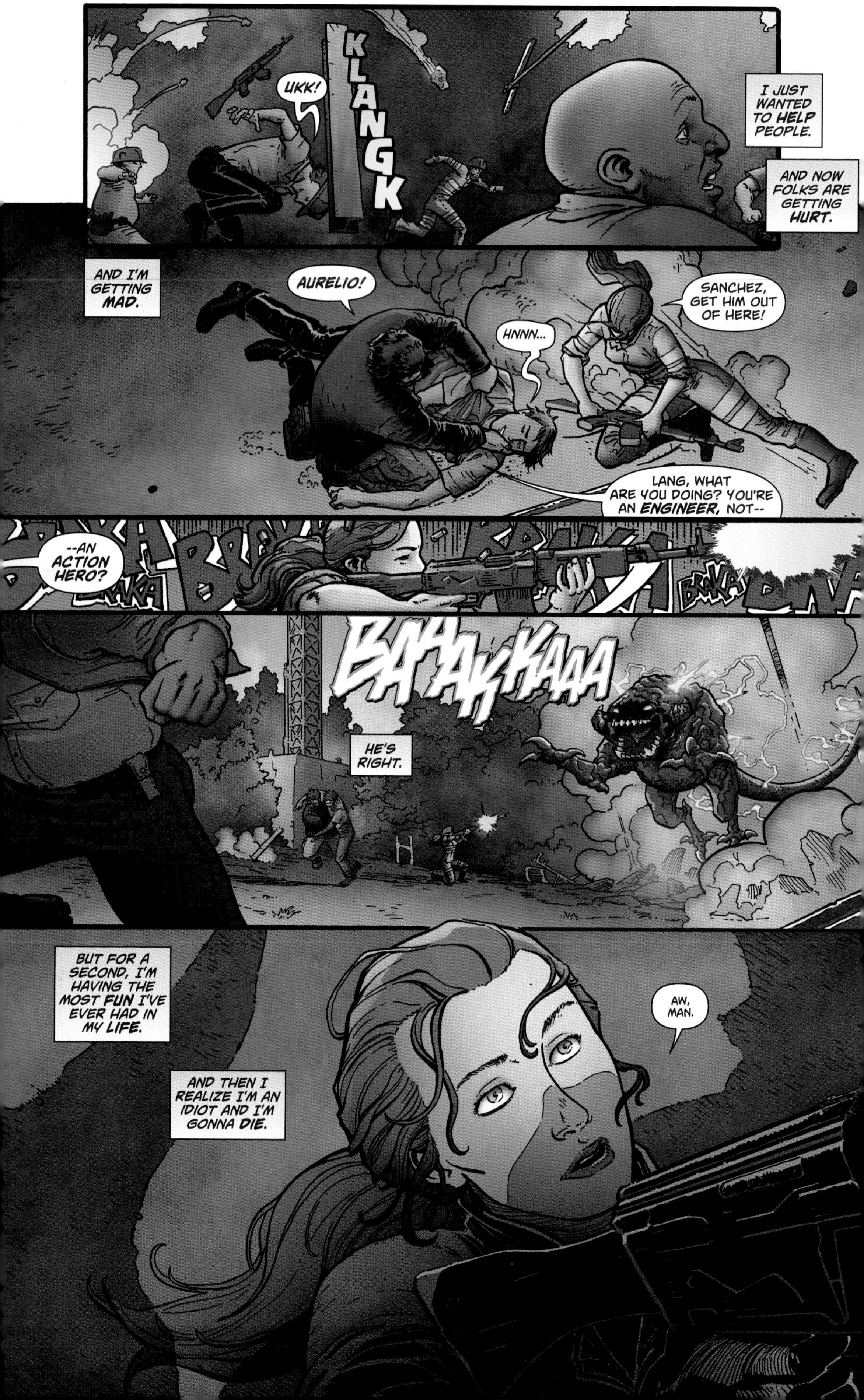
UKK!
KLANGK
I JUST WANTED TO HELP PEOPLE.
AND NOW FOLKS ARE GETTING HURT.
AND I'M GETTING MAD.
AURELIO!
HNNN...
SANCHEZ, GET HIM OUT OF HERE!
LANG, WHAT ARE YOU DOING? YOU'RE AN ENGINEER, NOT--
--AN ACTION HERO?
BAAKKAAA
HE'S RIGHT.
BUT FOR A SECOND, I'M HAVING THE MOST FUN I'VE EVER HAD IN MY LIFE.
AND THEN I REALIZE I'M AN IDIOT AND I'M GONNA DIE.
AW, MAN.

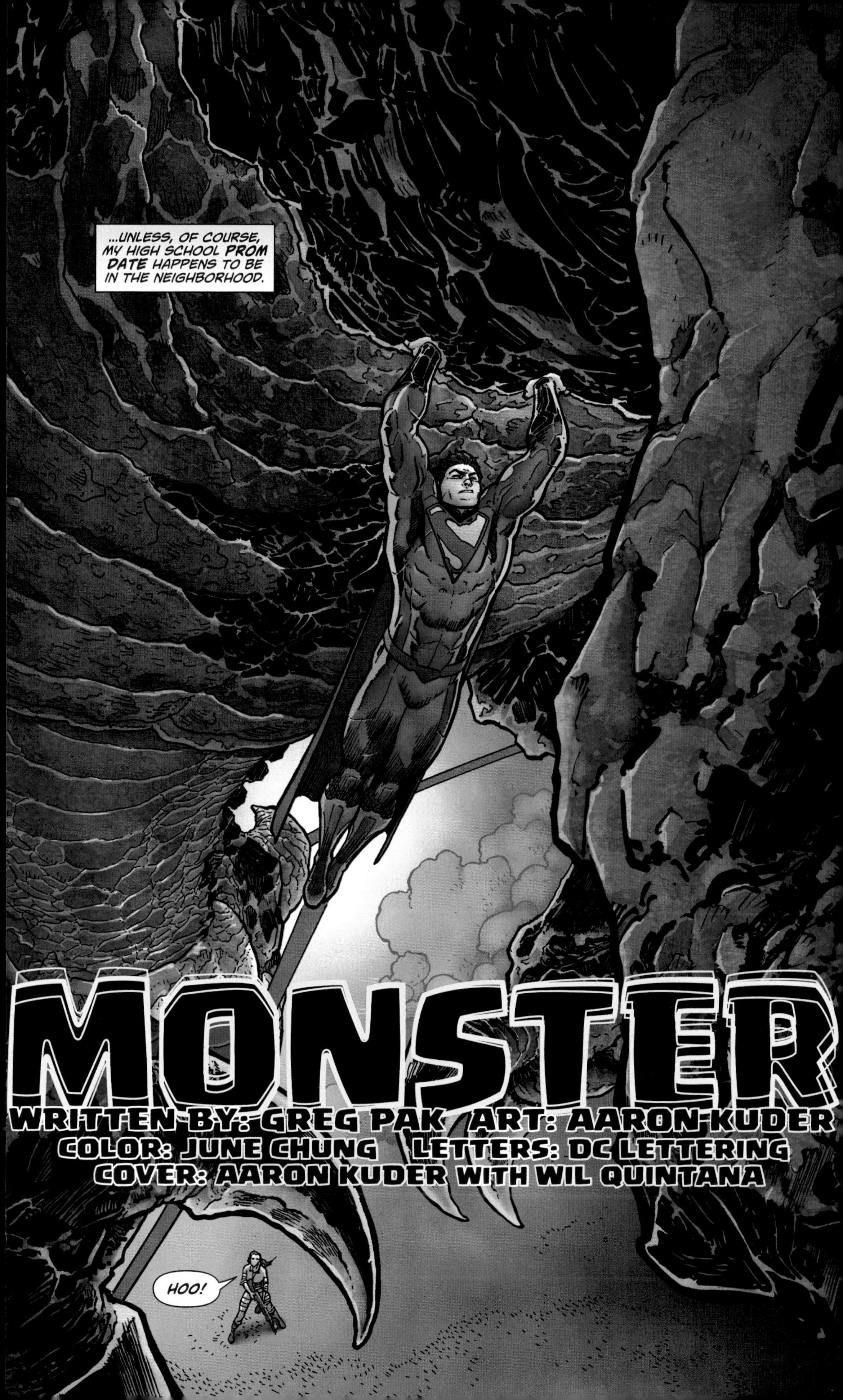

...UNLESS, OF COURSE, MY HIGH SCHOOL PROM DATE HAPPENS TO BE IN THE NEIGHBORHOOD.
MONSTER
WRITTEN BY: GREG PAK ART: AARON KUDER
COLOR: JUNE CHUNG LETTERS: DC LETTERING
COVER: AARON KUDER WITH WIL QUINTANA
HOO!

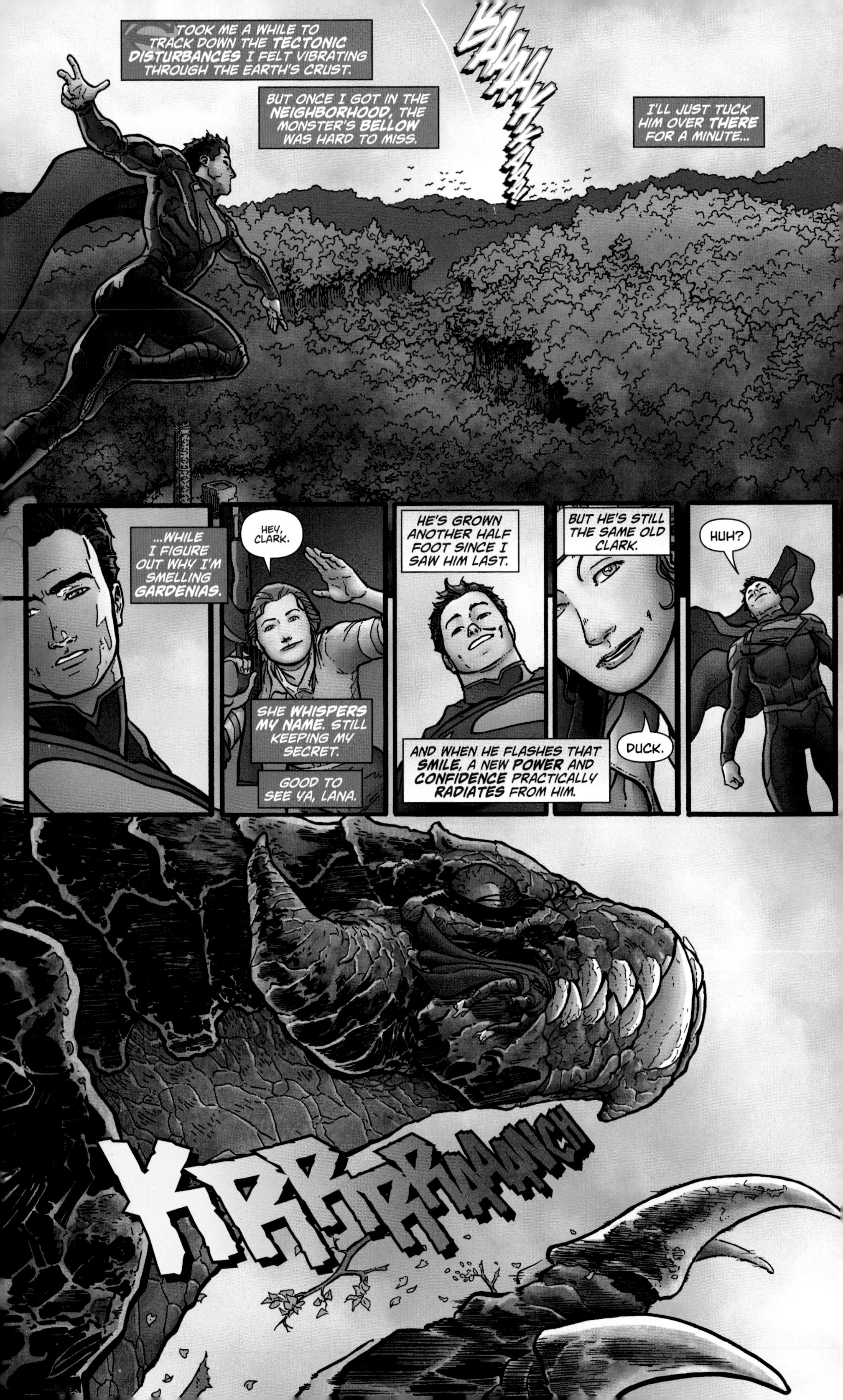

TOOK ME A WHILE TO TRACK DOWN THE TECTONIC DISTURBANCES I FELT VIBRATING THROUGH THE EARTH'S CRUST.
BUT ONCE I GOT IN THE NEIGHBORHOOD, THE MONSTER'S BELLOW WAS HARD TO MISS.
BAAAAKKAAAA
I'LL JUST TUCK HIM OVER THERE FOR A MINUTE...
...WHILE I FIGURE OUT WHY I'M SMELLING GARDENIAS.
HEY, CLARK.
SHE WHISPERS MY NAME. STILL KEEPING MY SECRET.
GOOD TO SEE YA, LANA.
HE'S GROWN ANOTHER HALF FOOT SINCE I SAW HIM LAST.
BUT HE'S STILL THE SAME OLD CLARK.
AND WHEN HE FLASHES THAT SMILE, A NEW POWER AND CONFIDENCE PRACTICALLY RADIATES FROM HIM.
DUCK.
HUH?
KRRBRRAAANCH

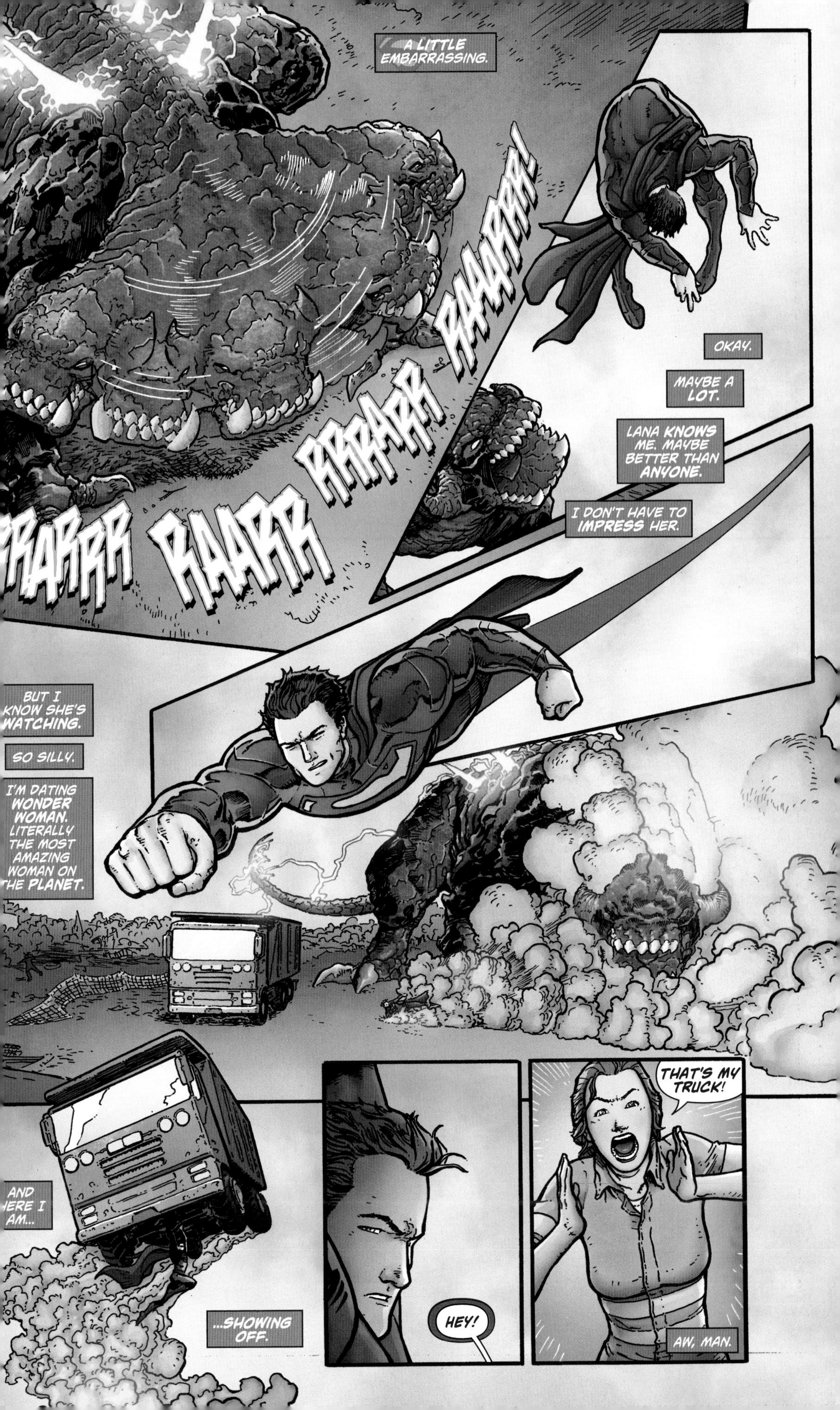

A LITTLE EMBARRASSING.
RRARRR RAARR RRRARR RAAARRR!
OKAY.
MAYBE A LOT.
LANA KNOWS ME. MAYBE BETTER THAN ANYONE.
I DON'T HAVE TO IMPRESS HER.
BUT I KNOW SHE'S WATCHING.
SO SILLY.
I'M DATING WONDER WOMAN. LITERALLY THE MOST AMAZING WOMAN ON THE PLANET.
AND HERE I AM...
...SHOWING OFF.
HEY!
THAT'S MY TRUCK!
AW, MAN.

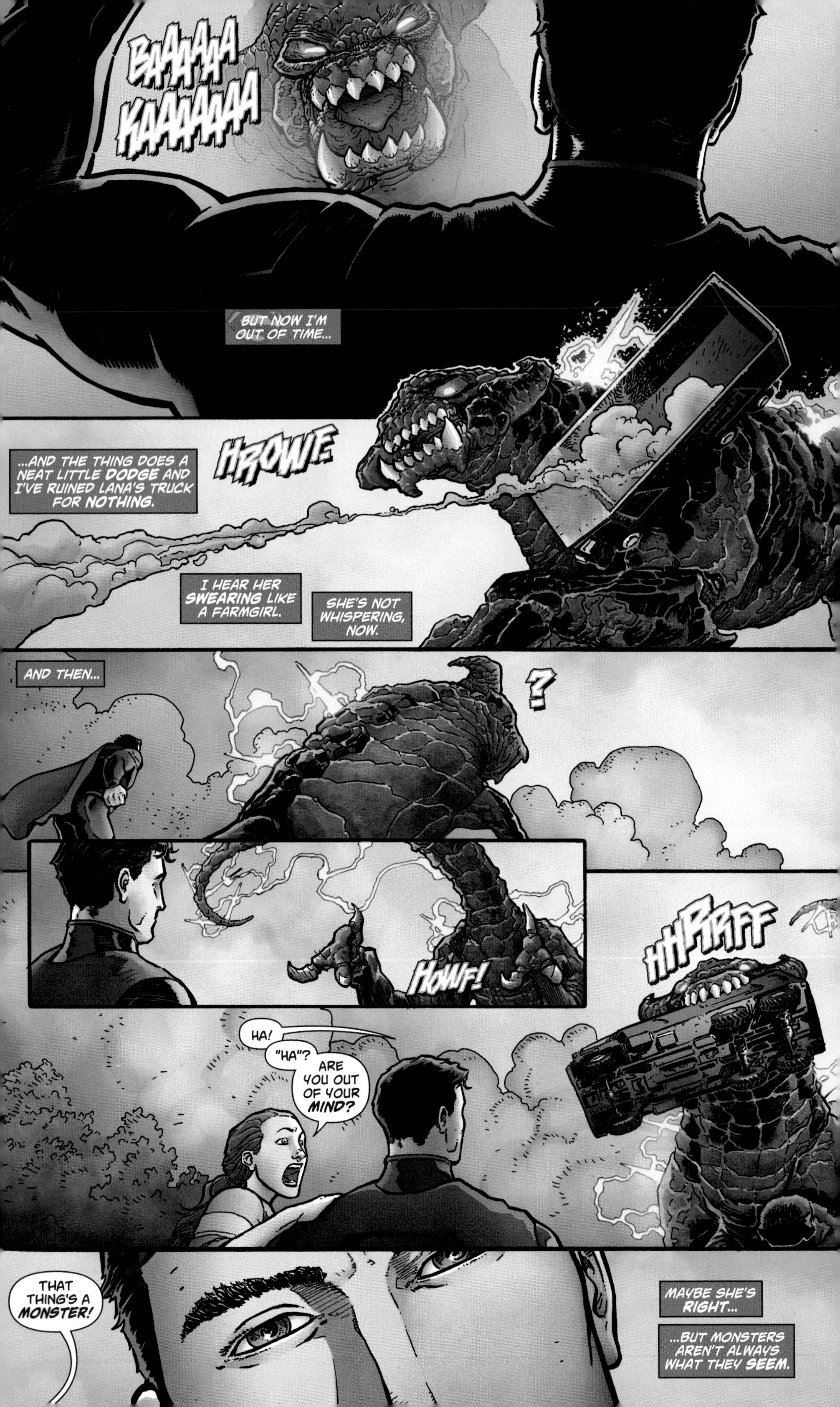
BAAAAAA KAAAAAAA
BUT NOW I'M OUT OF TIME...
...AND THE THING DOES A NEAT LITTLE DODGE AND I'VE RUINED LANA'S TRUCK FOR NOTHING.
HROWF
I HEAR HER SWEARING LIKE A FARMGIRL.
SHE'S NOT WHISPERING, NOW.
AND THEN...
?
HOWF!
HHRRFF
HA!
"HA"? ARE YOU OUT OF YOUR MIND?
THAT THING'S A MONSTER!
MAYBE SHE'S RIGHT...
...BUT MONSTERS AREN'T ALWAYS WHAT THEY SEEM.

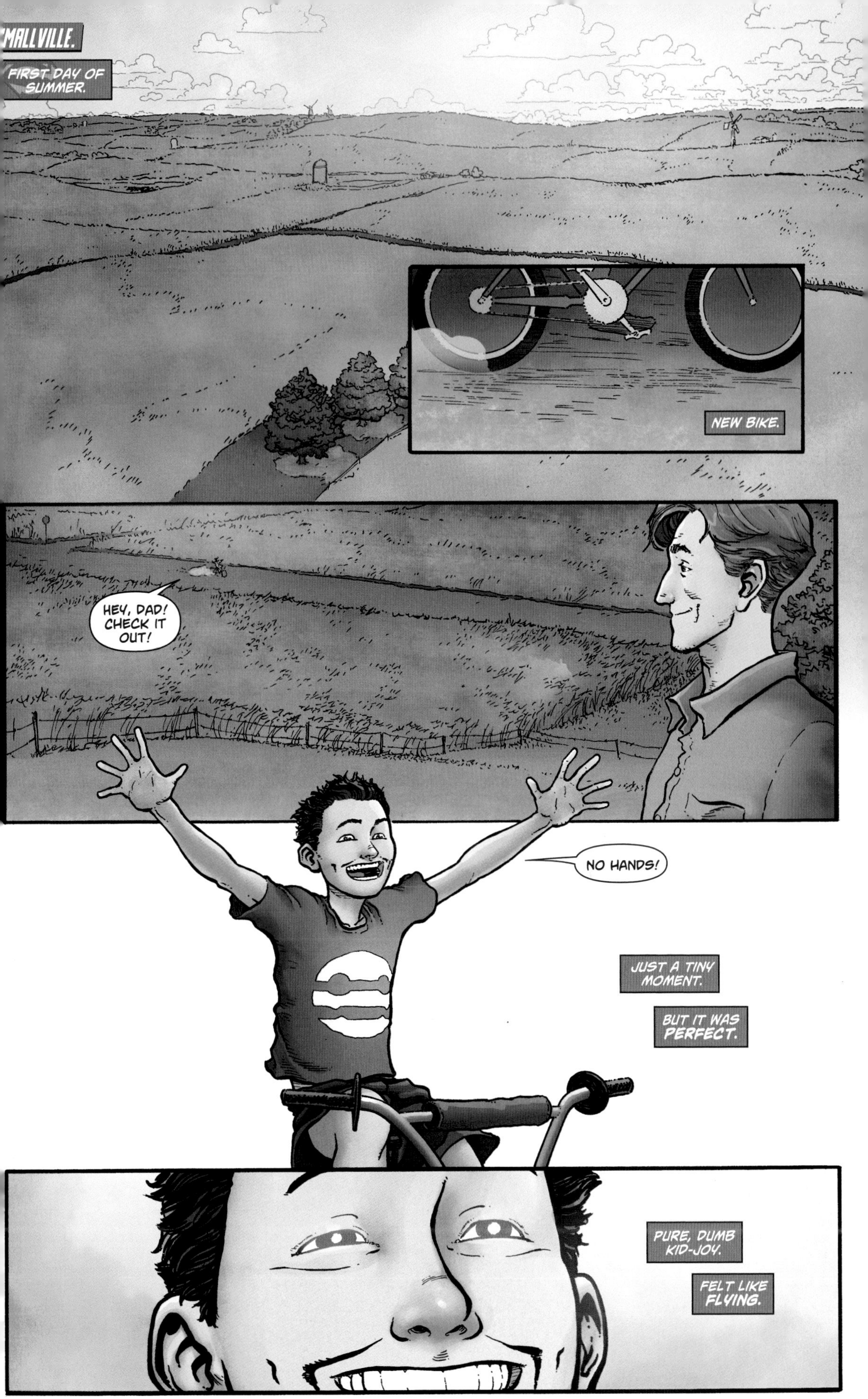
SMALLVILLE.
FIRST DAY OF SUMMER.
NEW BIKE.
HEY, DAD! CHECK IT OUT!
NO HANDS!
JUST A TINY MOMENT.
BUT IT WAS PERFECT.
PURE, DUMB KID-JOY.
FELT LIKE FLYING.

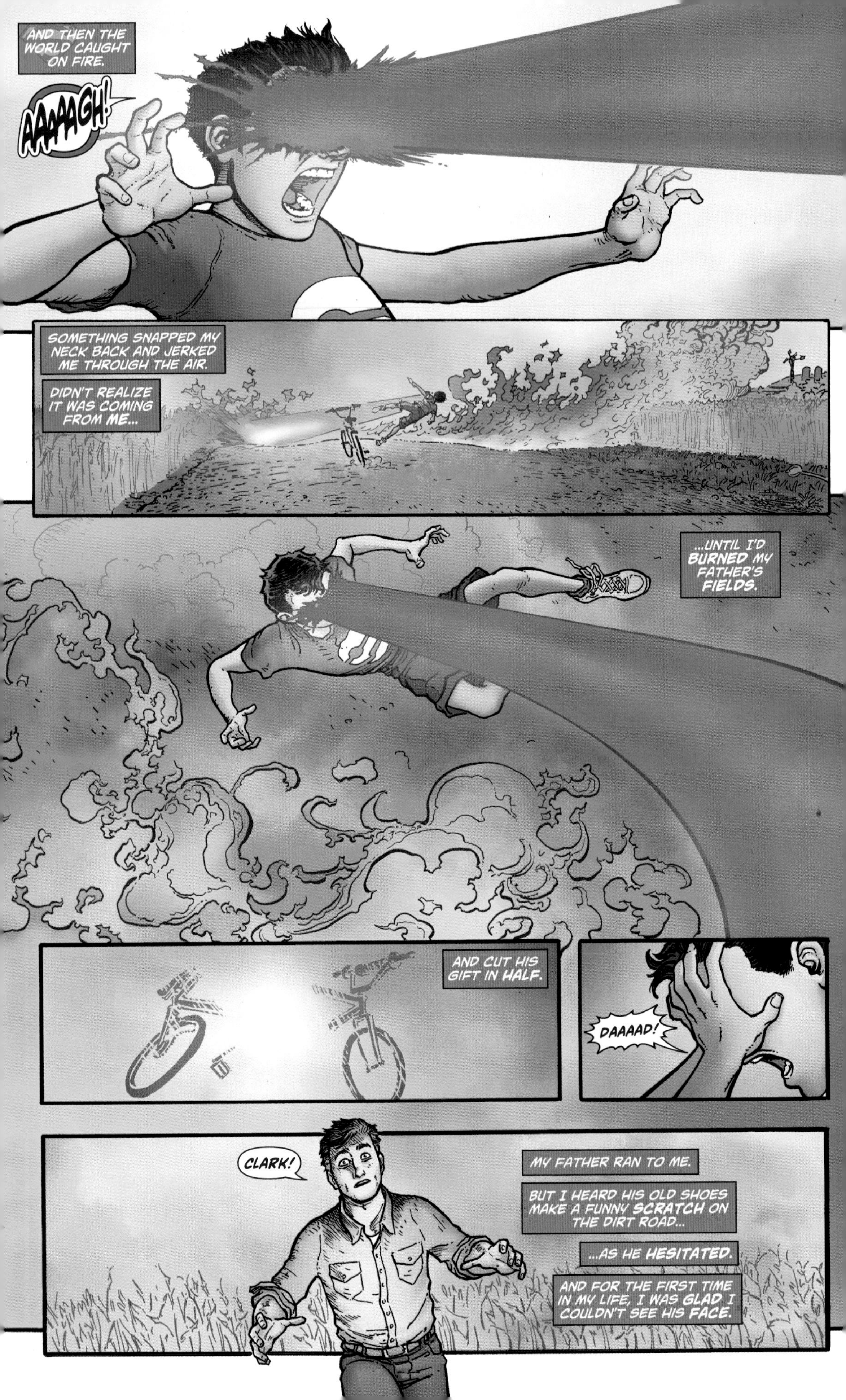
AND THEN THE WORLD CAUGHT ON FIRE.
AAAAAGH!
SOMETHING SNAPPED MY NECK BACK AND JERKED ME THROUGH THE AIR.
DIDN'T REALIZE IT WAS COMING FROM ME...
...UNTIL I'D BURNED MY FATHER'S FIELDS.
AND CUT HIS GIFT IN HALF.
DAAAAD!
CLARK!
MY FATHER RAN TO ME.
BUT I HEARD HIS OLD SHOES MAKE A FUNNY SCRATCH ON THE DIRT ROAD...
...AS HE HESITATED.
AND FOR THE FIRST TIME IN MY LIFE, I WAS GLAD I COULDN'T SEE HIS FACE.

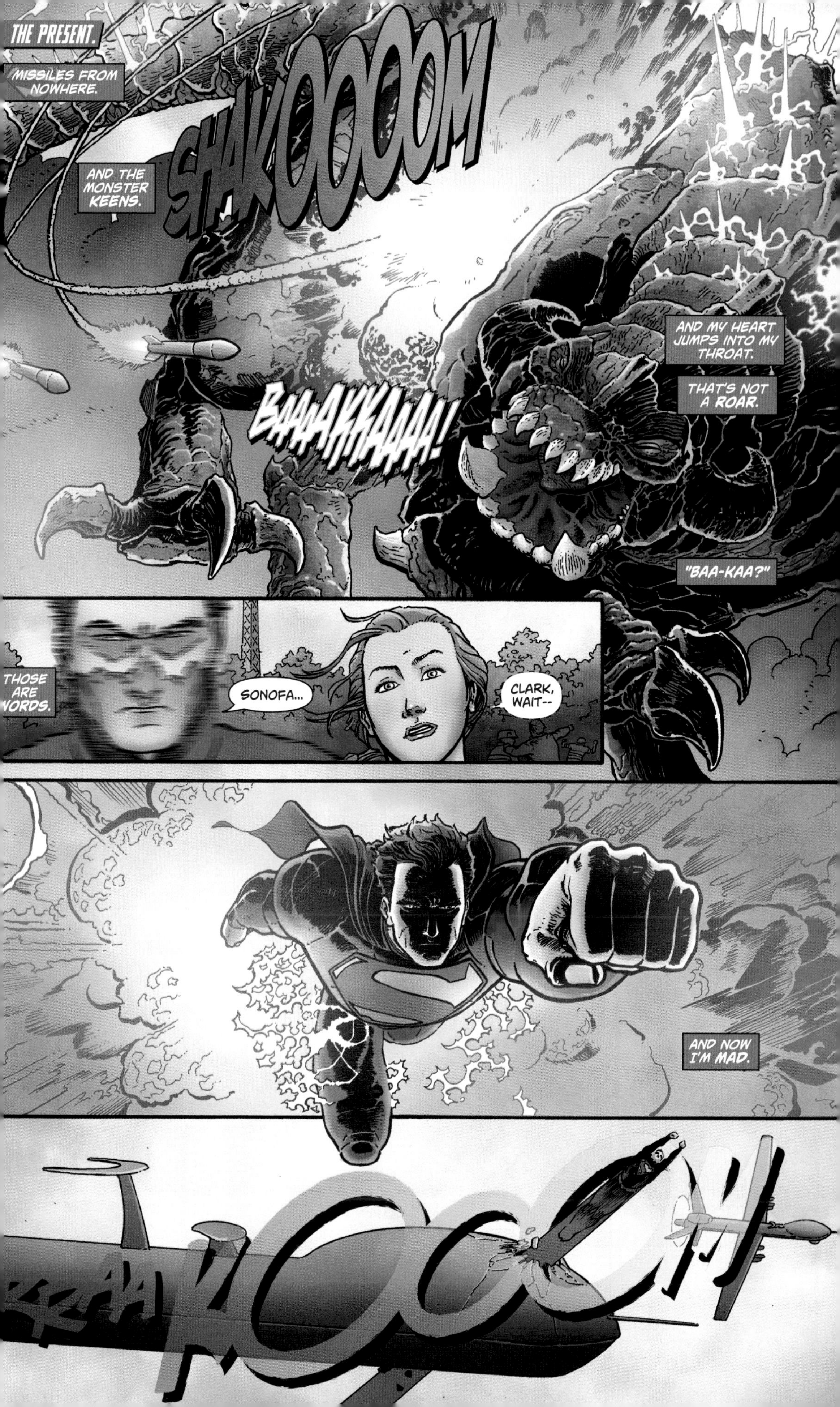
THE PRESENT.
MISSILES FROM NOWHERE.
SHAKOOOOM
AND THE MONSTER KEENS.
BAAAAKKAAAA!
AND MY HEART JUMPS INTO MY THROAT.
THAT'S NOT A ROAR.
"BAA-KAA?"
THOSE ARE WORDS.
SONOFA...
CLARK, WAIT--
AND NOW I'M MAD.

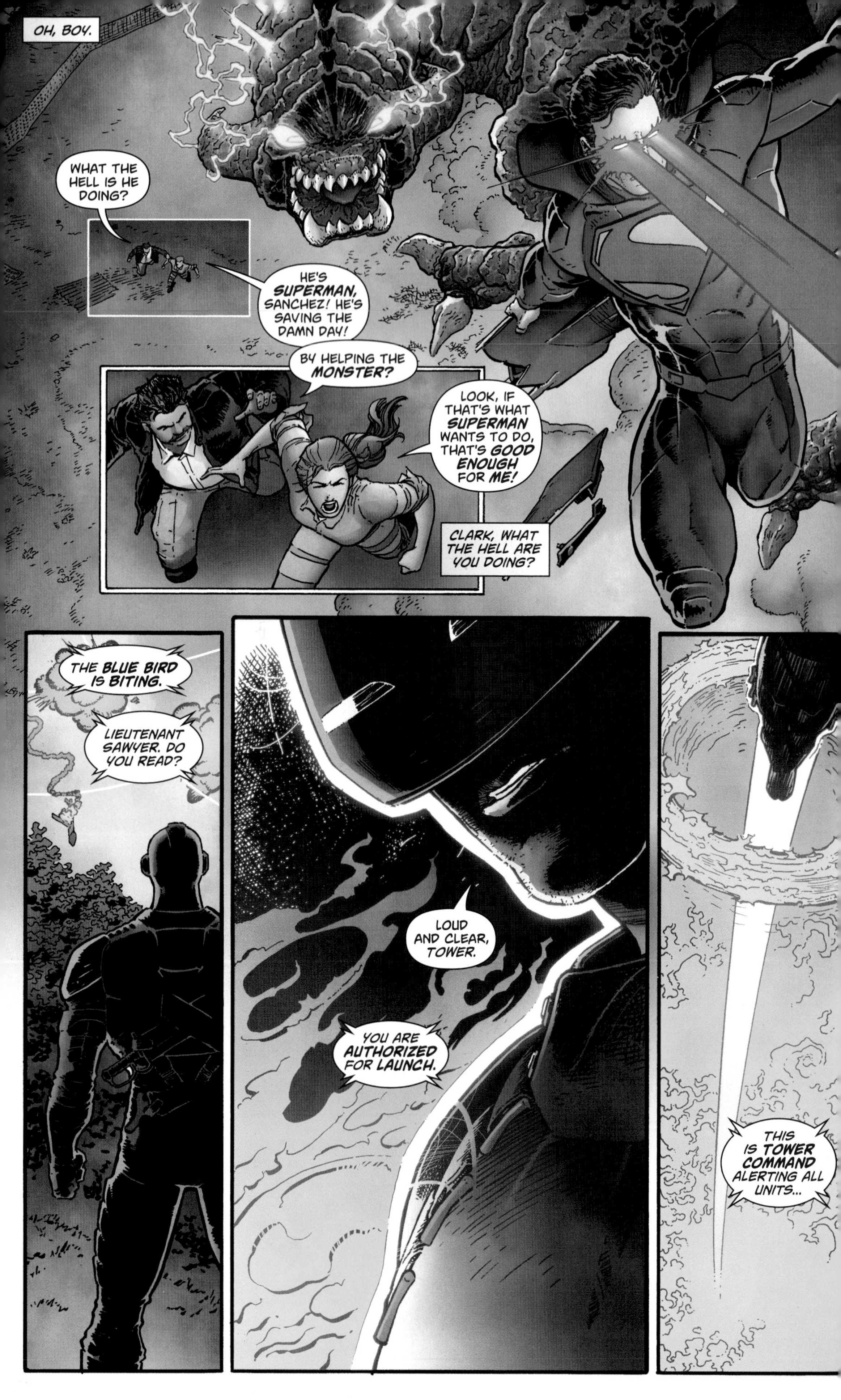
OH, BOY.
WHAT THE HELL IS HE DOING?
HE'S SUPERMAN, SANCHEZ! HE'S SAVING THE DAMN DAY!
BY HELPING THE MONSTER?
LOOK, IF THAT'S WHAT SUPERMAN WANTS TO DO, THAT'S GOOD ENOUGH FOR ME!
CLARK, WHAT THE HELL ARE YOU DOING?
THE BLUE BIRD IS BITING.
LIEUTENANT SAWYER. DO YOU READ?
LOUD AND CLEAR, TOWER.
YOU ARE AUTHORIZED FOR LAUNCH.
THIS IS TOWER COMMAND ALERTING ALL UNITS...

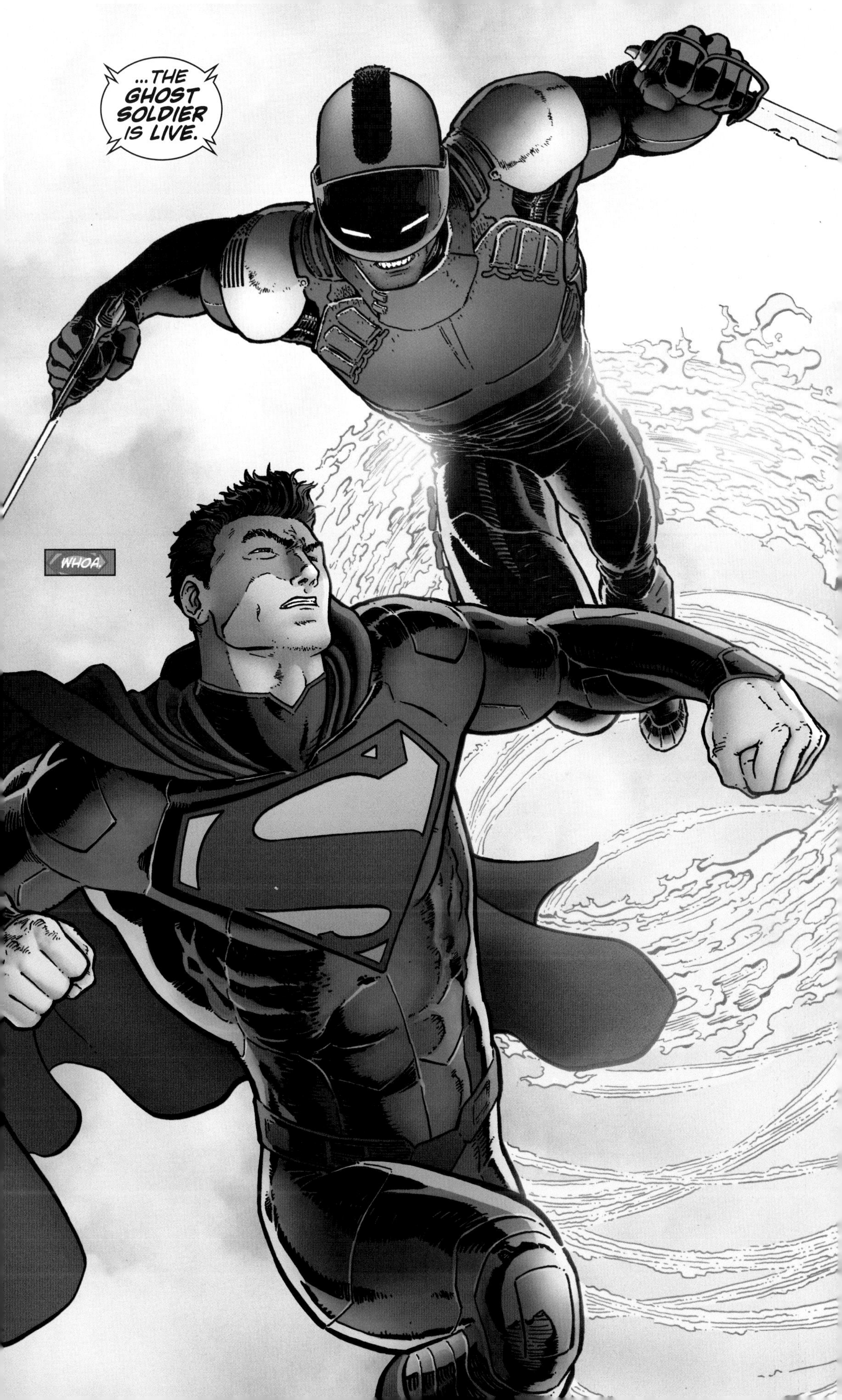
...THE GHOST SOLDIER IS LIVE.
WHOA.

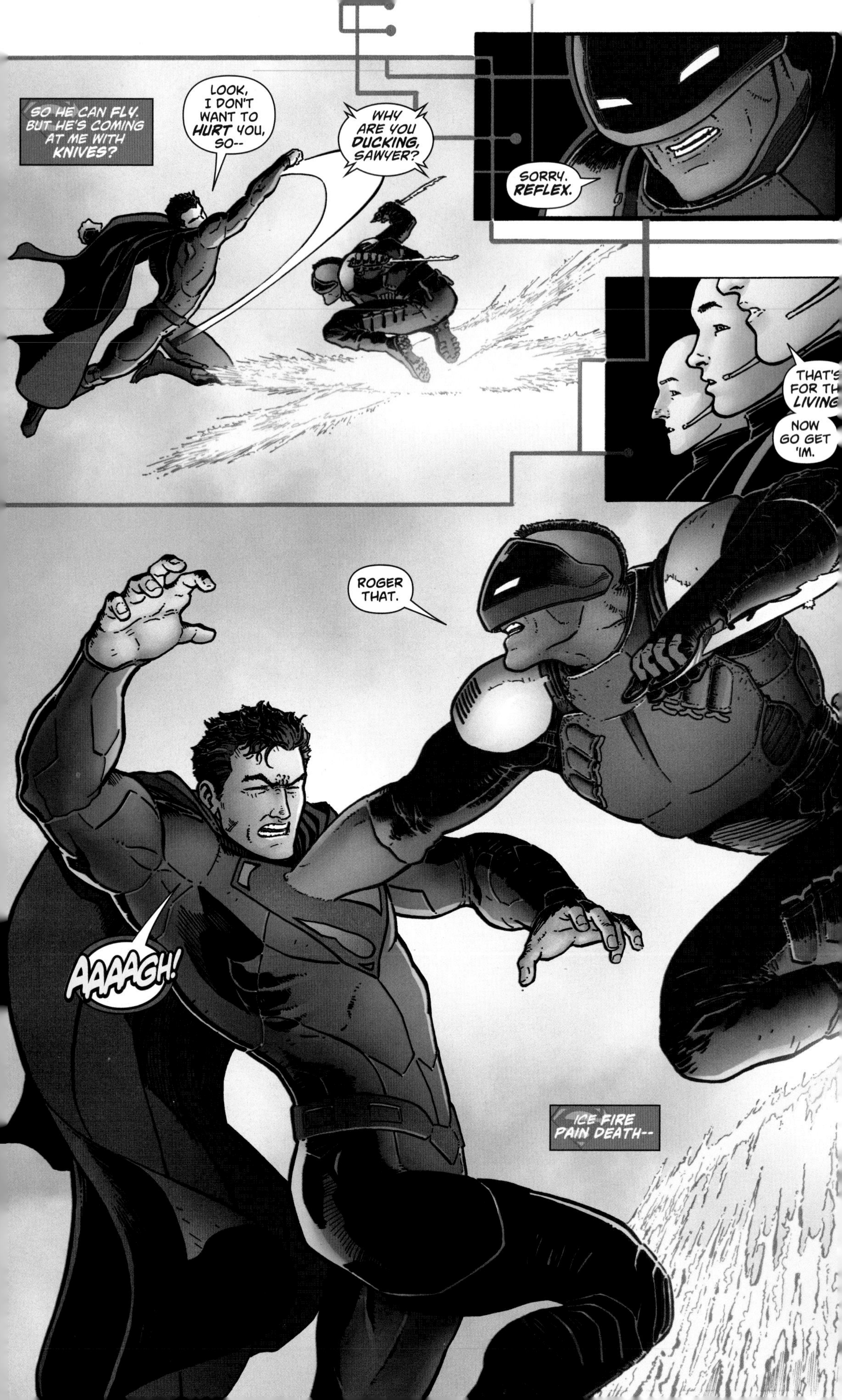

SO HE CAN FLY. BUT HE'S COMING AT ME WITH KNIVES?
LOOK, I DON'T WANT TO HURT YOU, SO--
WHY ARE YOU DUCKING, SAWYER?
SORRY. REFLEX.
NOW GO GET 'IM.
ROGER THAT.
AAAAGH!
ICE FIRE PAIN DEATH--

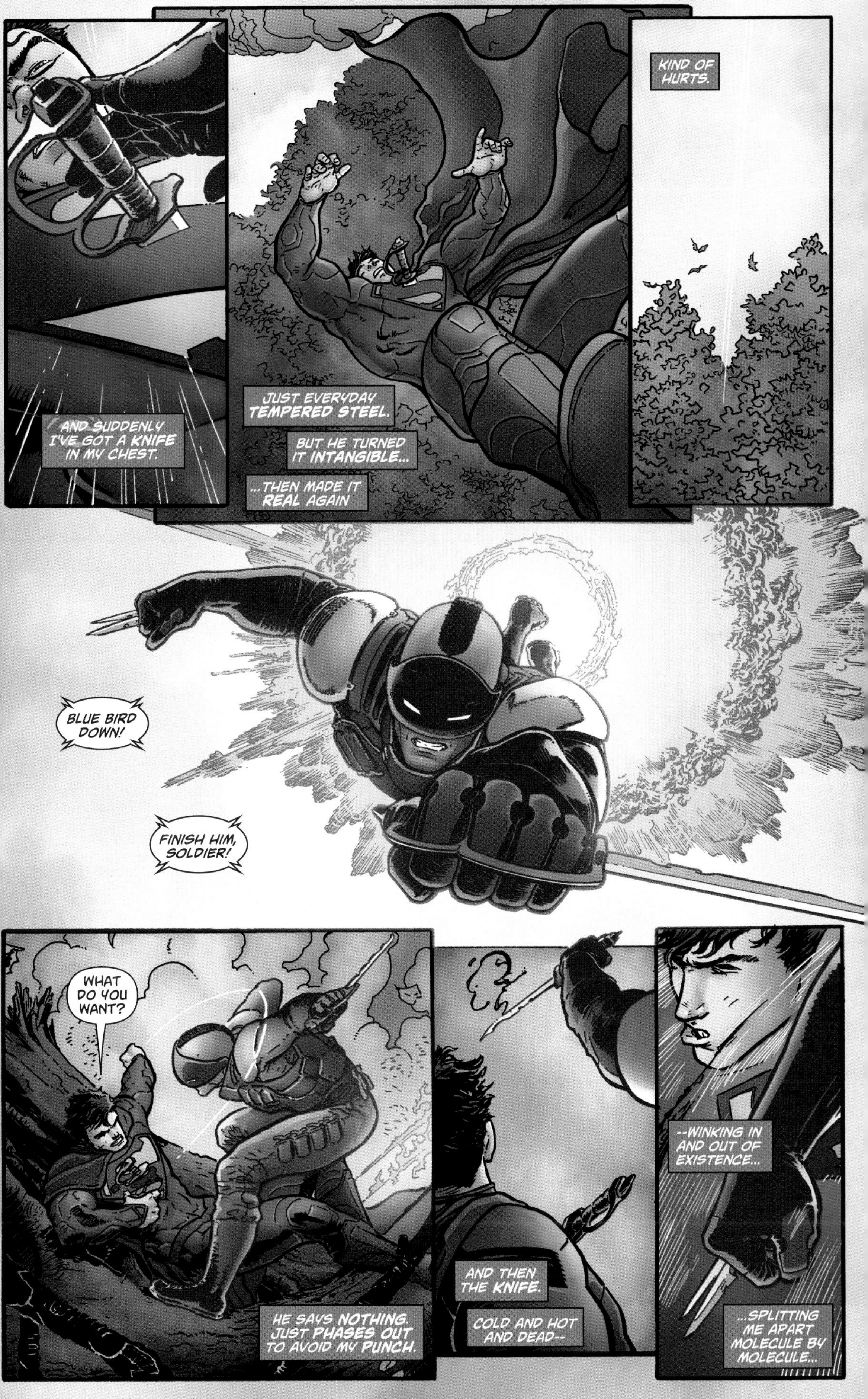

AND SUDDENLY I'VE GOT A KNIFE IN MY CHEST.
JUST EVERYDAY TEMPERED STEEL.
BUT HE TURNED IT INTANGIBLE...
...THEN MADE IT REAL AGAIN
KIND OF HURTS.
BLUE BIRD DOWN!
FINISH HIM, SOLDIER!
WHAT DO YOU WANT?
HE SAYS NOTHING. JUST PHASES OUT TO AVOID MY PUNCH.
AND THEN THE KNIFE.
COLD AND HOT AND DEAD--
--WINKING IN AND OUT OF EXISTENCE...
...SPLITTING ME APART MOLECULE BY MOLECULE...

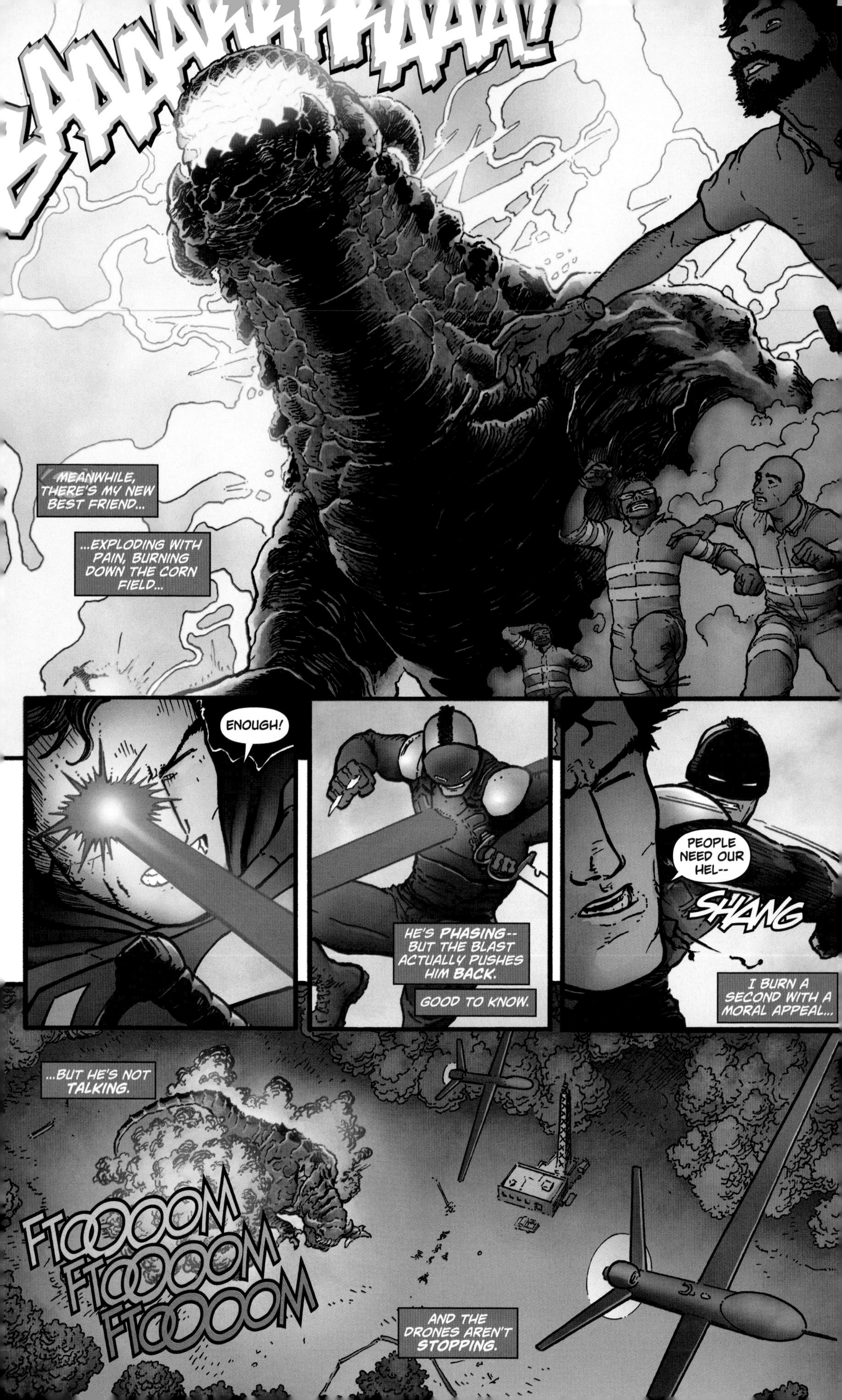
SKAAARRRRAAAA!
MEANWHILE, THERE'S MY NEW BEST FRIEND...
...EXPLODING WITH PAIN, BURNING DOWN THE CORN FIELD...
ENOUGH!
HE'S PHASING-- BUT THE BLAST ACTUALLY PUSHES HIM BACK.
GOOD TO KNOW.
PEOPLE NEED OUR HEL--
SHANG
I BURN A SECOND WITH A MORAL APPEAL...
...BUT HE'S NOT TALKING.
FTOOOOM FTOOOOM FTOOOOM
AND THE DRONES AREN'T STOPPING.

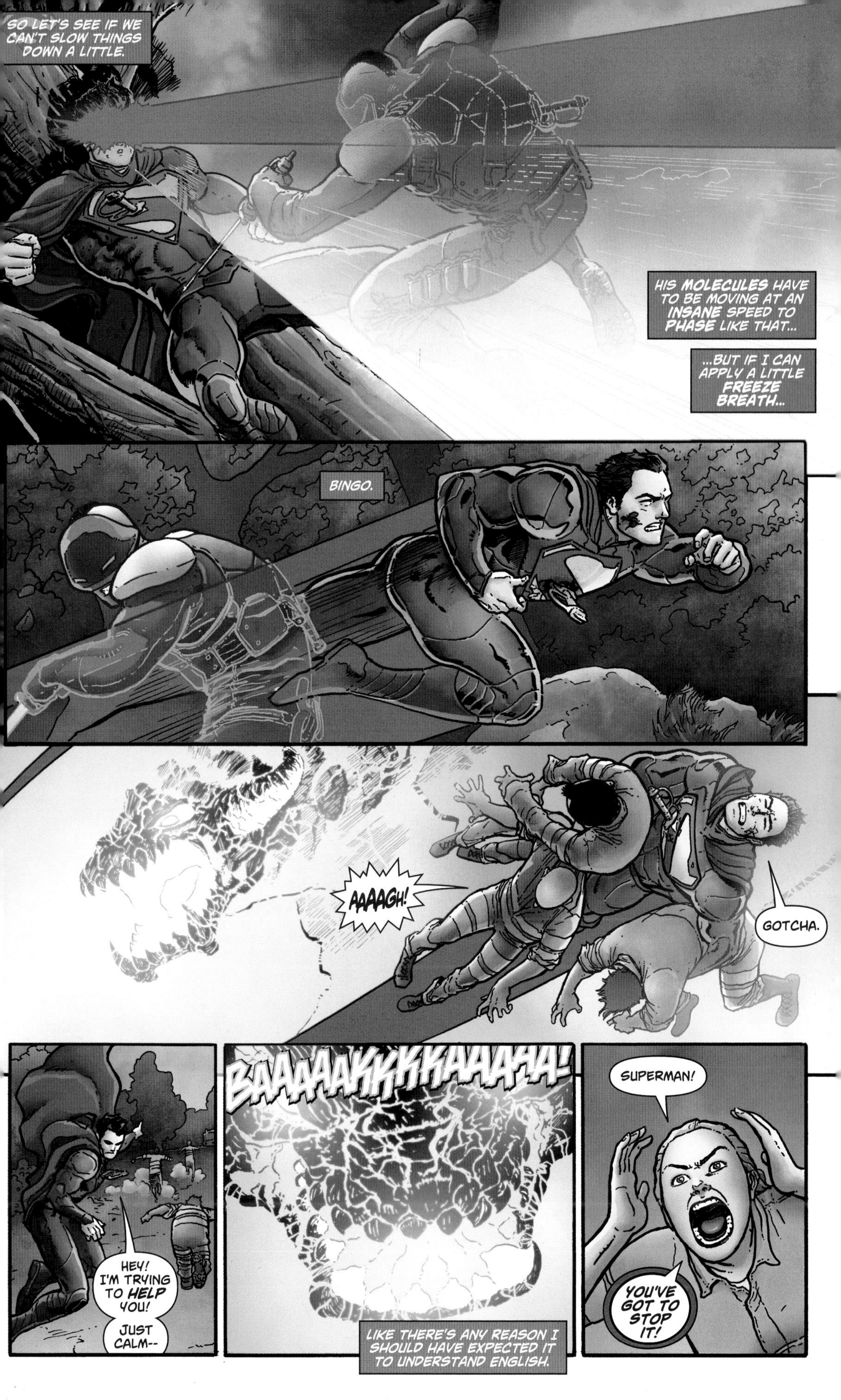
SO LET'S SEE IF WE CAN'T SLOW THINGS DOWN A LITTLE.
HIS MOLECULES HAVE TO BE MOVING AT AN INSANE SPEED TO PHASE LIKE THAT...
...BUT IF I CAN APPLY A LITTLE FREEZE BREATH...
BINGO.
AAAAGH!
GOTCHA.
HEY! I'M TRYING TO HELP YOU!
JUST CALM--
BAAAAAKKKKAAAAAA!
LIKE THERE'S ANY REASON I SHOULD HAVE EXPECTED IT TO UNDERSTAND ENGLISH.
SUPERMAN!
YOU'VE GOT TO STOP IT!

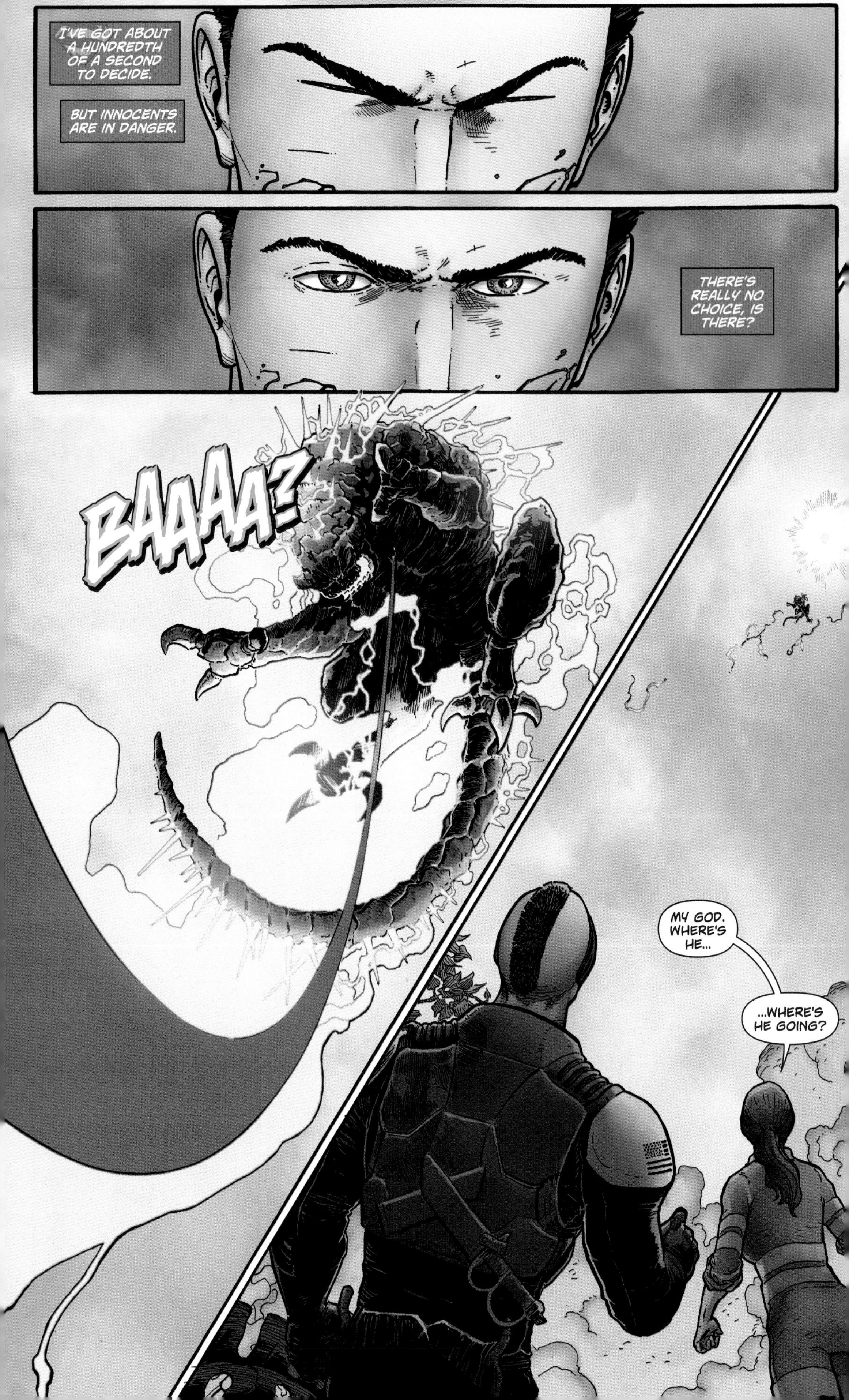
I'VE GOT ABOUT A HUNDREDTH OF A SECOND TO DECIDE.
BUT INNOCENTS ARE IN DANGER.
THERE'S REALLY NO CHOICE, IS THERE?
BAAAAA?
MY GOD. WHERE'S HE...
...WHERE'S HE GOING?

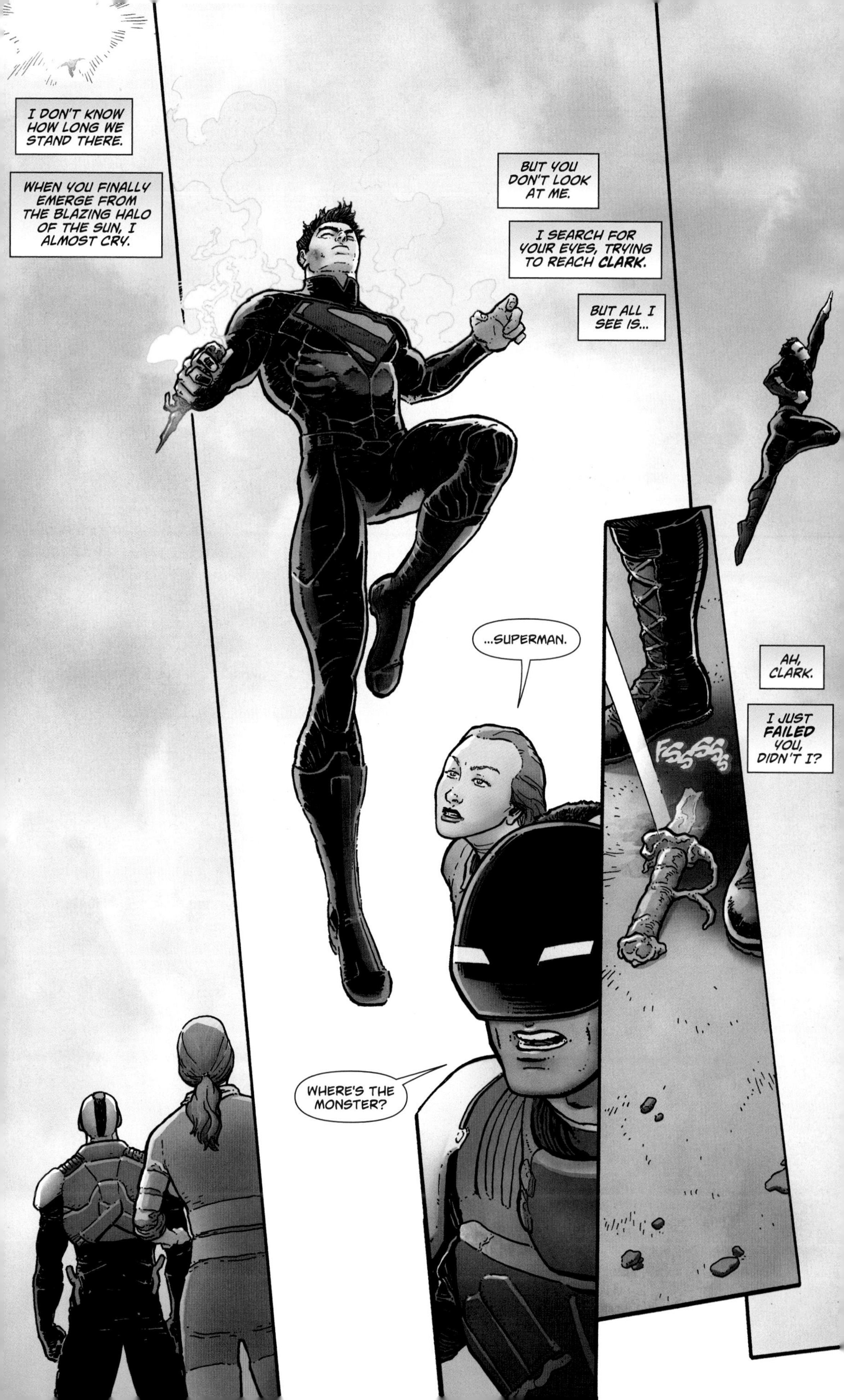
I DON'T KNOW HOW LONG WE STAND THERE.
WHEN YOU FINALLY EMERGE FROM THE BLAZING HALO OF THE SUN, I ALMOST CRY.
BUT YOU DON'T LOOK AT ME.
I SEARCH FOR YOUR EYES, TRYING TO REACH CLARK.
BUT ALL I SEE IS...
...SUPERMAN.
WHERE'S THE MONSTER?
FSSSSS
AH, CLARK.
I JUST FAILED YOU, DIDN'T I?

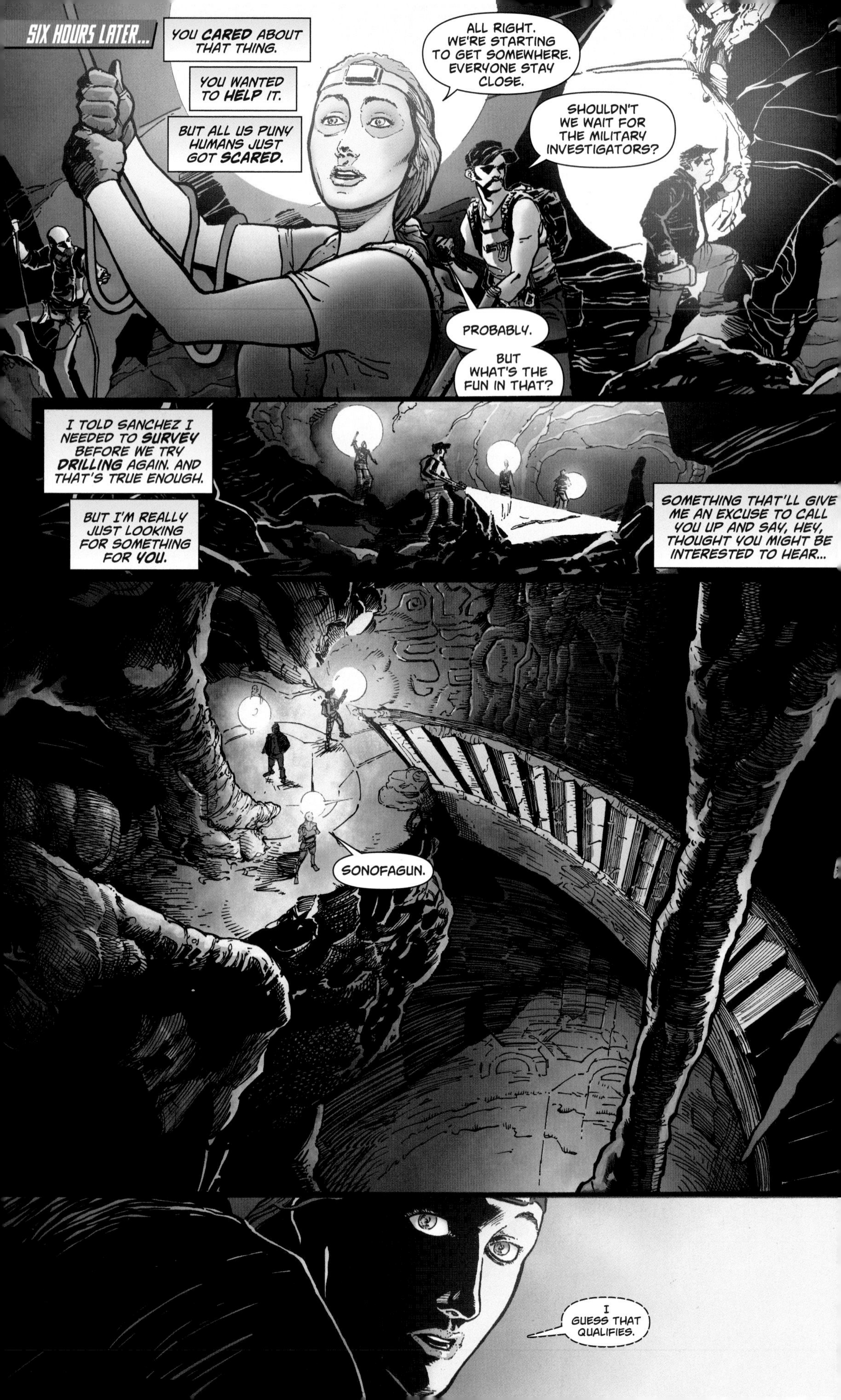
SIX HOURS LATER...
YOU CARED ABOUT THAT THING.
YOU WANTED TO HELP IT.
BUT ALL US PUNY HUMANS JUST GOT SCARED.
ALL RIGHT. WE'RE STARTING TO GET SOMEWHERE. EVERYONE STAY CLOSE.
SHOULDN'T WE WAIT FOR THE MILITARY INVESTIGATORS?
PROBABLY.
BUT WHAT'S THE FUN IN THAT?
I TOLD SANCHEZ I NEEDED TO SURVEY BEFORE WE TRY DRILLING AGAIN. AND THAT'S TRUE ENOUGH.
BUT I'M REALLY JUST LOOKING FOR SOMETHING FOR YOU.
SOMETHING THAT'LL GIVE ME AN EXCUSE TO CALL YOU UP AND SAY, HEY, THOUGHT YOU MIGHT BE INTERESTED TO HEAR...
SONOFAGUN.
I GUESS THAT QUALIFIES.

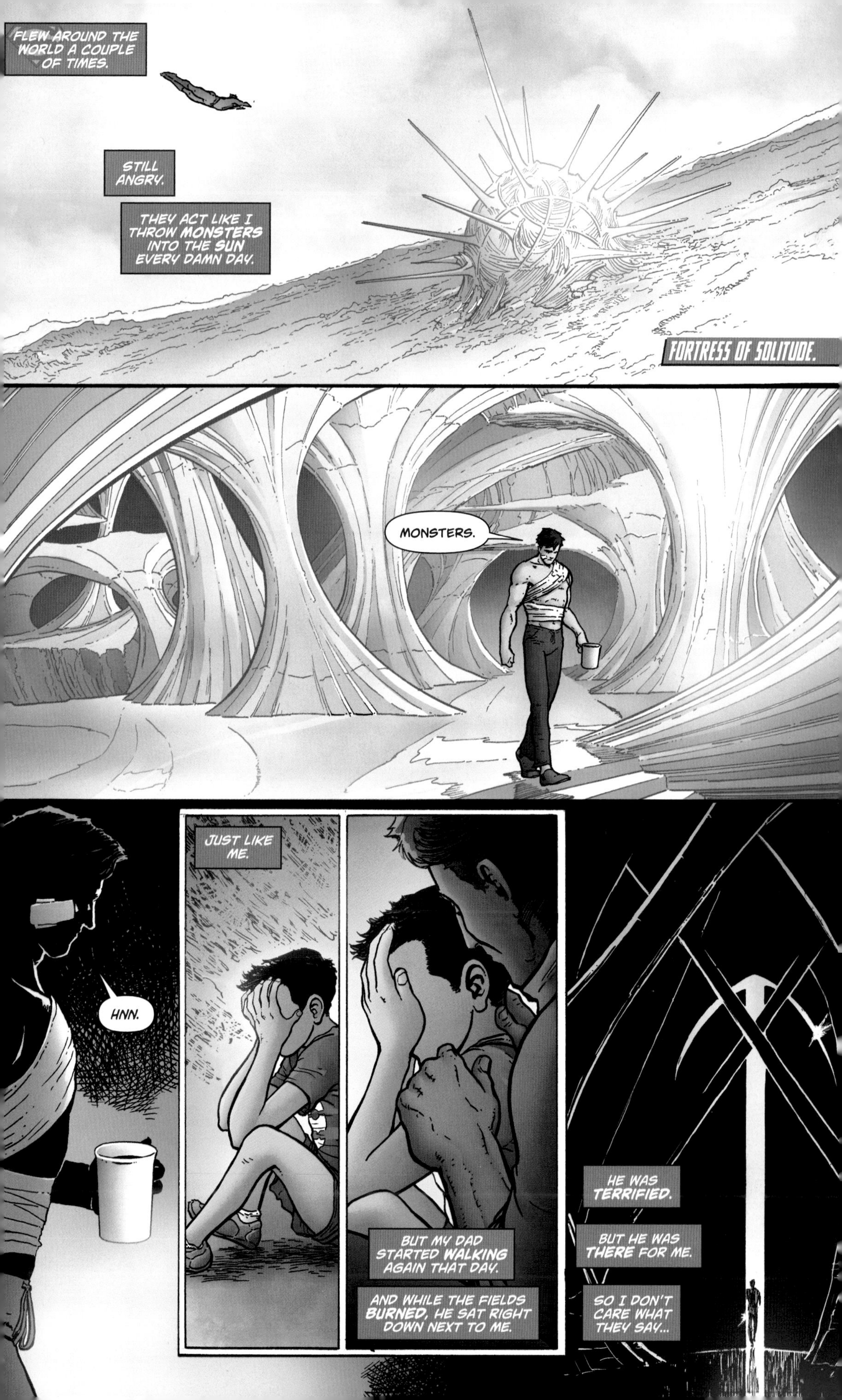
FLEW AROUND THE WORLD A COUPLE OF TIMES.
STILL ANGRY.
THEY ACT LIKE I THROW MONSTERS INTO THE SUN EVERY DAMN DAY.
FORTRESS OF SOLITUDE.
MONSTERS.
HNN.
JUST LIKE ME.
BUT MY DAD STARTED WALKING AGAIN THAT DAY.
AND WHILE THE FIELDS BURNED, HE SAT RIGHT DOWN NEXT TO ME.
HE WAS TERRIFIED.
BUT HE WAS THERE FOR ME.
SO I DON'T CARE WHAT THEY SAY...

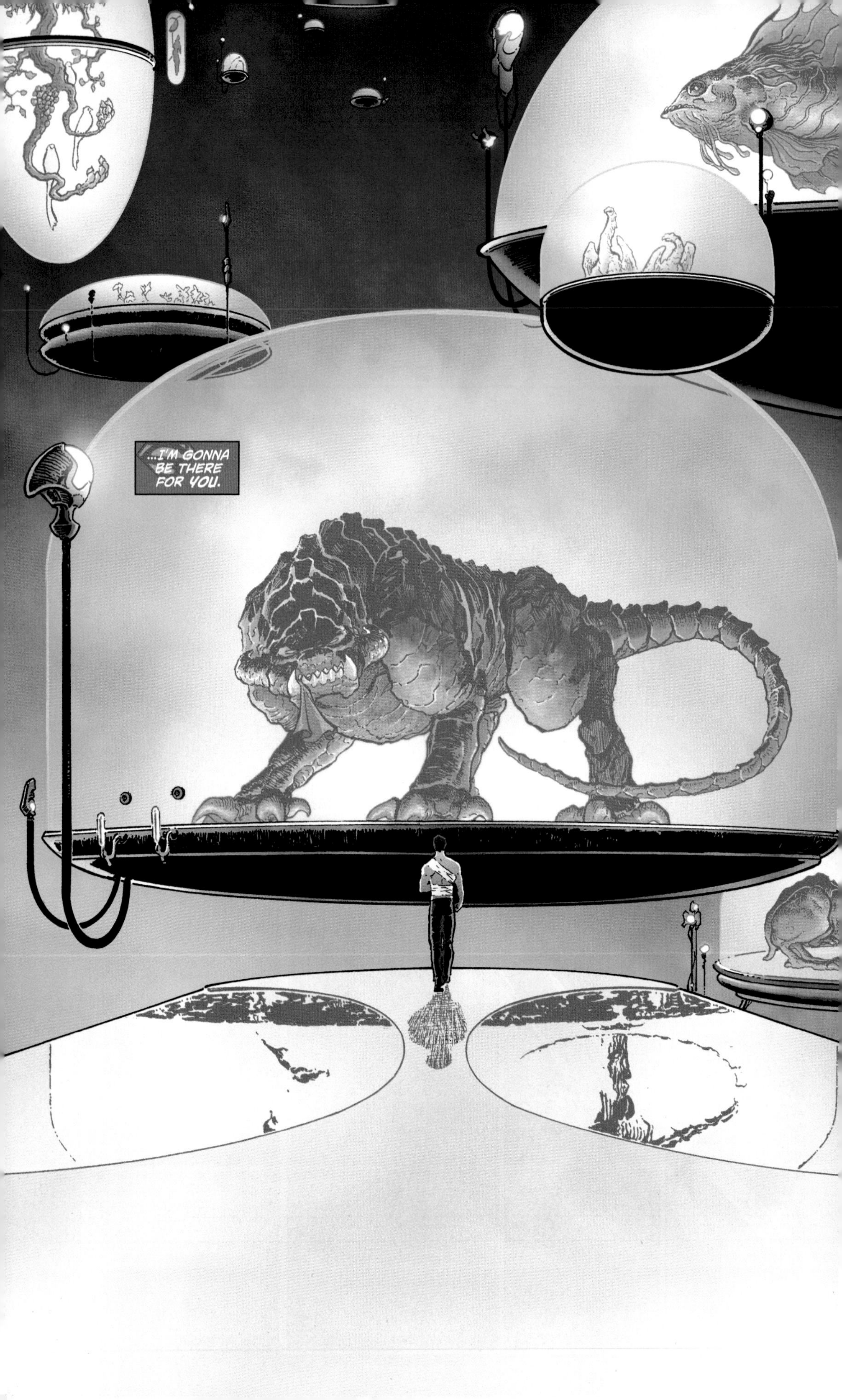
...I'M GONNA BE THERE FOR YOU.

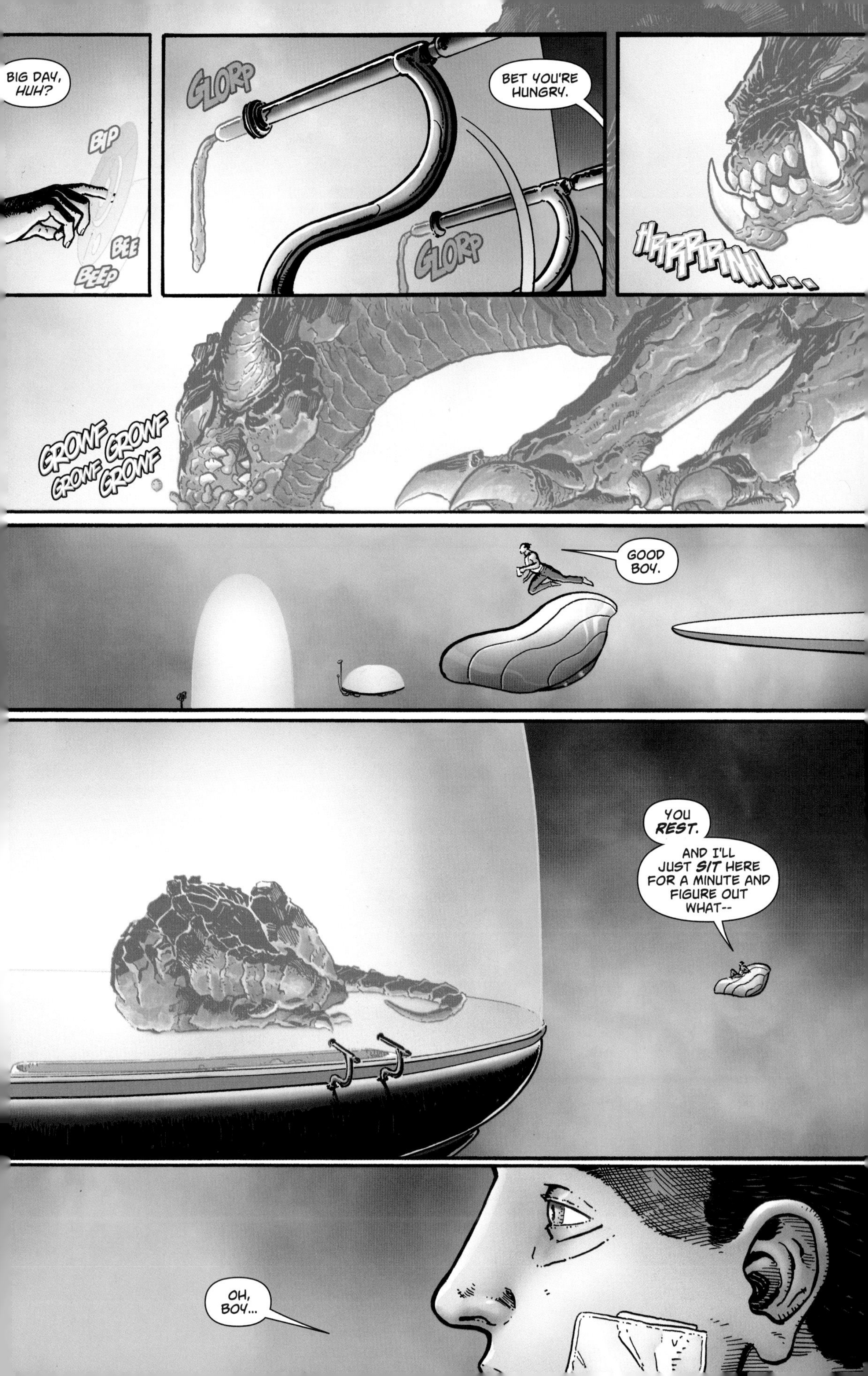
BIG DAY, HUH?
BIP
BEE
BEEP
GLORP
BET YOU'RE HUNGRY.
GLORP
HRRRRNN...
GRONF GRONF GRONF GRONF
GOOD BOY.
YOU REST.
AND I'LL JUST SIT HERE FOR A MINUTE AND FIGURE OUT WHAT--
OH, BOY...

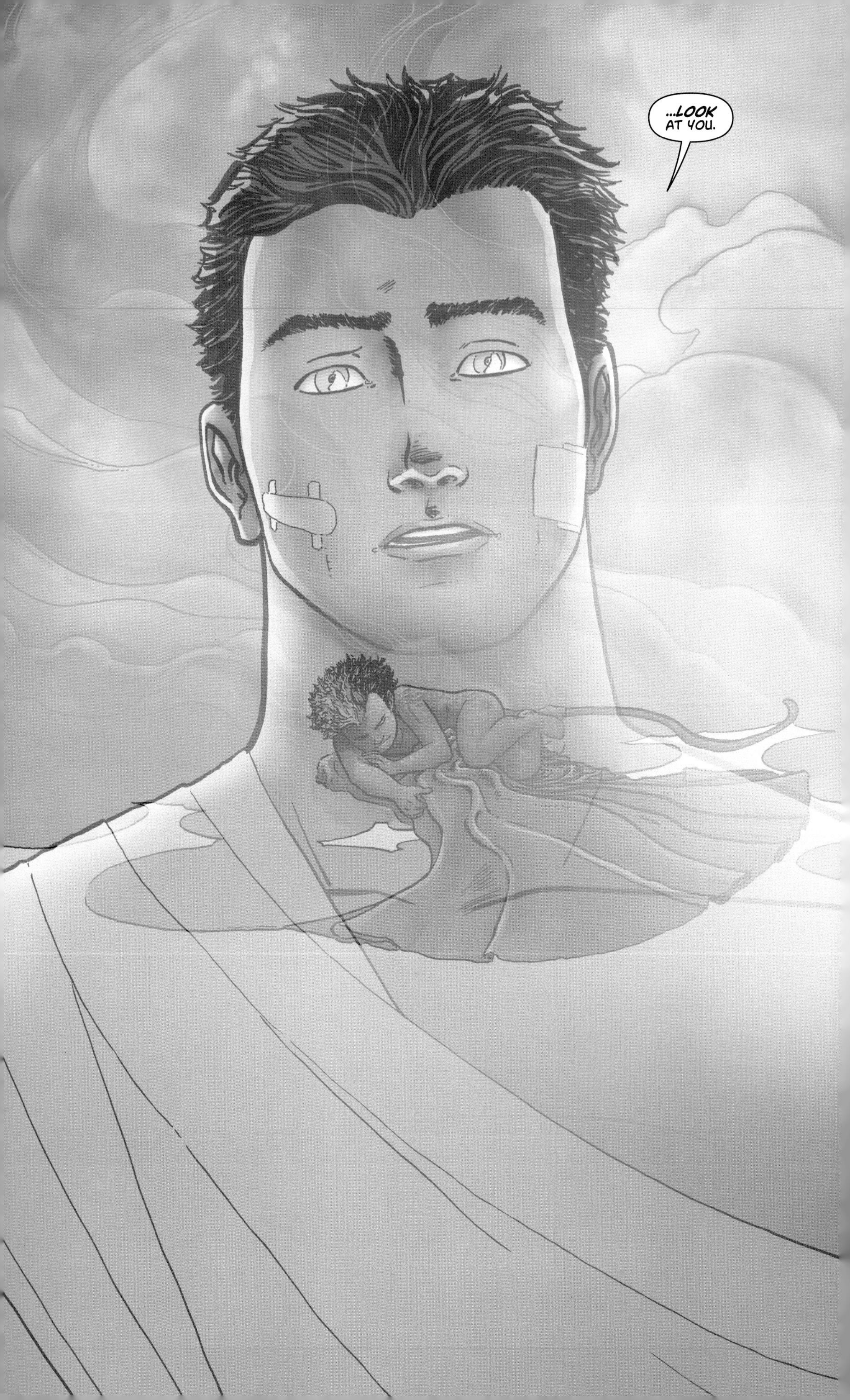
...LOOK AT YOU.

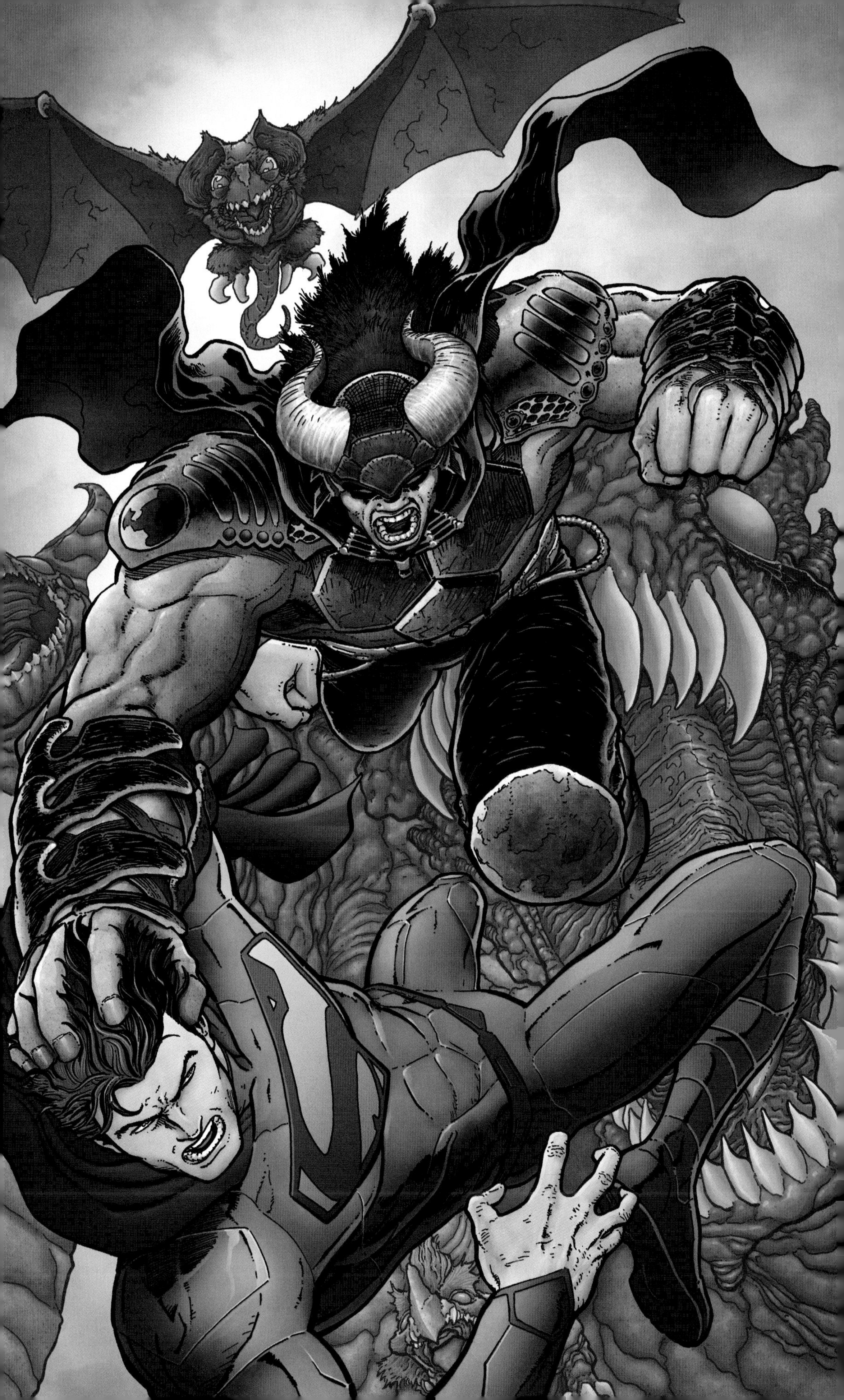

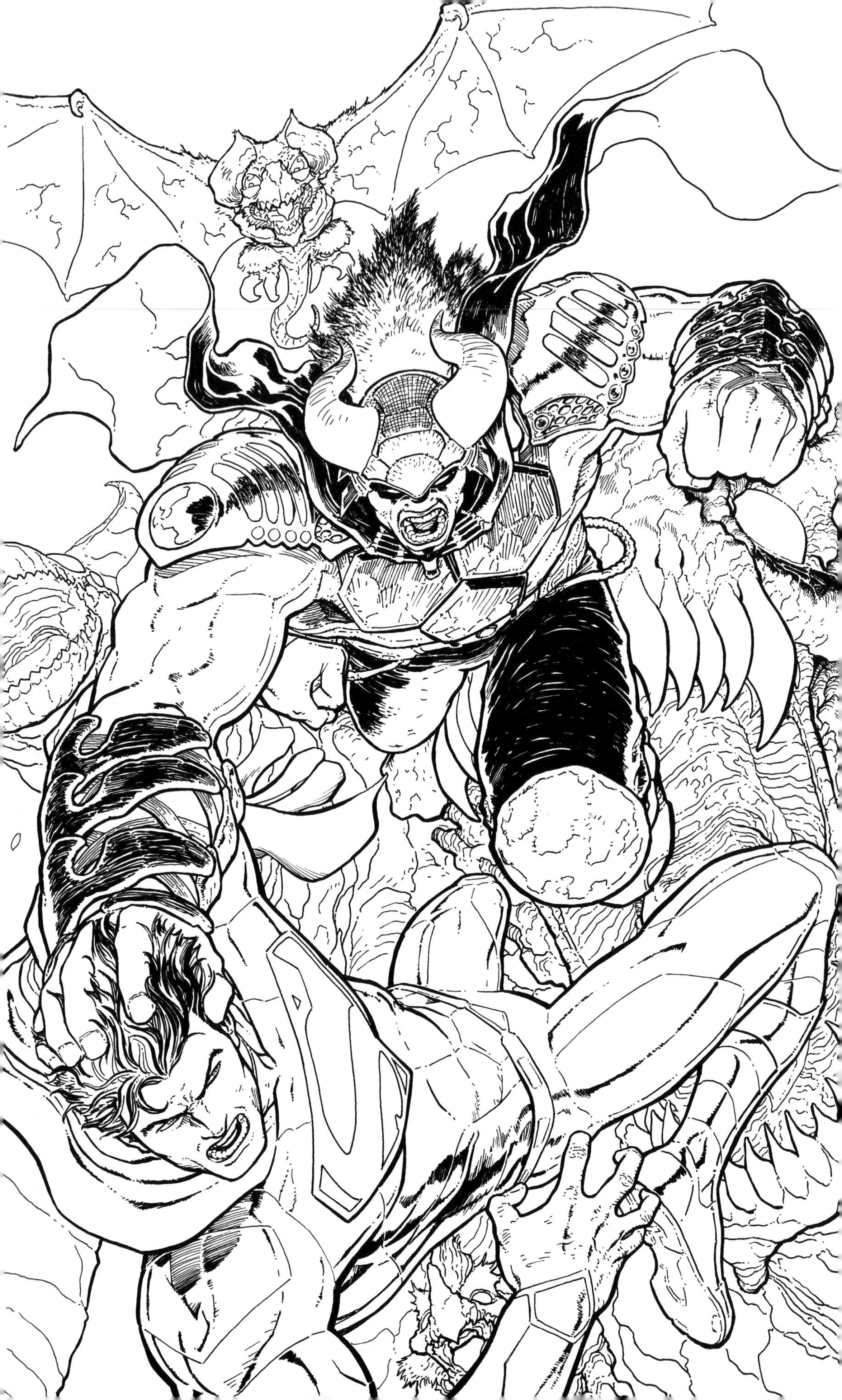

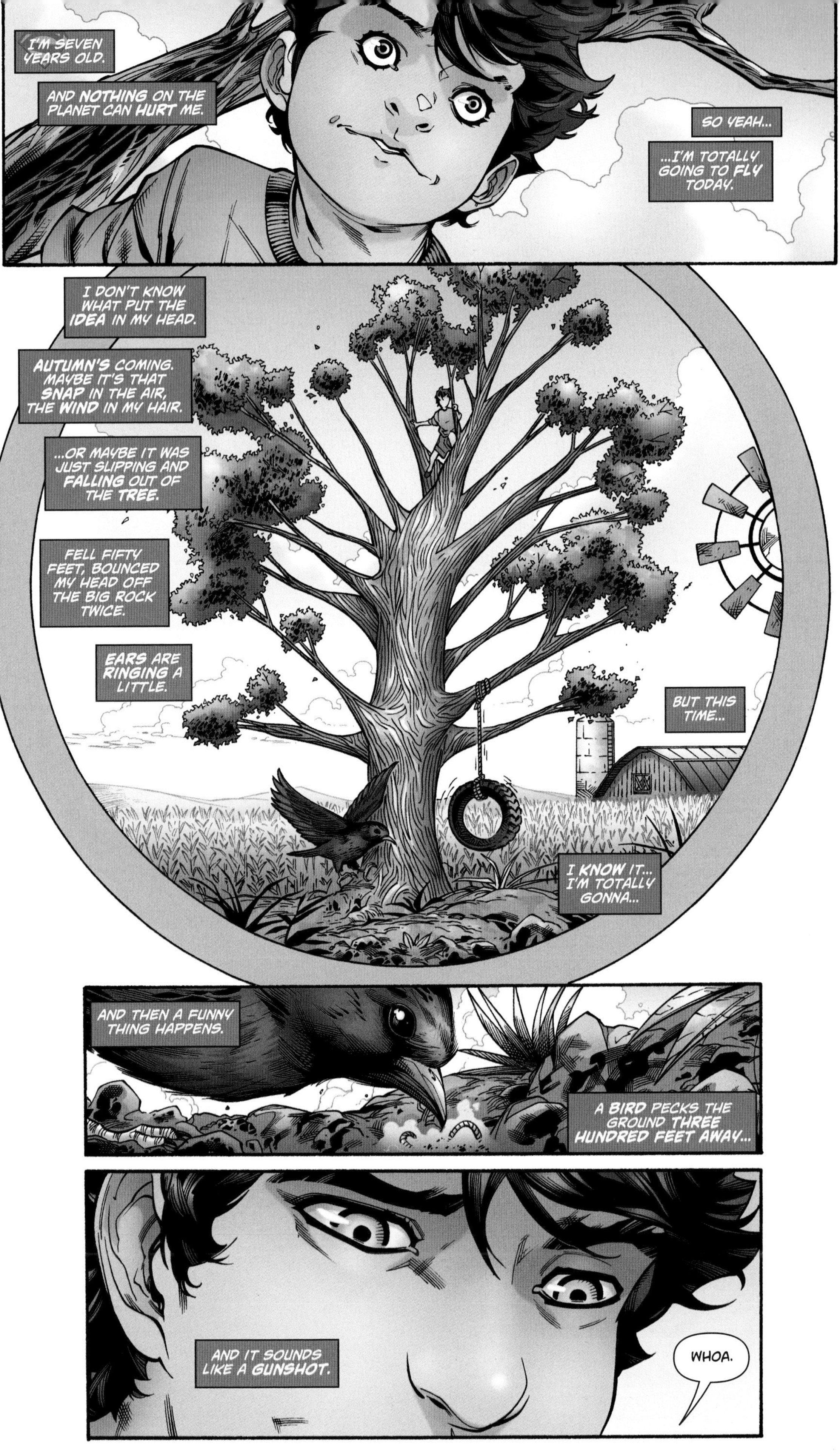

I'M SEVEN YEARS OLD.
AND NOTHING ON THE PLANET CAN HURT ME.
SO YEAH...
...I'M TOTALLY GOING TO FLY TODAY.
I DON'T KNOW WHAT PUT THE IDEA IN MY HEAD.
AUTUMN'S COMING. MAYBE IT'S THAT SNAP IN THE AIR, THE WIND IN MY HAIR.
...OR MAYBE IT WAS JUST SLIPPING AND FALLING OUT OF THE TREE.
FELL FIFTY FEET, BOUNCED MY HEAD OFF THE BIG ROCK TWICE.
EARS ARE RINGING A LITTLE.
BUT THIS TIME...
I KNOW IT... I'M TOTALLY GONNA...
AND THEN A FUNNY THING HAPPENS.
A BIRD PECKS THE GROUND THREE HUNDRED FEET AWAY...
AND IT SOUNDS LIKE A GUNSHOT.
WHOA.

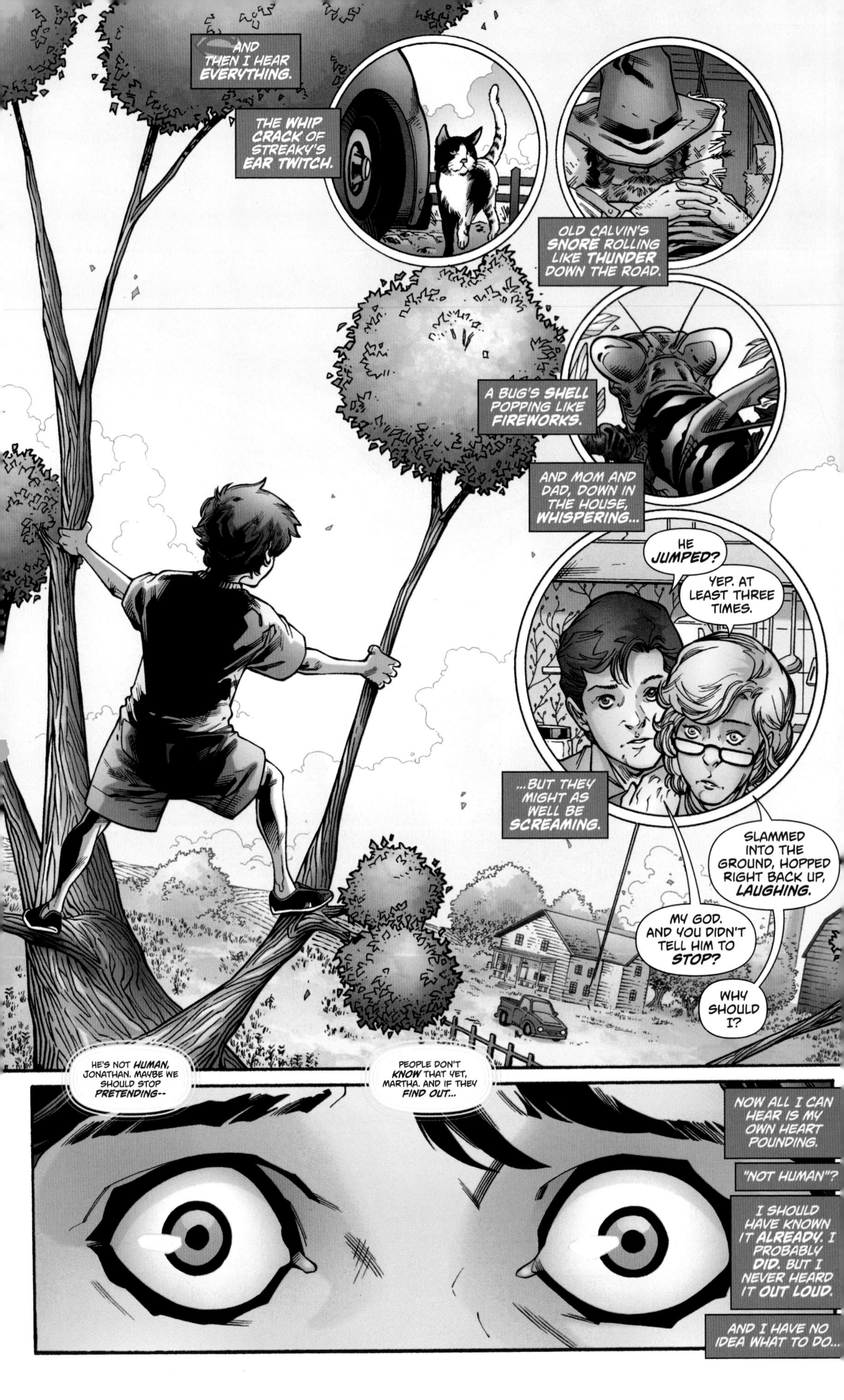

AND THEN I HEAR EVERYTHING.
THE WHIP CRACK OF STREAKY'S EAR TWITCH.
OLD CALVIN'S SNORE ROLLING LIKE THUNDER DOWN THE ROAD.
A BUG'S SHELL POPPING LIKE FIREWORKS.
AND MOM AND DAD, DOWN IN THE HOUSE, WHISPERING...
HE JUMPED?
YEP. AT LEAST THREE TIMES.
...BUT THEY MIGHT AS WELL BE SCREAMING.
SLAMMED INTO THE GROUND, HOPPED RIGHT BACK UP, LAUGHING.
MY GOD. AND YOU DIDN'T TELL HIM TO STOP?
WHY SHOULD I?
HE'S NOT HUMAN, JONATHAN. MAYBE WE SHOULD STOP PRETENDING--
PEOPLE DON'T KNOW THAT YET, MARTHA. AND IF THEY FIND OUT...
NOW ALL I CAN HEAR IS MY OWN HEART POUNDING.
"NOT HUMAN"?
I SHOULD HAVE KNOWN IT ALREADY. I PROBABLY DID. BUT I NEVER HEARD IT OUT LOUD.
AND I HAVE NO IDEA WHAT TO DO...

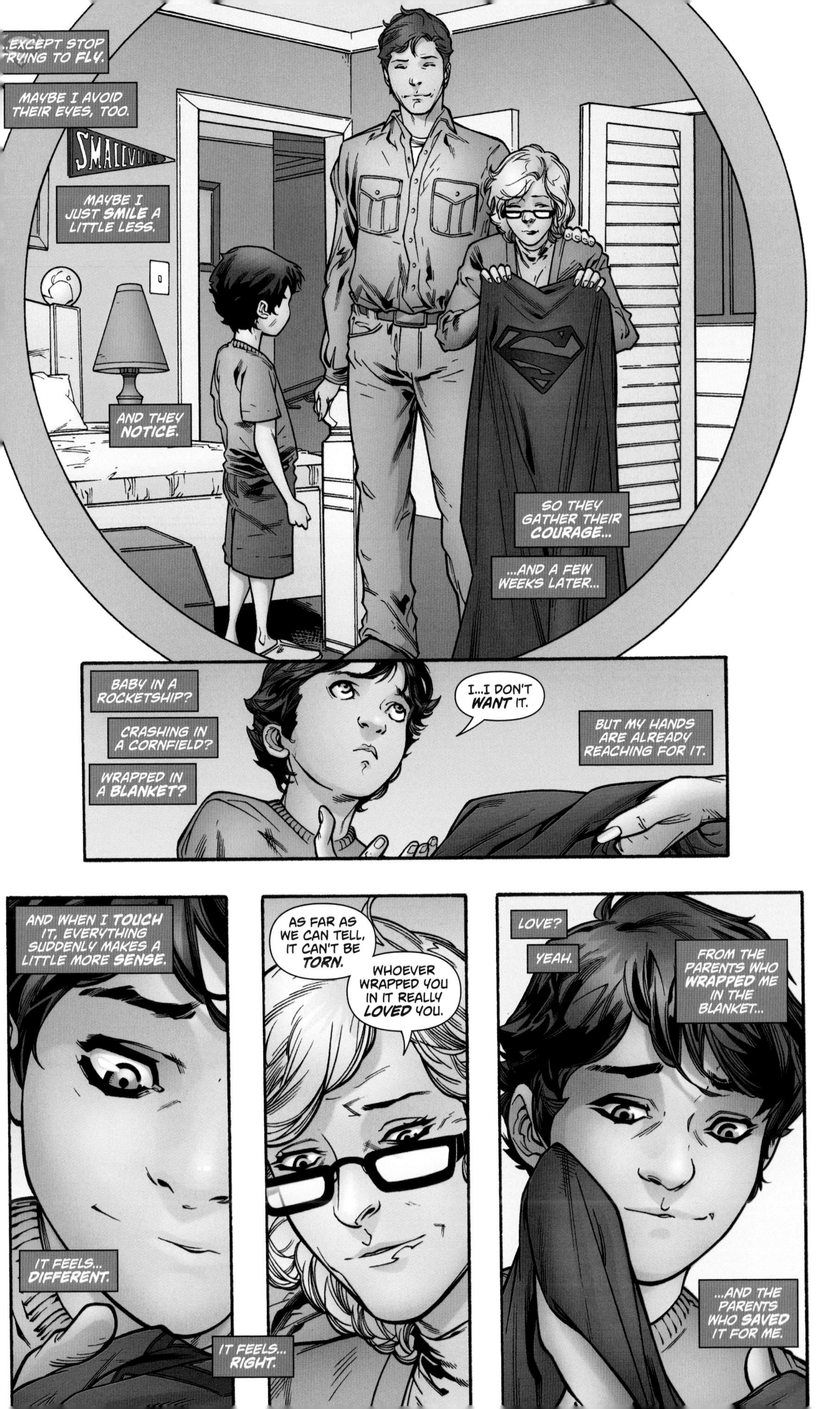
...EXCEPT STOP TRYING TO FLY.
MAYBE I AVOID THEIR EYES, TOO.
SMALLVILLE
MAYBE I JUST SMILE A LITTLE LESS.
AND THEY NOTICE.
SO THEY GATHER THEIR COURAGE...
...AND A FEW WEEKS LATER...
BABY IN A ROCKETSHIP?
CRASHING IN A CORNFIELD?
WRAPPED IN A BLANKET?
I...I DON'T WANT IT.
BUT MY HANDS ARE ALREADY REACHING FOR IT.
AND WHEN I TOUCH IT, EVERYTHING SUDDENLY MAKES A LITTLE MORE SENSE.
IT FEELS... DIFFERENT.
IT FEELS... RIGHT.
AS FAR AS WE CAN TELL, IT CAN'T BE TORN.
WHOEVER WRAPPED YOU IN IT REALLY LOVED YOU.
LOVE?
YEAH.
FROM THE PARENTS WHO WRAPPED ME IN THE BLANKET...
...AND THE PARENTS WHO SAVED IT FOR ME.

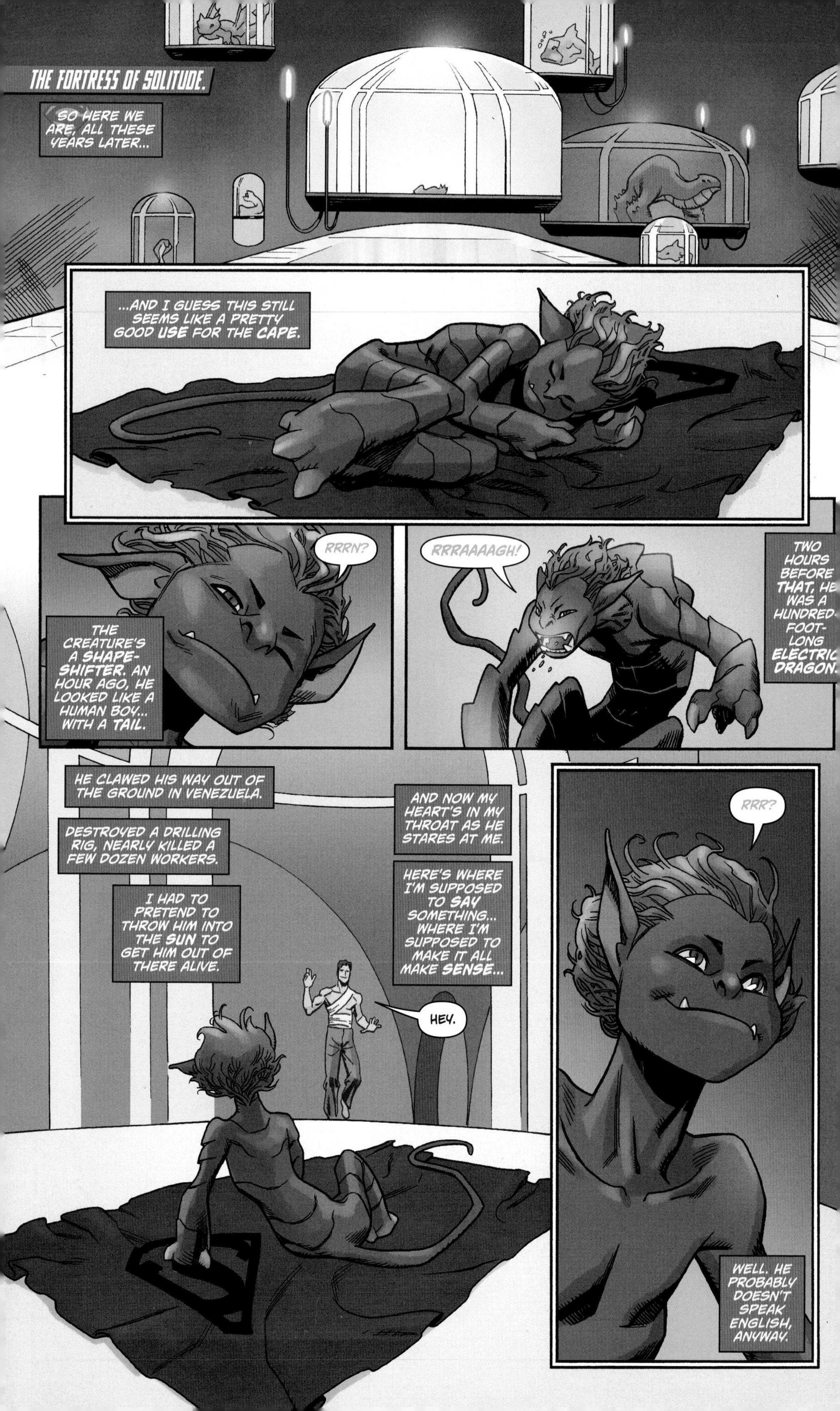
THE FORTRESS OF SOLITUDE.
SO HERE WE ARE, ALL THESE YEARS LATER...
...AND I GUESS THIS STILL SEEMS LIKE A PRETTY GOOD USE FOR THE CAPE.
RRRN?
THE CREATURE'S A SHAPE-SHIFTER. AN HOUR AGO, HE LOOKED LIKE A HUMAN BOY... WITH A TAIL.
RRRAAAAAGH!
TWO HOURS BEFORE THAT, HE WAS A HUNDRED-FOOT-LONG ELECTRIC DRAGON.
HE CLAWED HIS WAY OUT OF THE GROUND IN VENEZUELA.
DESTROYED A DRILLING RIG, NEARLY KILLED A FEW DOZEN WORKERS.
I HAD TO PRETEND TO THROW HIM INTO THE SUN TO GET HIM OUT OF THERE ALIVE.
AND NOW MY HEART'S IN MY THROAT AS HE STARES AT ME.
HERE'S WHERE I'M SUPPOSED TO SAY SOMETHING... WHERE I'M SUPPOSED TO MAKE IT ALL MAKE SENSE...
HEY.
RRR?
WELL. HE PROBABLY DOESN'T SPEAK ENGLISH, ANYWAY.

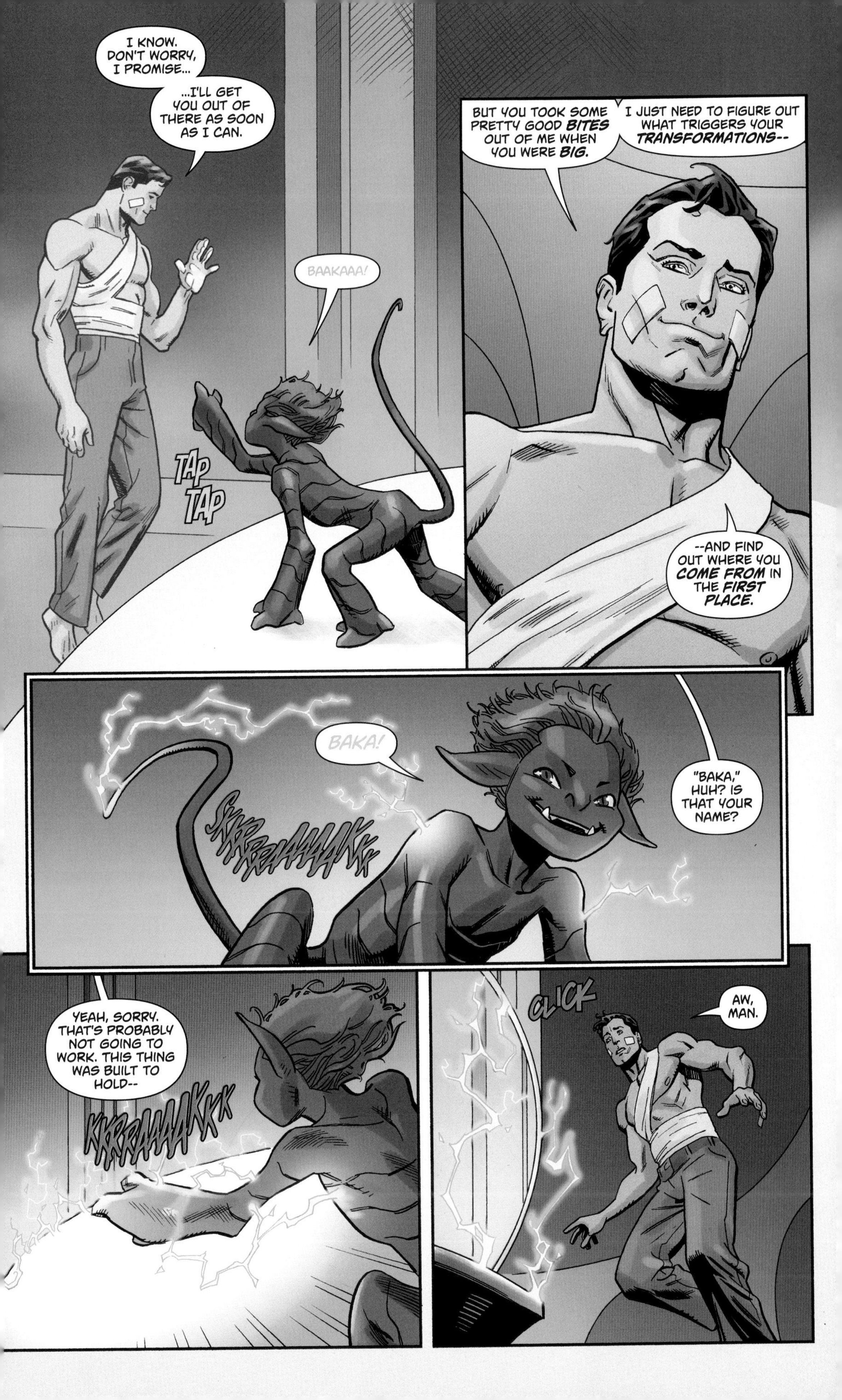
I KNOW. DON'T WORRY, I PROMISE...
...I'LL GET YOU OUT OF THERE AS SOON AS I CAN.
BAAKAAA!
TAP TAP
BUT YOU TOOK SOME PRETTY GOOD BITES OUT OF ME WHEN YOU WERE BIG.
I JUST NEED TO FIGURE OUT WHAT TRIGGERS YOUR TRANSFORMATIONS--
--AND FIND OUT WHERE YOU COME FROM IN THE FIRST PLACE.
BAKA!
SKRRRAAAAKKK
"BAKA," HUH? IS THAT YOUR NAME?
YEAH, SORRY. THAT'S PROBABLY NOT GOING TO WORK. THIS THING WAS BUILT TO HOLD--
KKRRAAAAKKK
CLICK
AW, MAN.

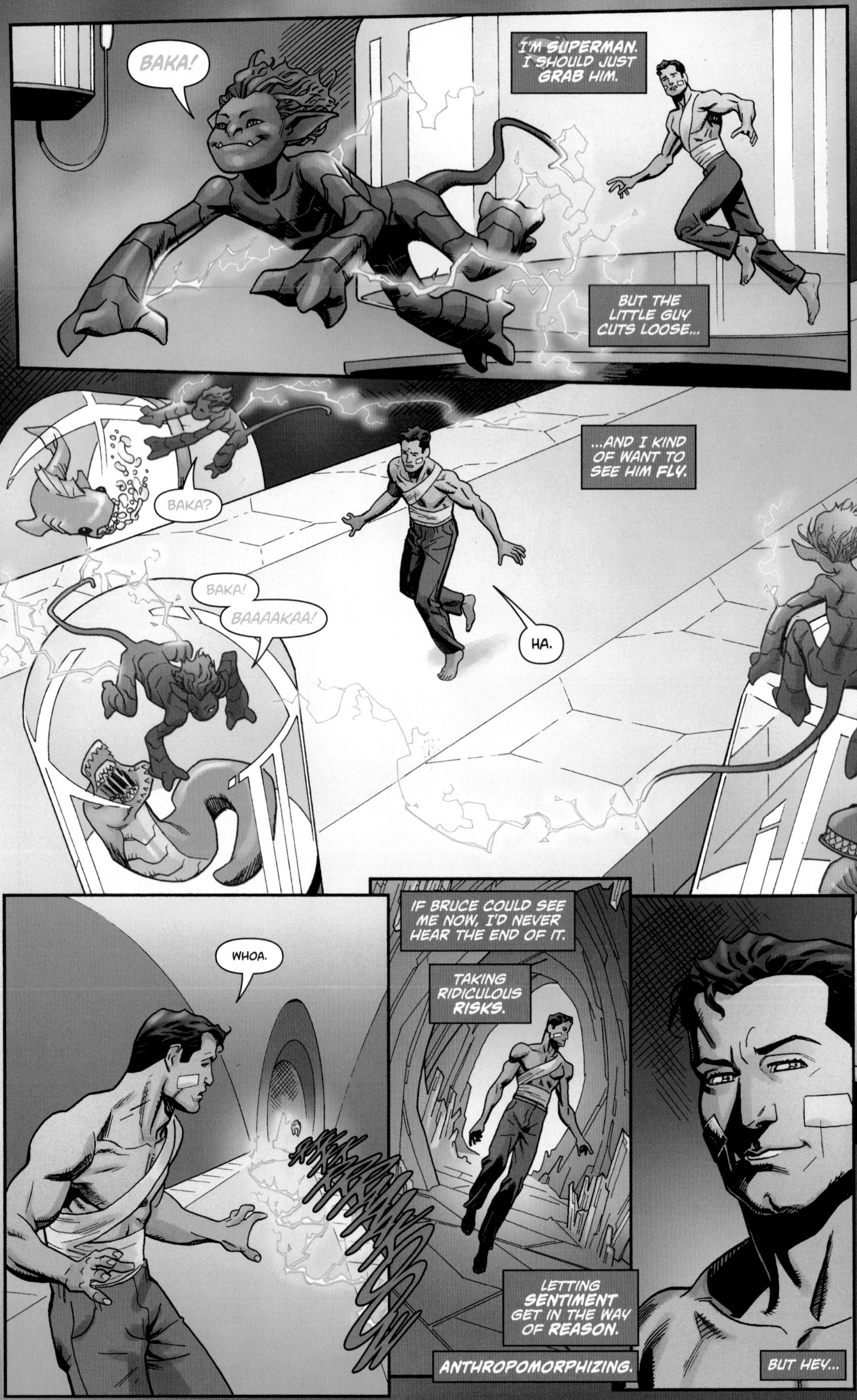

BAKA!
I'M SUPERMAN. I SHOULD JUST GRAB HIM.
BUT THE LITTLE GUY CUTS LOOSE...
...AND I KIND OF WANT TO SEE HIM FLY.
BAKA?
BAKA!
BAAAAKAA!
HA.
WHOA.
IF BRUCE COULD SEE ME NOW, I'D NEVER HEAR THE END OF IT.
TAKING RIDICULOUS RISKS.
LETTING SENTIMENT GET IN THE WAY OF REASON.
ANTHROPOMORPHIZING.
BUT HEY...

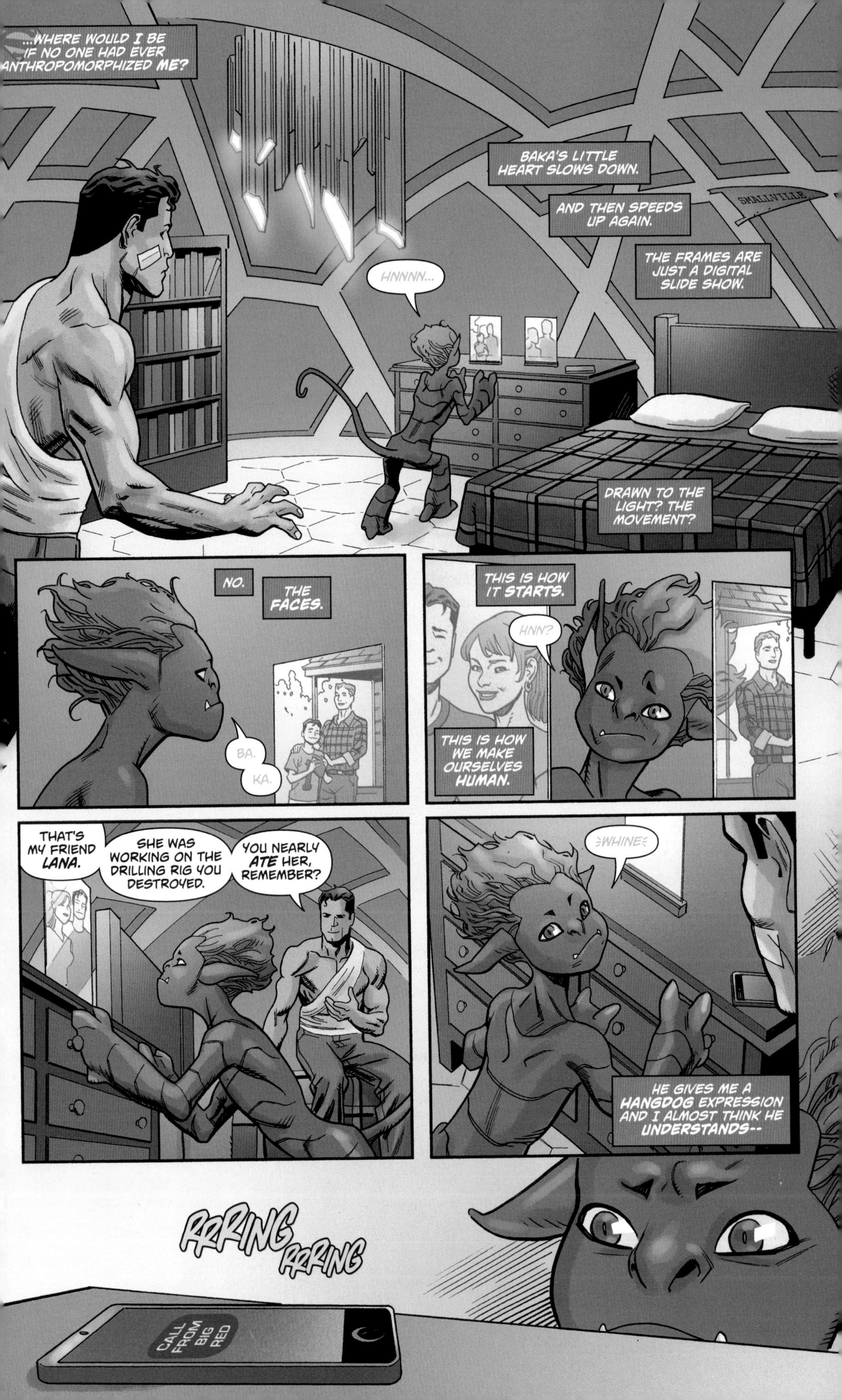
...WHERE WOULD I BE IF NO ONE HAD EVER ANTHROPOMORPHIZED ME?
BAKA'S LITTLE HEART SLOWS DOWN.
AND THEN SPEEDS UP AGAIN.
THE FRAMES ARE JUST A DIGITAL SLIDE SHOW.
HNNNN...
SMALLVILLE
DRAWN TO THE LIGHT? THE MOVEMENT?
NO.
THE FACES.
BA.
KA.
THIS IS HOW IT STARTS.
HNN?
THIS IS HOW WE MAKE OURSELVES HUMAN.
THAT'S MY FRIEND LANA.
SHE WAS WORKING ON THE DRILLING RIG YOU DESTROYED.
YOU NEARLY ATE HER, REMEMBER?
WHINE
HE GIVES ME A HANGDOG EXPRESSION AND I ALMOST THINK HE UNDERSTANDS--
RRRING RRRING
CALL FROM BIG RED

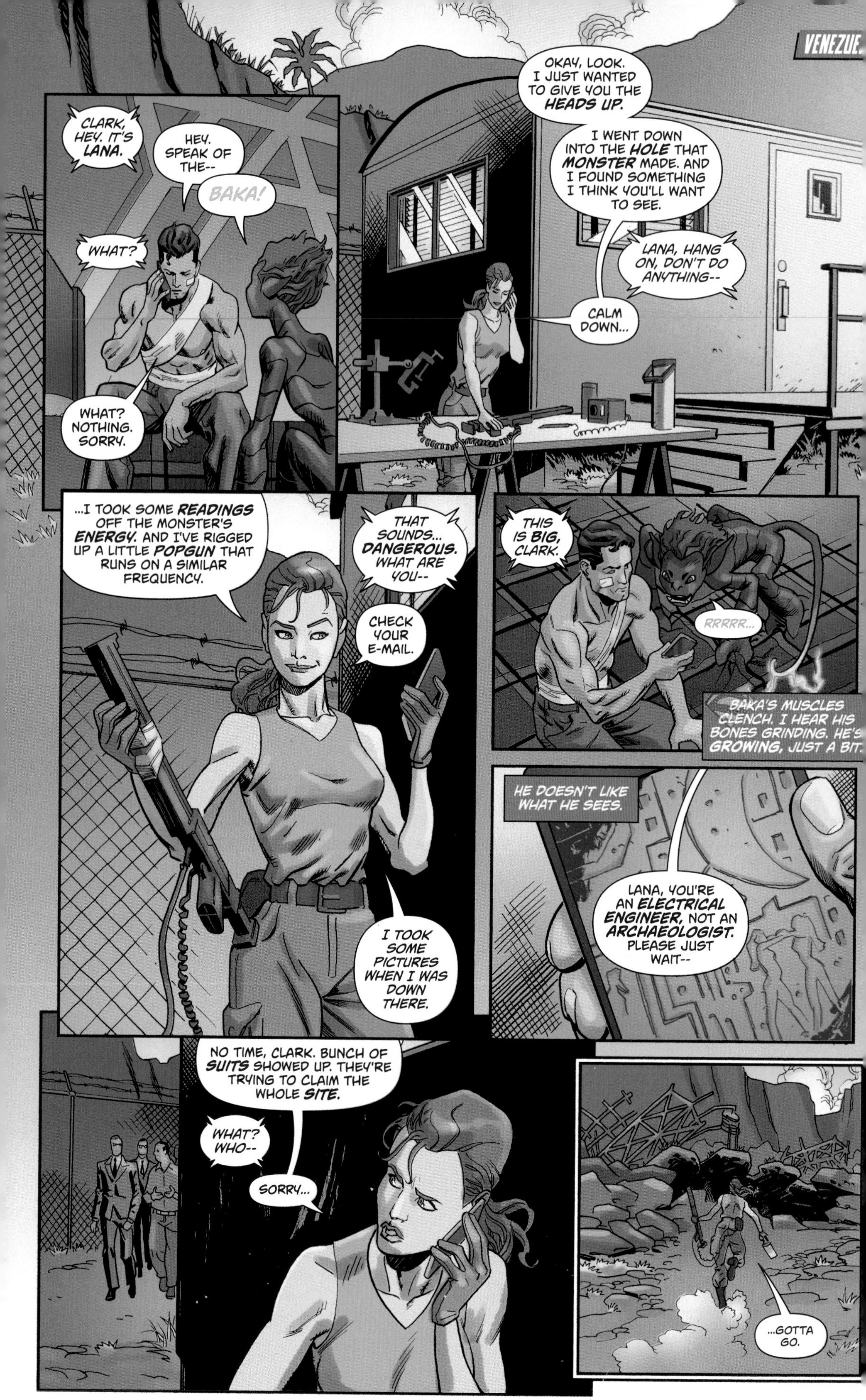
VENEZUE
CLARK, HEY. IT'S LANA.
HEY. SPEAK OF THE--
BAKA!
WHAT?
WHAT? NOTHING. SORRY.
OKAY, LOOK. I JUST WANTED TO GIVE YOU THE HEADS UP.
I WENT DOWN INTO THE HOLE THAT MONSTER MADE. AND I FOUND SOMETHING I THINK YOU'LL WANT TO SEE.
LANA, HANG ON, DON'T DO ANYTHING--
CALM DOWN...
...I TOOK SOME READINGS OFF THE MONSTER'S ENERGY. AND I'VE RIGGED UP A LITTLE POPGUN THAT RUNS ON A SIMILAR FREQUENCY.
THAT SOUNDS... DANGEROUS. WHAT ARE YOU--
CHECK YOUR E-MAIL.
I TOOK SOME PICTURES WHEN I WAS DOWN THERE.
THIS IS BIG, CLARK.
RRRRR...
BAKA'S MUSCLES CLENCH. I HEAR HIS BONES GRINDING. HE'S GROWING, JUST A BIT.
HE DOESN'T LIKE WHAT HE SEES.
LANA, YOU'RE AN ELECTRICAL ENGINEER, NOT AN ARCHAEOLOGIST. PLEASE JUST WAIT--
NO TIME, CLARK. BUNCH OF SUITS SHOWED UP. THEY'RE TRYING TO CLAIM THE WHOLE SITE.
WHAT? WHO--
SORRY...
...GOTTA GO.

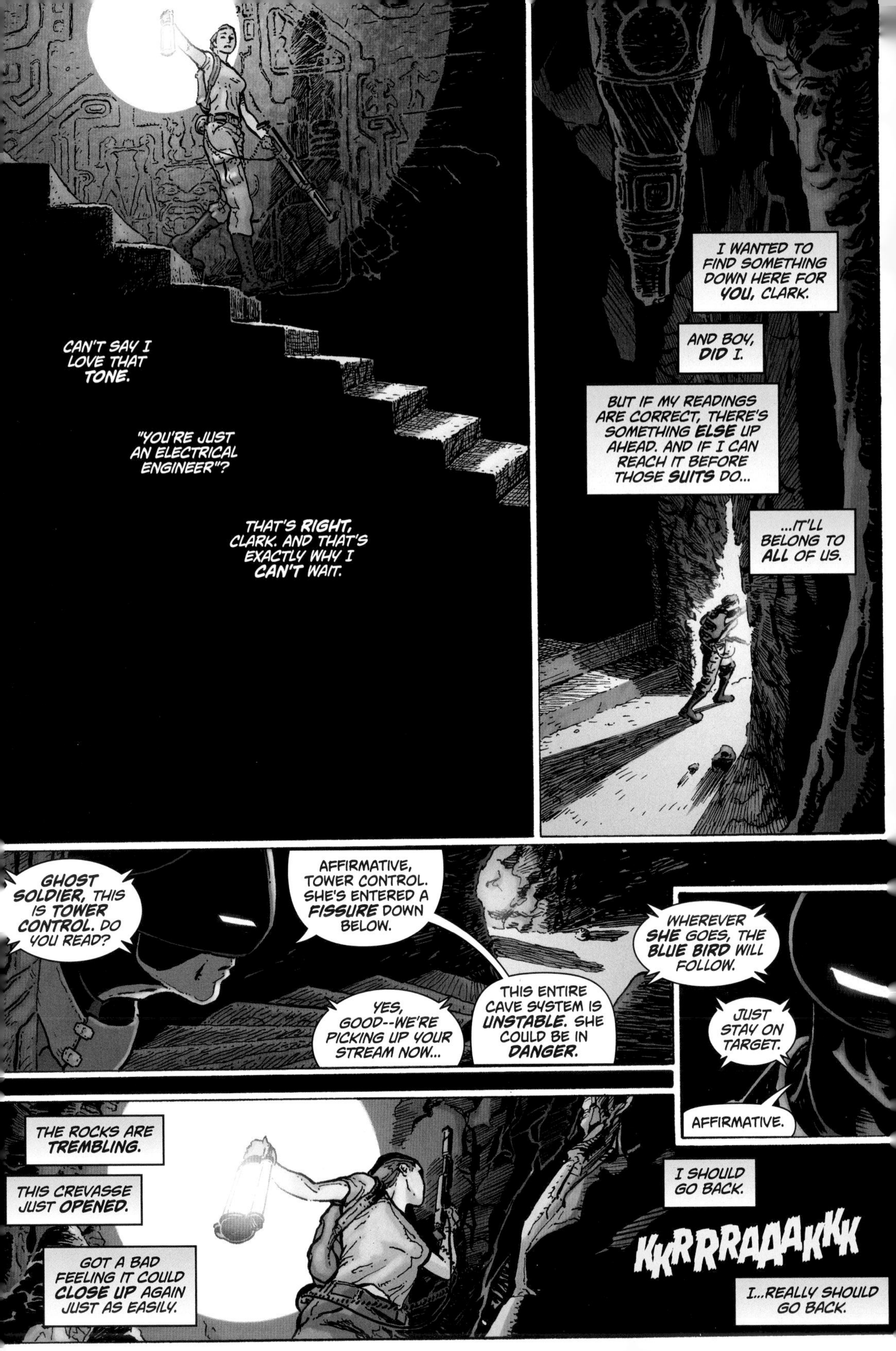
CAN'T SAY I LOVE THAT TONE.
"YOU'RE JUST AN ELECTRICAL ENGINEER"?
THAT'S RIGHT, CLARK. AND THAT'S EXACTLY WHY I CAN'T WAIT.
I WANTED TO FIND SOMETHING DOWN HERE FOR YOU, CLARK.
AND BOY, DID I.
BUT IF MY READINGS ARE CORRECT, THERE'S SOMETHING ELSE UP AHEAD. AND IF I CAN REACH IT BEFORE THOSE SUITS DO...
...IT'LL BELONG TO ALL OF US.
GHOST SOLDIER, THIS IS TOWER CONTROL. DO YOU READ?
AFFIRMATIVE, TOWER CONTROL. SHE'S ENTERED A FISSURE DOWN BELOW.
YES, GOOD--WE'RE PICKING UP YOUR STREAM NOW...
THIS ENTIRE CAVE SYSTEM IS UNSTABLE. SHE COULD BE IN DANGER.
WHEREVER SHE GOES, THE BLUE BIRD WILL FOLLOW.
JUST STAY ON TARGET.
AFFIRMATIVE.
THE ROCKS ARE TREMBLING.
THIS CREVASSE JUST OPENED.
GOT A BAD FEELING IT COULD CLOSE UP AGAIN JUST AS EASILY.
I SHOULD GO BACK.
KKRRRAAAKKK
I...REALLY SHOULD GO BACK.

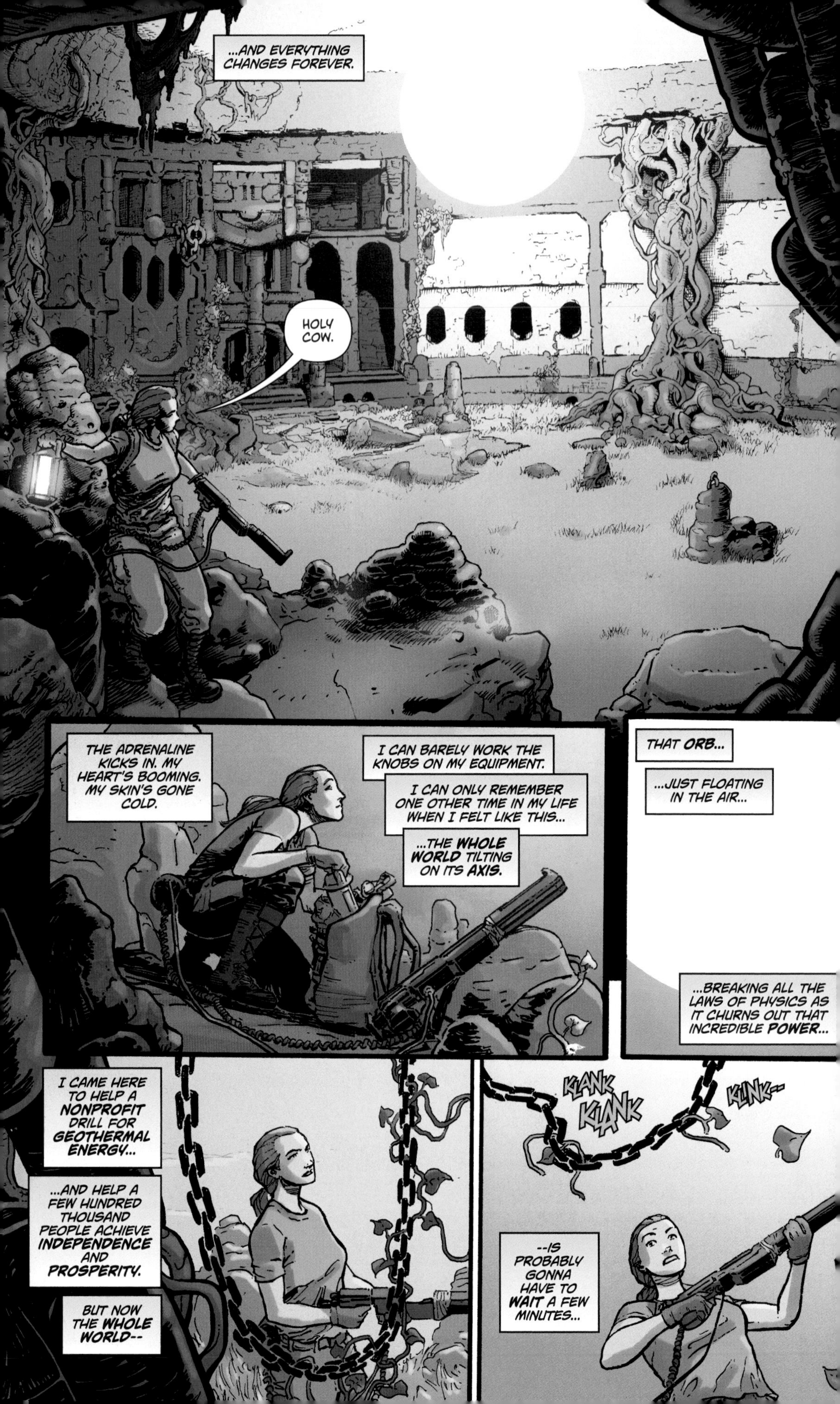

...AND EVERYTHING CHANGES FOREVER.
HOLY COW.
THE ADRENALINE KICKS IN. MY HEART'S BOOMING. MY SKIN'S GONE COLD.
I CAN BARELY WORK THE KNOBS ON MY EQUIPMENT.
I CAN ONLY REMEMBER ONE OTHER TIME IN MY LIFE WHEN I FELT LIKE THIS...
...THE WHOLE WORLD TILTING ON ITS AXIS.
THAT ORB...
...JUST FLOATING IN THE AIR...
...BREAKING ALL THE LAWS OF PHYSICS AS IT CHURNS OUT THAT INCREDIBLE POWER...
I CAME HERE TO HELP A NONPROFIT DRILL FOR GEOTHERMAL ENERGY...
...AND HELP A FEW HUNDRED THOUSAND PEOPLE ACHIEVE INDEPENDENCE AND PROSPERITY.
BUT NOW THE WHOLE WORLD--
KLANK
KLANK
KLINK--
--IS PROBABLY GONNA HAVE TO WAIT A FEW MINUTES...

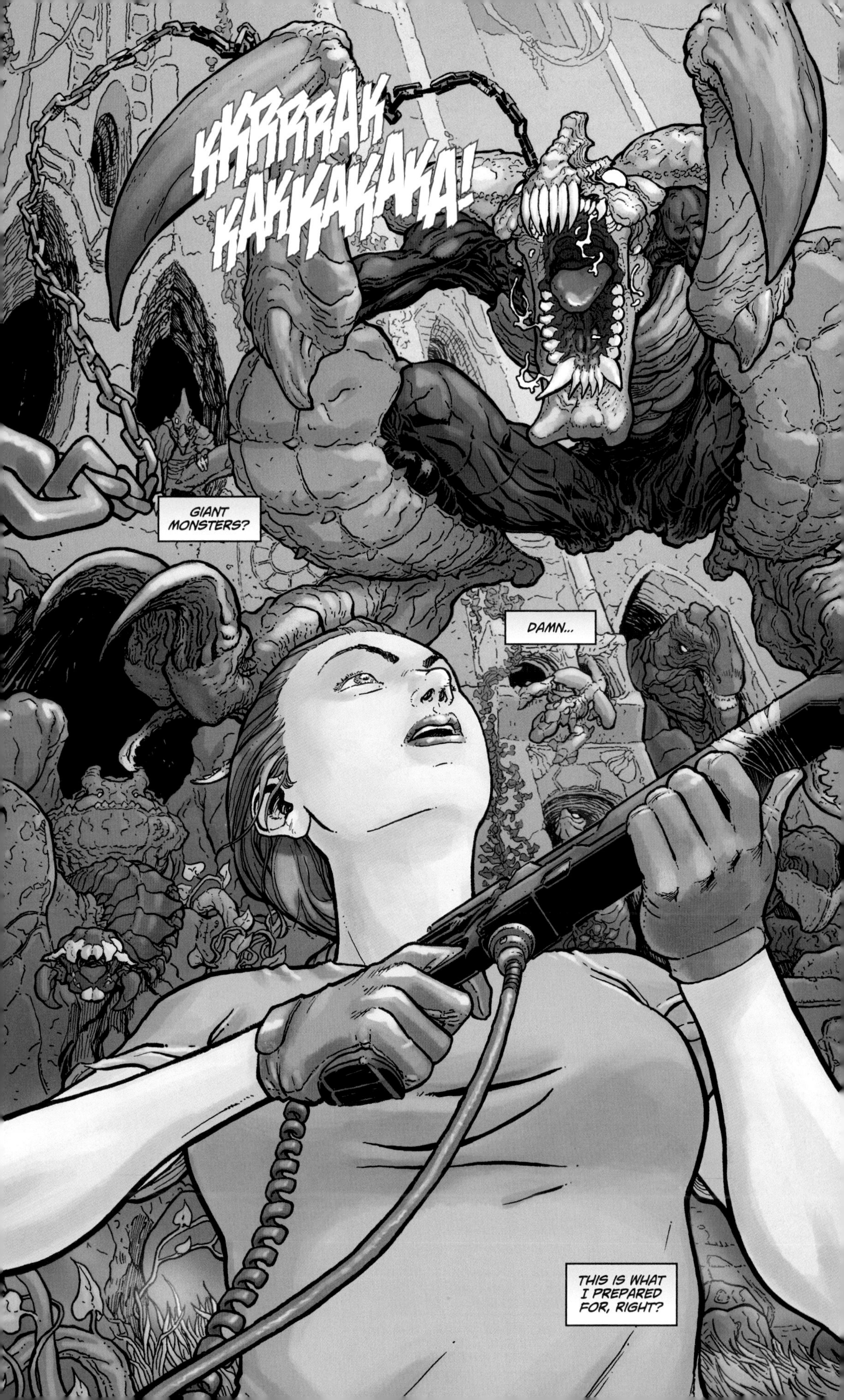
KKRRRAK KAKKAKAKA!
GIANT MONSTERS?
DAMN...
THIS IS WHAT I PREPARED FOR, RIGHT?

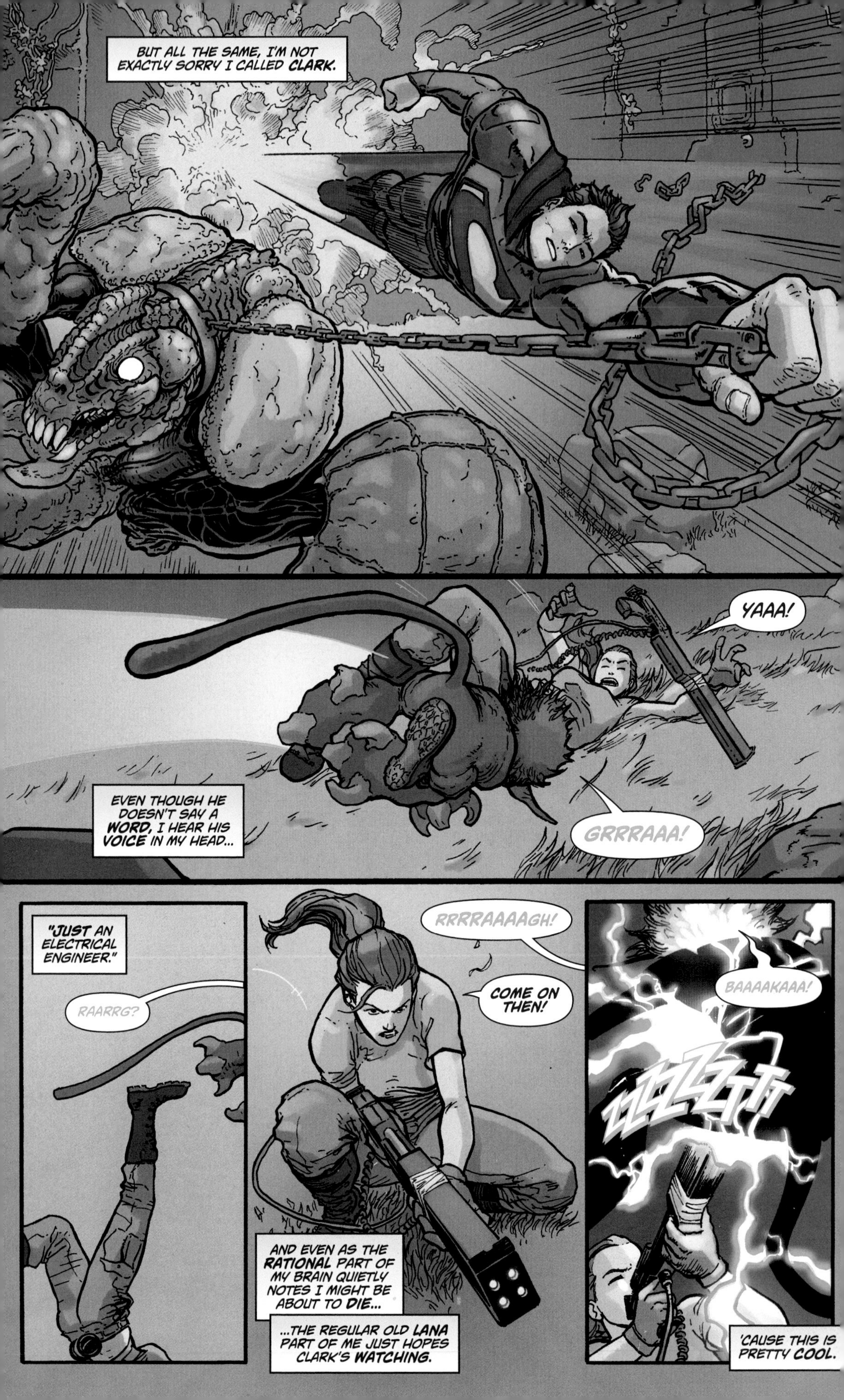
BUT ALL THE SAME, I'M NOT EXACTLY SORRY I CALLED CLARK.
YAAA!
EVEN THOUGH HE DOESN'T SAY A WORD, I HEAR HIS VOICE IN MY HEAD...
GRRRAAA!
"JUST AN ELECTRICAL ENGINEER."
RAARRG?
COME ON THEN!
AND EVEN AS THE RATIONAL PART OF MY BRAIN QUIETLY NOTES I MIGHT BE ABOUT TO DIE...
...THE REGULAR OLD LANA PART OF ME JUST HOPES CLARK'S WATCHING.
RRRRAAAAGH!
BAAAAKAAA!
ZZZZZTTT
'CAUSE THIS IS PRETTY COOL.

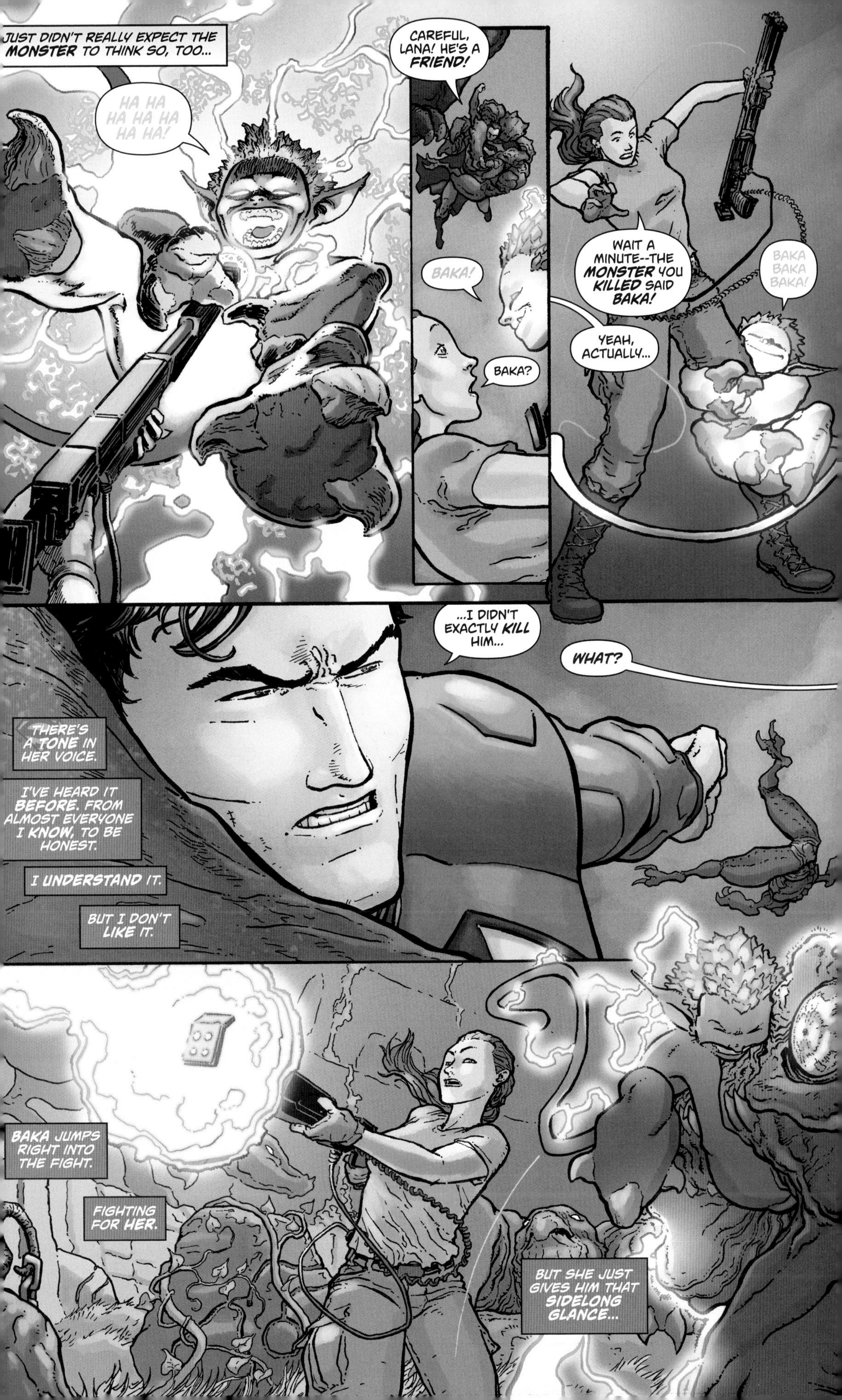
JUST DIDN'T REALLY EXPECT THE MONSTER TO THINK SO, TOO...
HA HA HA HA HA HA HA!
CAREFUL, LANA! HE'S A FRIEND!
BAKA!
BAKA?
WAIT A MINUTE--THE MONSTER YOU KILLED SAID BAKA!
YEAH, ACTUALLY...
BAKA BAKA BAKA!
...I DIDN'T EXACTLY KILL HIM...
WHAT?
THERE'S A TONE IN HER VOICE.
I'VE HEARD IT BEFORE. FROM ALMOST EVERYONE I KNOW, TO BE HONEST.
I UNDERSTAND IT.
BUT I DON'T LIKE IT.
BAKA JUMPS RIGHT INTO THE FIGHT.
FIGHTING FOR HER.
BUT SHE JUST GIVES HIM THAT SIDELONG GLANCE...

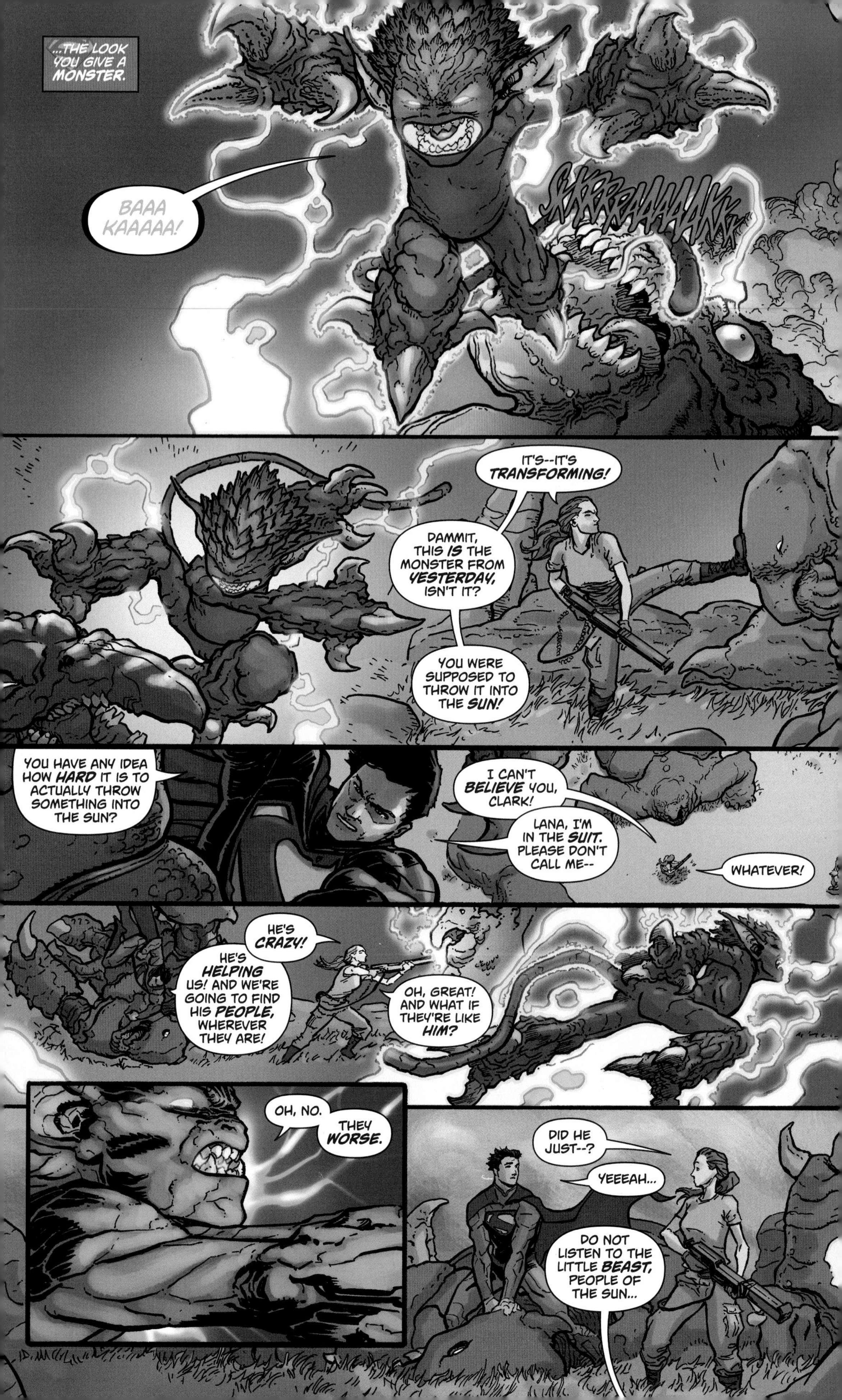

...THE LOOK YOU GIVE A MONSTER.
BAAA KAAAAA!
SKRRAAAAAKK
IT'S--IT'S TRANSFORMING!
DAMMIT, THIS IS THE MONSTER FROM YESTERDAY, ISN'T IT?
YOU WERE SUPPOSED TO THROW IT INTO THE SUN!
YOU HAVE ANY IDEA HOW HARD IT IS TO ACTUALLY THROW SOMETHING INTO THE SUN?
I CAN'T BELIEVE YOU, CLARK!
LANA, I'M IN THE SUIT. PLEASE DON'T CALL ME--
WHATEVER!
HE'S CRAZY!
HE'S HELPING US! AND WE'RE GOING TO FIND HIS PEOPLE, WHEREVER THEY ARE!
OH, GREAT! AND WHAT IF THEY'RE LIKE HIM?
OH, NO.
THEY WORSE.
DID HE JUST--?
YEEEAH...
DO NOT LISTEN TO THE LITTLE BEAST, PEOPLE OF THE SUN...

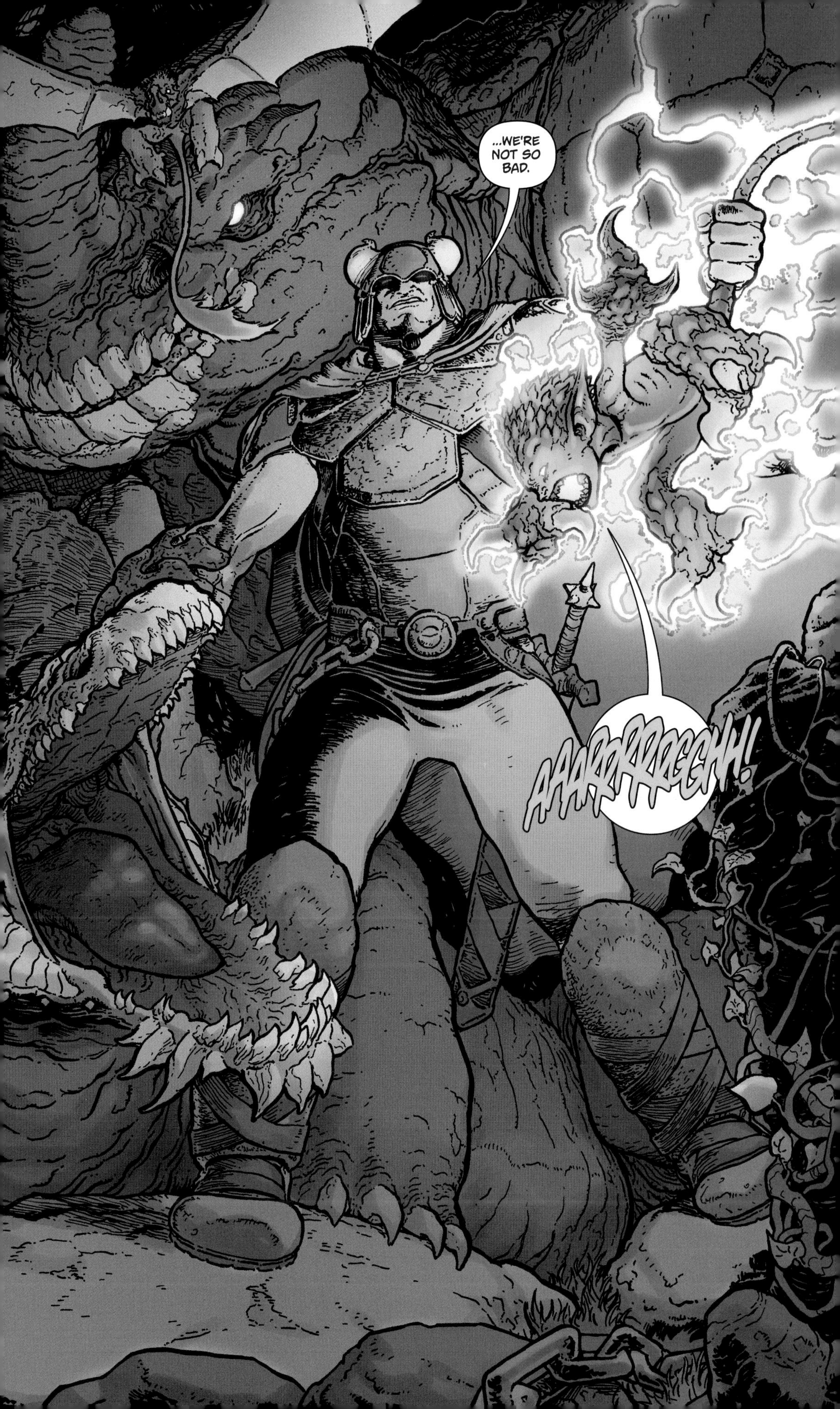

...WE'RE NOT SO BAD.
AAARRRRGGHH!

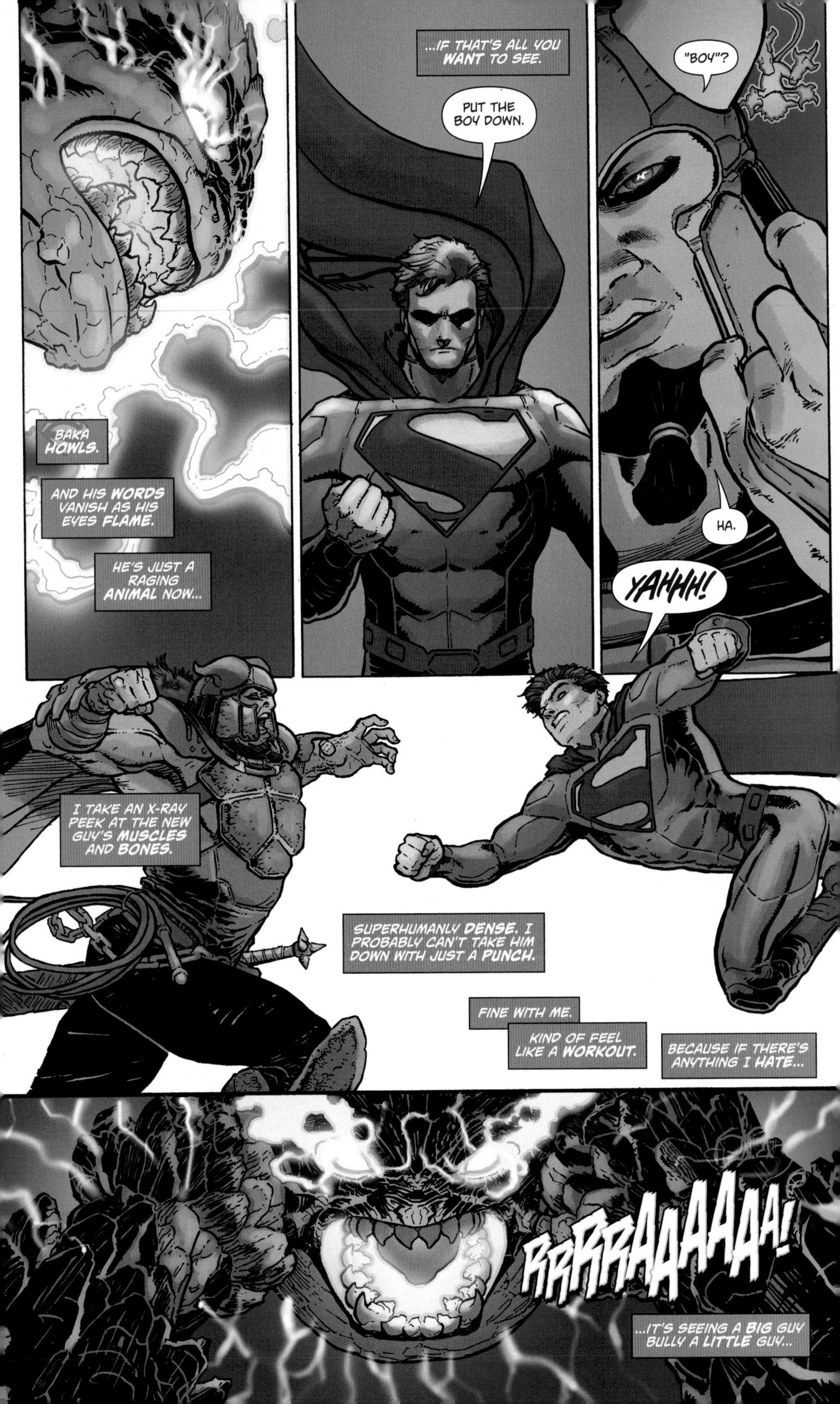

BAKA HOWLS.
AND HIS WORDS VANISH AS HIS EYES FLAME.
HE'S JUST A RAGING ANIMAL NOW...
...IF THAT'S ALL YOU WANT TO SEE.
PUT THE BOY DOWN.
"BOY"?
HA.
YAHHH!
I TAKE AN X-RAY PEEK AT THE NEW GUY'S MUSCLES AND BONES.
SUPERHUMANLY DENSE. I PROBABLY CAN'T TAKE HIM DOWN WITH JUST A PUNCH.
FINE WITH ME.
KIND OF FEEL LIKE A WORKOUT.
BECAUSE IF THERE'S ANYTHING I HATE...
RRRRAAAAAA!
...IT'S SEEING A BIG GUY BULLY A LITTLE GUY...

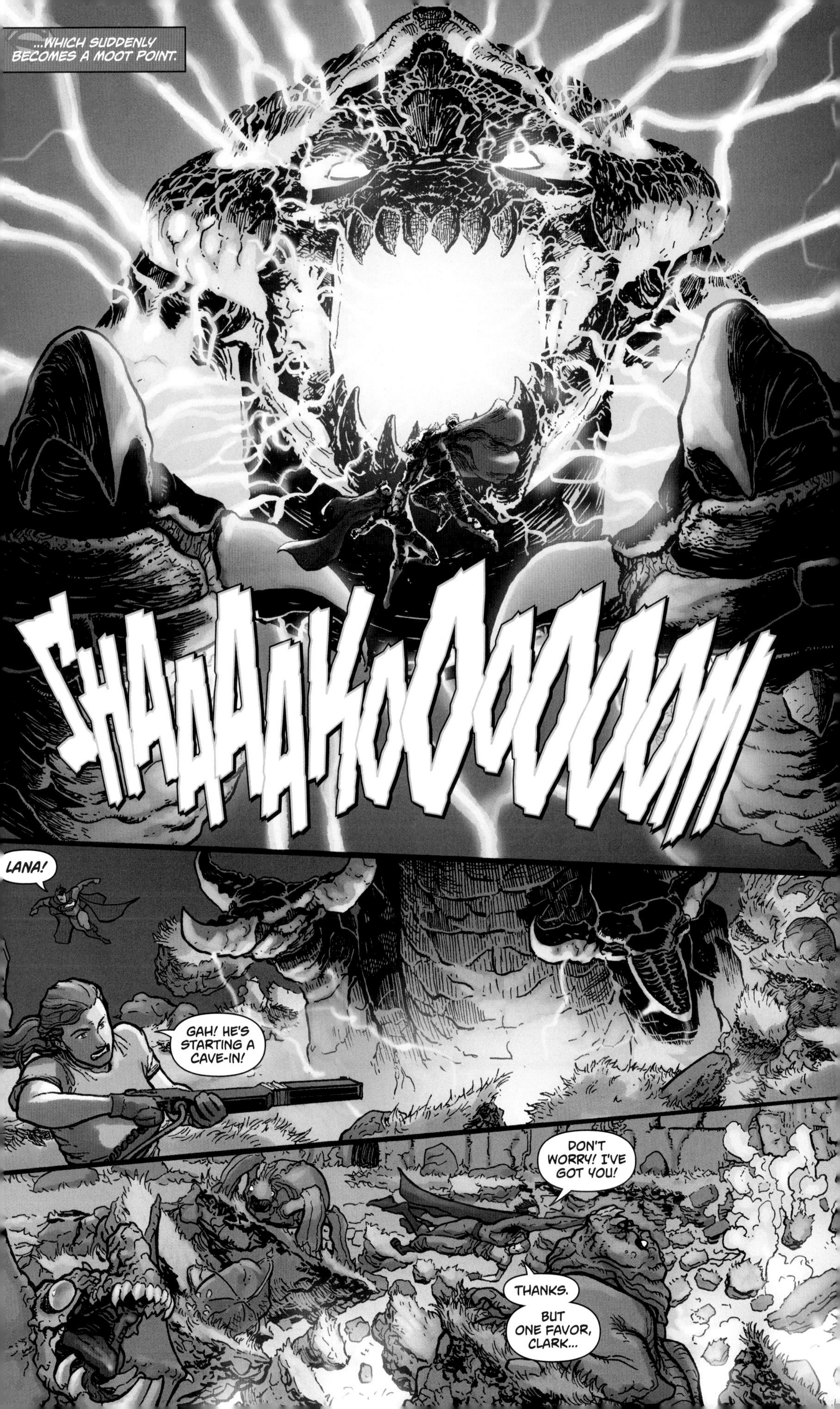
...WHICH SUDDENLY BECOMES A MOOT POINT.
SHAAAAKOOOOOOM
LANA!
GAH! HE'S STARTING A CAVE-IN!
DON'T WORRY! I'VE GOT YOU!
THANKS.
BUT ONE FAVOR, CLARK...

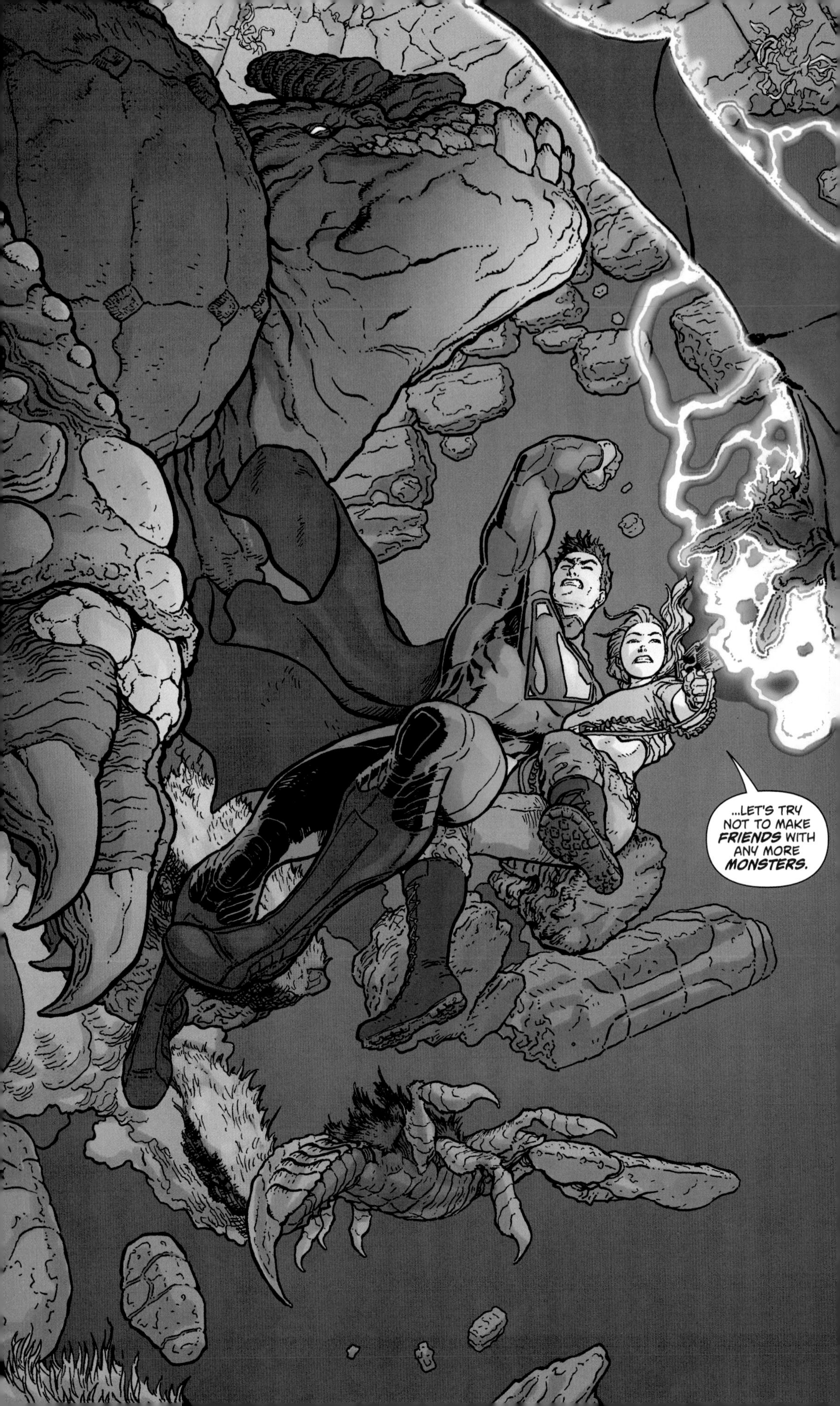
...LET'S TRY NOT TO MAKE **FRIENDS** WITH ANY MORE **MONSTERS.**

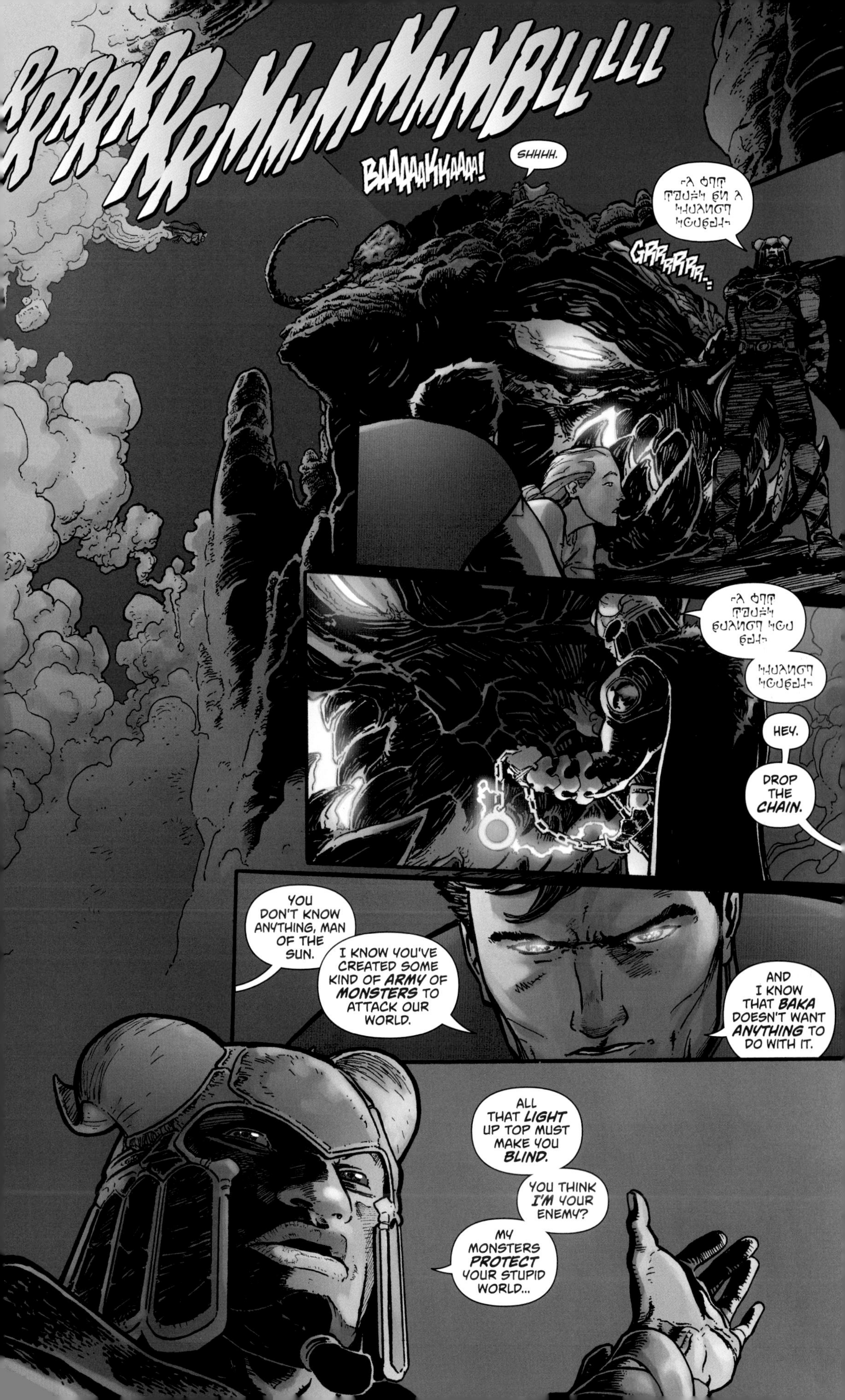
RRRRRRMMMMMMMMBLLLLL
BAAAAKKAAAA!
SHHHH.
GRRRRRR..
HEY.
DROP THE *CHAIN.*
YOU DON'T KNOW ANYTHING, MAN OF THE SUN.
I KNOW YOU'VE CREATED SOME KIND OF *ARMY* OF *MONSTERS* TO ATTACK OUR WORLD.
AND I KNOW THAT *BAKA* DOESN'T WANT *ANYTHING* TO DO WITH IT.
ALL THAT *LIGHT* UP TOP MUST MAKE YOU *BLIND.*
YOU THINK *I'M* YOUR ENEMY?
MY MONSTERS *PROTECT* YOUR STUPID WORLD...

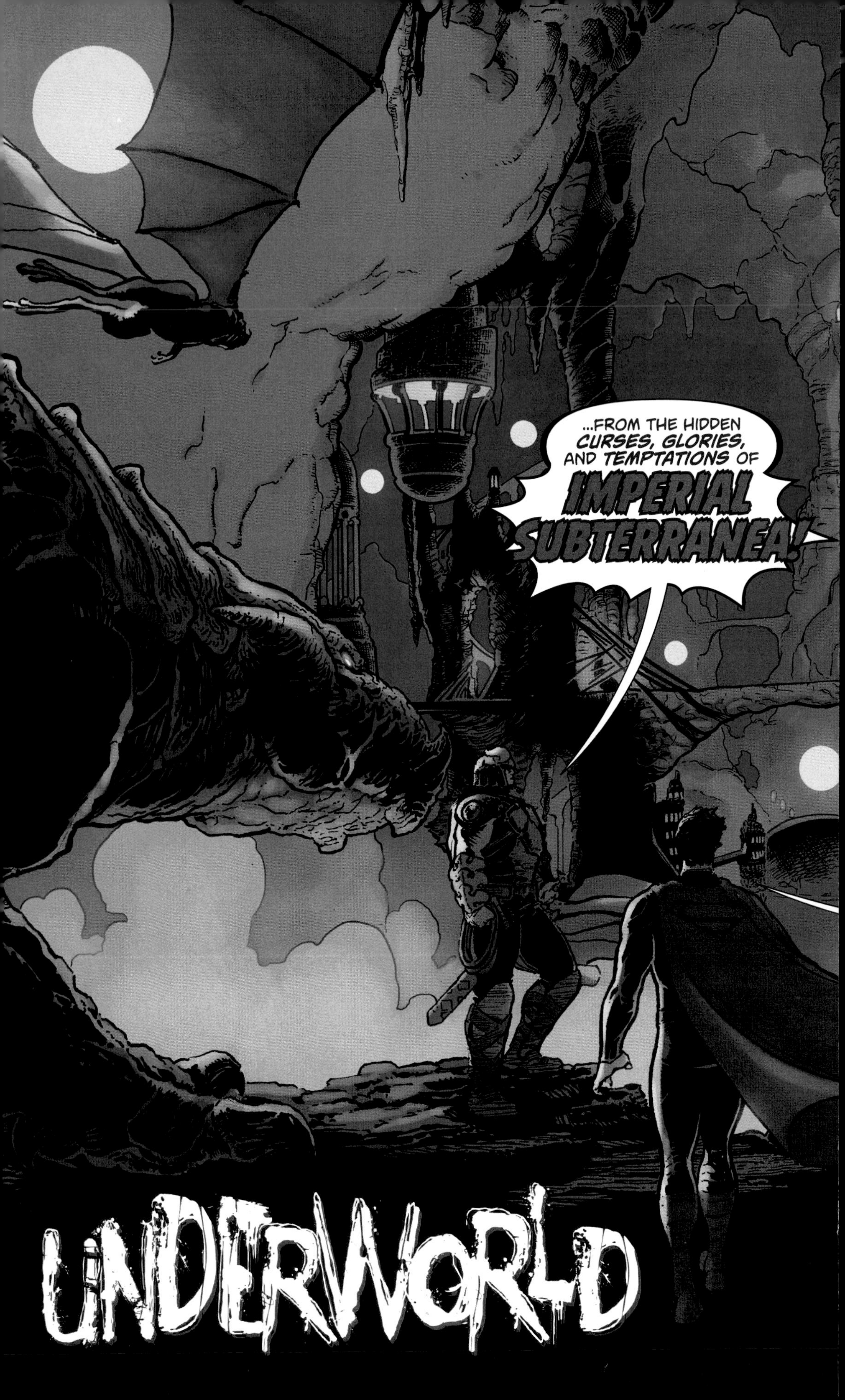
...FROM THE HIDDEN CURSES, GLORIES, AND TEMPTATIONS OF IMPERIAL SUBTERRANEA!
UNDERWORLD

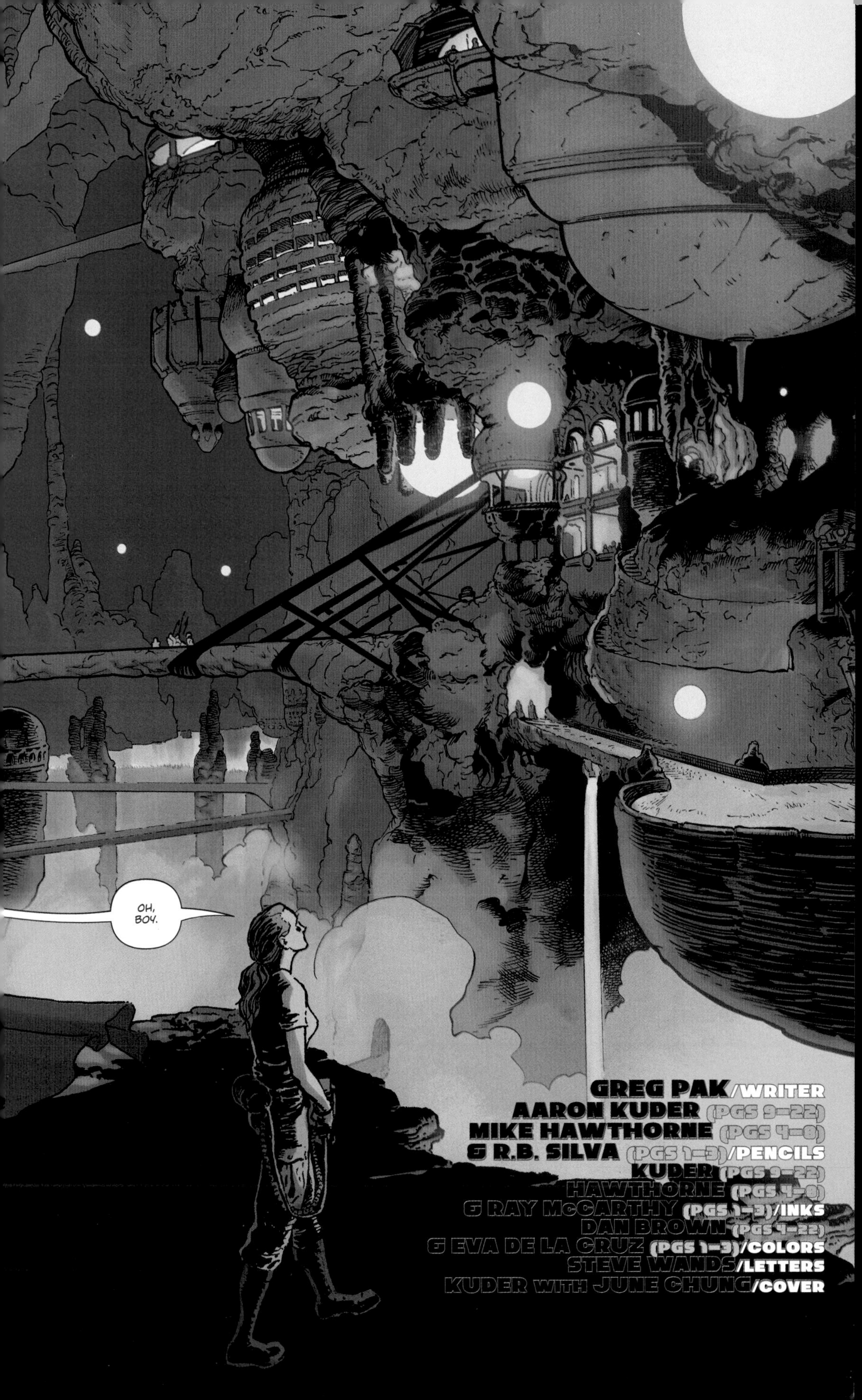
OH, BOY.
GREG PAK/WRITER
AARON KUDER (PGS 9-22)
MIKE HAWTHORNE (PGS 4-8)
& R.B. SILVA (PGS 1-3)/PENCILS
KUDER (PGS 9-22)
HAWTHORNE (PGS 4-8)
& RAY McCARTHY (PGS 1-3)/INKS
DAN BROWN (PGS 4-22)
& EVA DE LA CRUZ (PGS 1-3)/COLORS
STEVE WANDS/LETTERS
KUDER with JUNE CHUNG/COVER

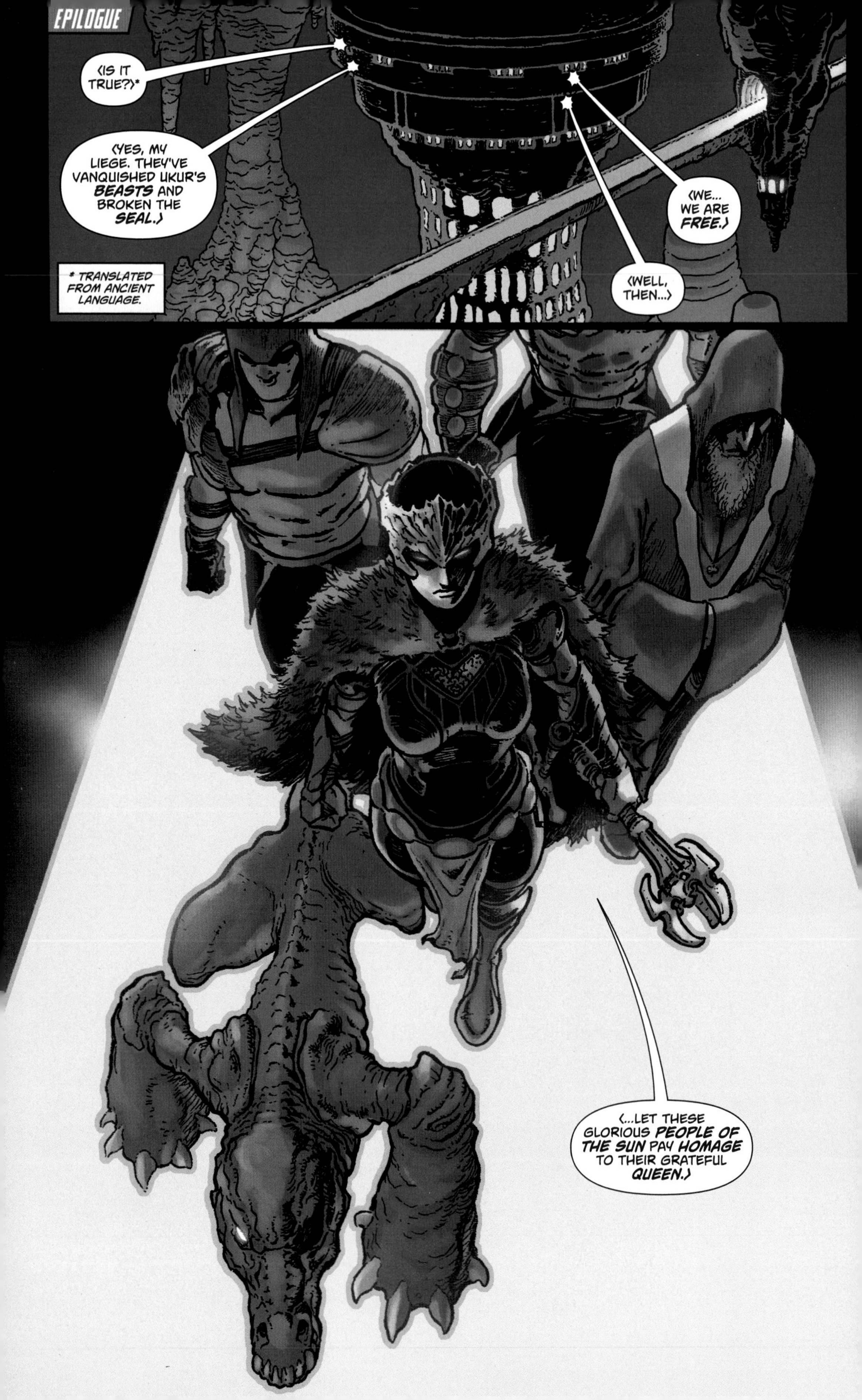
EPILOGUE
‹IS IT TRUE?›*
‹YES, MY LIEGE. THEY'VE VANQUISHED UKUR'S BEASTS AND BROKEN THE SEAL.›
‹WE... WE ARE FREE.›
‹WELL, THEN...›
* TRANSLATED FROM ANCIENT LANGUAGE.
‹...LET THESE GLORIOUS PEOPLE OF THE SUN PAY HOMAGE TO THEIR GRATEFUL QUEEN.›

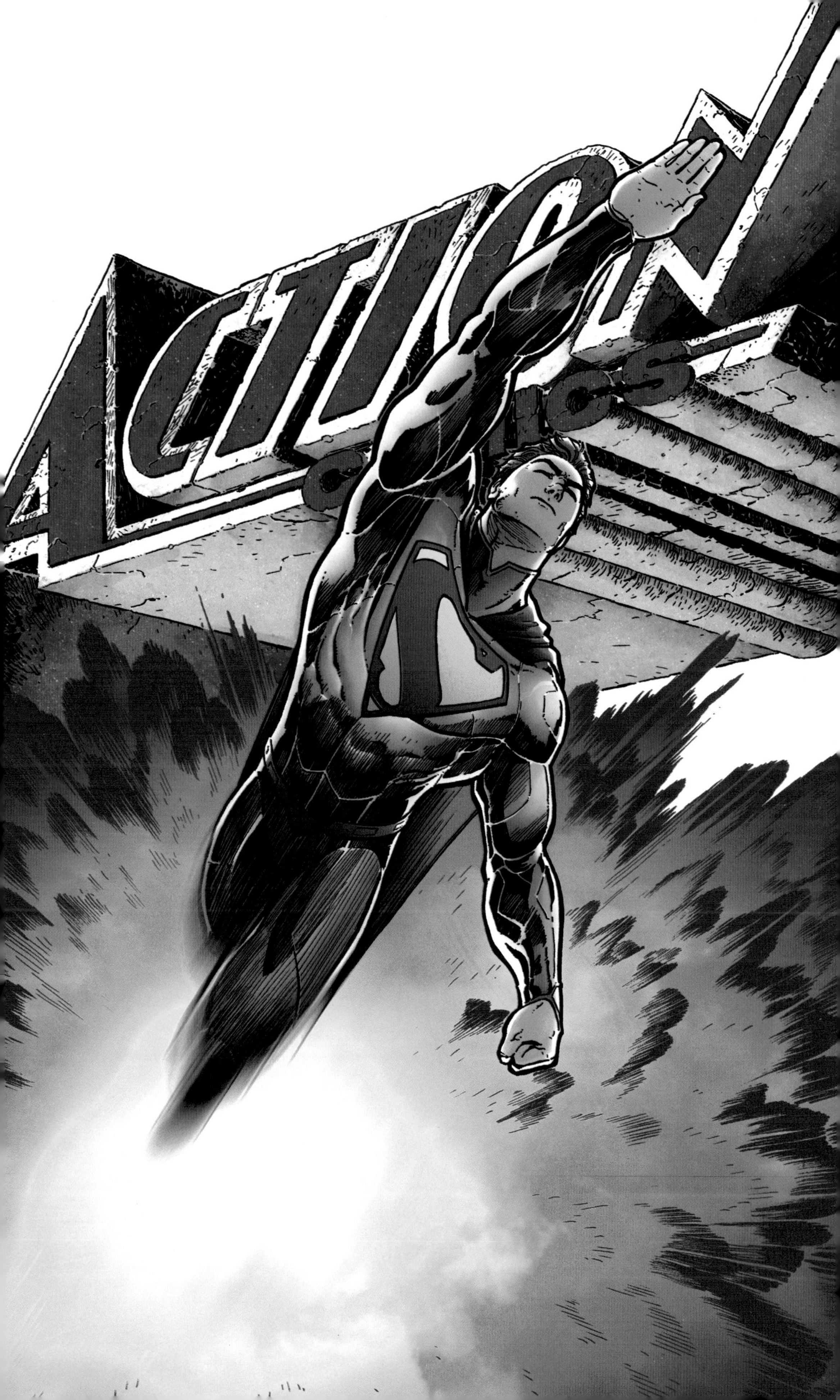
ACTION

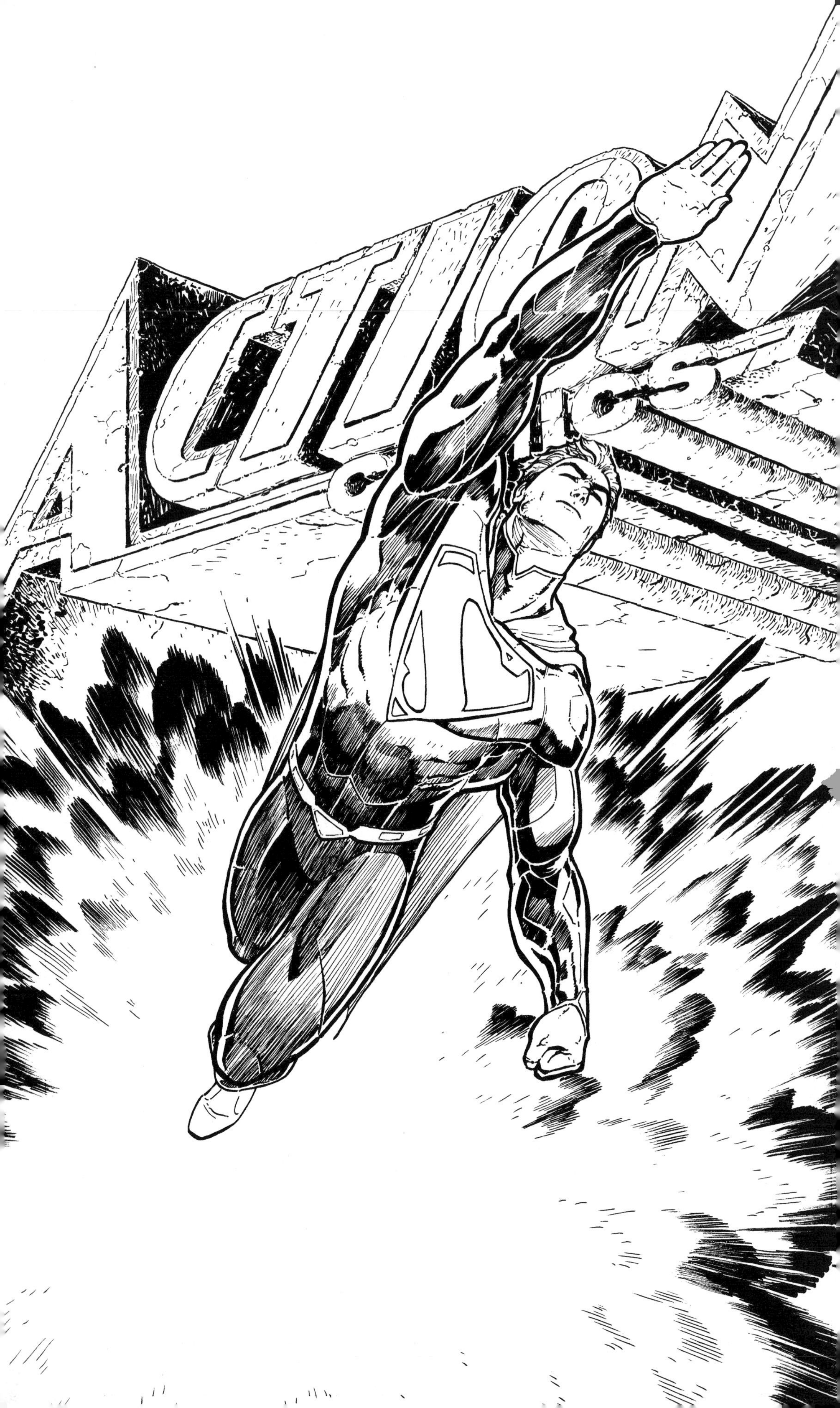

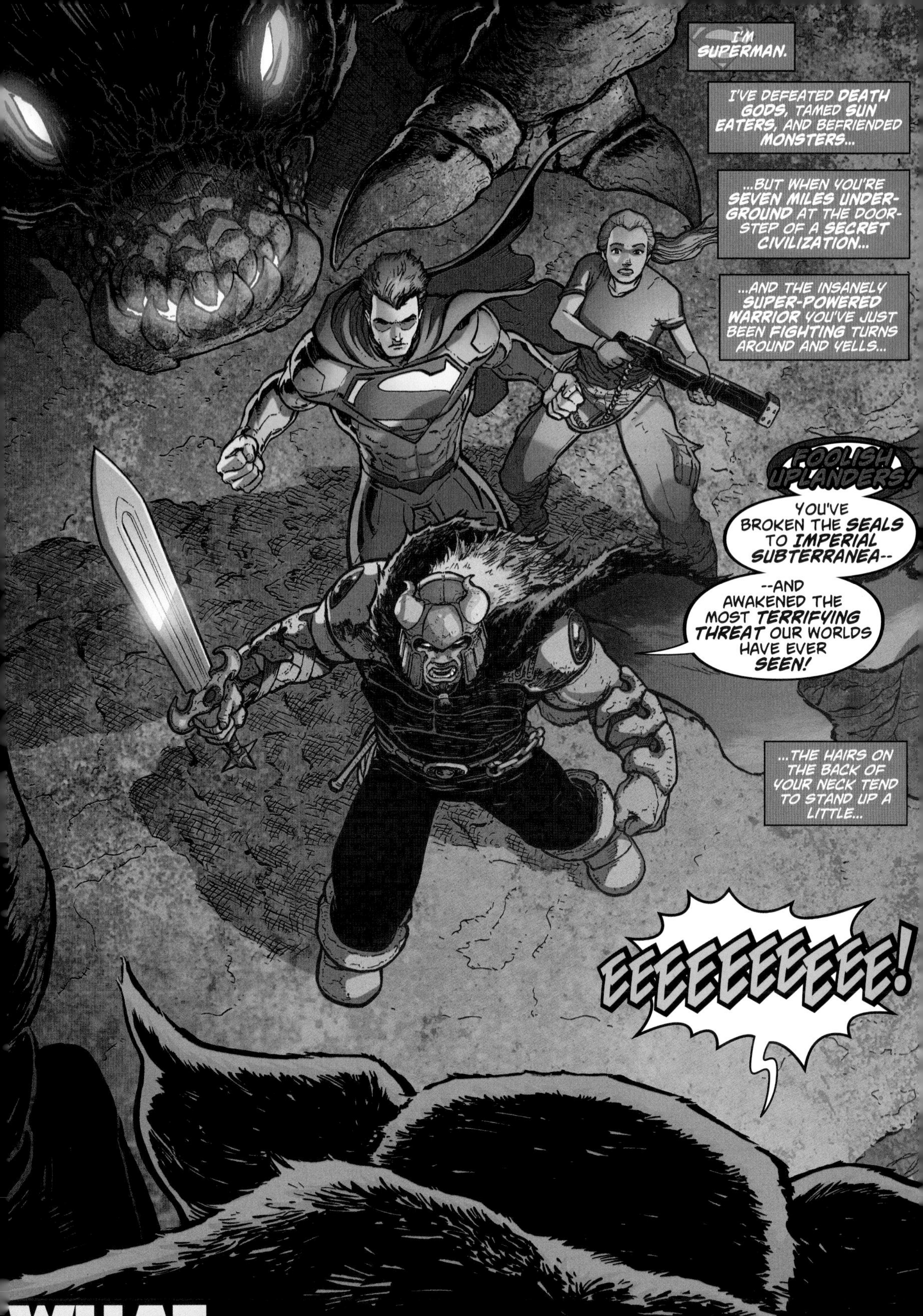
I'M SUPERMAN.
I'VE DEFEATED DEATH GODS, TAMED SUN EATERS, AND BEFRIENDED MONSTERS...
...BUT WHEN YOU'RE SEVEN MILES UNDERGROUND AT THE DOORSTEP OF A SECRET CIVILIZATION...
...AND THE INSANELY SUPER-POWERED WARRIOR YOU'VE JUST BEEN FIGHTING TURNS AROUND AND YELLS...
FOOLISH UPLANDERS!
YOU'VE BROKEN THE SEALS TO IMPERIAL SUBTERRANEA--
--AND AWAKENED THE MOST TERRIFYING THREAT OUR WORLDS HAVE EVER SEEN!
...THE HAIRS ON THE BACK OF YOUR NECK TEND TO STAND UP A LITTLE...
EEEEEEEEEEE!

WHAT LIES BENEATH

WRITTEN BY GREG PAK ART BY AARON KUDER COLORS BY WIL QUINTANA
LETTERS BY DC L[illegible]TERING COVER BY AARON KUDER AND WIL QUINTANA

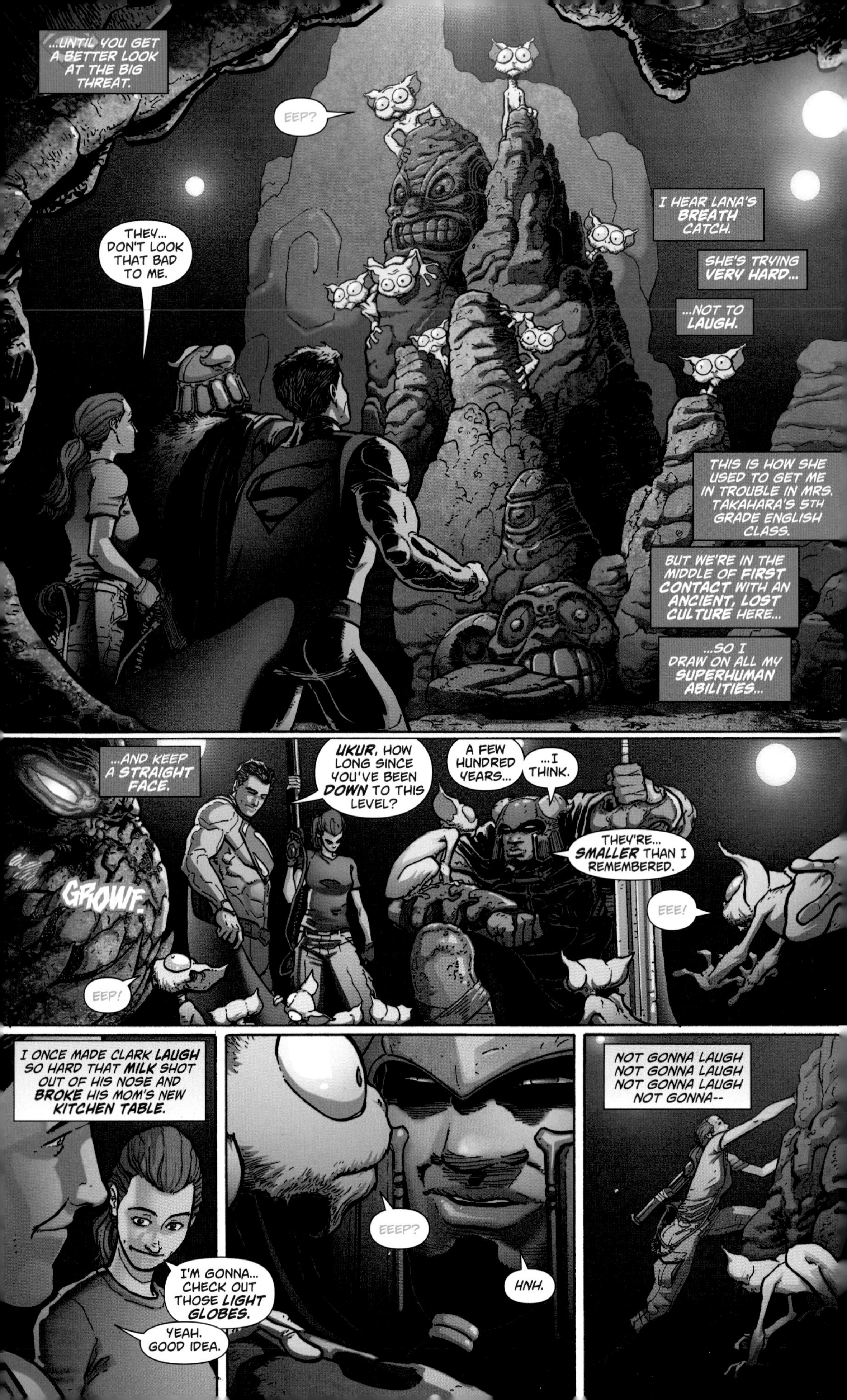
...UNTIL YOU GET A BETTER LOOK AT THE BIG THREAT.
EEP?
THEY... DON'T LOOK THAT BAD TO ME.
I HEAR LANA'S BREATH CATCH.
SHE'S TRYING VERY HARD...
...NOT TO LAUGH.
THIS IS HOW SHE USED TO GET ME IN TROUBLE IN MRS. TAKAHARA'S 5TH GRADE ENGLISH CLASS.
BUT WE'RE IN THE MIDDLE OF FIRST CONTACT WITH AN ANCIENT, LOST CULTURE HERE...
...SO I DRAW ON ALL MY SUPERHUMAN ABILITIES...
...AND KEEP A STRAIGHT FACE.
GROWF.
UKUR, HOW LONG SINCE YOU'VE BEEN DOWN TO THIS LEVEL?
A FEW HUNDRED YEARS...
...I THINK.
THEY'RE... SMALLER THAN I REMEMBERED.
EEE!
EEP!
I ONCE MADE CLARK LAUGH SO HARD THAT MILK SHOT OUT OF HIS NOSE AND BROKE HIS MOM'S NEW KITCHEN TABLE.
I'M GONNA... CHECK OUT THOSE LIGHT GLOBES.
YEAH. GOOD IDEA.
EEEP?
HNH.
NOT GONNA LAUGH NOT GONNA LAUGH NOT GONNA LAUGH NOT GONNA--

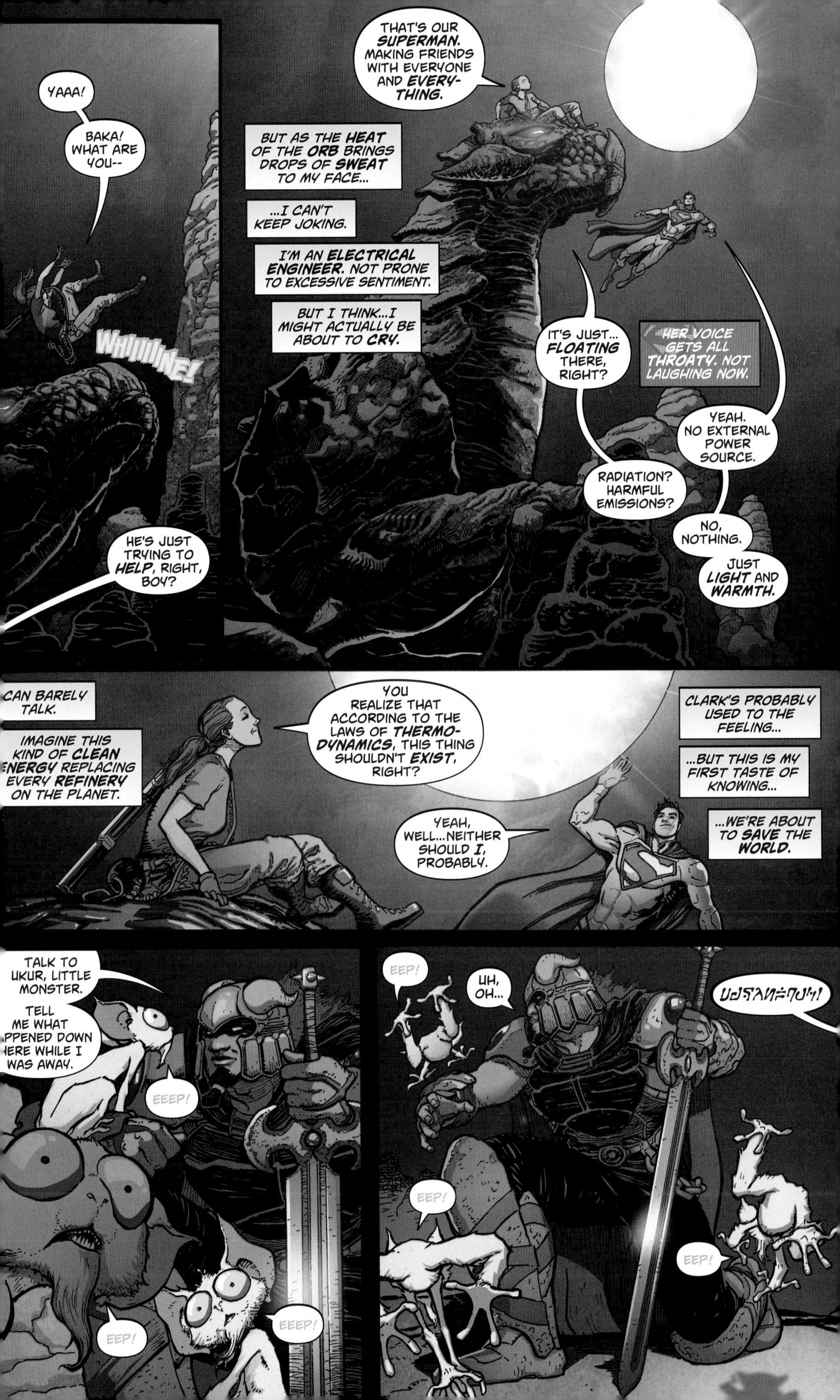

YAAA!
BAKA! WHAT ARE YOU--
WHIIIIIINE!
HE'S JUST TRYING TO HELP, RIGHT, BOY?
THAT'S OUR SUPERMAN. MAKING FRIENDS WITH EVERYONE AND EVERY-THING.
BUT AS THE HEAT OF THE ORB BRINGS DROPS OF SWEAT TO MY FACE...
...I CAN'T KEEP JOKING.
I'M AN ELECTRICAL ENGINEER. NOT PRONE TO EXCESSIVE SENTIMENT.
BUT I THINK...I MIGHT ACTUALLY BE ABOUT TO CRY.
IT'S JUST... FLOATING THERE, RIGHT?
HER VOICE GETS ALL THROATY. NOT LAUGHING NOW.
YEAH. NO EXTERNAL POWER SOURCE.
RADIATION? HARMFUL EMISSIONS?
NO, NOTHING.
JUST LIGHT AND WARMTH.
CAN BARELY TALK.
IMAGINE THIS KIND OF CLEAN ENERGY REPLACING EVERY REFINERY ON THE PLANET.
YOU REALIZE THAT ACCORDING TO THE LAWS OF THERMO-DYNAMICS, THIS THING SHOULDN'T EXIST, RIGHT?
YEAH, WELL...NEITHER SHOULD I, PROBABLY.
CLARK'S PROBABLY USED TO THE FEELING...
...BUT THIS IS MY FIRST TASTE OF KNOWING...
...WE'RE ABOUT TO SAVE THE WORLD.
TALK TO UKUR, LITTLE MONSTER.
TELL ME WHAT PPENED DOWN HERE WHILE I WAS AWAY.
EEEP!
EEP!
EEEP!
EEP!
UH, OH...
EEP!
EEP!

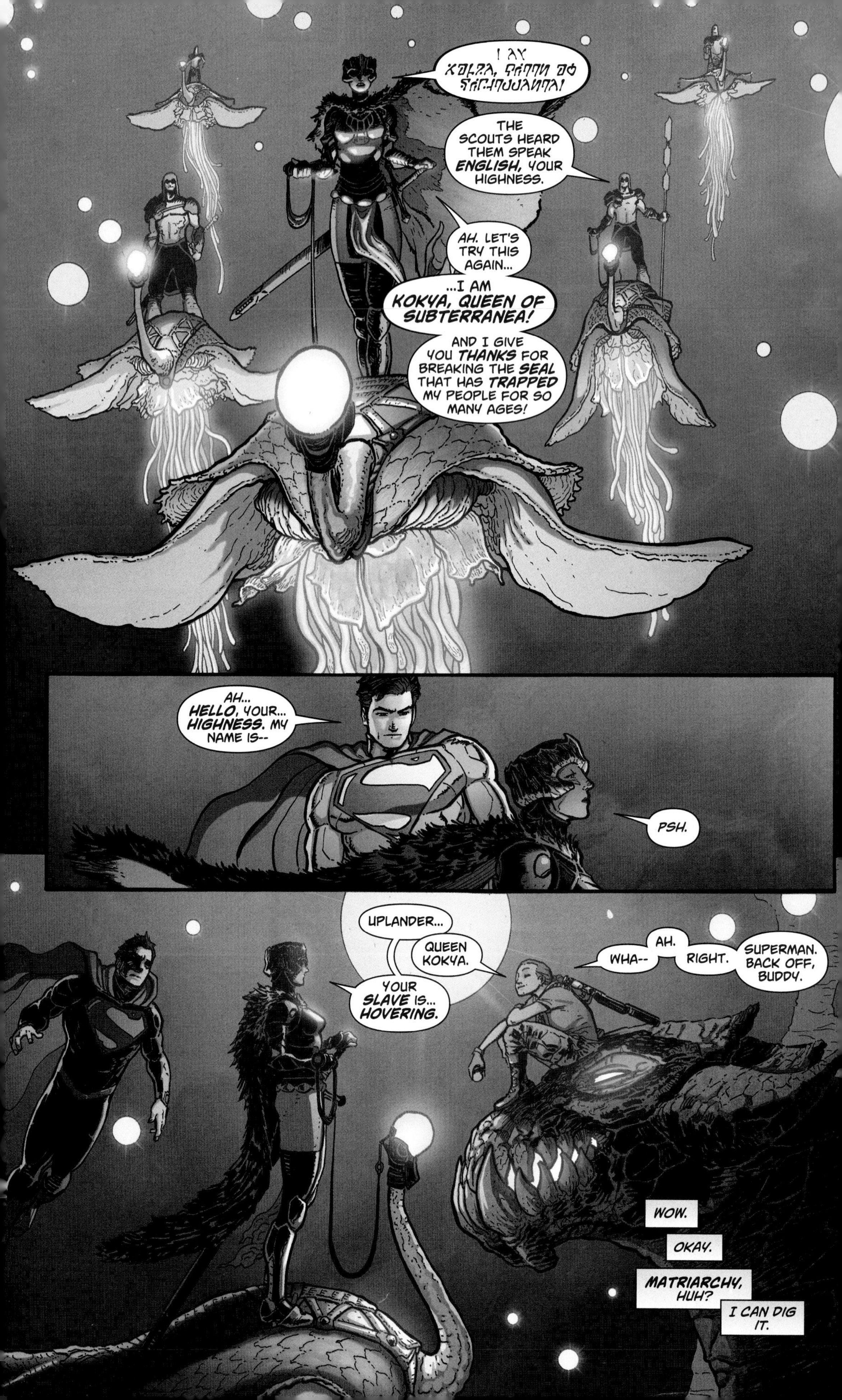
THE SCOUTS HEARD THEM SPEAK ENGLISH, YOUR HIGHNESS.
AH. LET'S TRY THIS AGAIN...
...I AM KOKYA, QUEEN OF SUBTERRANEA!
AND I GIVE YOU THANKS FOR BREAKING THE SEAL THAT HAS TRAPPED MY PEOPLE FOR SO MANY AGES!
AH... HELLO, YOUR... HIGHNESS. MY NAME IS--
PSH.
UPLANDER...
QUEEN KOKYA.
YOUR SLAVE IS... HOVERING.
WHA--
AH.
RIGHT.
SUPERMAN. BACK OFF, BUDDY.
WOW.
OKAY.
MATRIARCHY, HUH?
I CAN DIG IT.

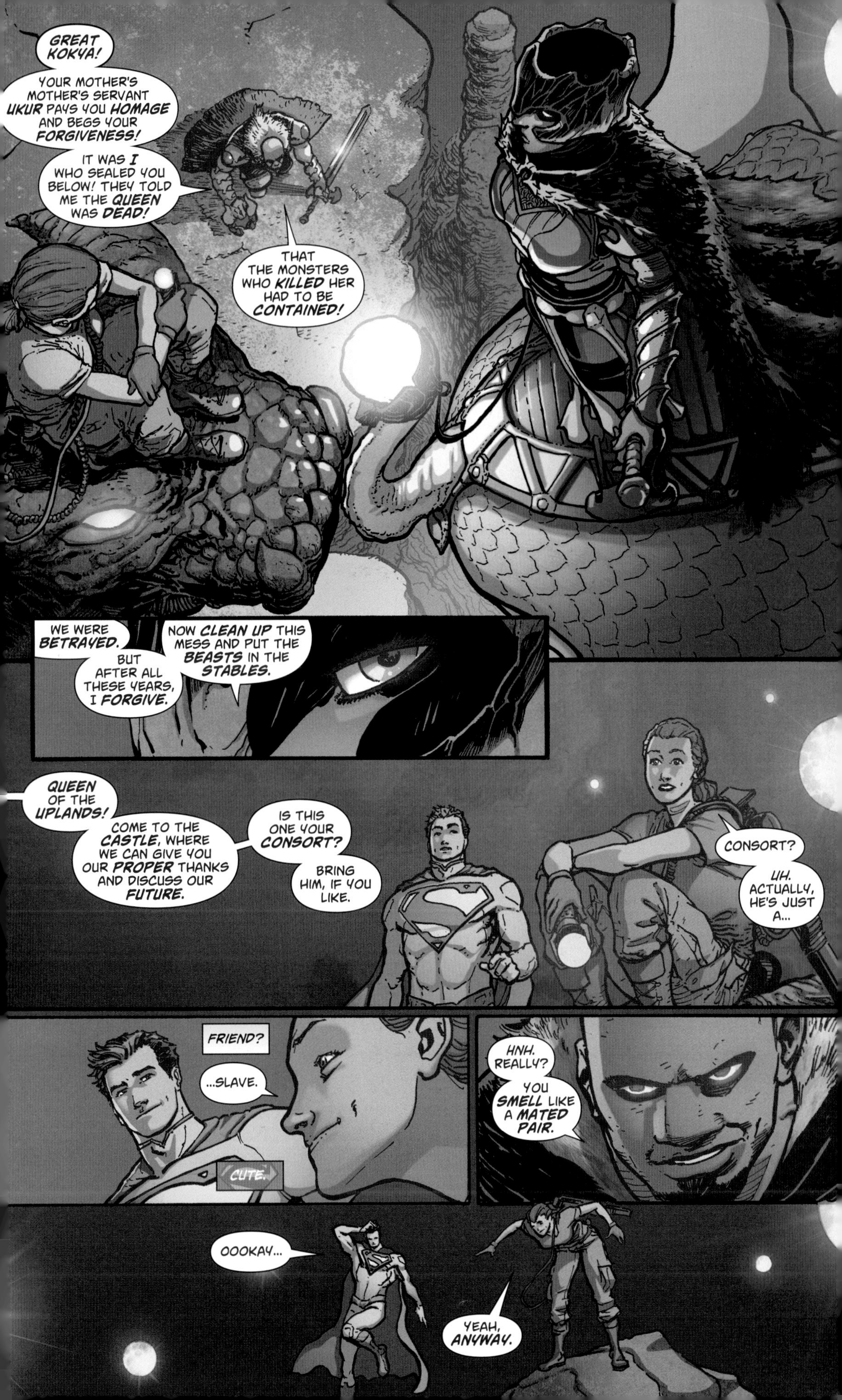

GREAT KOKYA!
YOUR MOTHER'S MOTHER'S SERVANT UKUR PAYS YOU HOMAGE AND BEGS YOUR FORGIVENESS!
IT WAS I WHO SEALED YOU BELOW! THEY TOLD ME THE QUEEN WAS DEAD!
THAT THE MONSTERS WHO KILLED HER HAD TO BE CONTAINED!
WE WERE BETRAYED.
BUT AFTER ALL THESE YEARS, I FORGIVE.
NOW CLEAN UP THIS MESS AND PUT THE BEASTS IN THE STABLES.
QUEEN OF THE UPLANDS!
COME TO THE CASTLE, WHERE WE CAN GIVE YOU OUR PROPER THANKS AND DISCUSS OUR FUTURE.
IS THIS ONE YOUR CONSORT?
BRING HIM, IF YOU LIKE.
CONSORT?
UH. ACTUALLY, HE'S JUST A...
FRIEND?
...SLAVE.
CUTE.
HNH. REALLY?
YOU SMELL LIKE A MATED PAIR.
OOOKAY...
YEAH, ANYWAY.

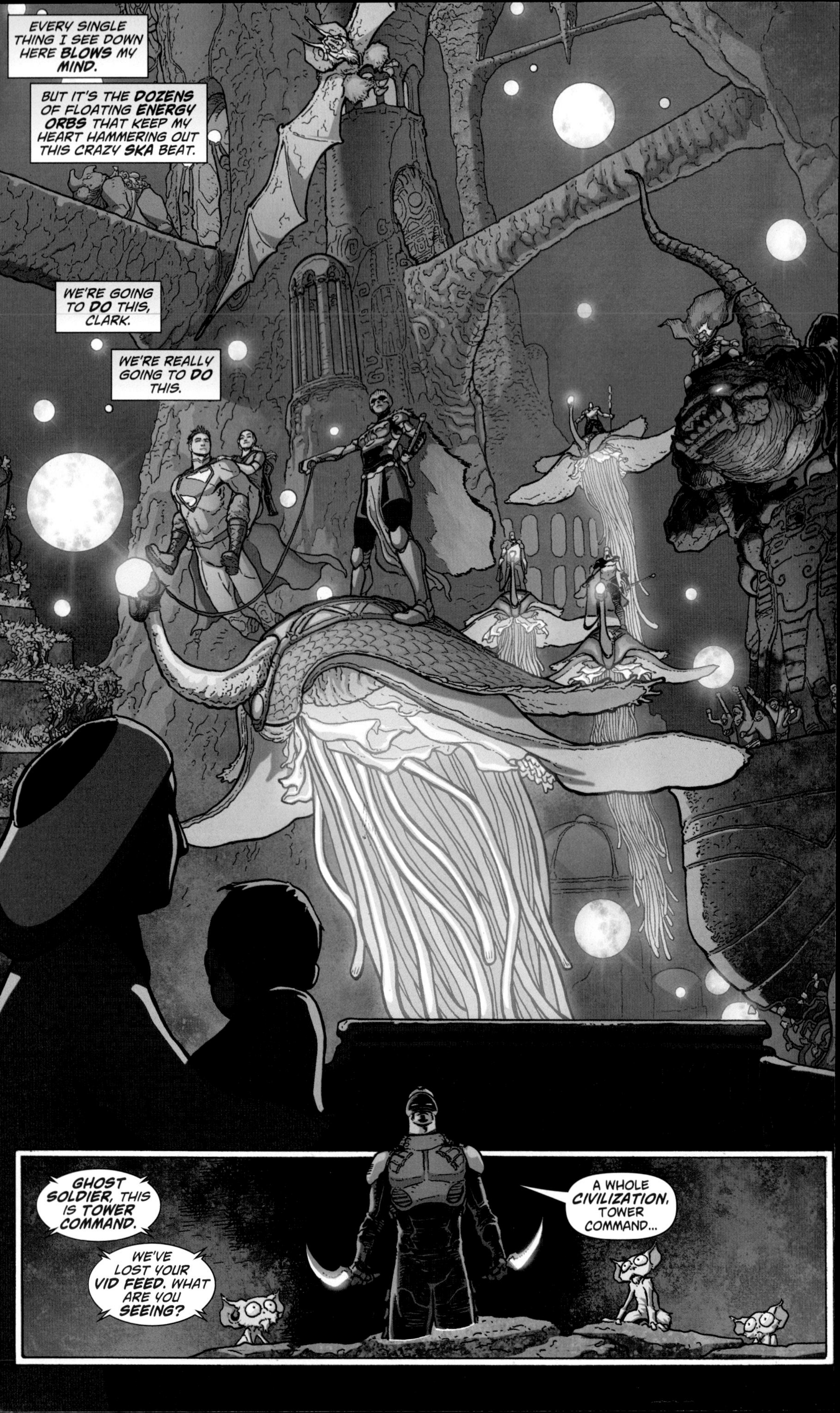
EVERY SINGLE THING I SEE DOWN HERE BLOWS MY MIND.
BUT IT'S THE DOZENS OF FLOATING ENERGY ORBS THAT KEEP MY HEART HAMMERING OUT THIS CRAZY SKA BEAT.
WE'RE GOING TO DO THIS, CLARK.
WE'RE REALLY GOING TO DO THIS.
GHOST SOLDIER, THIS IS TOWER COMMAND.
WE'VE LOST YOUR VID FEED. WHAT ARE YOU SEEING?
A WHOLE CIVILIZATION, TOWER COMMAND...

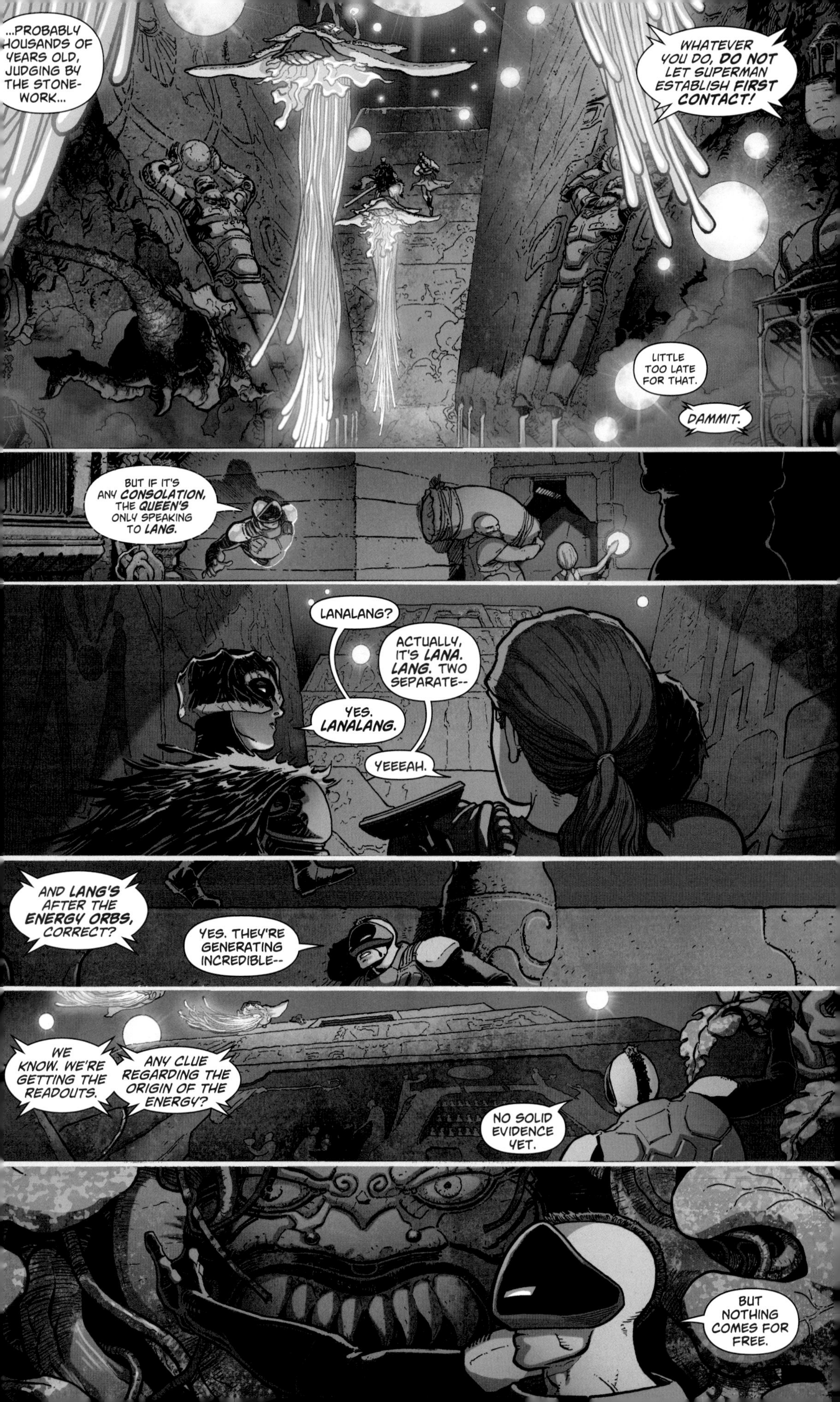
...PROBABLY HOUSANDS OF YEARS OLD, JUDGING BY THE STONE-WORK...
WHATEVER YOU DO, DO NOT LET SUPERMAN ESTABLISH FIRST CONTACT!
LITTLE TOO LATE FOR THAT.
DAMMIT.
BUT IF IT'S ANY CONSOLATION, THE QUEEN'S ONLY SPEAKING TO LANG.
LANALANG?
ACTUALLY, IT'S LANA. LANG. TWO SEPARATE--
YES. LANALANG.
YEEEAH.
AND LANG'S AFTER THE ENERGY ORBS, CORRECT?
YES. THEY'RE GENERATING INCREDIBLE--
WE KNOW. WE'RE GETTING THE READOUTS.
ANY CLUE REGARDING THE ORIGIN OF THE ENERGY?
NO SOLID EVIDENCE YET.
BUT NOTHING COMES FOR FREE.

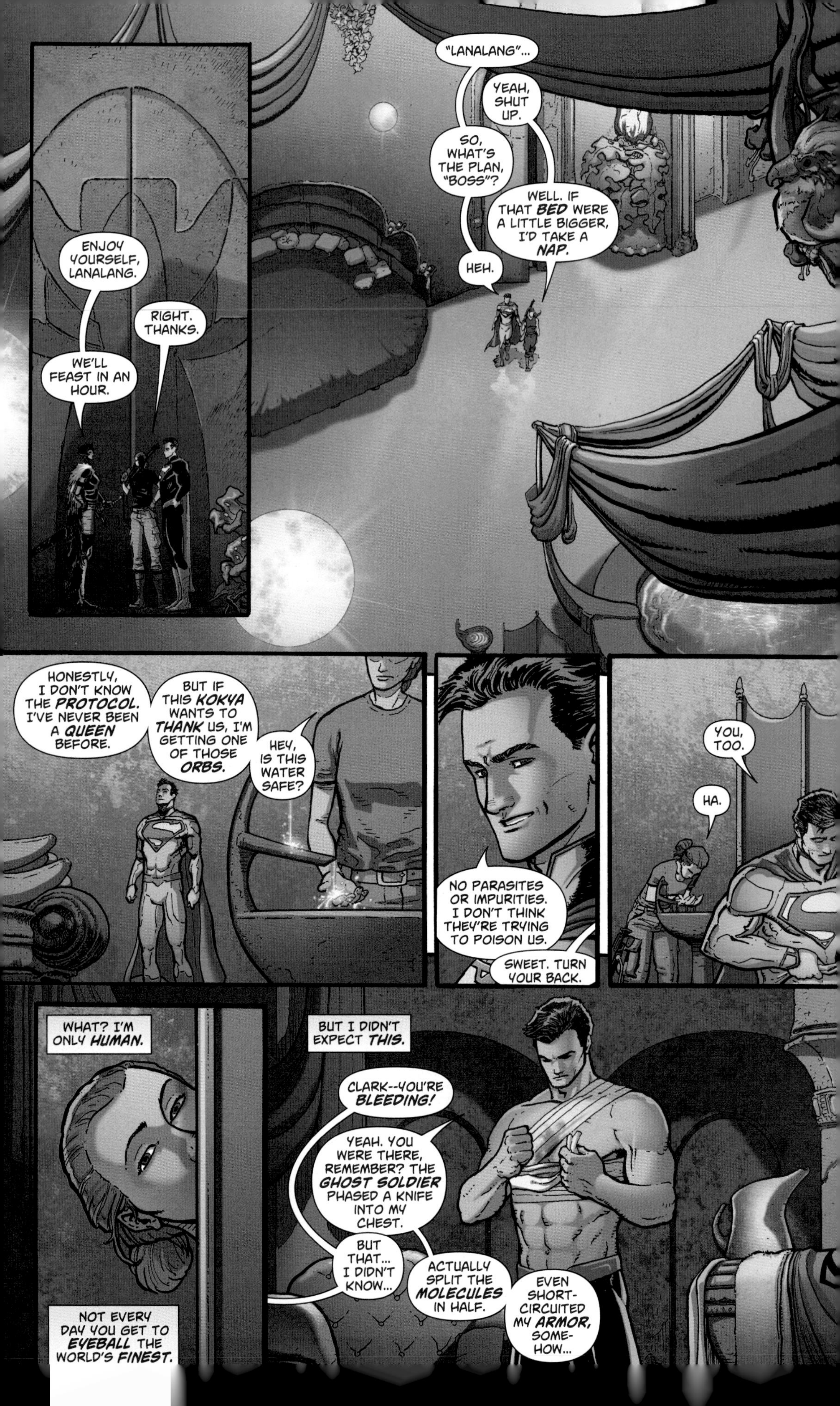
ENJOY YOURSELF, LANALANG.
WE'LL FEAST IN AN HOUR.
RIGHT. THANKS.
"LANALANG"...
YEAH, SHUT UP.
SO, WHAT'S THE PLAN, "BOSS"?
WELL. IF THAT BED WERE A LITTLE BIGGER, I'D TAKE A NAP.
HEH.
HONESTLY, I DON'T KNOW THE PROTOCOL. I'VE NEVER BEEN A QUEEN BEFORE.
BUT IF THIS KOKYA WANTS TO THANK US, I'M GETTING ONE OF THOSE ORBS.
HEY, IS THIS WATER SAFE?
NO PARASITES OR IMPURITIES. I DON'T THINK THEY'RE TRYING TO POISON US.
SWEET. TURN YOUR BACK.
YOU, TOO.
HA.
WHAT? I'M ONLY HUMAN.
NOT EVERY DAY YOU GET TO EYEBALL THE WORLD'S FINEST.
BUT I DIDN'T EXPECT THIS.
CLARK--YOU'RE BLEEDING!
YEAH. YOU WERE THERE, REMEMBER? THE GHOST SOLDIER PHASED A KNIFE INTO MY CHEST.
BUT THAT... I DIDN'T KNOW...
ACTUALLY SPLIT THE MOLECULES IN HALF.
EVEN SHORT-CIRCUITED MY ARMOR, SOMEHOW...

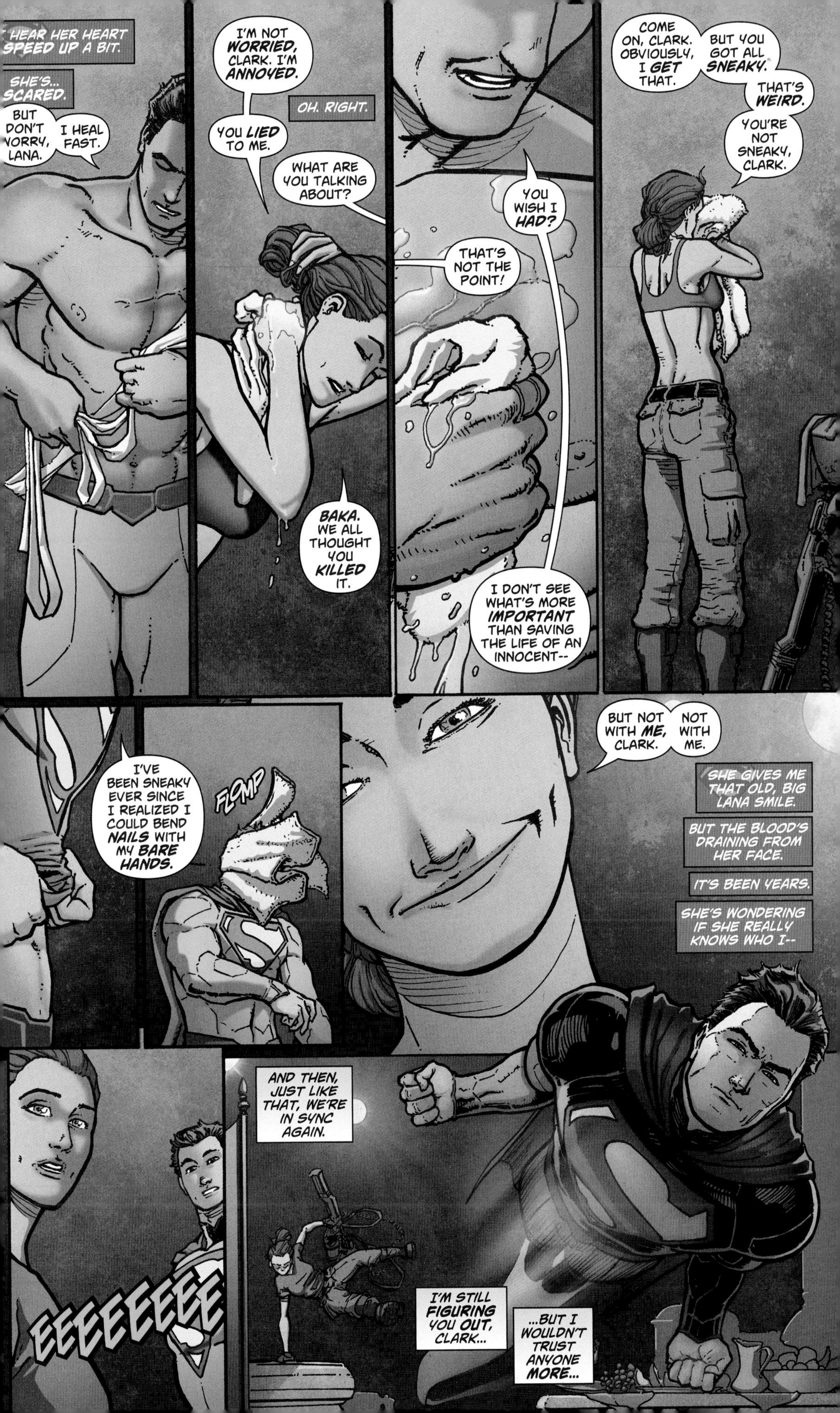

I HEAR HER HEART SPEED UP A BIT.
SHE'S... SCARED.
BUT DON'T WORRY, LANA.
I HEAL FAST.
I'M NOT WORRIED, CLARK. I'M ANNOYED.
OH. RIGHT.
YOU LIED TO ME.
WHAT ARE YOU TALKING ABOUT?
BAKA. WE ALL THOUGHT YOU KILLED IT.
YOU WISH I HAD?
THAT'S NOT THE POINT!
I DON'T SEE WHAT'S MORE IMPORTANT THAN SAVING THE LIFE OF AN INNOCENT--
COME ON, CLARK. OBVIOUSLY, I GET THAT.
BUT YOU GOT ALL SNEAKY.
THAT'S WEIRD.
YOU'RE NOT SNEAKY, CLARK.
I'VE BEEN SNEAKY EVER SINCE I REALIZED I COULD BEND NAILS WITH MY BARE HANDS.
FLOMP
BUT NOT WITH ME, CLARK.
NOT WITH ME.
SHE GIVES ME THAT OLD, BIG LANA SMILE.
BUT THE BLOOD'S DRAINING FROM HER FACE.
IT'S BEEN YEARS.
SHE'S WONDERING IF SHE REALLY KNOWS WHO I--
EEEEEEEE
AND THEN, JUST LIKE THAT, WE'RE IN SYNC AGAIN.
I'M STILL FIGURING YOU OUT, CLARK...
...BUT I WOULDN'T TRUST ANYONE MORE...

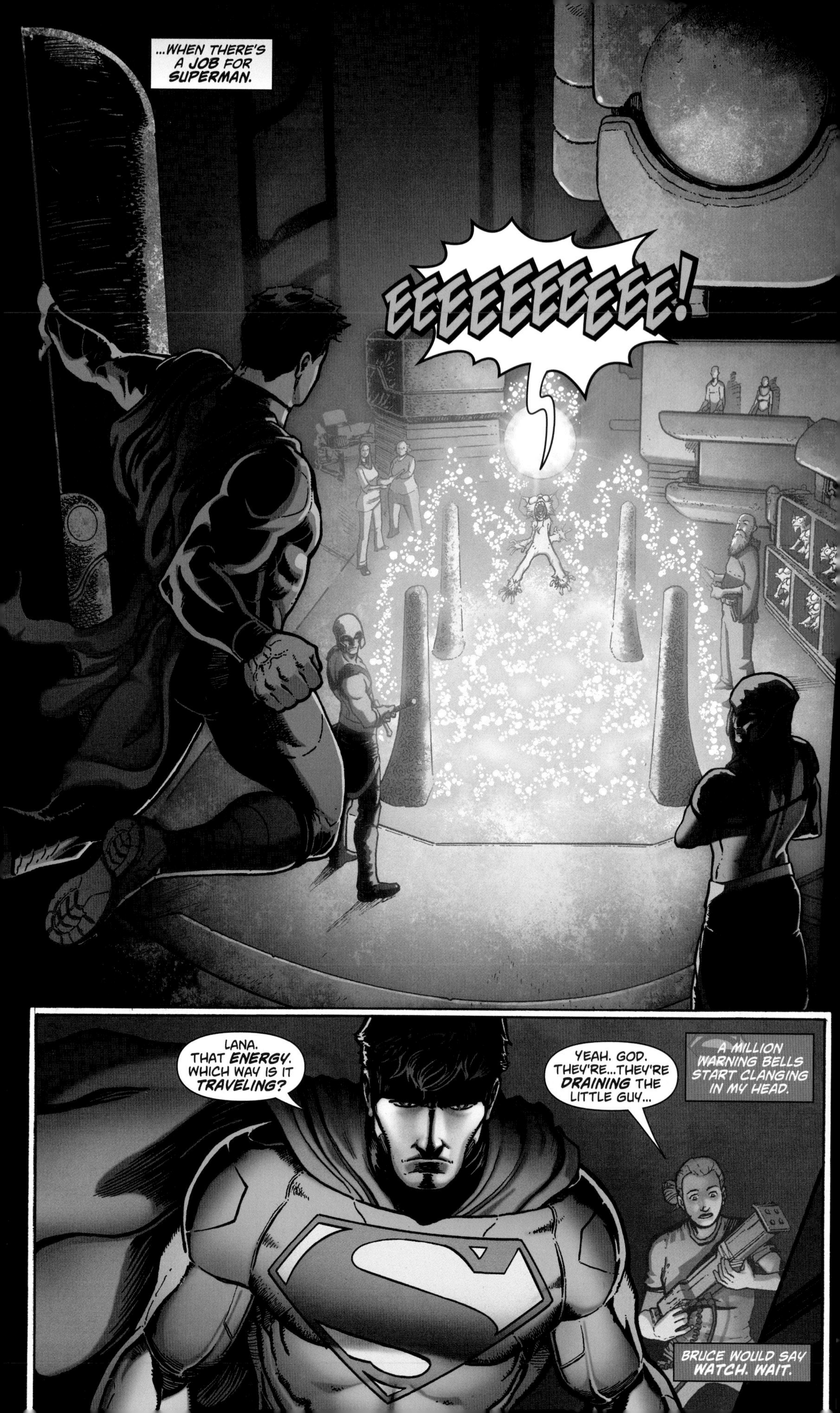
...WHEN THERE'S A JOB FOR SUPERMAN.
EEEEEEEEEEE!
LANA. THAT ENERGY. WHICH WAY IS IT TRAVELING?
YEAH. GOD. THEY'RE...THEY'RE DRAINING THE LITTLE GUY...
A MILLION WARNING BELLS START CLANGING IN MY HEAD.
BRUCE WOULD SAY WATCH. WAIT.

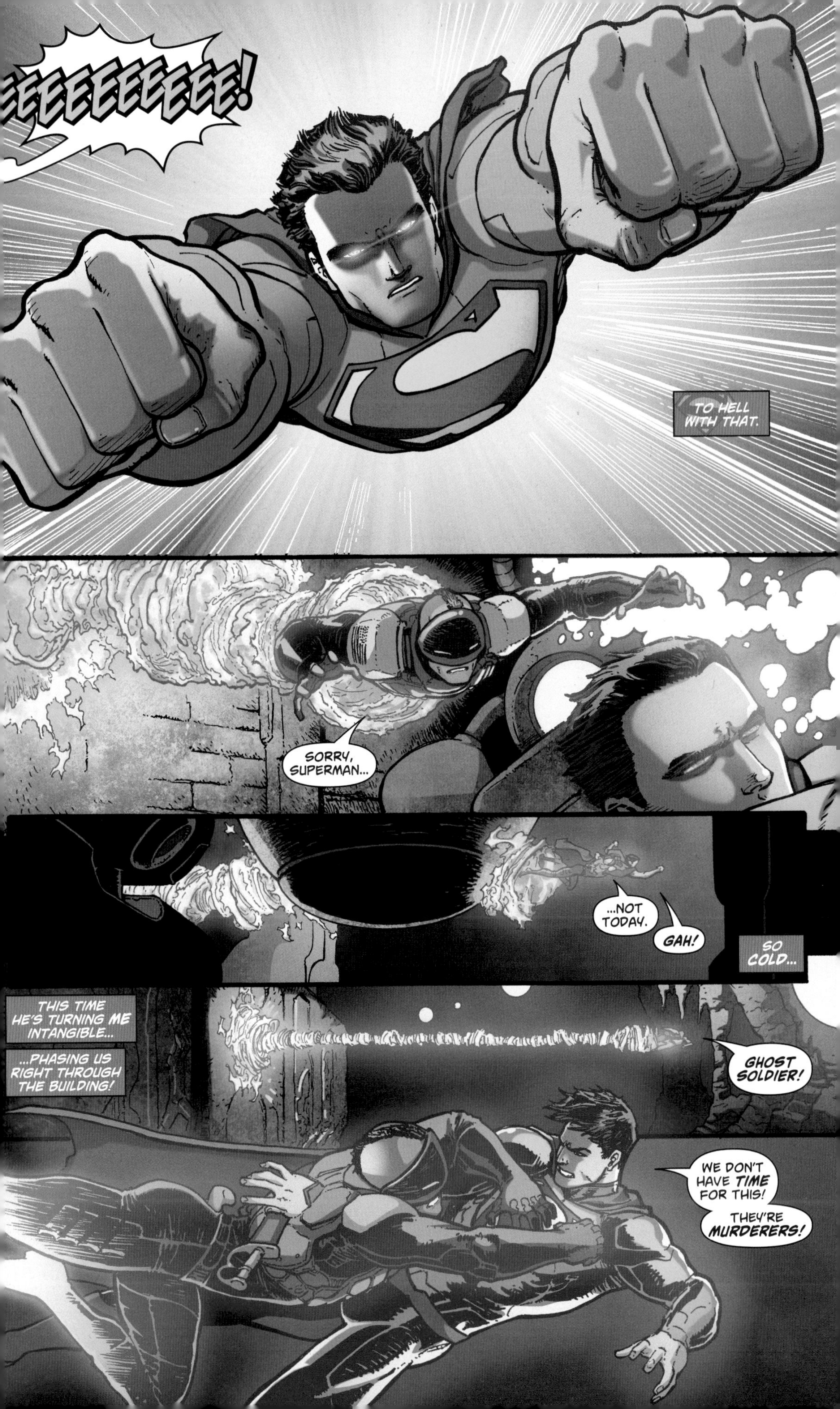
EEEEEEEEEEEE!
TO HELL WITH THAT.
SORRY, SUPERMAN...
...NOT TODAY.
GAH!
SO COLD...
THIS TIME HE'S TURNING *ME* INTANGIBLE...
...PHASING US RIGHT THROUGH THE BUILDING!
GHOST SOLDIER!
WE DON'T HAVE *TIME* FOR THIS!
THEY'RE *MURDERERS!*

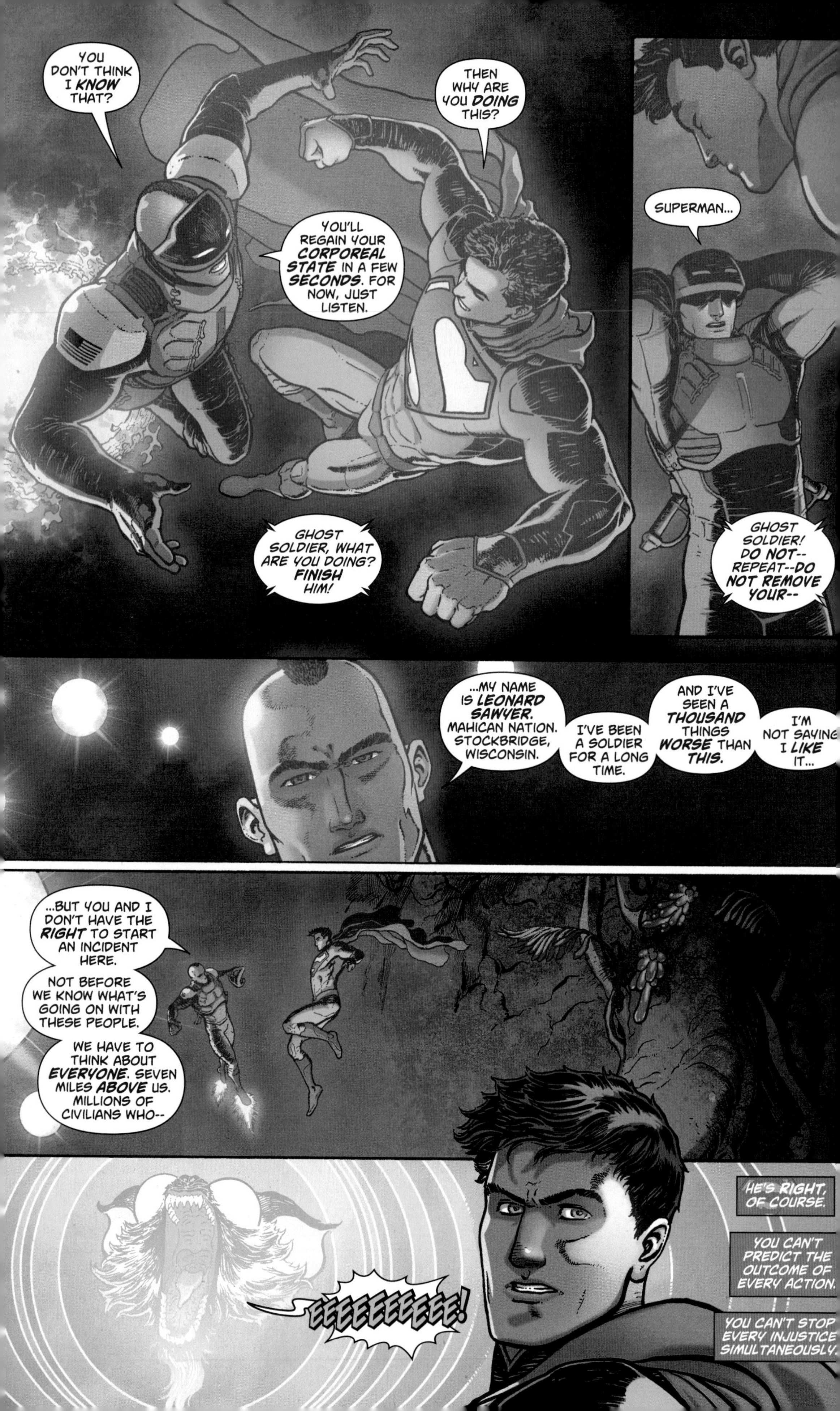

YOU DON'T THINK I KNOW THAT?
THEN WHY ARE YOU DOING THIS?
YOU'LL REGAIN YOUR CORPOREAL STATE IN A FEW SECONDS. FOR NOW, JUST LISTEN.
GHOST SOLDIER, WHAT ARE YOU DOING? FINISH HIM!
SUPERMAN...
GHOST SOLDIER! DO NOT--REPEAT--DO NOT REMOVE YOUR--
...MY NAME IS LEONARD SAWYER. MAHICAN NATION. STOCKBRIDGE, WISCONSIN.
I'VE BEEN A SOLDIER FOR A LONG TIME.
AND I'VE SEEN A THOUSAND THINGS WORSE THAN THIS.
I'M NOT SAYING I LIKE IT...
...BUT YOU AND I DON'T HAVE THE RIGHT TO START AN INCIDENT HERE.
NOT BEFORE WE KNOW WHAT'S GOING ON WITH THESE PEOPLE.
WE HAVE TO THINK ABOUT EVERYONE. SEVEN MILES ABOVE US. MILLIONS OF CIVILIANS WHO--
EEEEEEEEEEEE!
HE'S RIGHT, OF COURSE.
YOU CAN'T PREDICT THE OUTCOME OF EVERY ACTION.
YOU CAN'T STOP EVERY INJUSTICE SIMULTANEOUSLY.

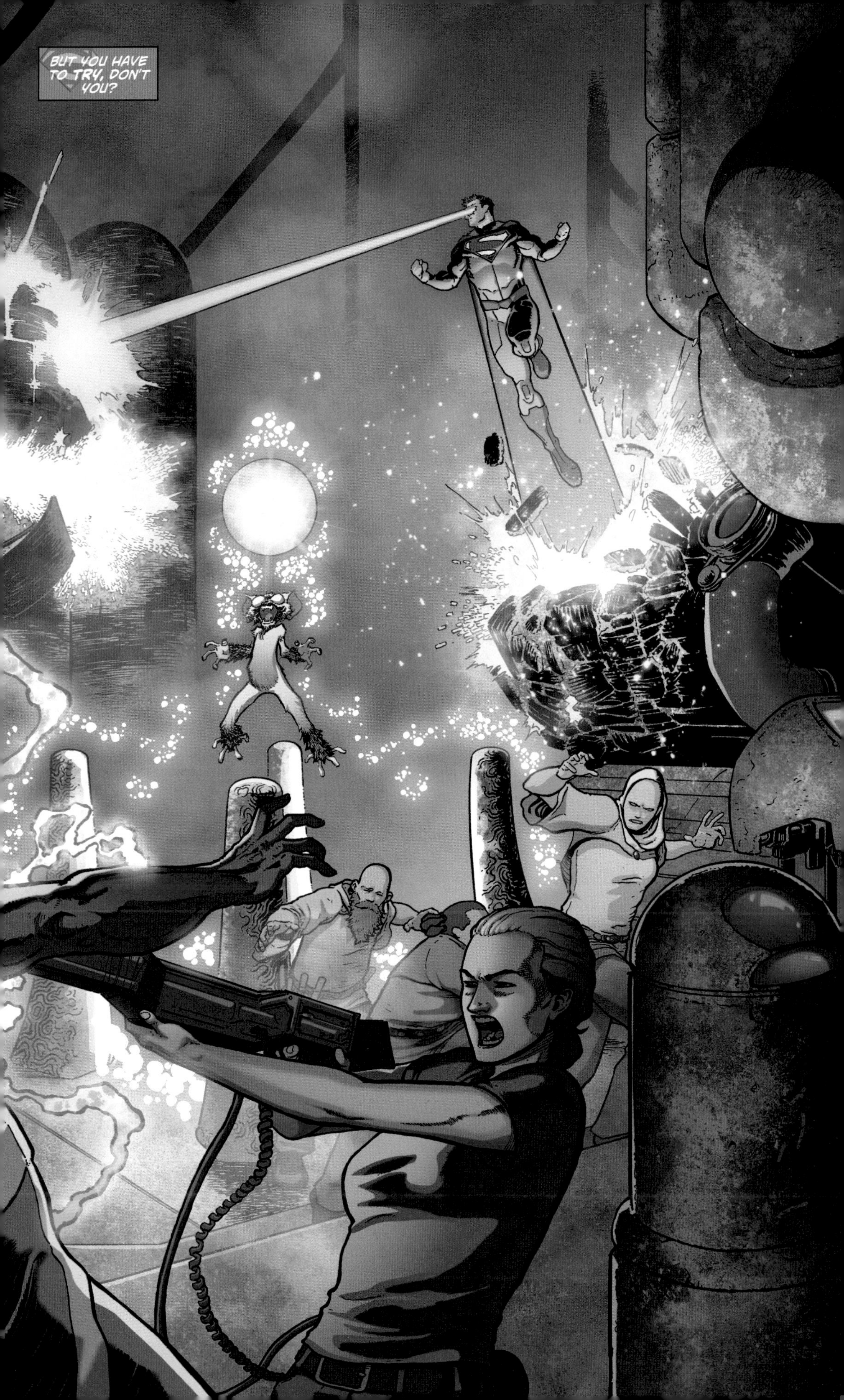
BUT YOU HAVE TO TRY, DON'T YOU?

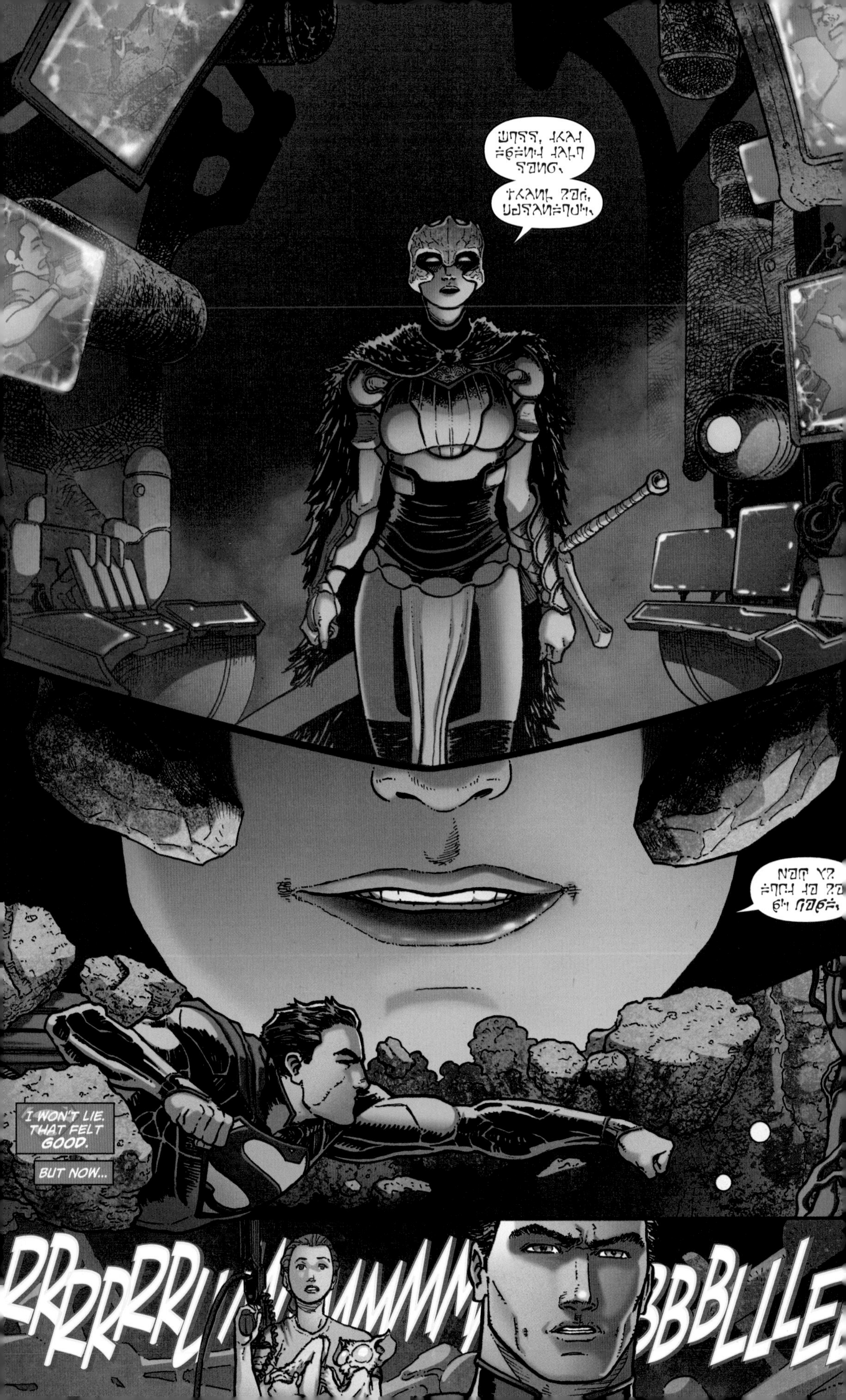
I WON'T LIE. THAT FELT GOOD.
BUT NOW...
RRRRRRRUMMMMMMBBBLLLEE

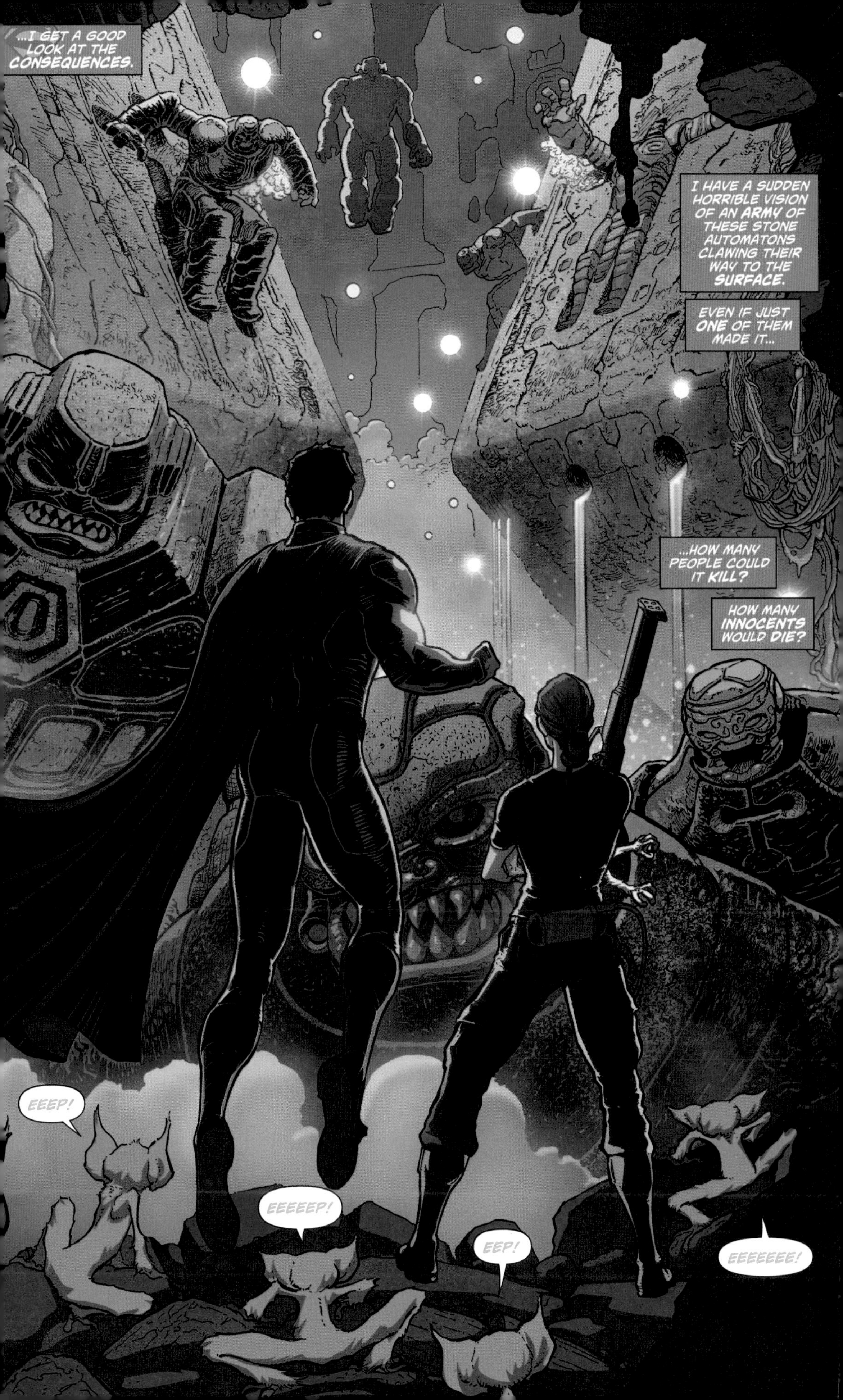
...I GET A GOOD LOOK AT THE CONSEQUENCES.
I HAVE A SUDDEN HORRIBLE VISION OF AN ARMY OF THESE STONE AUTOMATONS CLAWING THEIR WAY TO THE SURFACE.
EVEN IF JUST ONE OF THEM MADE IT...
...HOW MANY PEOPLE COULD IT KILL?
HOW MANY INNOCENTS WOULD DIE?
EEEP!
EEEEEP!
EEP!
EEEEEEE!

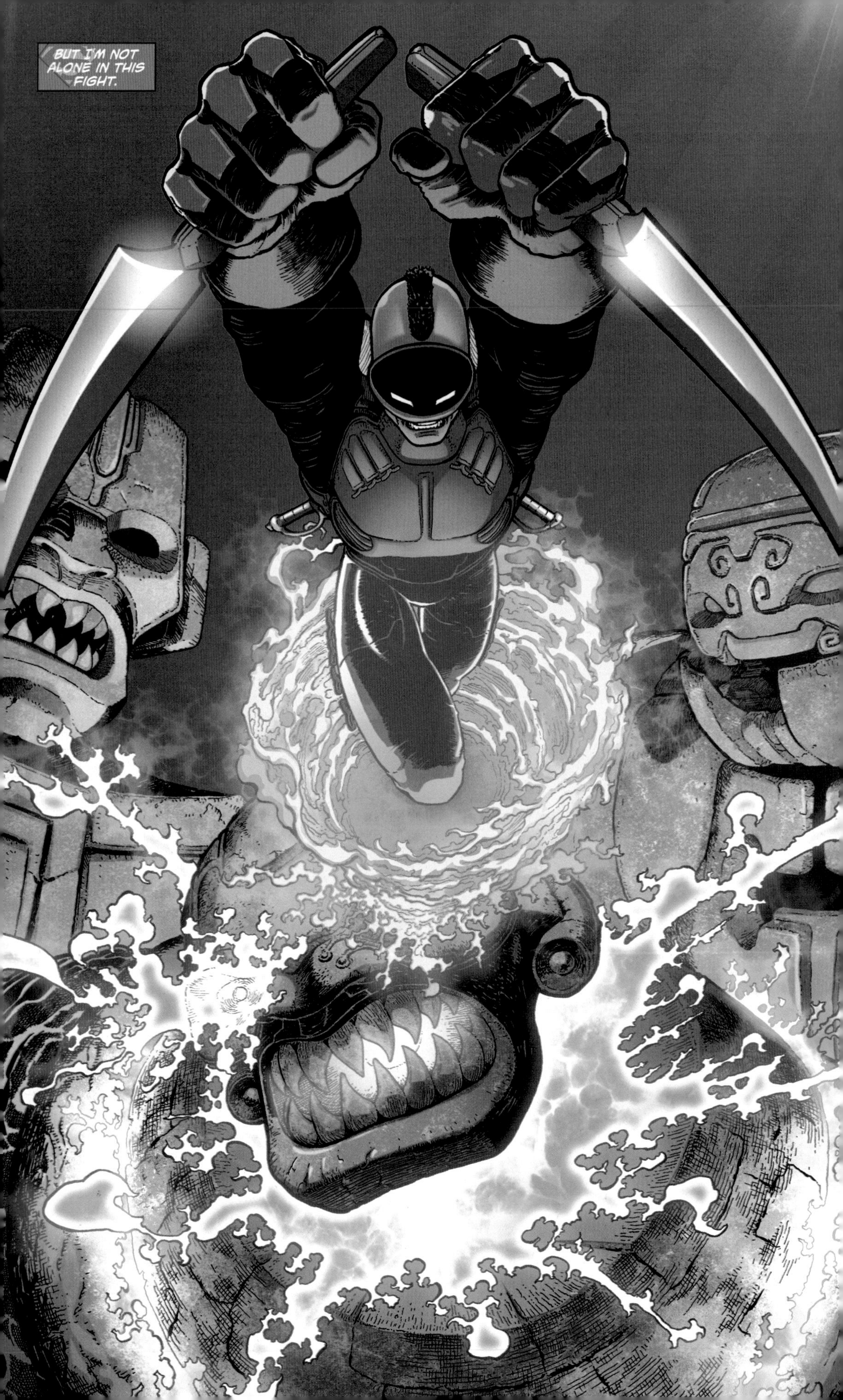
BUT I'M NOT ALONE IN THIS FIGHT.

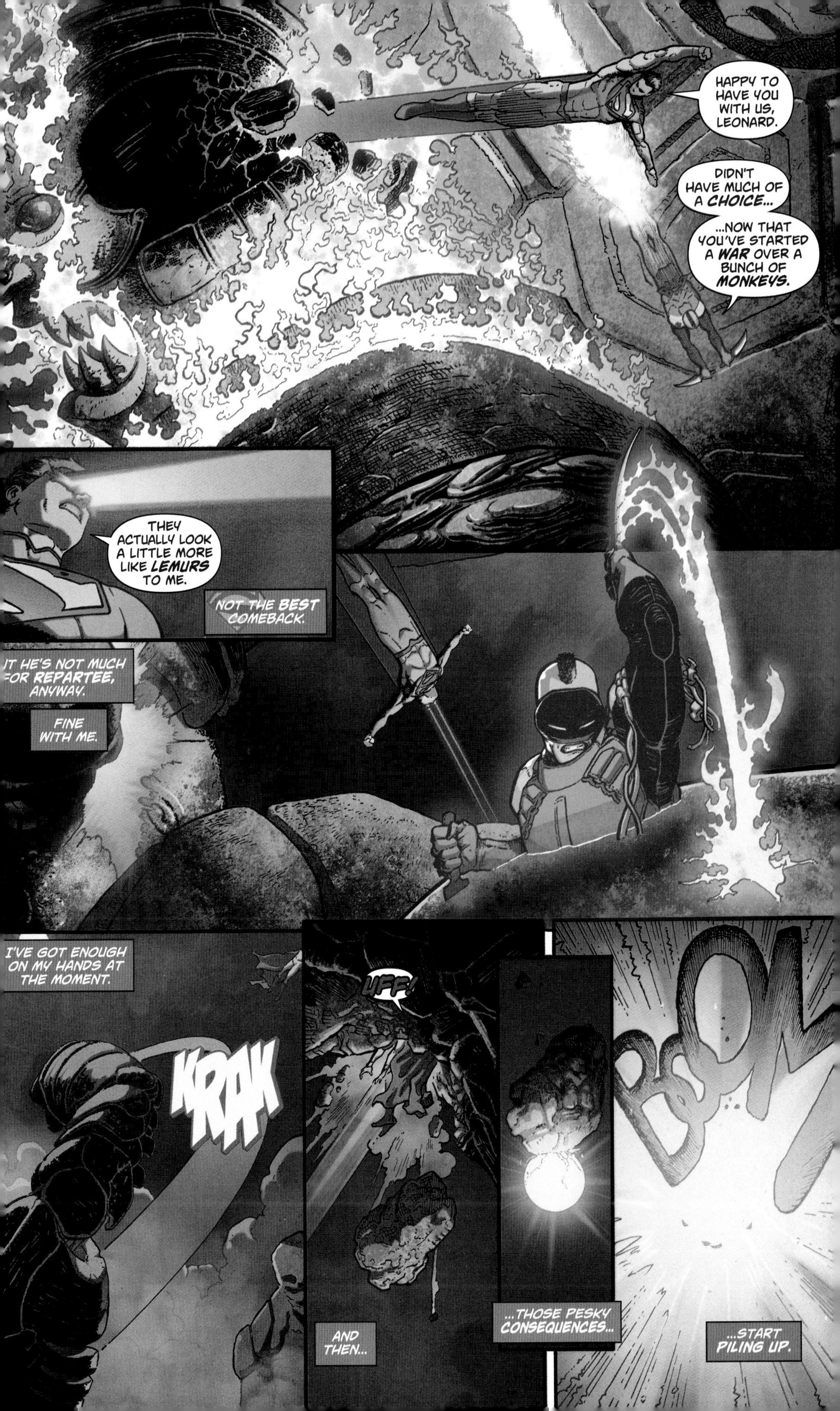
HAPPY TO HAVE YOU WITH US, LEONARD.
DIDN'T HAVE MUCH OF A CHOICE...
...NOW THAT YOU'VE STARTED A WAR OVER A BUNCH OF MONKEYS.
THEY ACTUALLY LOOK A LITTLE MORE LIKE LEMURS TO ME.
NOT THE BEST COMEBACK.
IT HE'S NOT MUCH FOR REPARTEE, ANYWAY.
FINE WITH ME.
I'VE GOT ENOUGH ON MY HANDS AT THE MOMENT.
KRAK
UFF!
AND THEN...
...THOSE PESKY CONSEQUENCES...
BOOM
...START PILING UP.

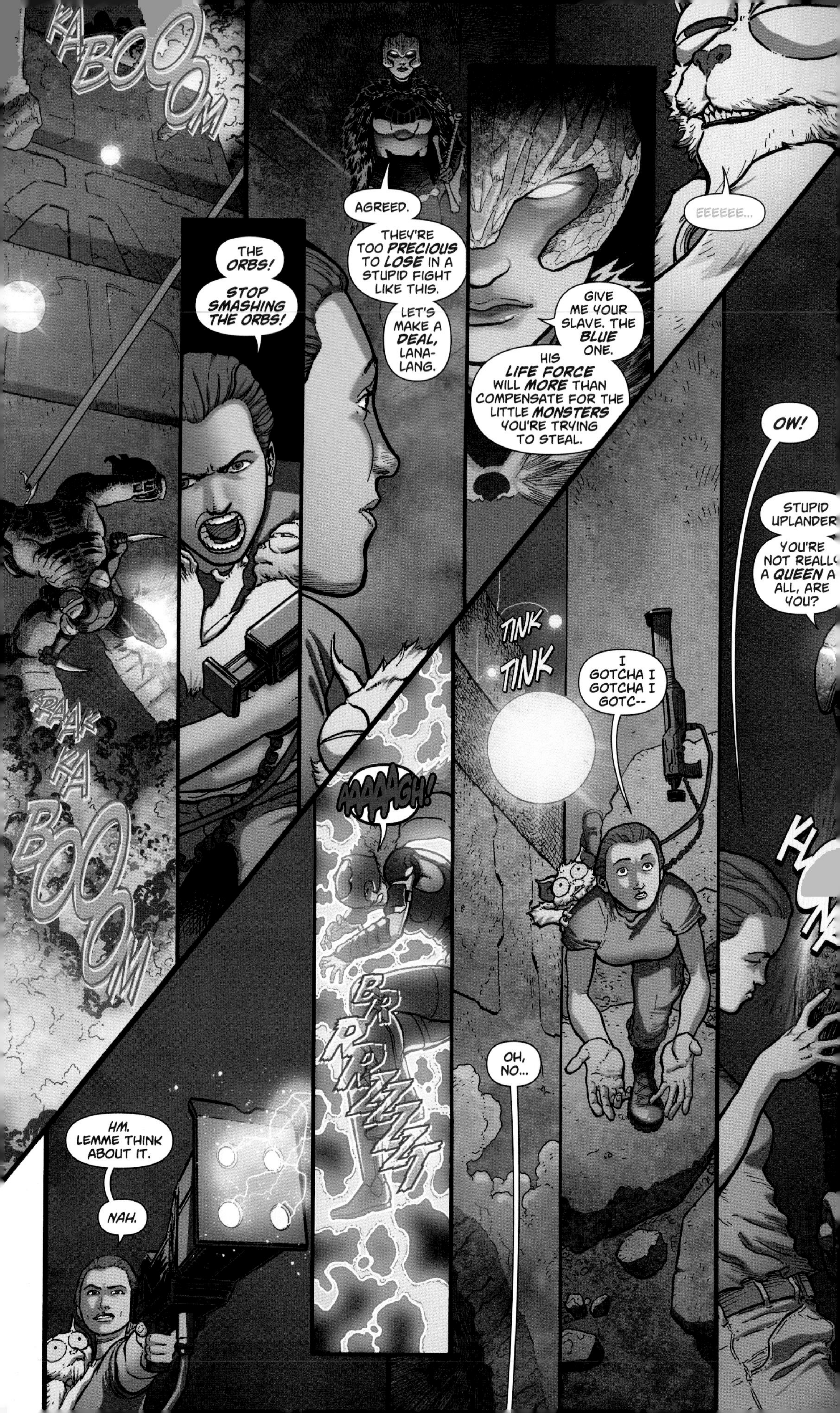
KA-BOOOOM
THE ORBS!
STOP SMASHING THE ORBS!
AGREED.
THEY'RE TOO PRECIOUS TO LOSE IN A STUPID FIGHT LIKE THIS.
LET'S MAKE A DEAL, LANA-LANG.
GIVE ME YOUR SLAVE. THE BLUE ONE.
HIS LIFE FORCE WILL MORE THAN COMPENSATE FOR THE LITTLE MONSTERS YOU'RE TRYING TO STEAL.
EEEEEE...
KRAAK KA BOOOOM
AAAAAGH!
BRRRZZZZT
TINK
TINK
I GOTCHA I GOTCHA I GOTC--
OH, NO...
OW!
STUPID UPLANDER
YOU'RE NOT REALLY A QUEEN AT ALL, ARE YOU?
HM. LEMME THINK ABOUT IT.
NAH.

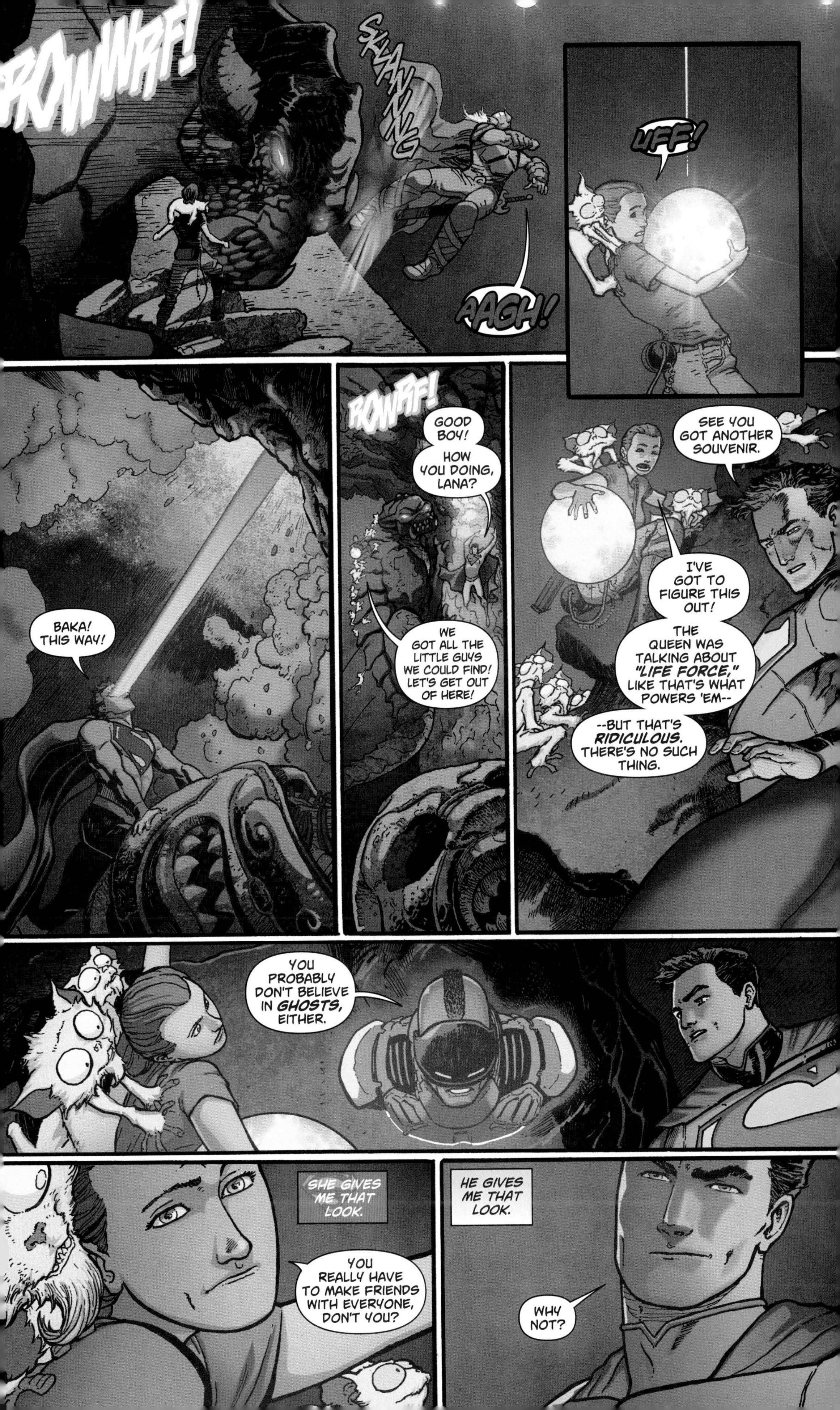

ROWWRF!
SKRANNNG
AAGH!
UFF!
BAKA! THIS WAY!
ROWRF!
GOOD BOY!
HOW YOU DOING, LANA?
WE GOT ALL THE LITTLE GUYS WE COULD FIND! LET'S GET OUT OF HERE!
SEE YOU GOT ANOTHER SOUVENIR.
I'VE GOT TO FIGURE THIS OUT!
THE QUEEN WAS TALKING ABOUT "LIFE FORCE," LIKE THAT'S WHAT POWERS 'EM--
--BUT THAT'S RIDICULOUS. THERE'S NO SUCH THING.
YOU PROBABLY DON'T BELIEVE IN GHOSTS, EITHER.
SHE GIVES ME THAT LOOK.
YOU REALLY HAVE TO MAKE FRIENDS WITH EVERYONE, DON'T YOU?
HE GIVES ME THAT LOOK.
WHY NOT?

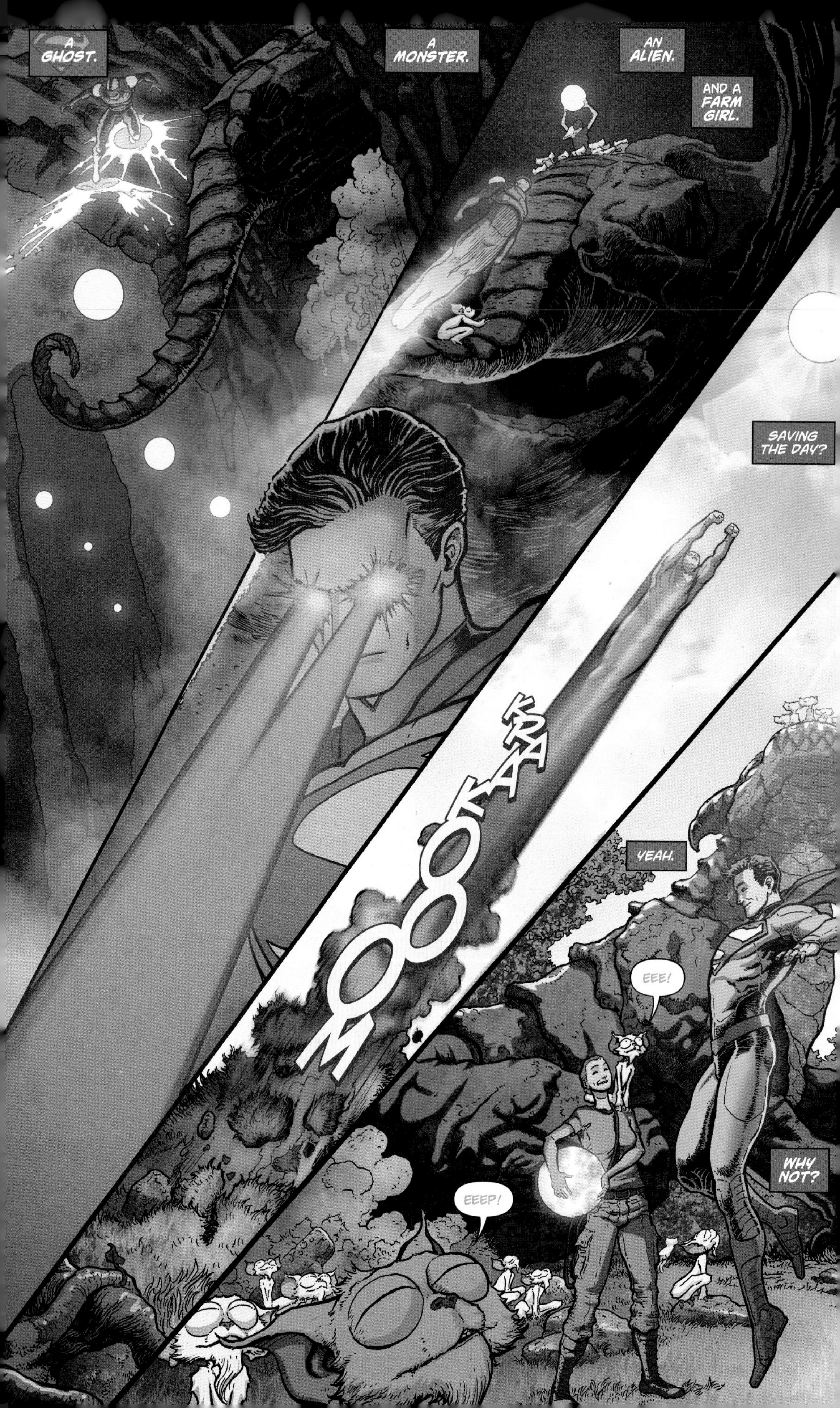
A GHOST.
A MONSTER.
AN ALIEN.
AND A FARM GIRL.
SAVING THE DAY?
KRAKOOOOM
YEAH.
EEE!
EEEP!
WHY NOT?

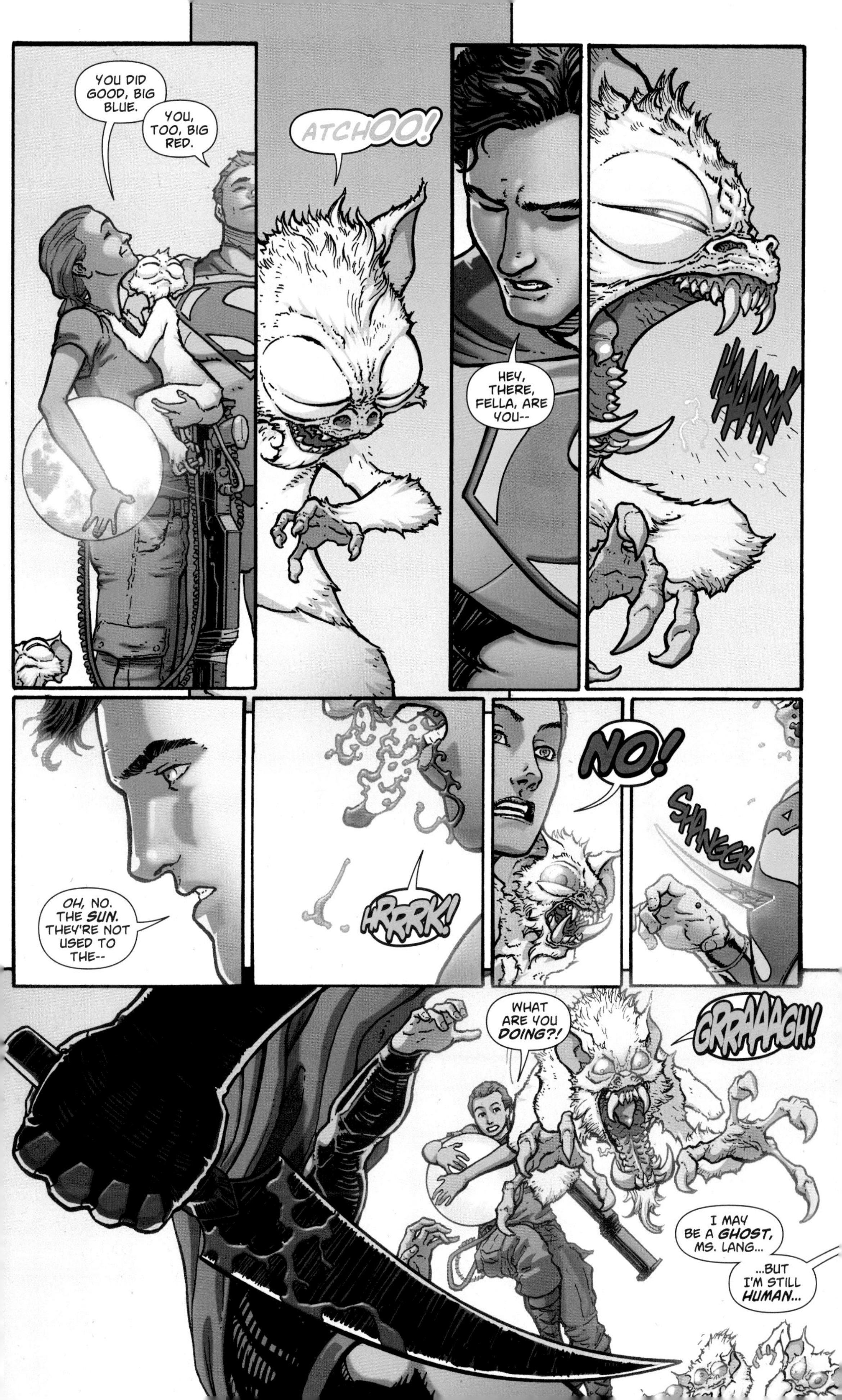

YOU DID GOOD, BIG BLUE.
YOU, TOO, BIG RED.
ATCHOO!
HEY, THERE, FELLA, ARE YOU--
HAAAKKK
OH, NO. THE *SUN*. THEY'RE NOT USED TO THE--
HRRRK!
NO!
SHANGGK
WHAT ARE YOU *DOING?!*
GRRAAAGH!
I MAY BE A *GHOST*, MS. LANG...
...BUT I'M STILL *HUMAN*...

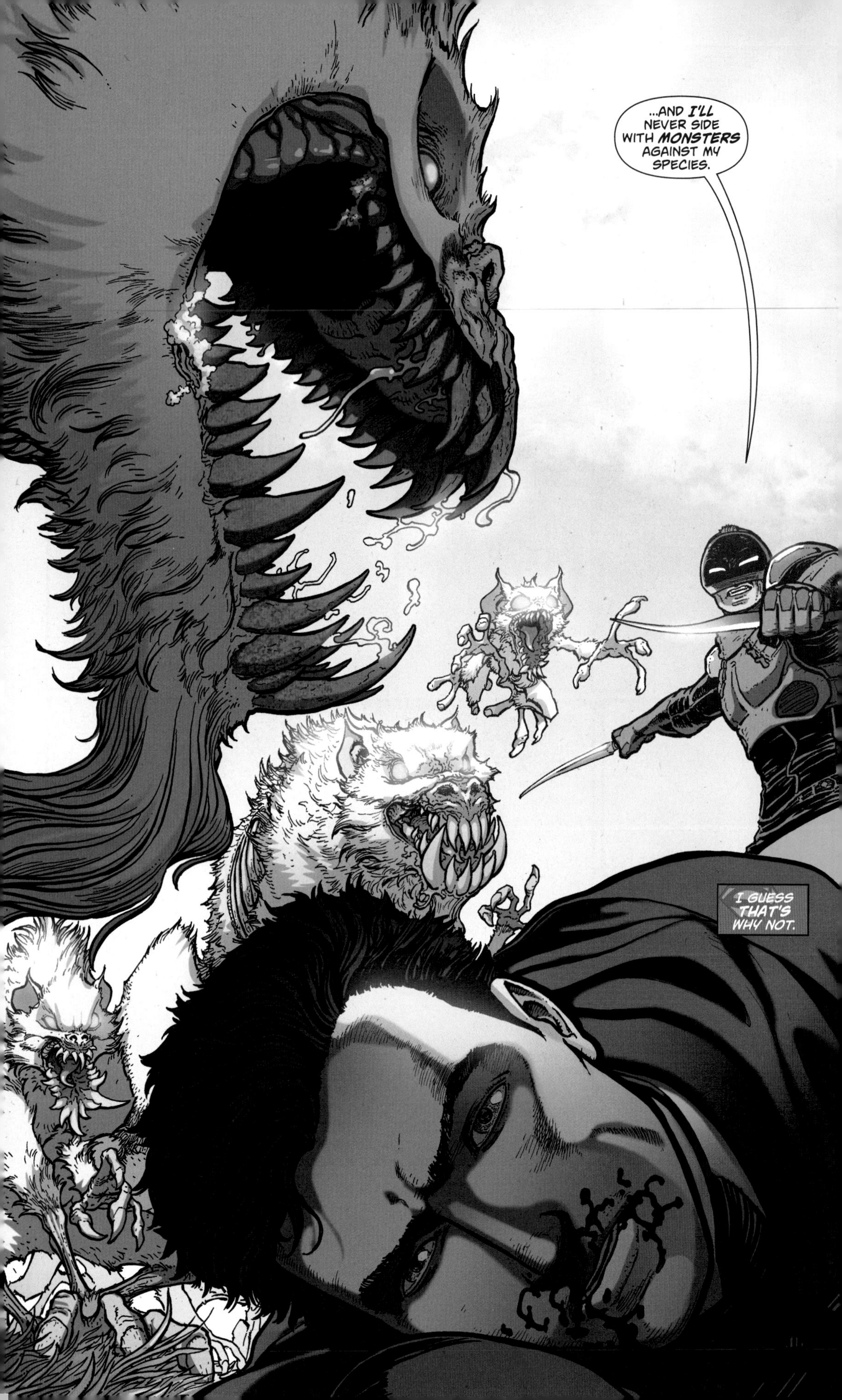

...AND I'LL NEVER SIDE WITH MONSTERS AGAINST MY SPECIES.
I GUESS THAT'S WHY NOT.

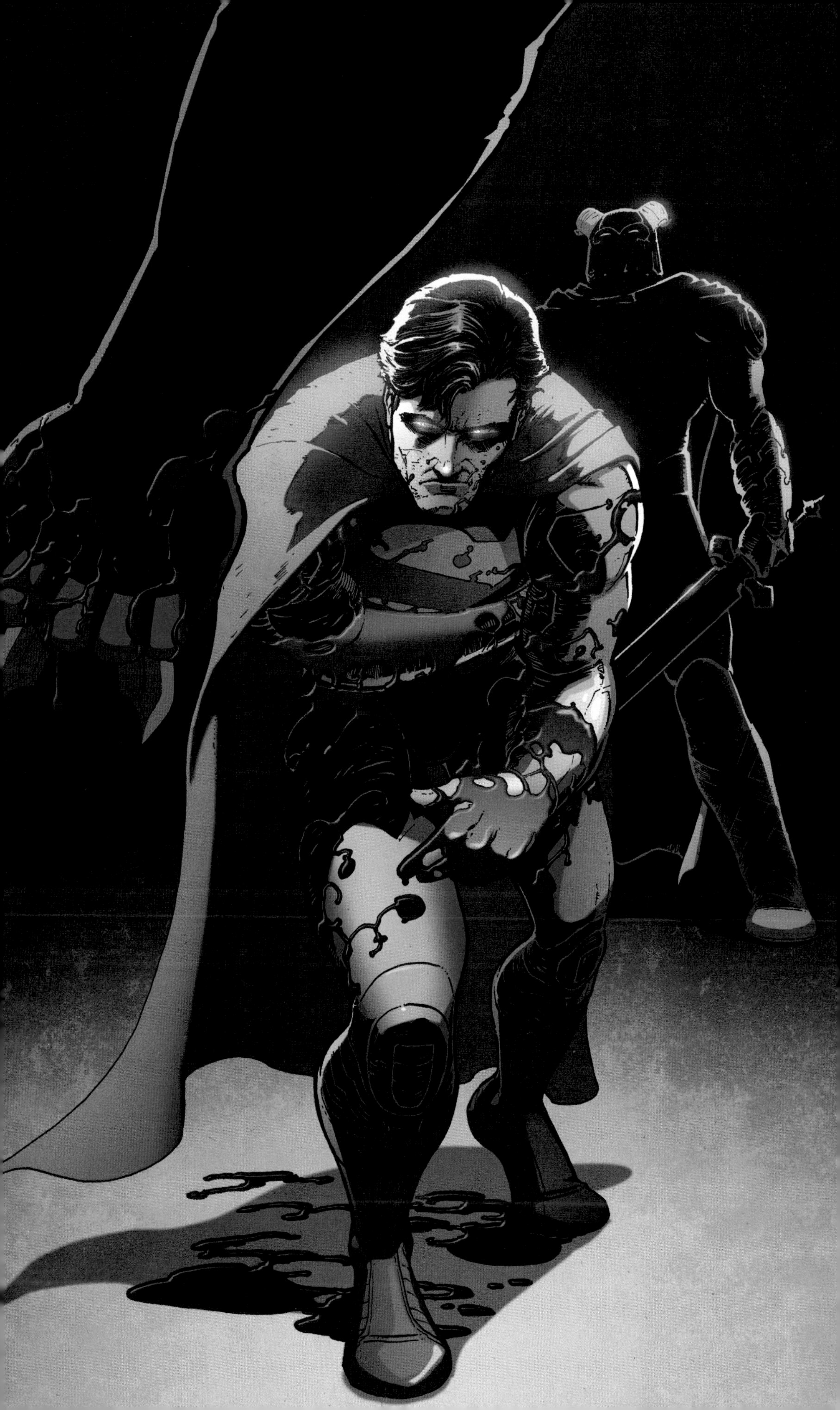

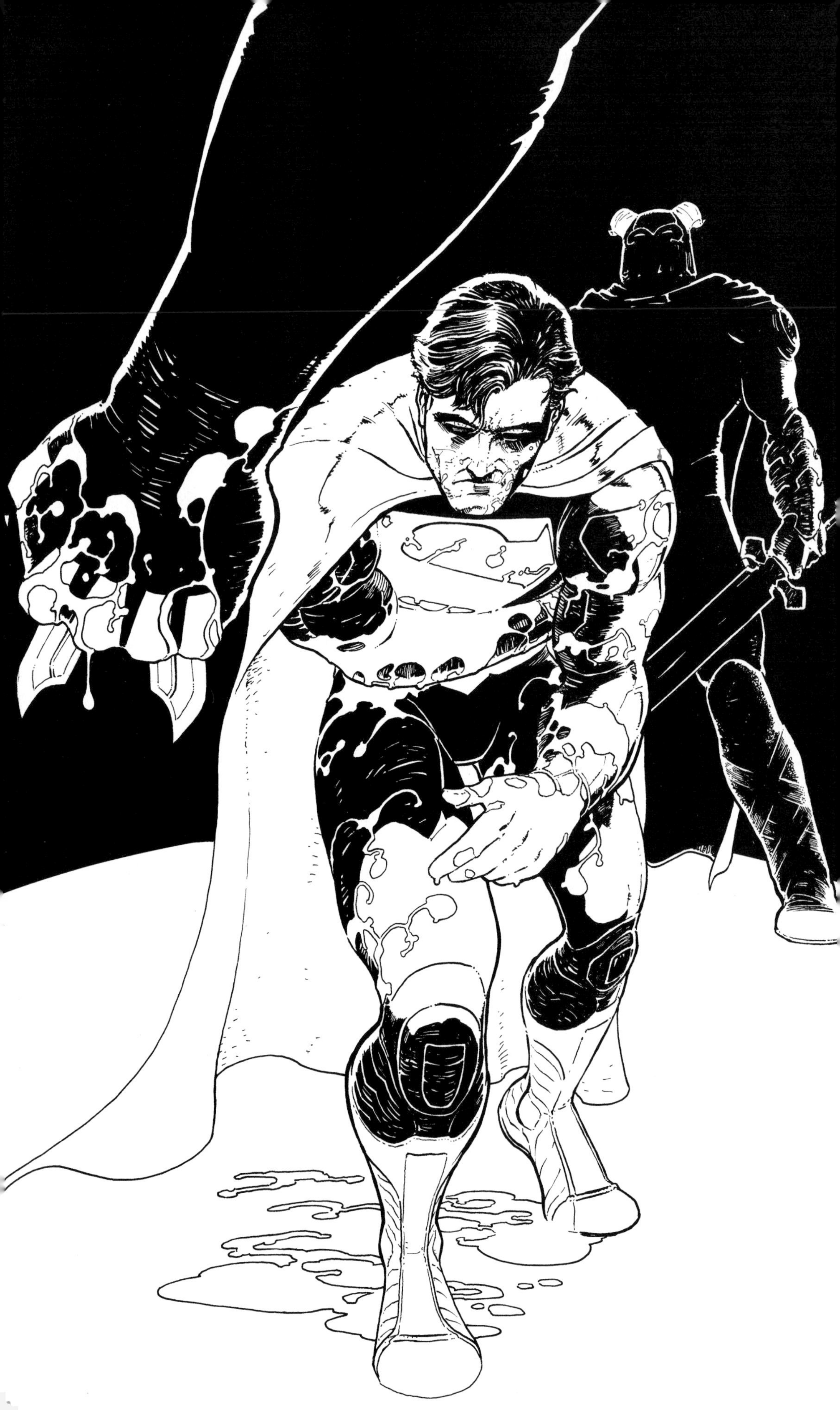

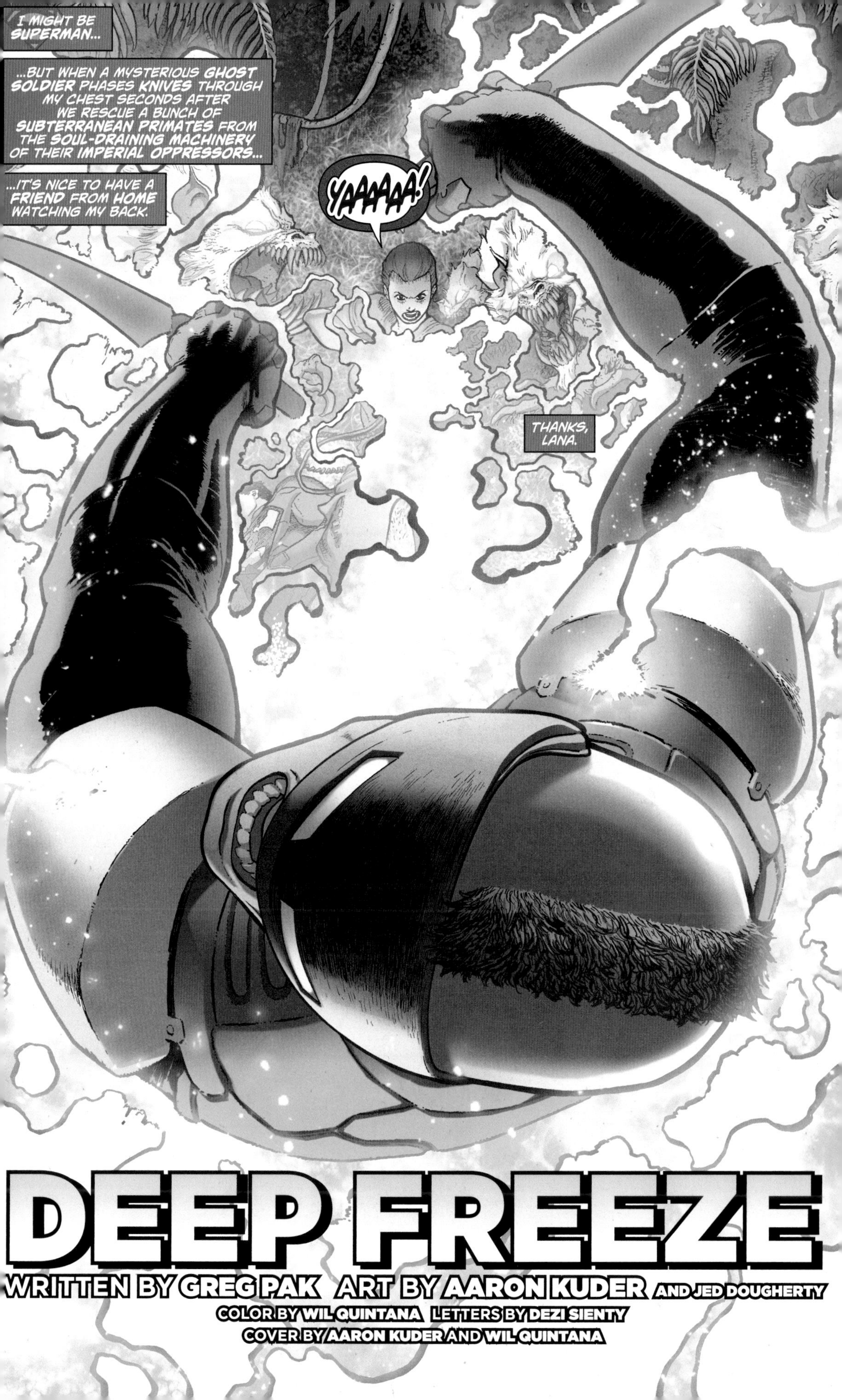
I MIGHT BE SUPERMAN...
...BUT WHEN A MYSTERIOUS GHOST SOLDIER PHASES KNIVES THROUGH MY CHEST SECONDS AFTER WE RESCUE A BUNCH OF SUBTERRANEAN PRIMATES FROM THE SOUL-DRAINING MACHINERY OF THEIR IMPERIAL OPPRESSORS...
...IT'S NICE TO HAVE A FRIEND FROM HOME WATCHING MY BACK.
YAAAAAA!
THANKS, LANA.
DEEP FREEZE
WRITTEN BY GREG PAK ART BY AARON KUDER AND JED DOUGHERTY
COLOR BY WIL QUINTANA LETTERS BY DEZI SIENTY
COVER BY AARON KUDER AND WIL QUINTANA

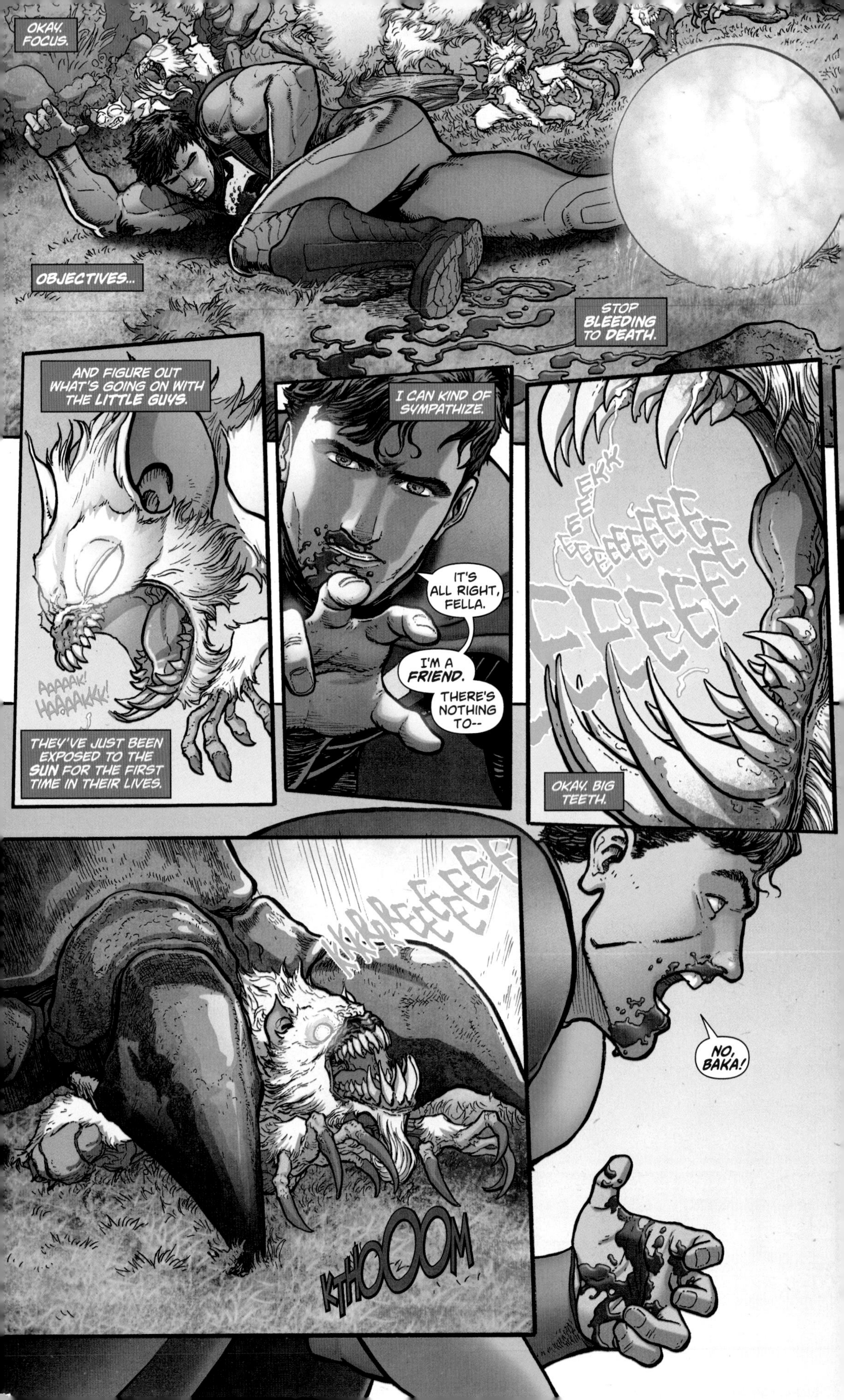
OKAY. FOCUS.
OBJECTIVES...
STOP BLEEDING TO DEATH.
AND FIGURE OUT WHAT'S GOING ON WITH THE LITTLE GUYS.
AAAAAK! HAAAAKKK!
THEY'VE JUST BEEN EXPOSED TO THE SUN FOR THE FIRST TIME IN THEIR LIVES.
I CAN KIND OF SYMPATHIZE.
IT'S ALL RIGHT, FELLA.
I'M A FRIEND.
THERE'S NOTHING TO--
OKAY. BIG TEETH.
NO, BAKA!
KTHOOOM

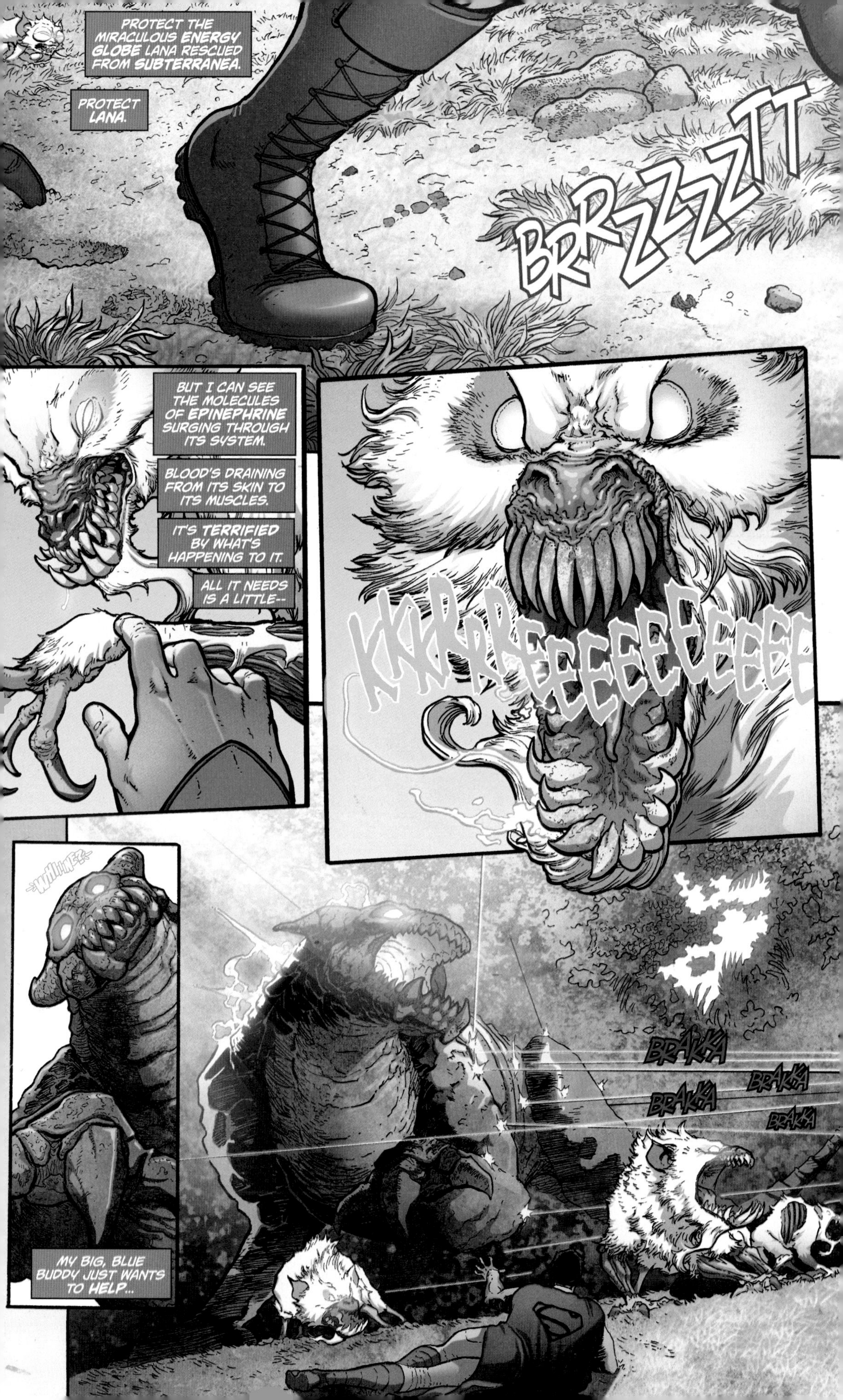
PROTECT THE MIRACULOUS ENERGY GLOBE LANA RESCUED FROM SUBTERRANEA.
PROTECT LANA.
BRRZZZZZTT
BUT I CAN SEE THE MOLECULES OF EPINEPHRINE SURGING THROUGH ITS SYSTEM.
BLOOD'S DRAINING FROM ITS SKIN TO ITS MUSCLES.
IT'S TERRIFIED BY WHAT'S HAPPENING TO IT.
ALL IT NEEDS IS A LITTLE--
KKKRRREEEEEEEEEEE
WHINE
BRAKKA
BRAKKA
BRAKKA
BRAKKA
MY BIG, BLUE BUDDY JUST WANTS TO HELP...

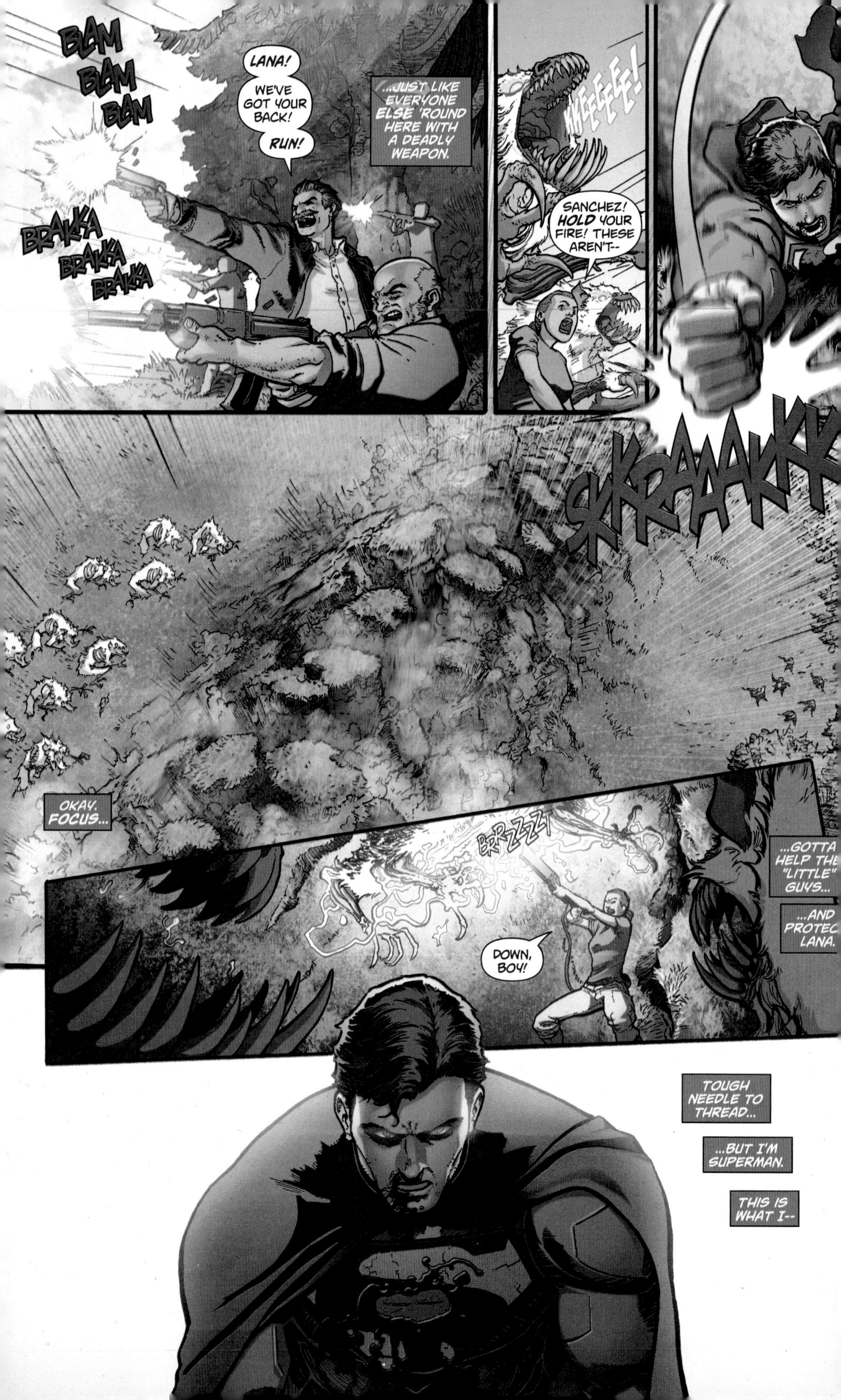
BLAM
BLAM
BLAM
BRAKKA
BRAKKA
BRAKKA
LANA!
WE'VE GOT YOUR BACK!
RUN!
...JUST LIKE EVERYONE ELSE 'ROUND HERE WITH A DEADLY WEAPON.
KKEEEEEE!
SANCHEZ! HOLD YOUR FIRE! THESE AREN'T--
SKRAAAKK
OKAY. FOCUS...
BRRZZZT
DOWN, BOY!
...GOTTA HELP THE "LITTLE" GUYS...
...AND PROTEC LANA.
TOUGH NEEDLE TO THREAD...
...BUT I'M SUPERMAN.
THIS IS WHAT I--

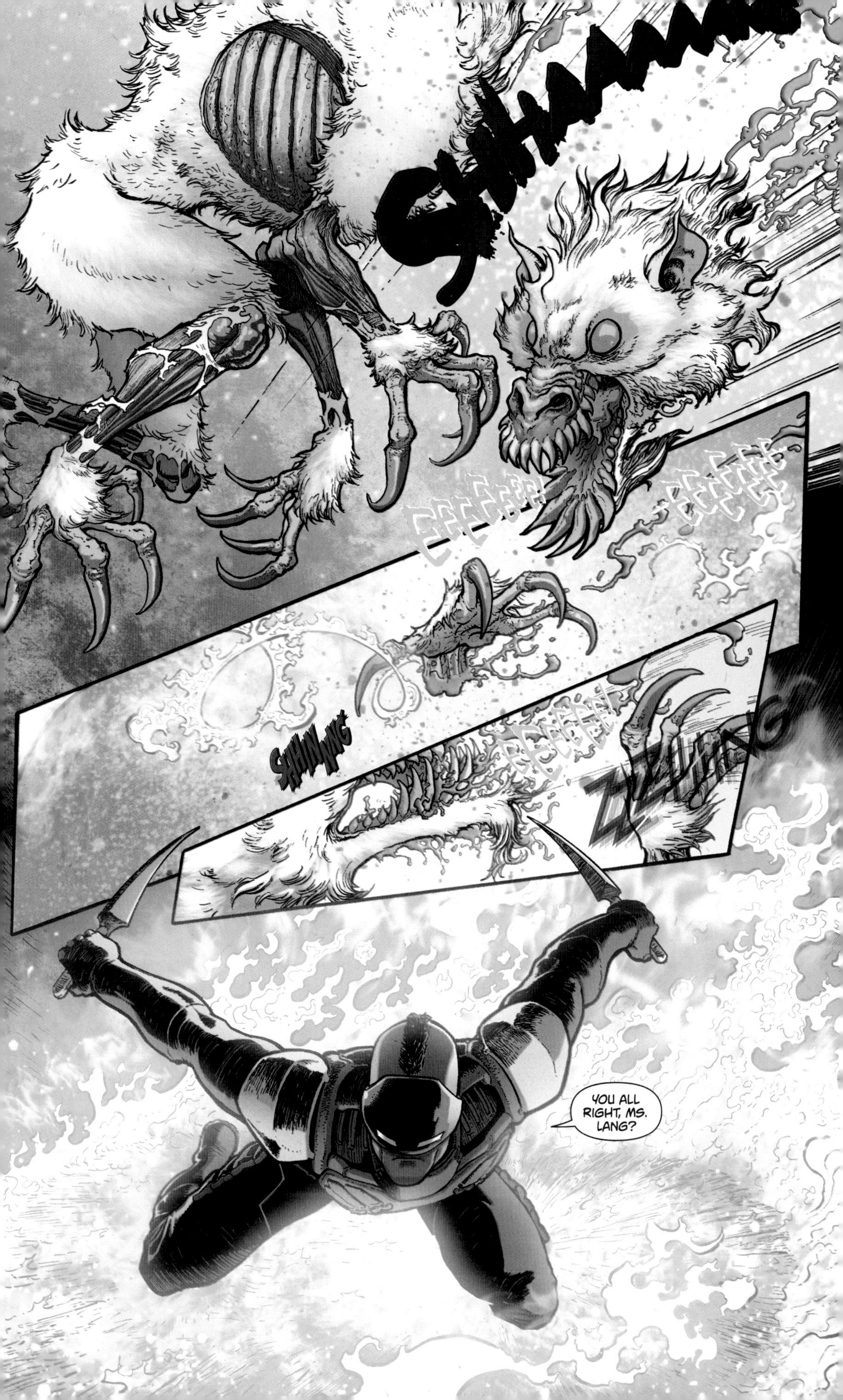
SHHAAAAANG
EEEEEE
EEEEEE
SHHING
EEEEEE
ZZZING
YOU ALL RIGHT, MS. LANG?

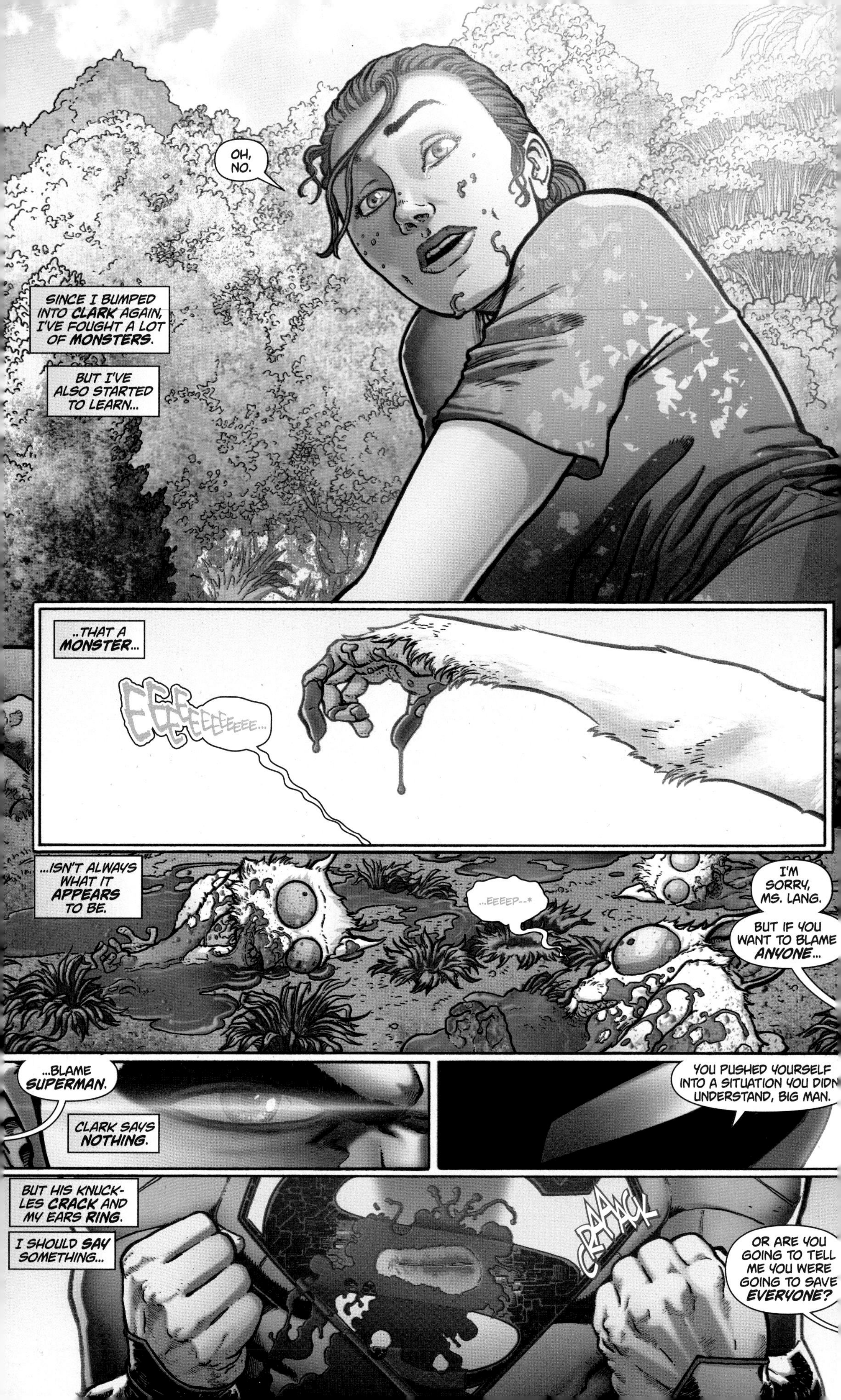
OH, NO.
SINCE I BUMPED INTO CLARK AGAIN, I'VE FOUGHT A LOT OF MONSTERS.
BUT I'VE ALSO STARTED TO LEARN...
..THAT A MONSTER...
EEEEEEEEEEEE...
...ISN'T ALWAYS WHAT IT APPEARS TO BE.
...EEEEP--*
I'M SORRY, MS. LANG.
BUT IF YOU WANT TO BLAME ANYONE...
...BLAME SUPERMAN.
CLARK SAYS NOTHING.
YOU PUSHED YOURSELF INTO A SITUATION YOU DIDN UNDERSTAND, BIG MAN.
BUT HIS KNUCK-LES CRACK AND MY EARS RING.
I SHOULD SAY SOMETHING...
CRAAACK
OR ARE YOU GOING TO TELL ME YOU WERE GOING TO SAVE EVERYONE?

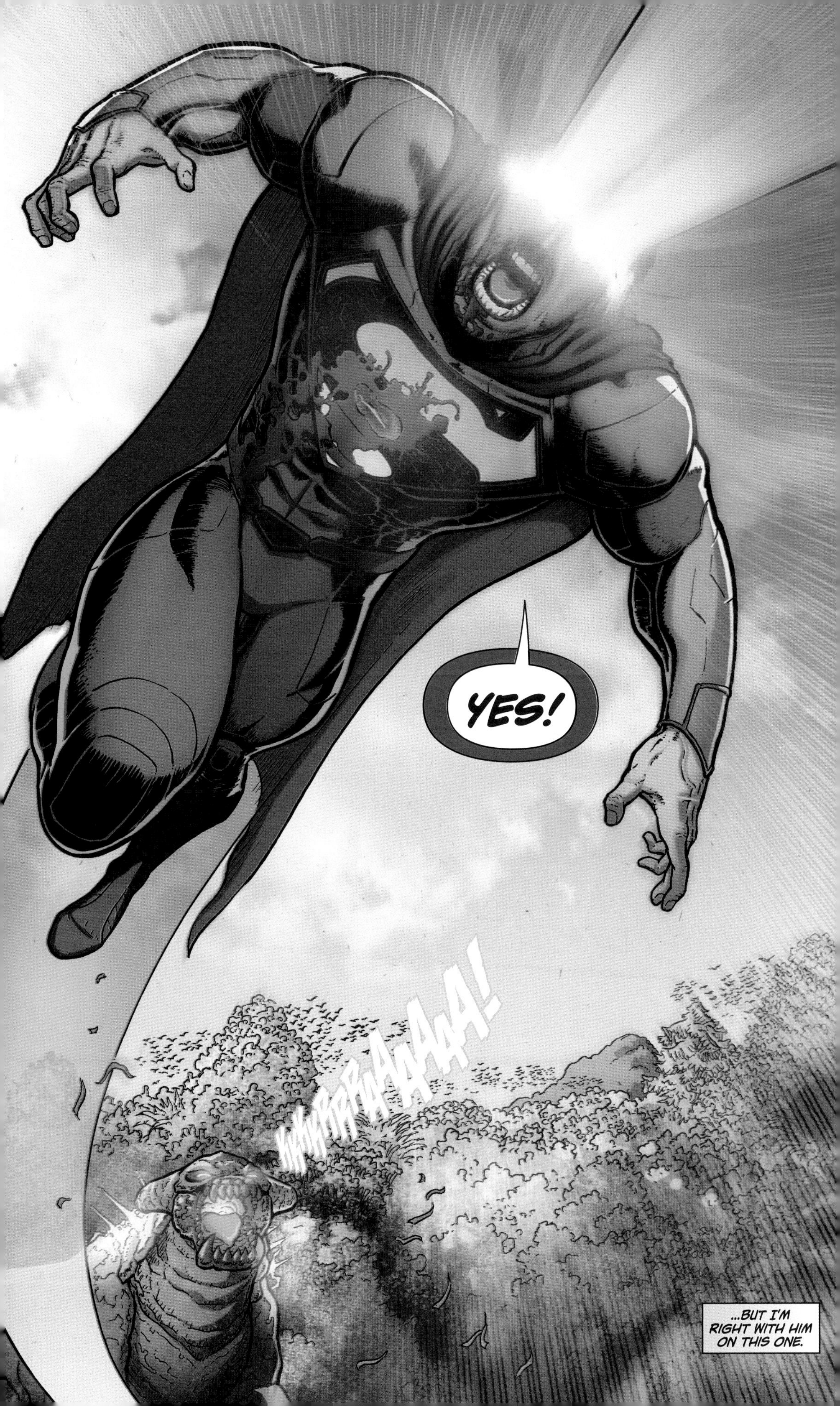
YES!
KKKKRRRAAAAAA!
...BUT I'M RIGHT WITH HIM ON THIS ONE.

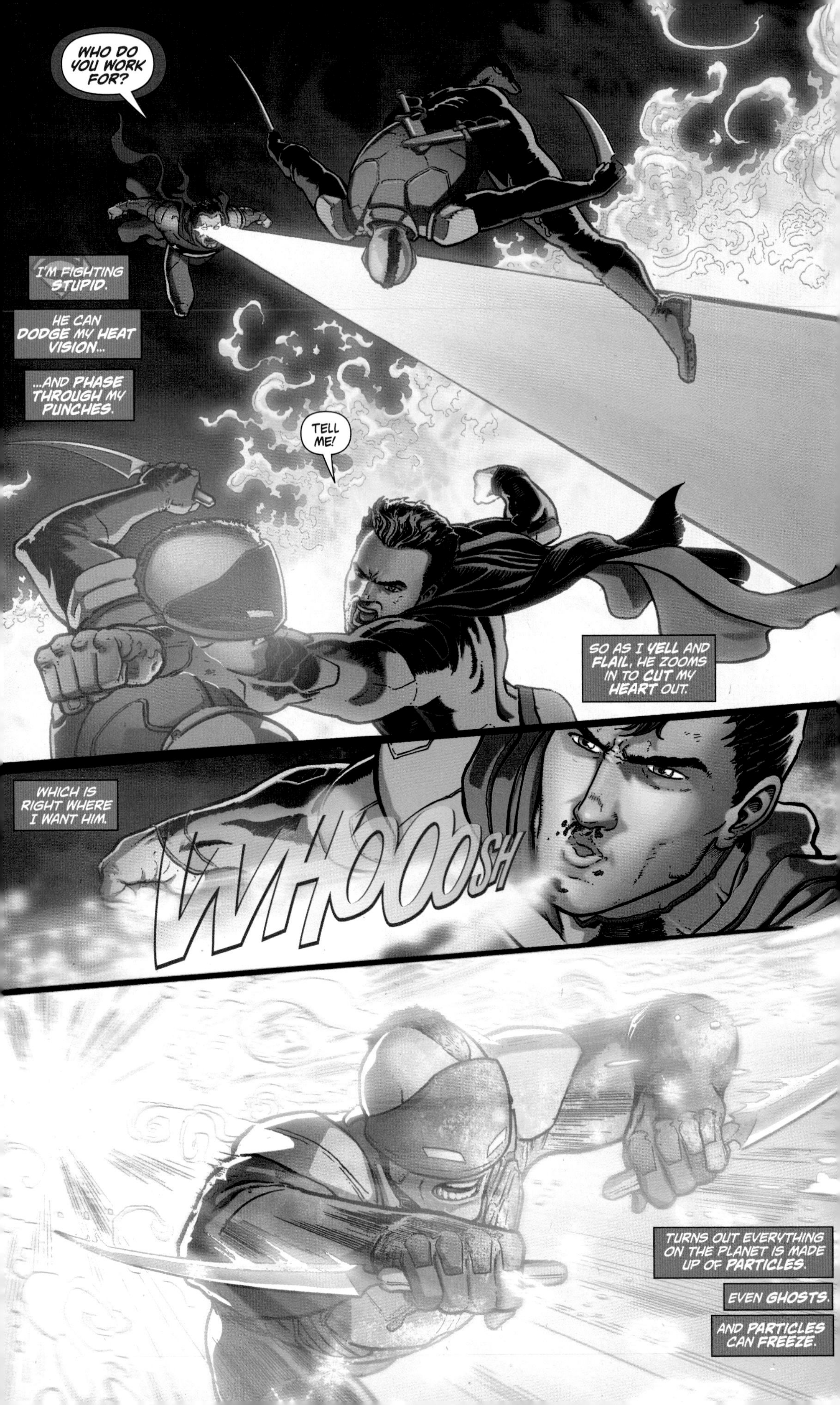
WHO DO YOU WORK FOR?
I'M FIGHTING STUPID.
HE CAN DODGE MY HEAT VISION...
...AND PHASE THROUGH MY PUNCHES.
TELL ME!
SO AS I YELL AND FLAIL, HE ZOOMS IN TO CUT MY HEART OUT.
WHICH IS RIGHT WHERE I WANT HIM.
WHOOOOSH
TURNS OUT EVERYTHING ON THE PLANET IS MADE UP OF PARTICLES.
EVEN GHOSTS.
AND PARTICLES CAN FREEZE.

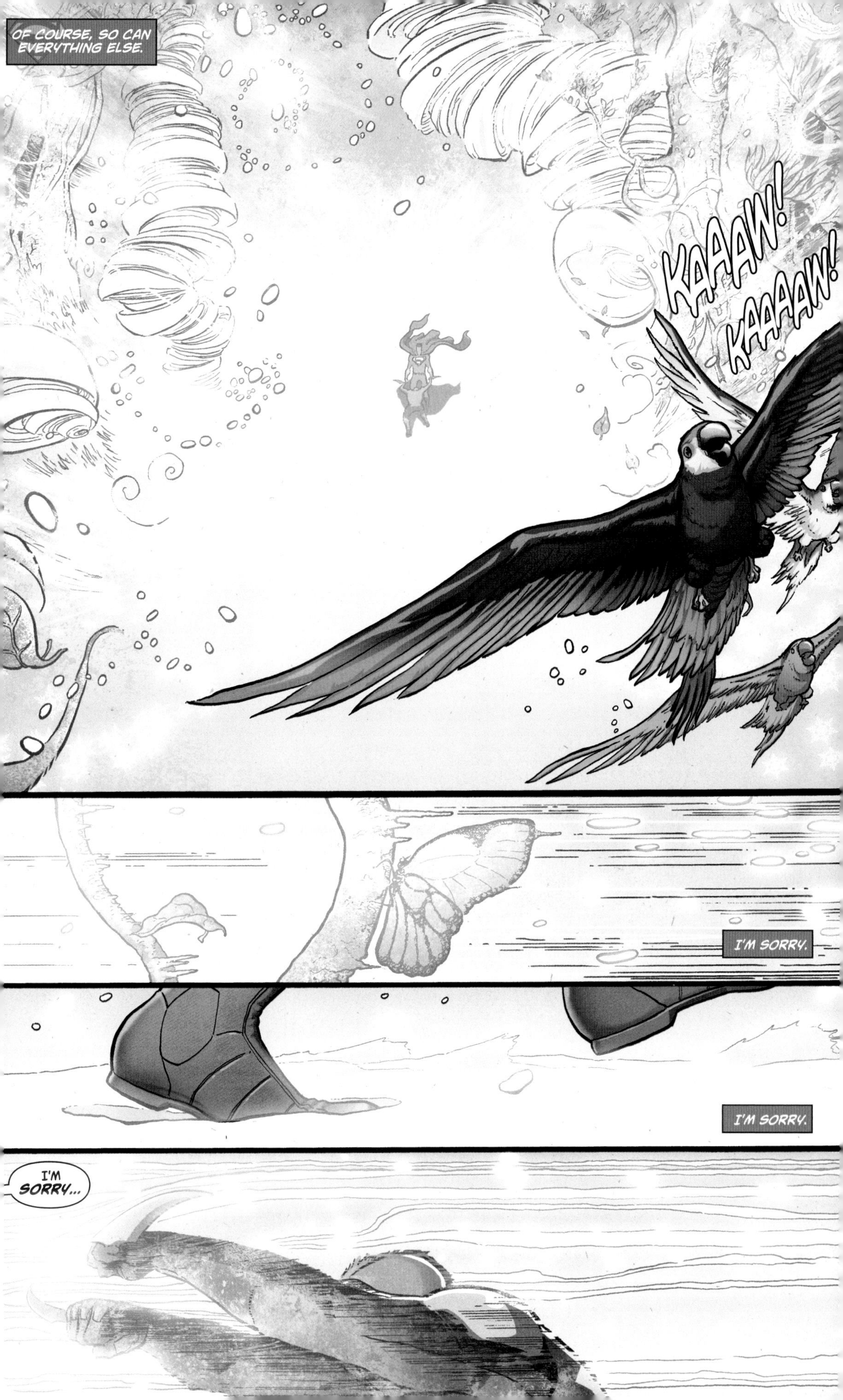
OF COURSE, SO CAN EVERYTHING ELSE.
KAAAW!
KAAAAW!
I'M SORRY.
I'M SORRY.
I'M SORRY...

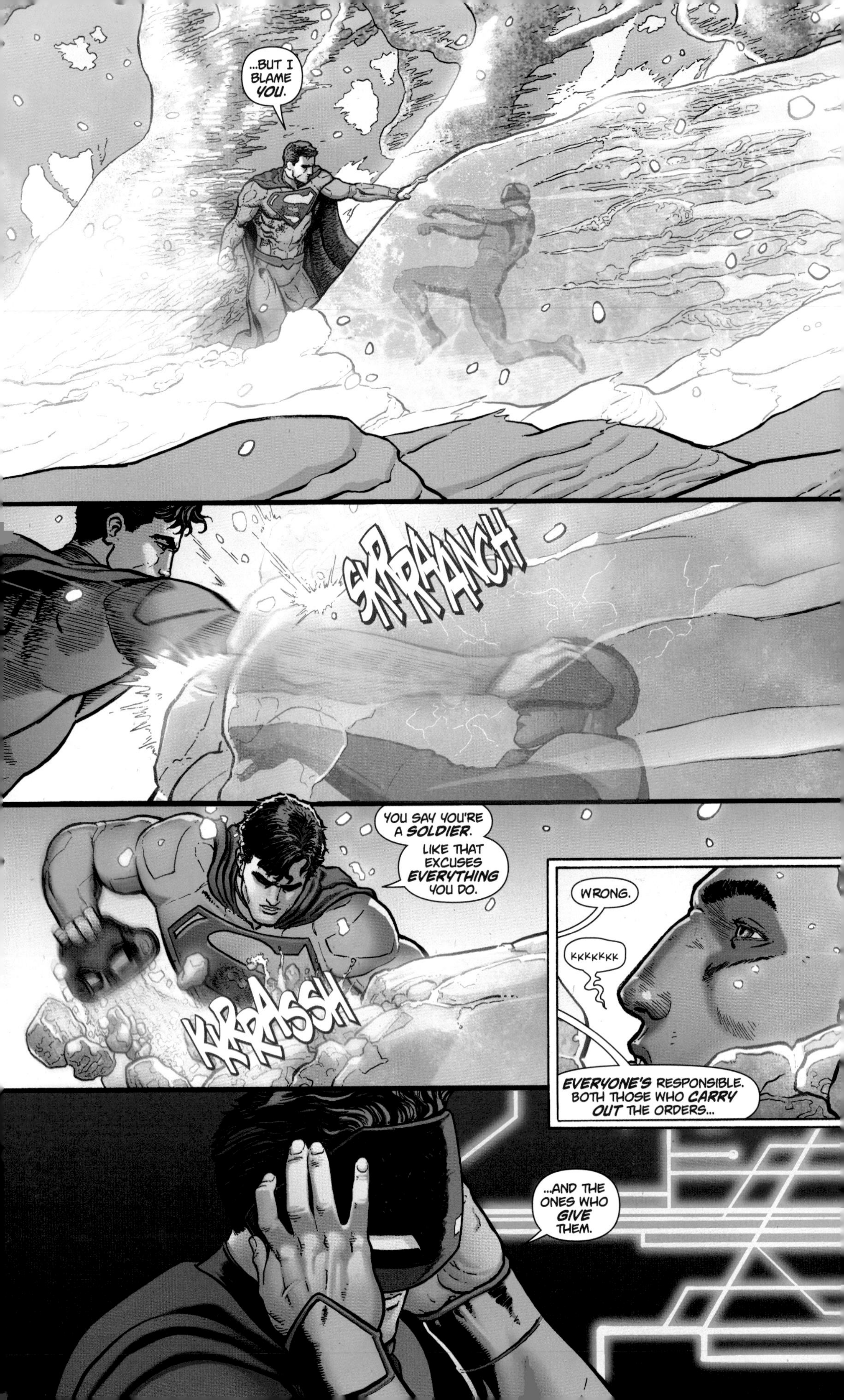
...BUT I BLAME YOU.
SKRANCH
YOU SAY YOU'RE A SOLDIER.
LIKE THAT EXCUSES EVERYTHING YOU DO.
KRASSH
WRONG.
KKKKKKK
EVERYONE'S RESPONSIBLE. BOTH THOSE WHO CARRY OUT THE ORDERS...
...AND THE ONES WHO GIVE THEM.

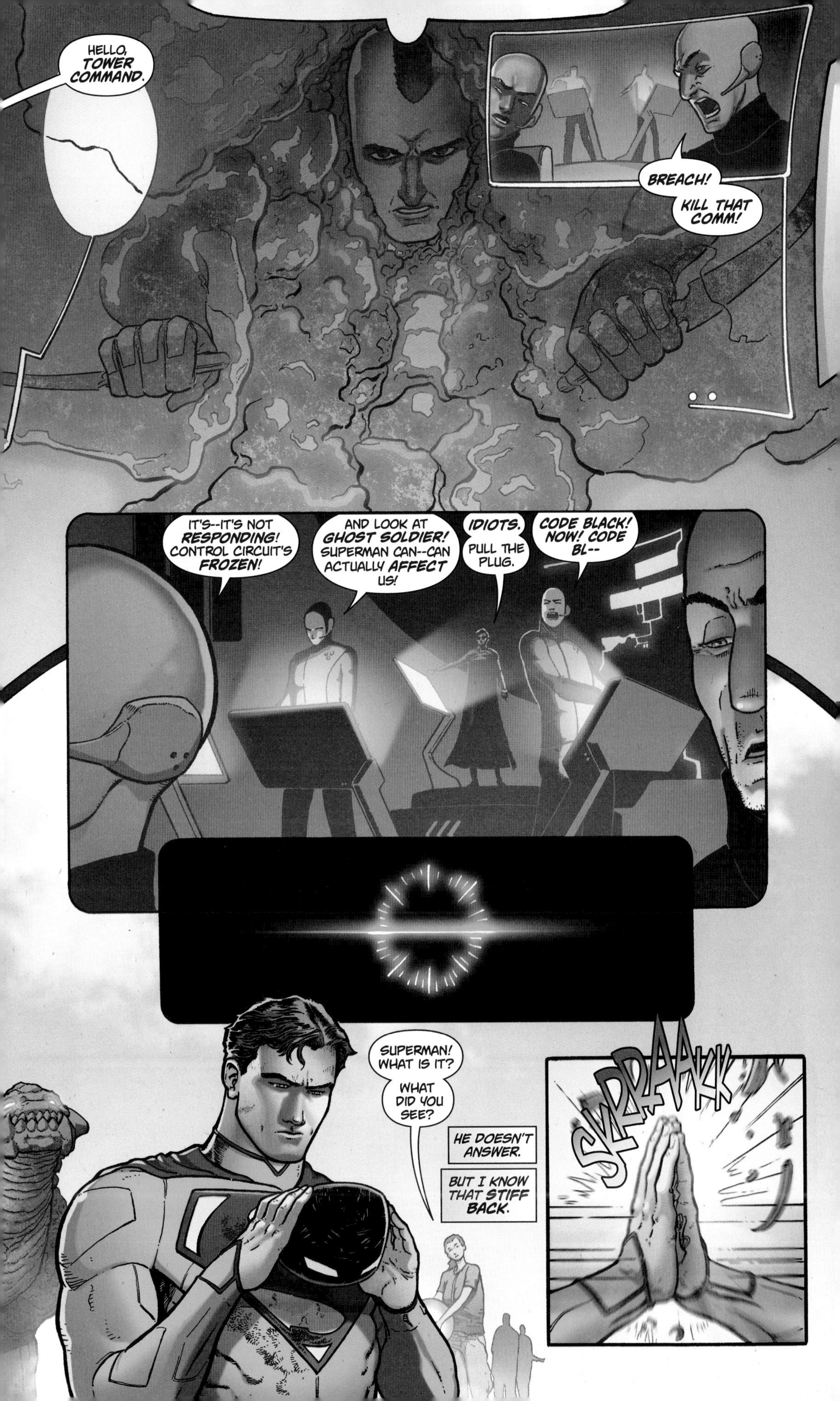
HELLO, TOWER COMMAND.
BREACH!
KILL THAT COMM!
IT'S--IT'S NOT RESPONDING! CONTROL CIRCUIT'S FROZEN!
AND LOOK AT GHOST SOLDIER! SUPERMAN CAN--CAN ACTUALLY AFFECT US!
IDIOTS.
PULL THE PLUG.
CODE BLACK! NOW! CODE BL--
SUPERMAN! WHAT IS IT?
WHAT DID YOU SEE?
HE DOESN'T ANSWER.
BUT I KNOW THAT STIFF BACK.
SKRRAAKK

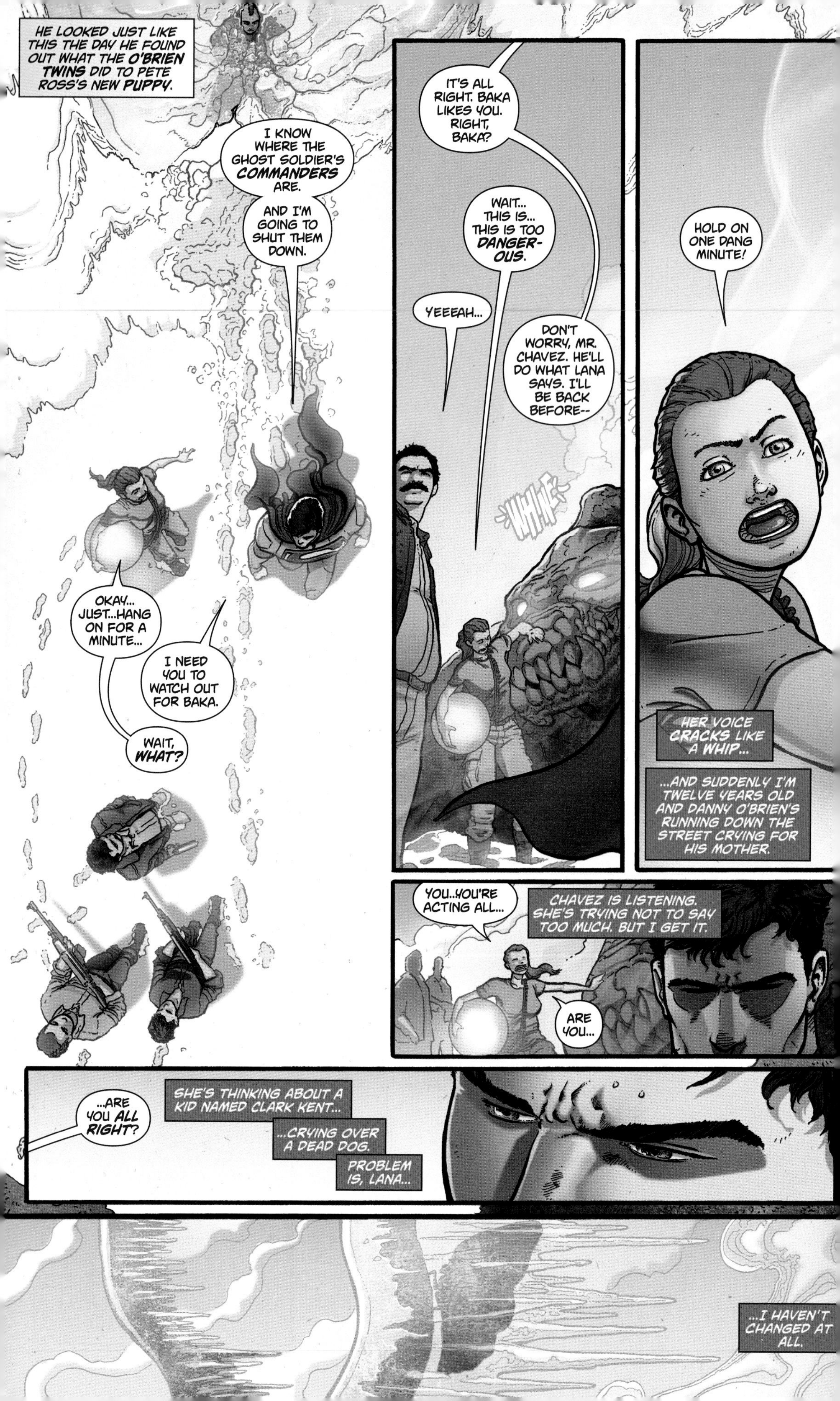

HE LOOKED JUST LIKE THIS THE DAY HE FOUND OUT WHAT THE O'BRIEN TWINS DID TO PETE ROSS'S NEW PUPPY.
I KNOW WHERE THE GHOST SOLDIER'S COMMANDERS ARE.
AND I'M GOING TO SHUT THEM DOWN.
OKAY... JUST...HANG ON FOR A MINUTE...
I NEED YOU TO WATCH OUT FOR BAKA.
WAIT, WHAT?
IT'S ALL RIGHT. BAKA LIKES YOU. RIGHT, BAKA?
WAIT... THIS IS... THIS IS TOO DANGER-OUS.
YEEEAH...
DON'T WORRY, MR. CHAVEZ. HE'LL DO WHAT LANA SAYS. I'LL BE BACK BEFORE--
WHIP
HOLD ON ONE DANG MINUTE!
HER VOICE CRACKS LIKE A WHIP...
...AND SUDDENLY I'M TWELVE YEARS OLD AND DANNY O'BRIEN'S RUNNING DOWN THE STREET CRYING FOR HIS MOTHER.
YOU...YOU'RE ACTING ALL...
CHAVEZ IS LISTENING. SHE'S TRYING NOT TO SAY TOO MUCH. BUT I GET IT.
ARE YOU...
...ARE YOU ALL RIGHT?
SHE'S THINKING ABOUT A KID NAMED CLARK KENT...
...CRYING OVER A DEAD DOG.
PROBLEM IS, LANA...
...I HAVEN'T CHANGED AT ALL.

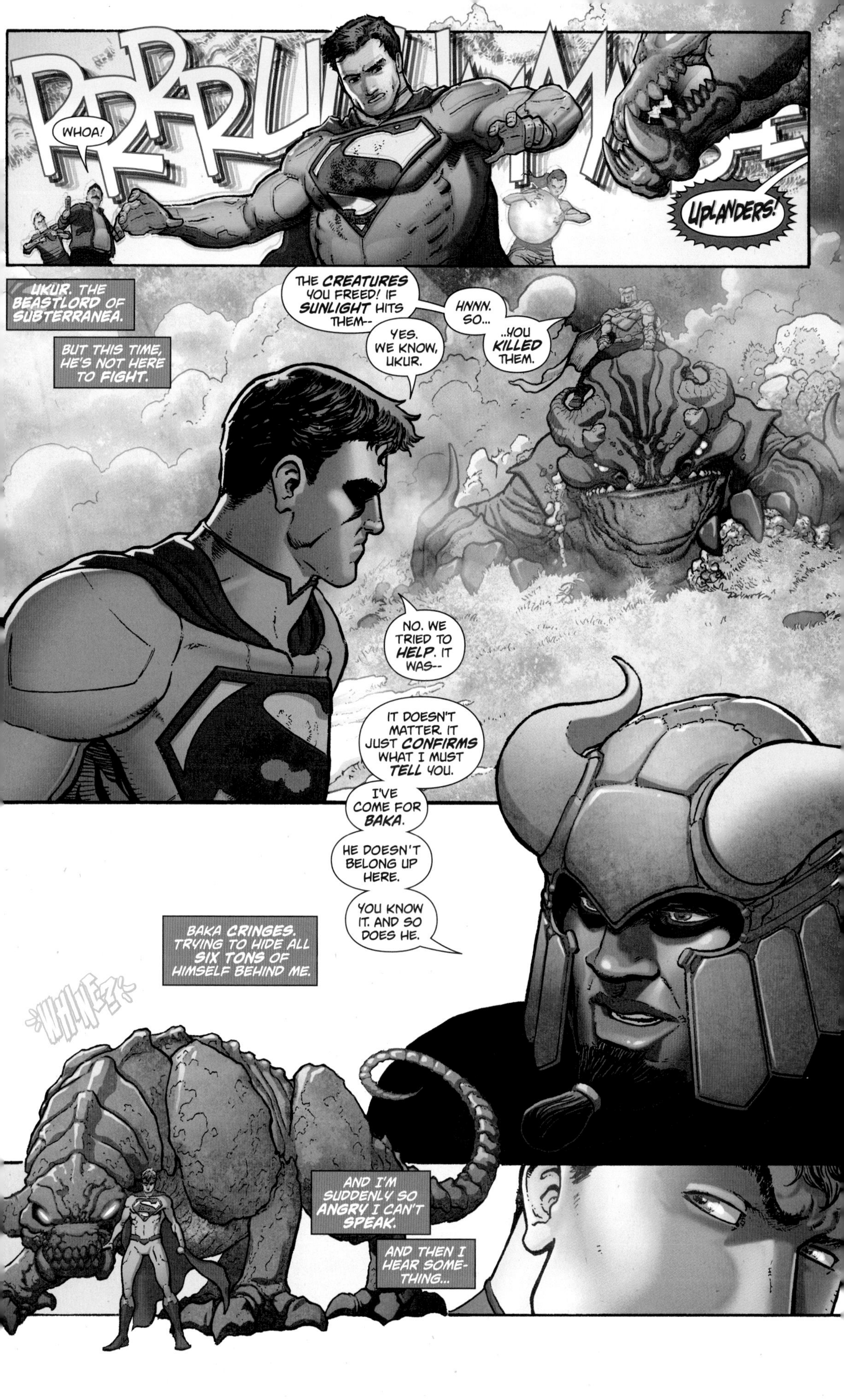
PRRUMMM
WHOA!
UPLANDERS!
UKUR. THE BEASTLORD OF SUBTERRANEA.
BUT THIS TIME, HE'S NOT HERE TO FIGHT.
THE CREATURES YOU FREED! IF SUNLIGHT HITS THEM--
YES. WE KNOW, UKUR.
HNNN. SO...
...YOU KILLED THEM.
NO. WE TRIED TO HELP. IT WAS--
IT DOESN'T MATTER. IT JUST CONFIRMS WHAT I MUST TELL YOU.
I'VE COME FOR BAKA.
HE DOESN'T BELONG UP HERE.
YOU KNOW IT. AND SO DOES HE.
BAKA CRINGES. TRYING TO HIDE ALL SIX TONS OF HIMSELF BEHIND ME.
WHINE?
AND I'M SUDDENLY SO ANGRY I CAN'T SPEAK.
AND THEN I HEAR SOME-THING...

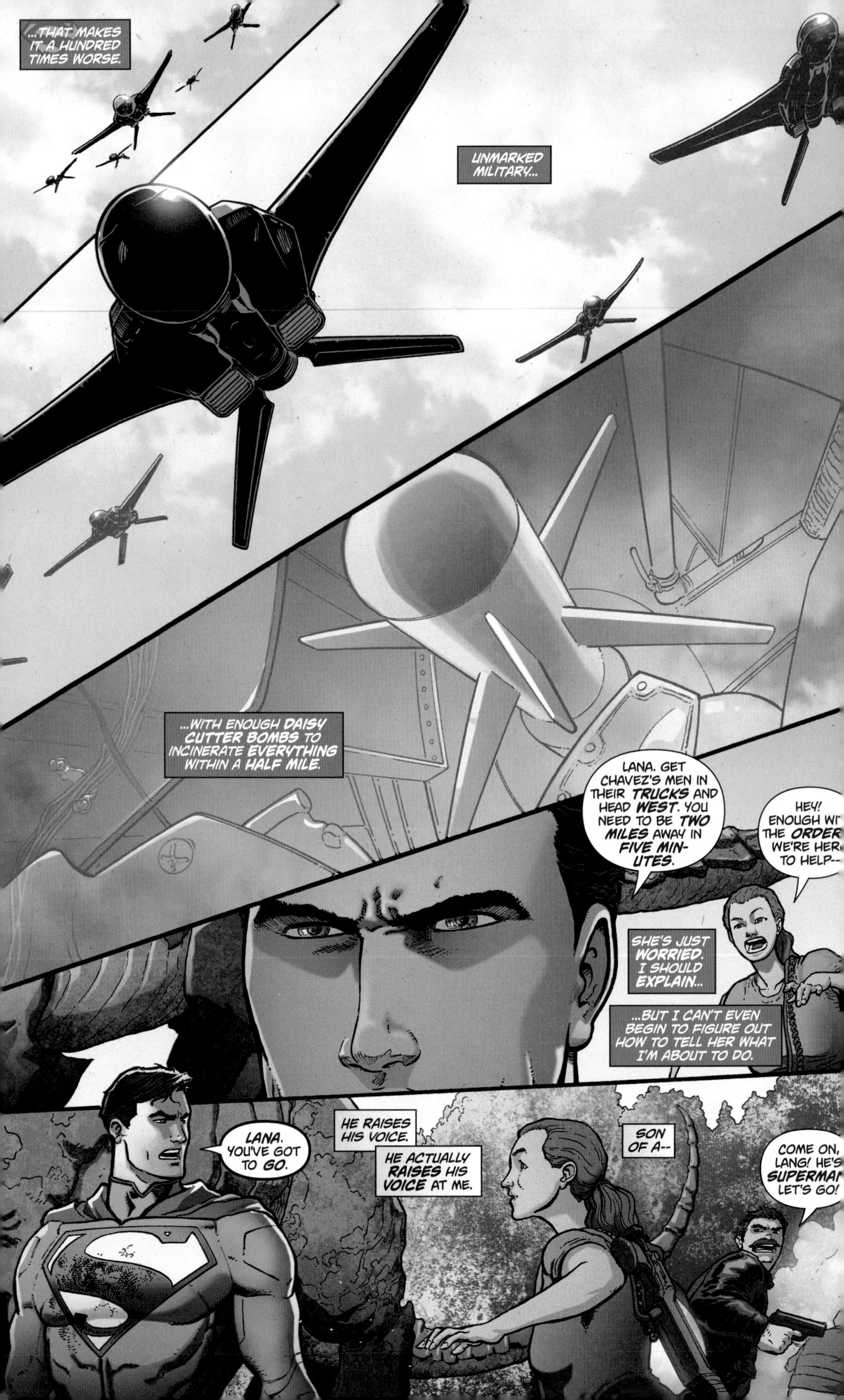

...THAT MAKES IT A HUNDRED TIMES WORSE.
UNMARKED MILITARY...
...WITH ENOUGH DAISY CUTTER BOMBS TO INCINERATE EVERYTHING WITHIN A HALF MILE.
LANA. GET CHAVEZ'S MEN IN THEIR TRUCKS AND HEAD WEST. YOU NEED TO BE TWO MILES AWAY IN FIVE MIN-UTES.
HEY! ENOUGH WI THE ORDER WE'RE HER TO HELP--
SHE'S JUST WORRIED. I SHOULD EXPLAIN...
...BUT I CAN'T EVEN BEGIN TO FIGURE OUT HOW TO TELL HER WHAT I'M ABOUT TO DO.
LANA. YOU'VE GOT TO GO.
HE RAISES HIS VOICE.
HE ACTUALLY RAISES HIS VOICE AT ME.
SON OF A--
COME ON, LANG! HE'S SUPERMAN LET'S GO!

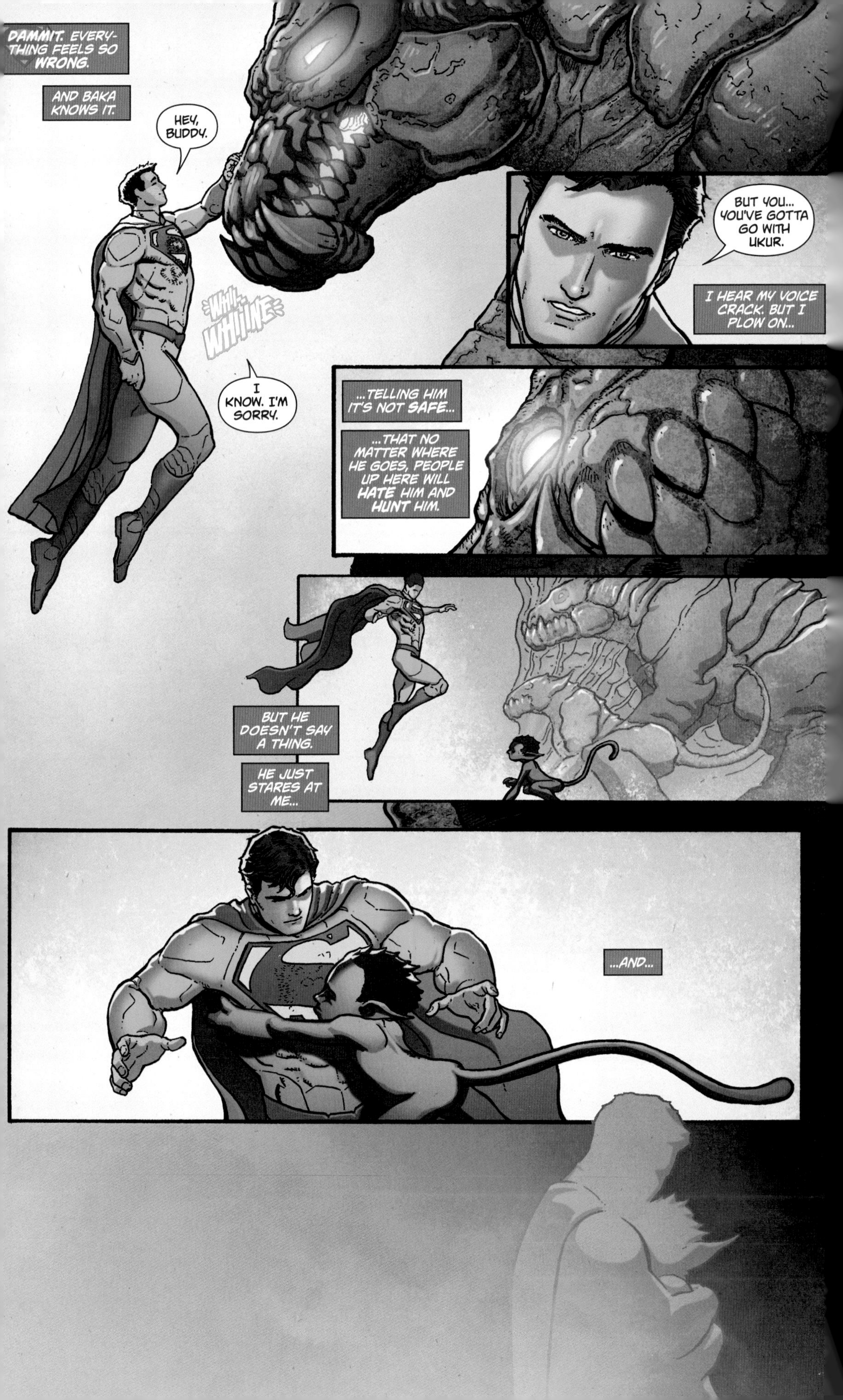
DAMMIT. EVERY-THING FEELS SO WRONG.
AND BAKA KNOWS IT.
HEY, BUDDY.
BUT YOU... YOU'VE GOTTA GO WITH UKUR.
I HEAR MY VOICE CRACK. BUT I PLOW ON...
WHIIIN WHIIINE
I KNOW. I'M SORRY.
...TELLING HIM IT'S NOT SAFE...
...THAT NO MATTER WHERE HE GOES, PEOPLE UP HERE WILL HATE HIM AND HUNT HIM.
BUT HE DOESN'T SAY A THING.
HE JUST STARES AT ME...
...AND...

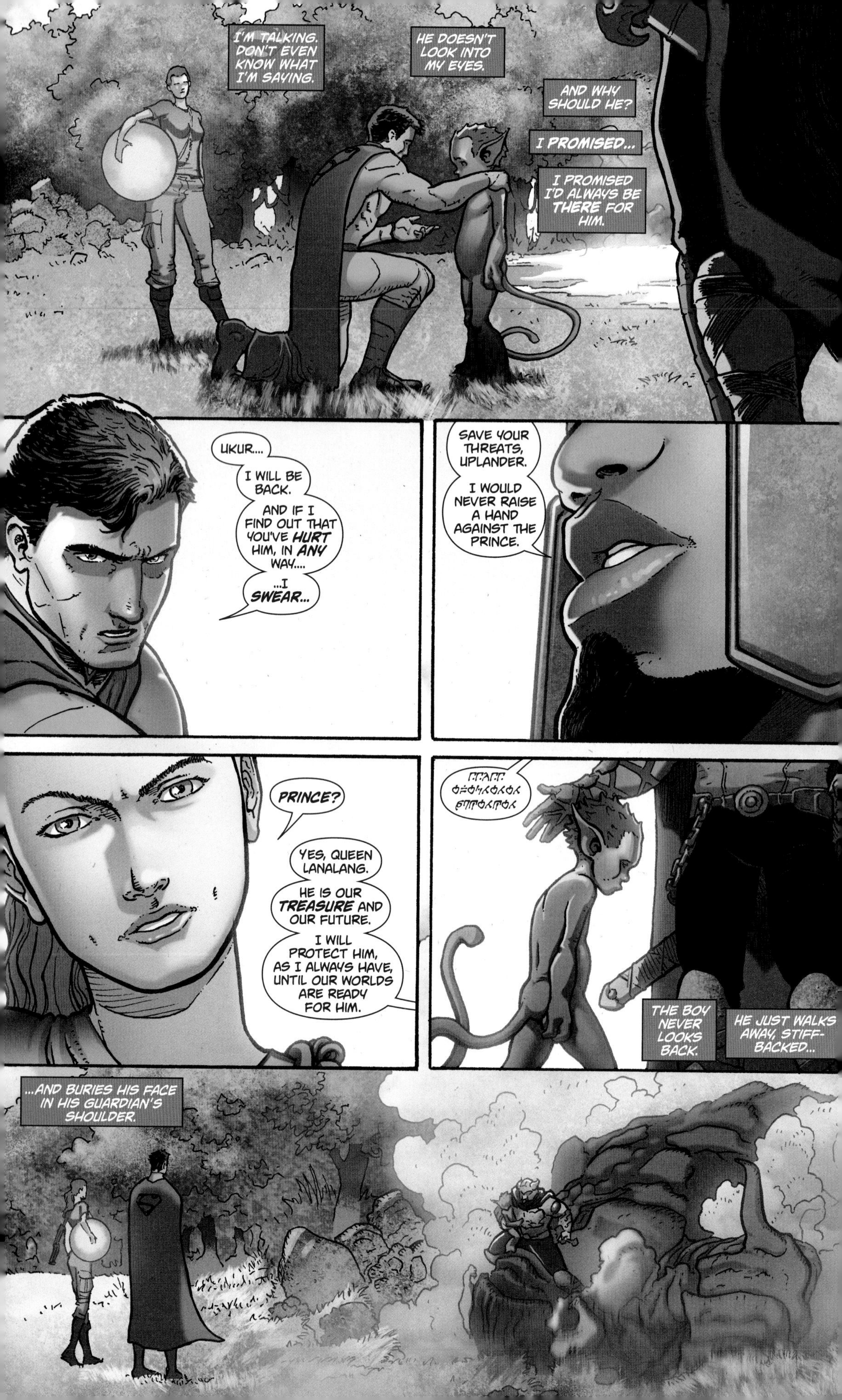

I'M TALKING. DON'T EVEN KNOW WHAT I'M SAYING.
HE DOESN'T LOOK INTO MY EYES.
AND WHY SHOULD HE?
I PROMISED...
I PROMISED I'D ALWAYS BE THERE FOR HIM.
UKUR....
I WILL BE BACK.
AND IF I FIND OUT THAT YOU'VE HURT HIM, IN ANY WAY....
...I SWEAR...
SAVE YOUR THREATS, UPLANDER.
I WOULD NEVER RAISE A HAND AGAINST THE PRINCE.
PRINCE?
YES, QUEEN LANALANG.
HE IS OUR TREASURE AND OUR FUTURE.
I WILL PROTECT HIM, AS I ALWAYS HAVE, UNTIL OUR WORLDS ARE READY FOR HIM.
THE BOY NEVER LOOKS BACK.
HE JUST WALKS AWAY, STIFF-BACKED...
...AND BURIES HIS FACE IN HIS GUARDIAN'S SHOULDER.

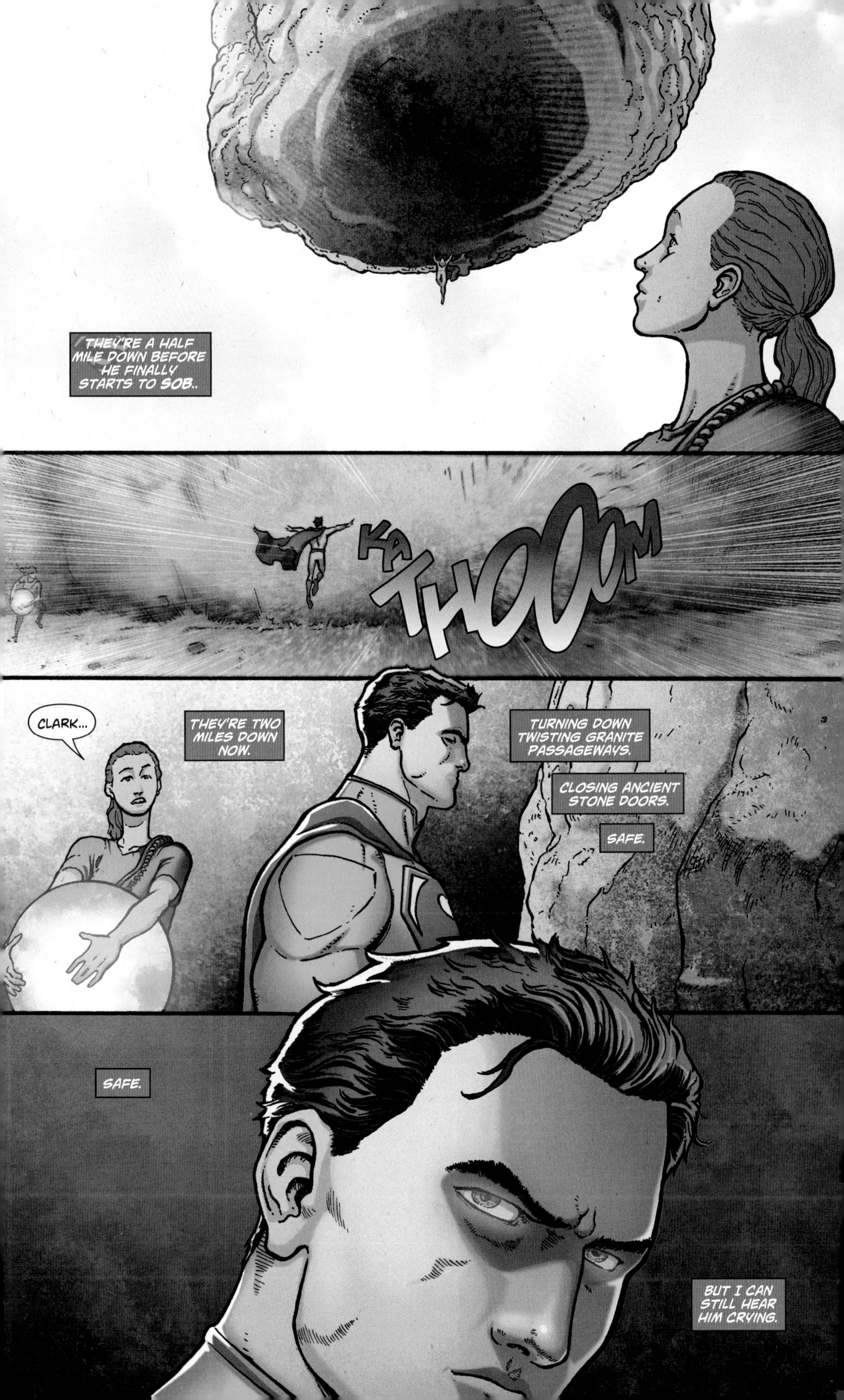
THEY'RE A HALF MILE DOWN BEFORE HE FINALLY STARTS TO SOB..
KA THOOOOM
CLARK...
THEY'RE TWO MILES DOWN NOW.
TURNING DOWN TWISTING GRANITE PASSAGEWAYS.
CLOSING ANCIENT STONE DOORS.
SAFE.
SAFE.
BUT I CAN STILL HEAR HIM CRYING.

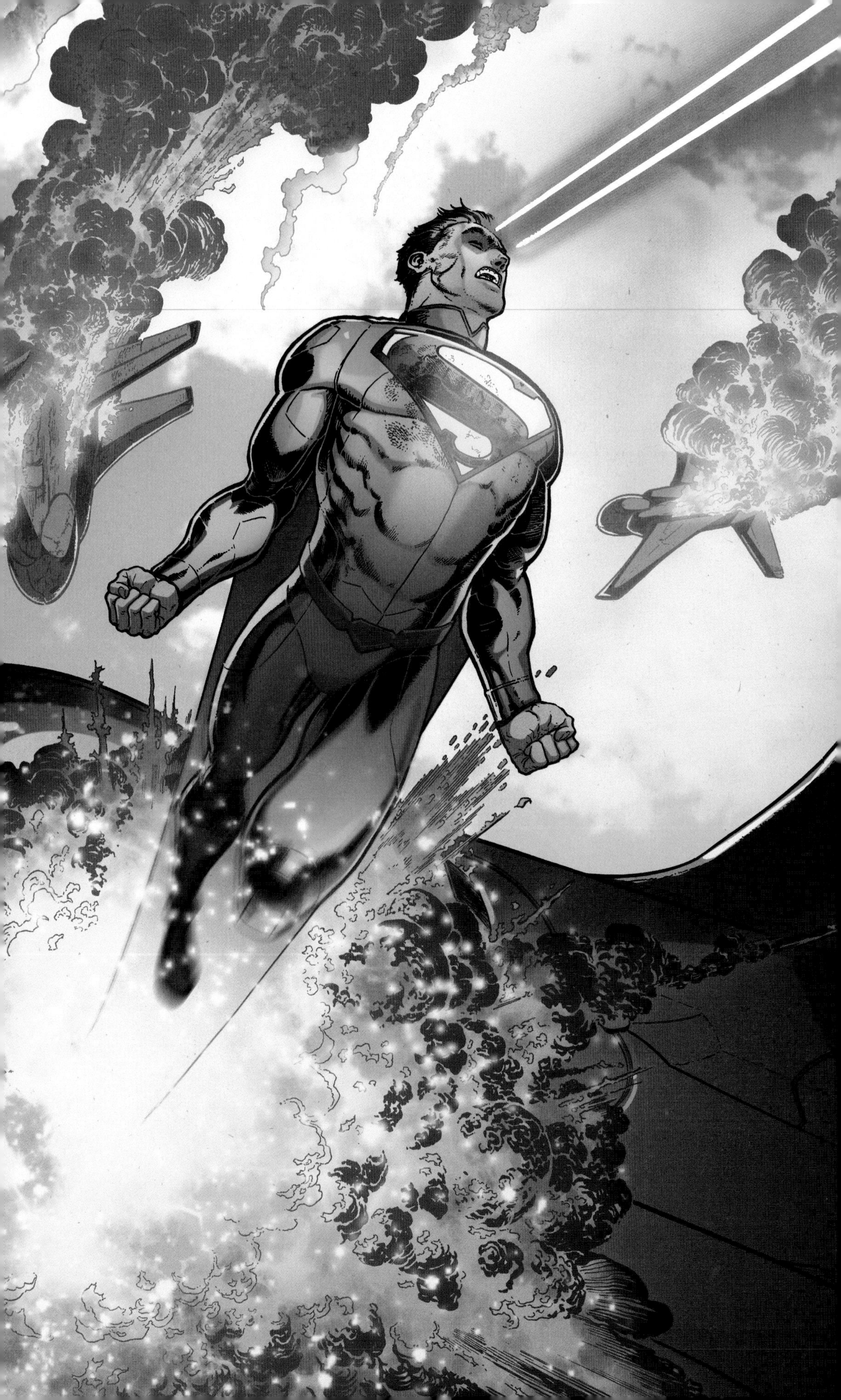

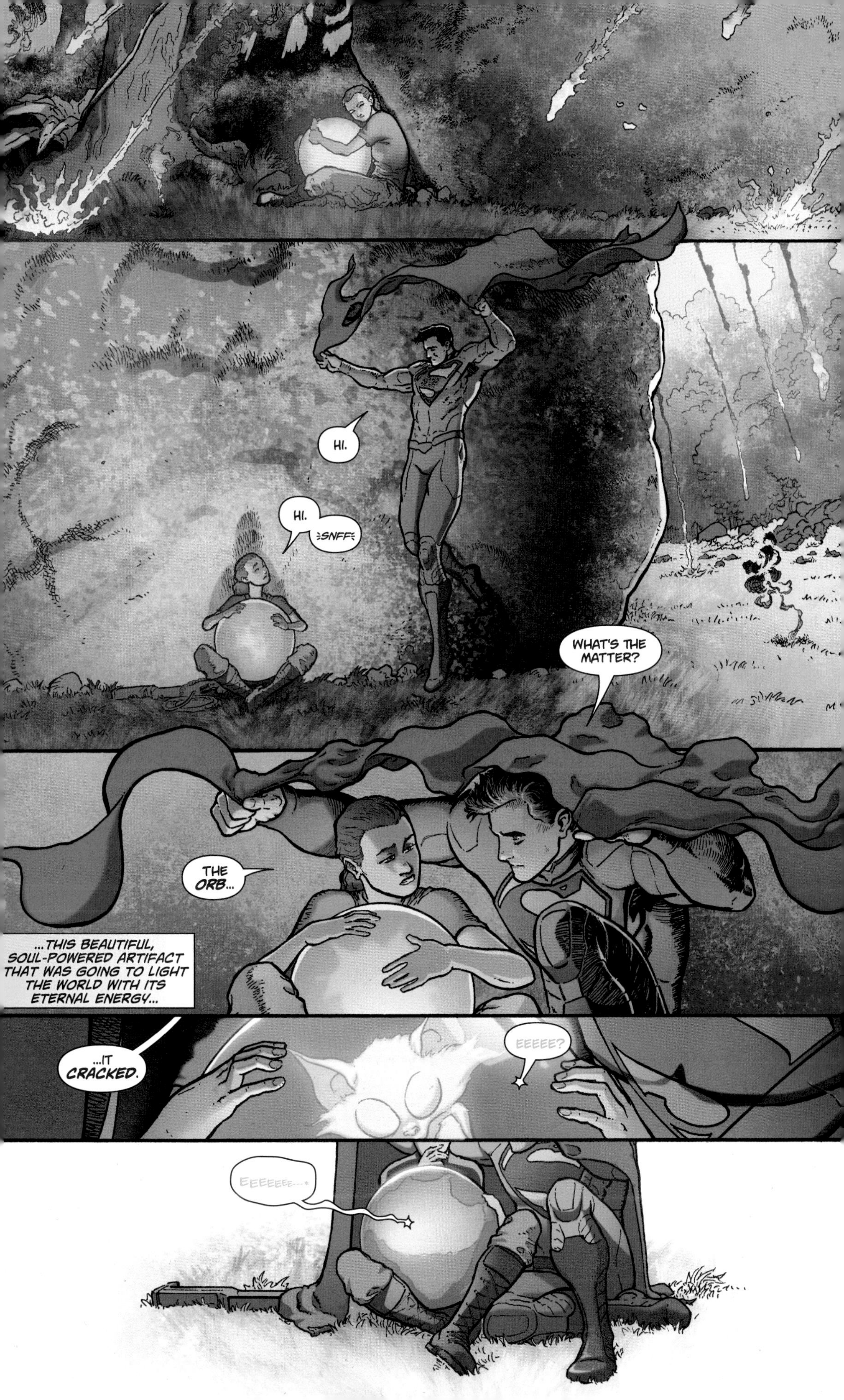
HI.
HI.
SNFF
WHAT'S THE MATTER?
THE ORB...
...THIS BEAUTIFUL, SOUL-POWERED ARTIFACT THAT WAS GOING TO LIGHT THE WORLD WITH ITS ETERNAL ENERGY...
...IT CRACKED.
EEEEE?
EEEEEEE...

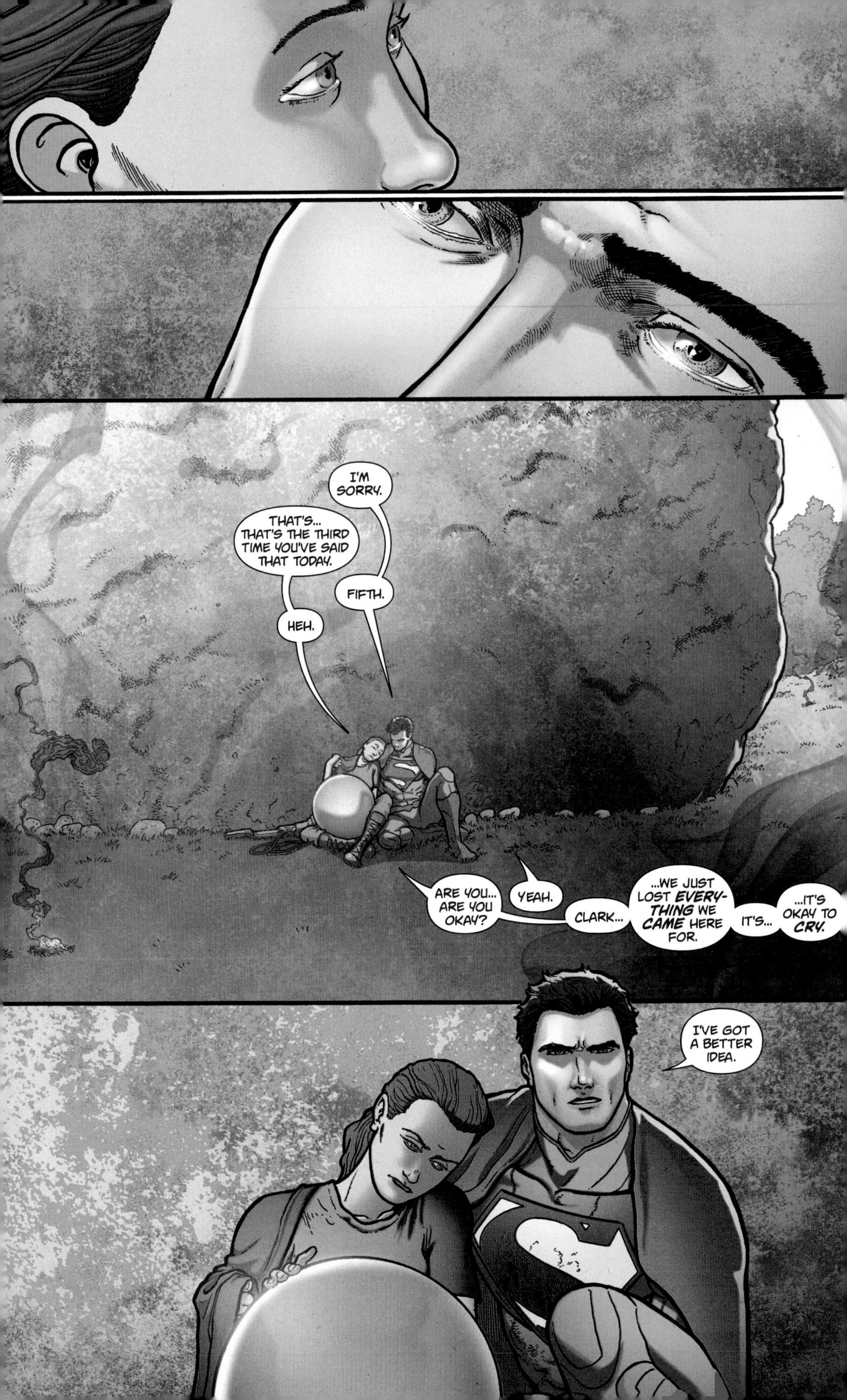
I'M SORRY.
THAT'S... THAT'S THE THIRD TIME YOU'VE SAID THAT TODAY.
FIFTH.
HEH.
ARE YOU... ARE YOU OKAY?
YEAH.
CLARK...
...WE JUST LOST EVERY-THING WE CAME HERE FOR.
IT'S...
...IT'S OKAY TO CRY.
I'VE GOT A BETTER IDEA.

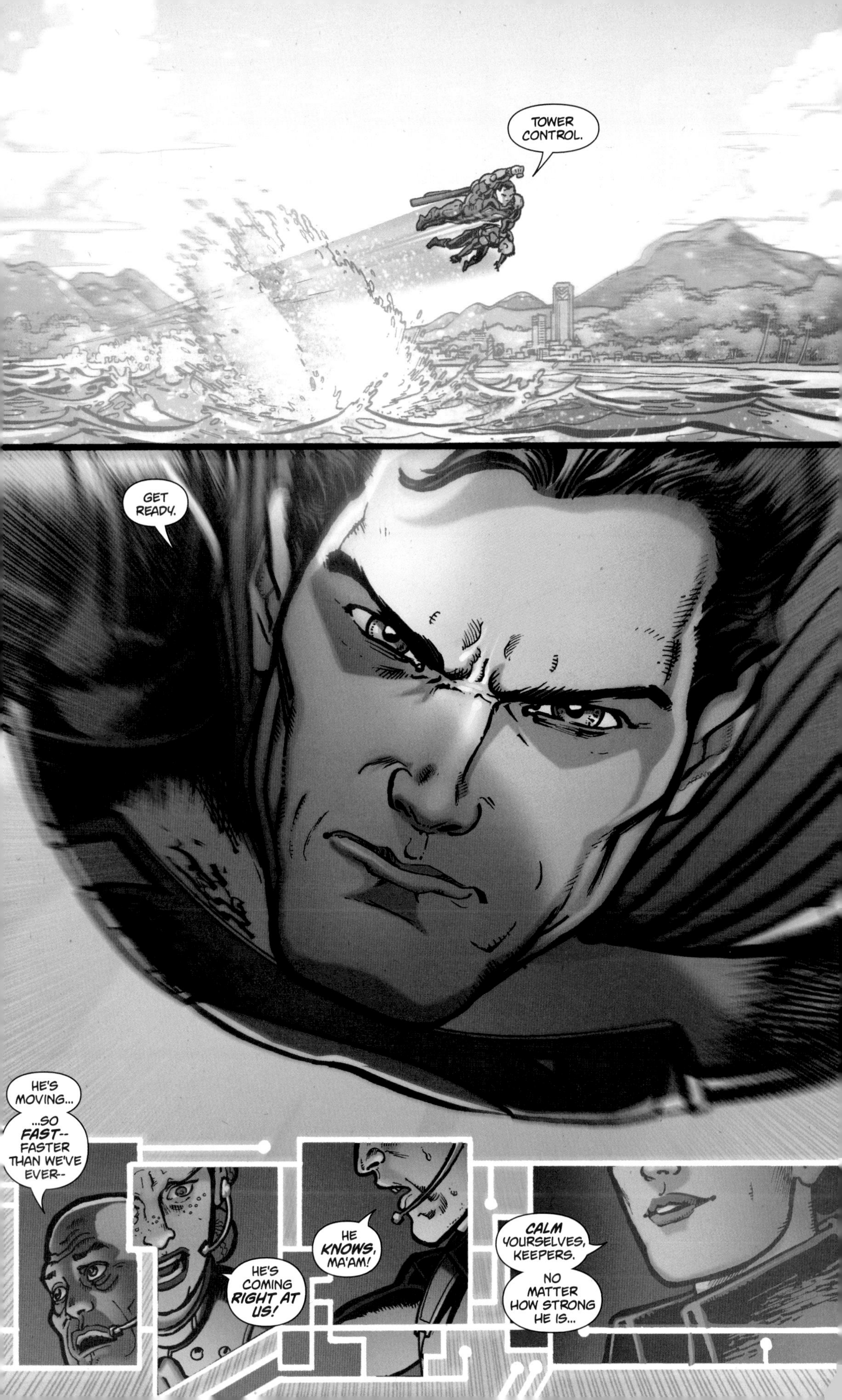
TOWER CONTROL.
GET READY.
HE'S MOVING... ...SO FAST--FASTER THAN WE'VE EVER--
HE'S COMING RIGHT AT US!
HE KNOWS, MA'AM!
CALM YOURSELVES, KEEPERS.
NO MATTER HOW STRONG HE IS...

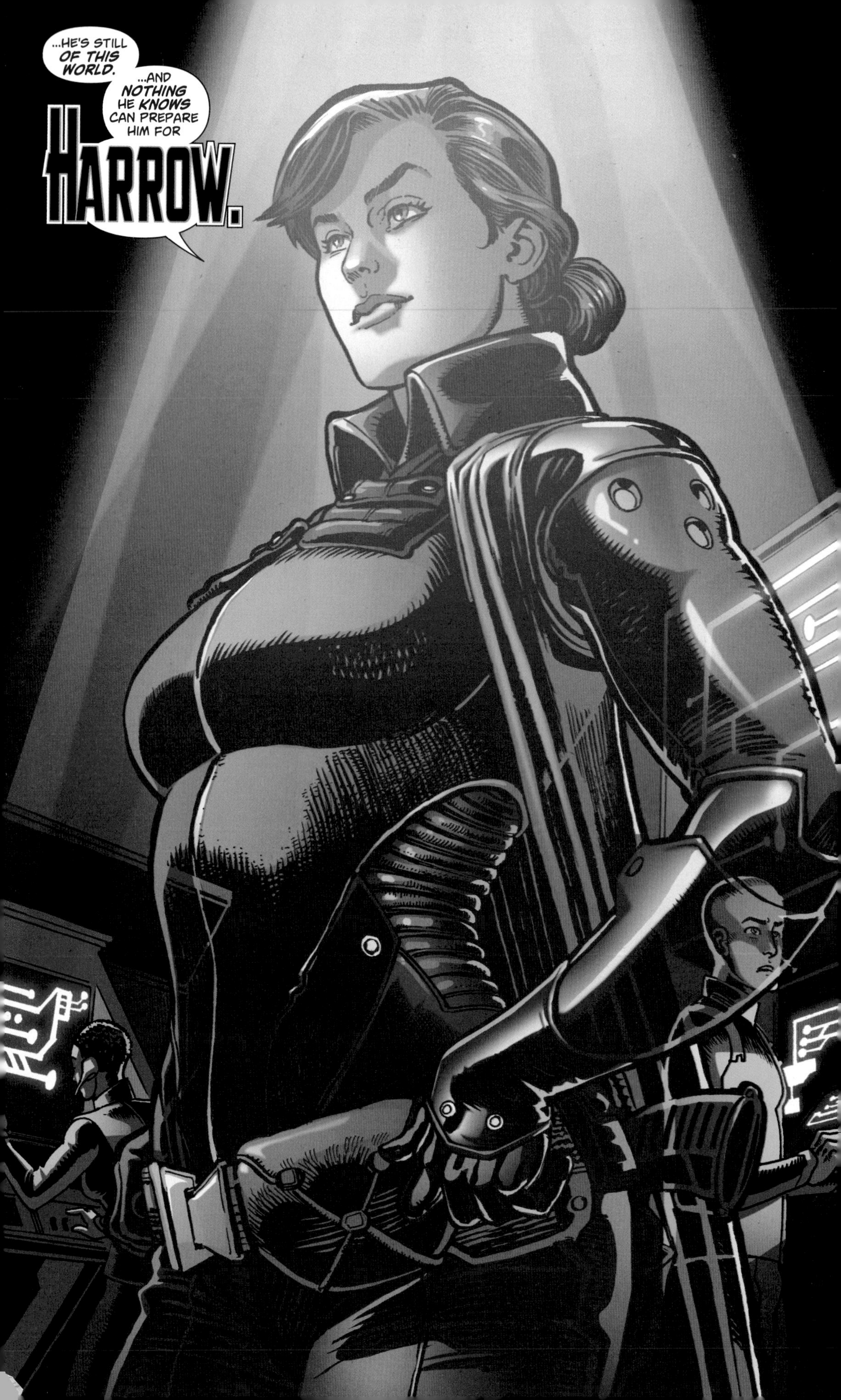
...HE'S STILL OF THIS WORLD.
...AND NOTHING HE KNOWS CAN PREPARE HIM FOR
HARROW.

ACTION COMICS #27

SCRIBBLENAUTS VARIANT COVER BY JON KATZ, AFTER JOE SHUSTER

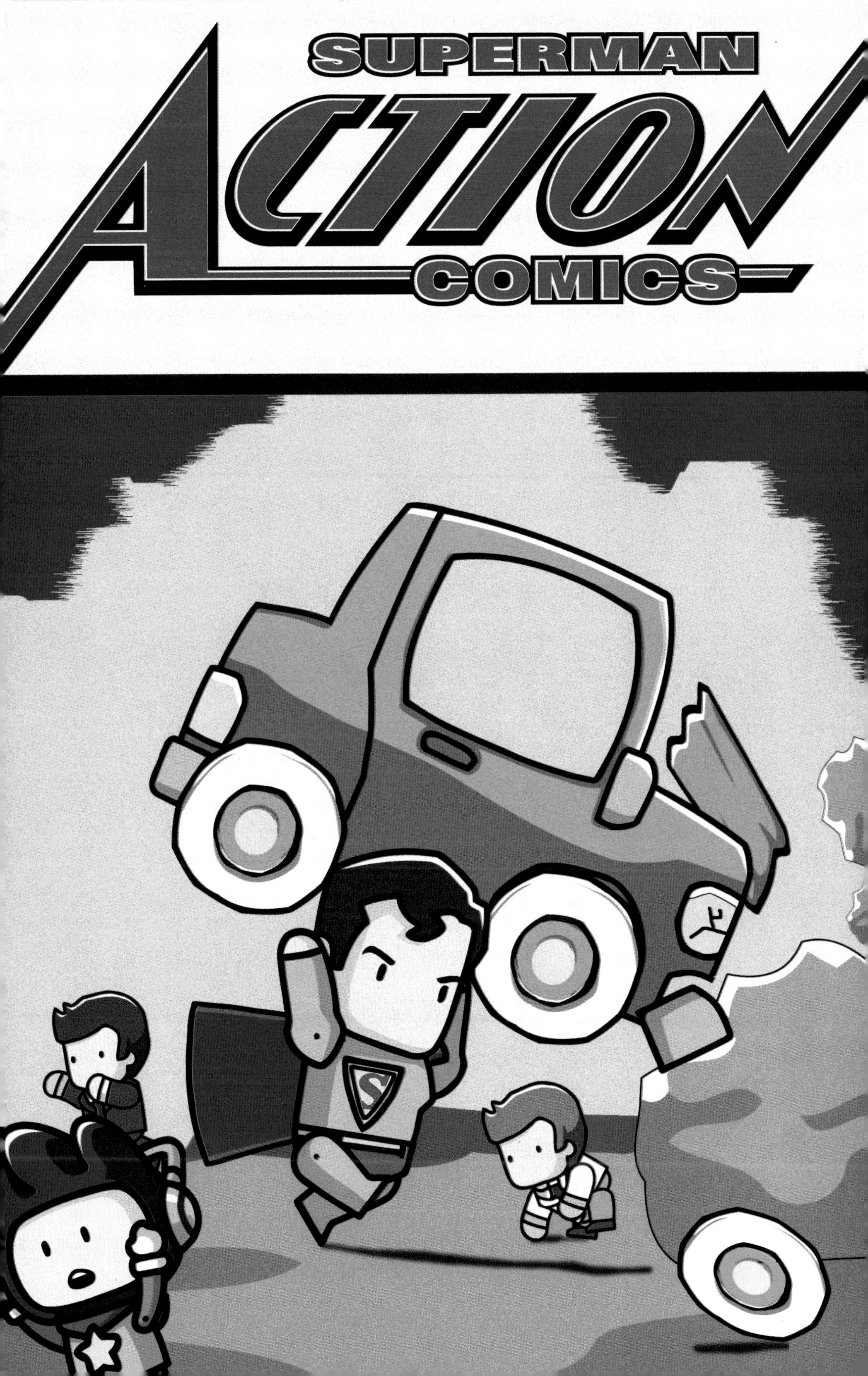
SUPERMAN
ACTION
COMICS

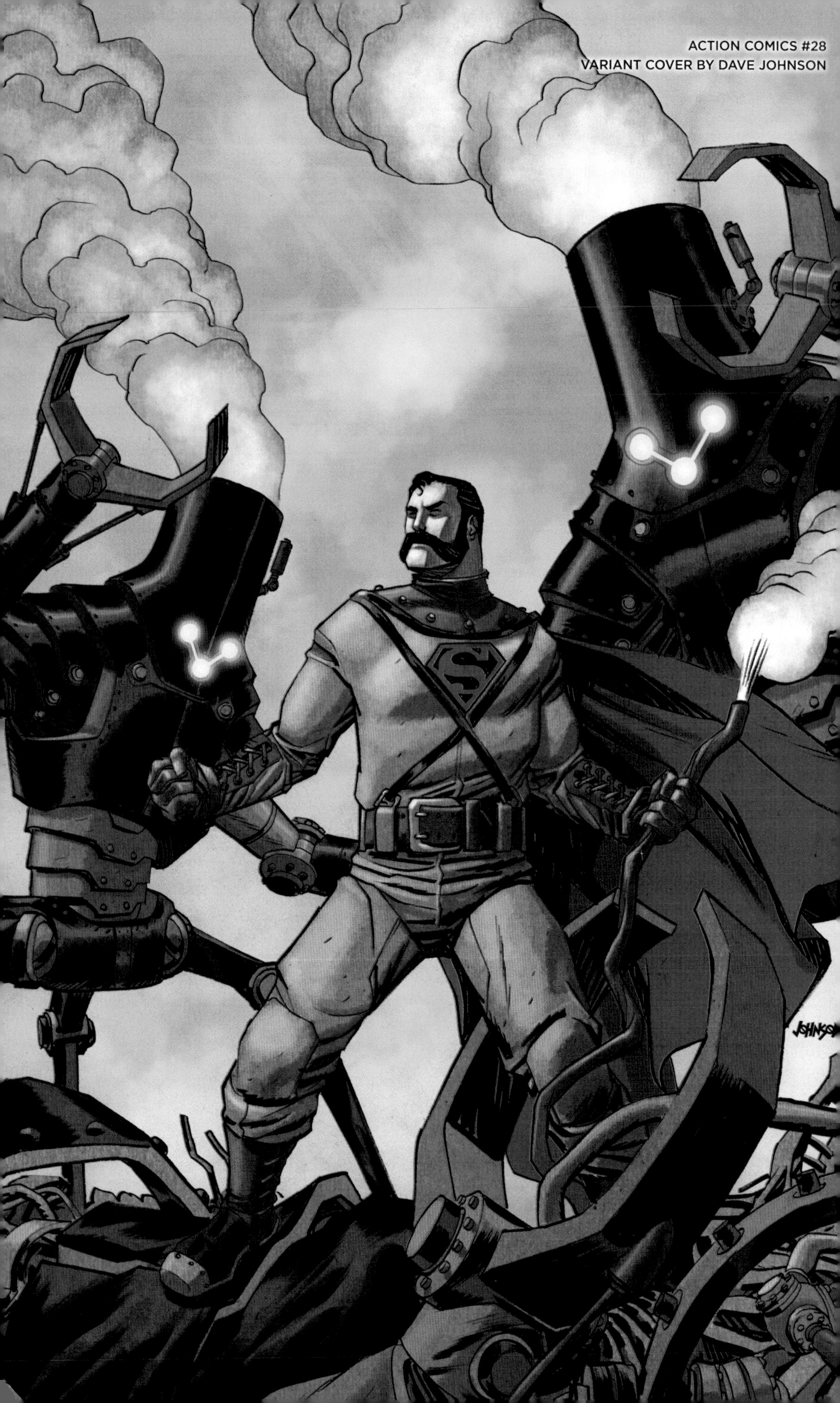

ACTION COMICS #28
VARIANT COVER BY DAVE JOHNSON

ACTION COMICS #29
ROBOT CHICKEN VARIANT COVER BY RC STOODIOS

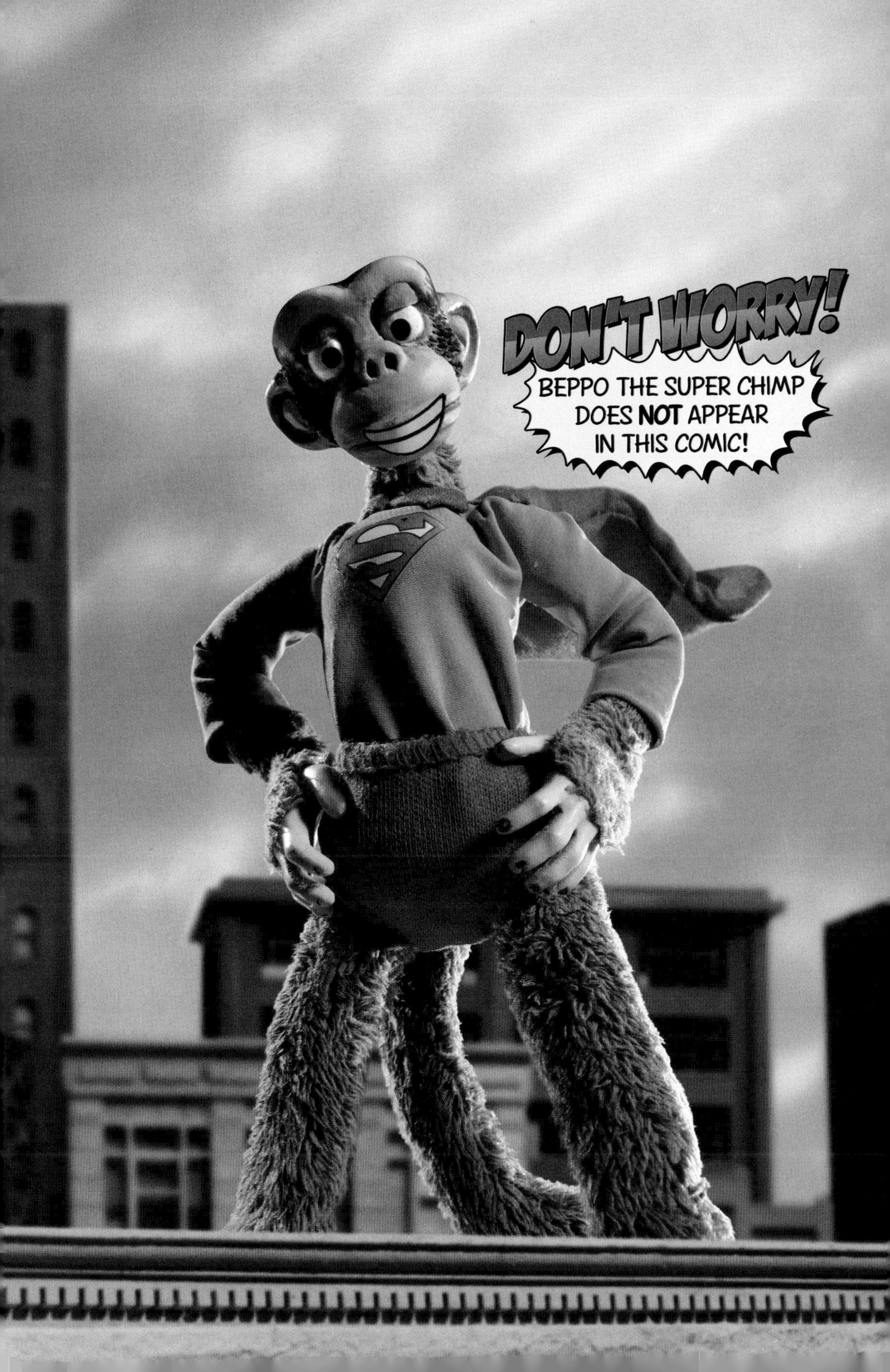
DON'T WORRY!
BEPPO THE SUPER CHIMP DOES **NOT** APPEAR IN THIS COMIC!

Beast Lord

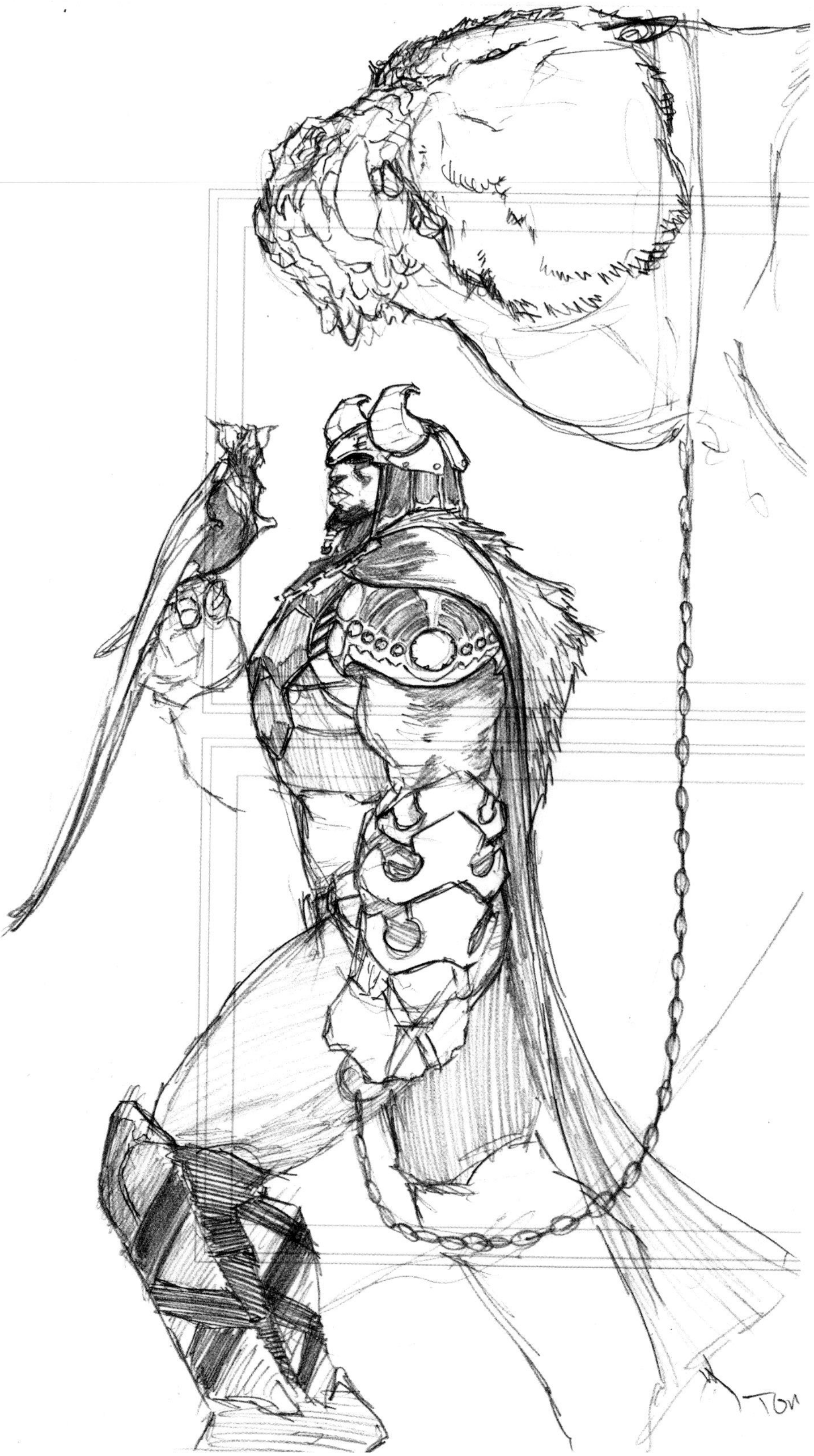

Early Beast Lord concept

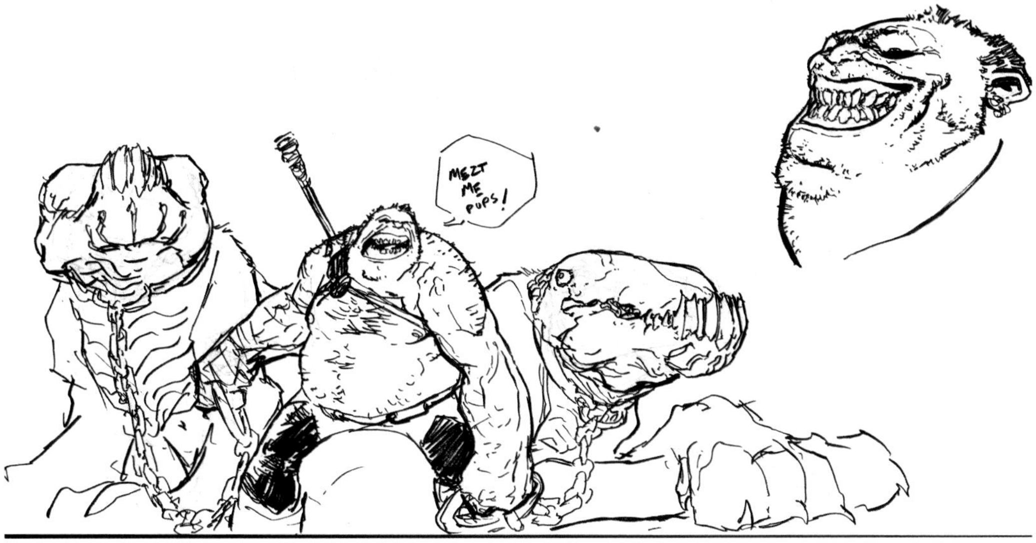
MEET ME PUPS!

Ghost soldier designs

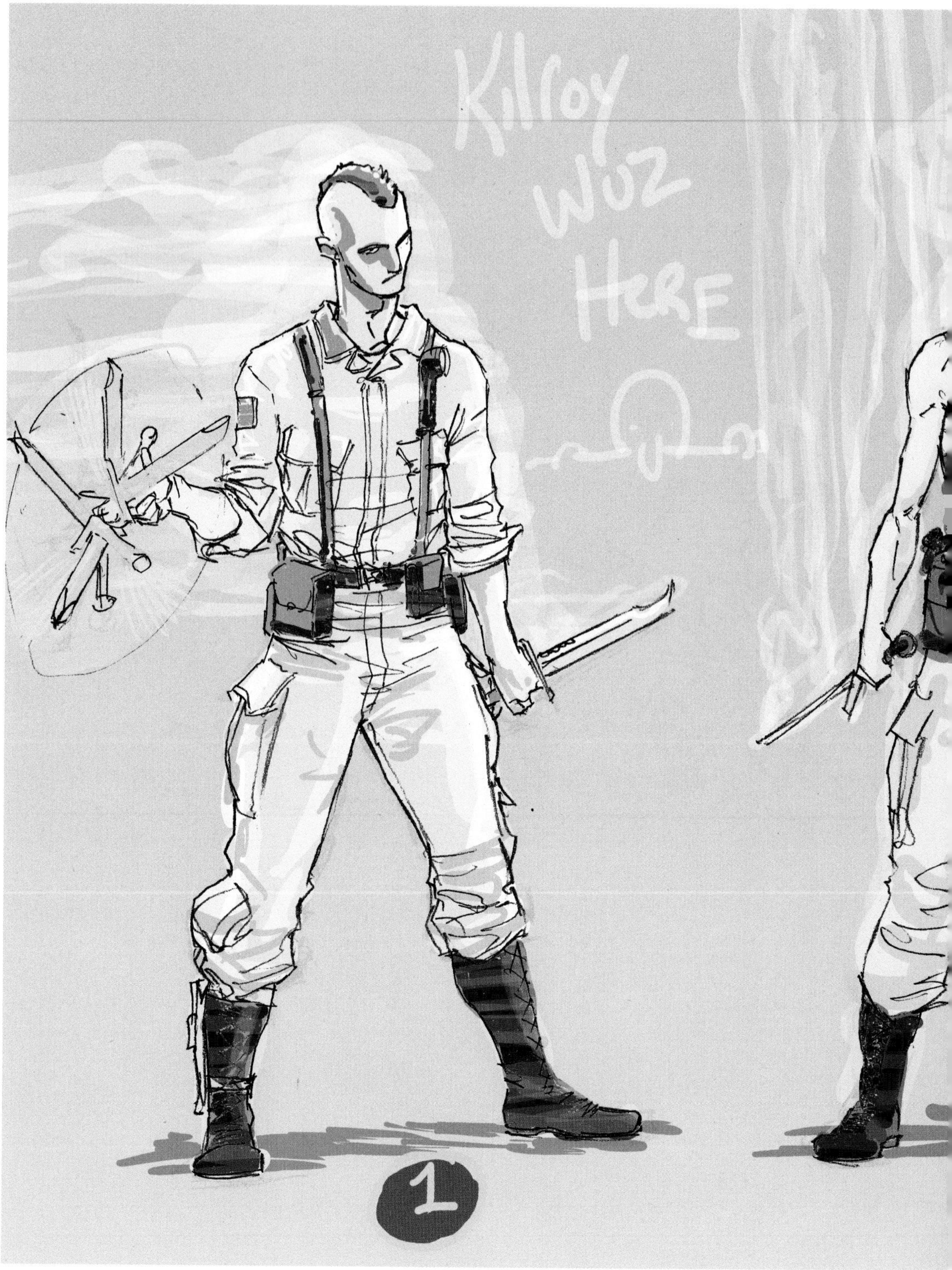
Kilroy
Wuz
Here
1

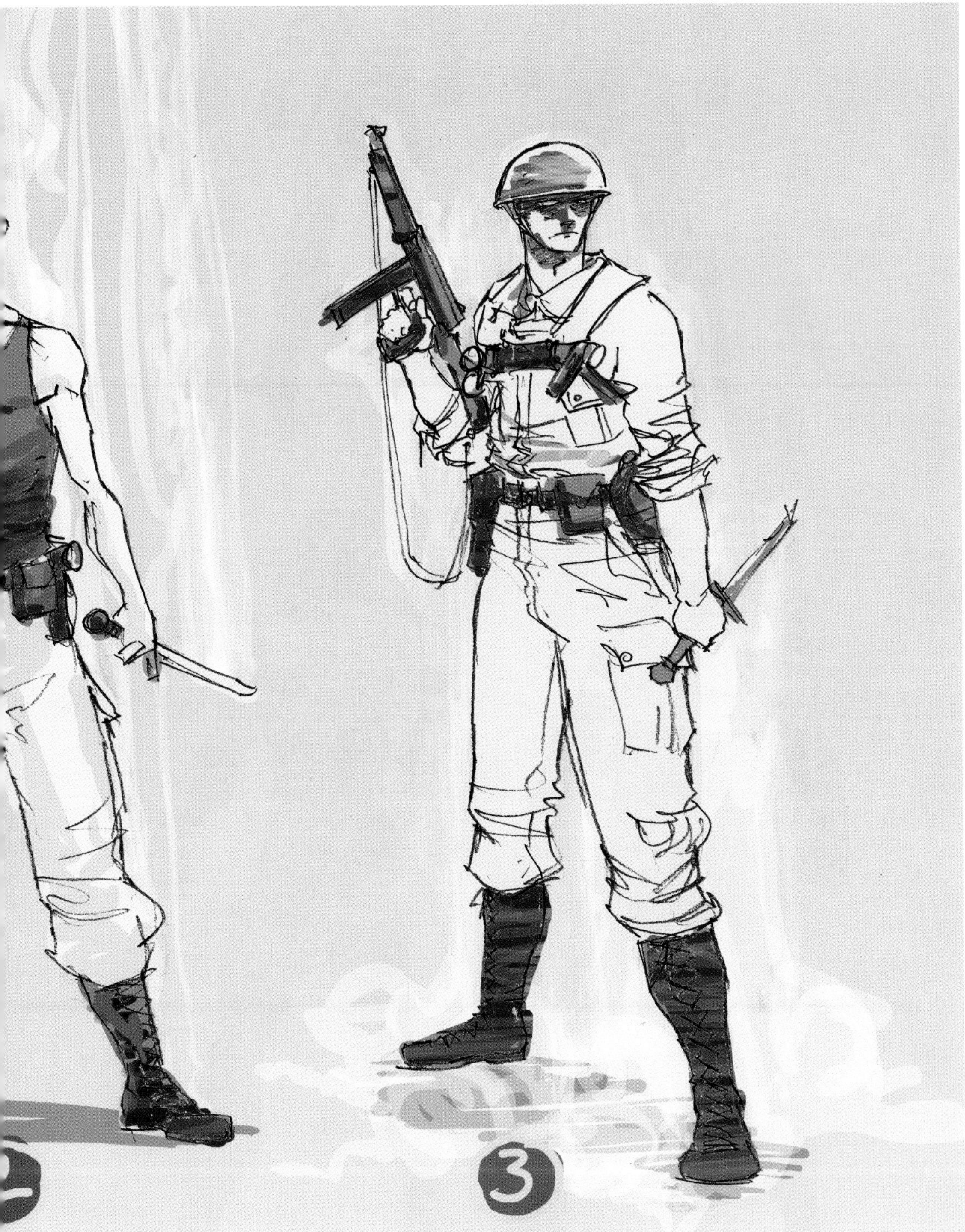
3

Soldier designs

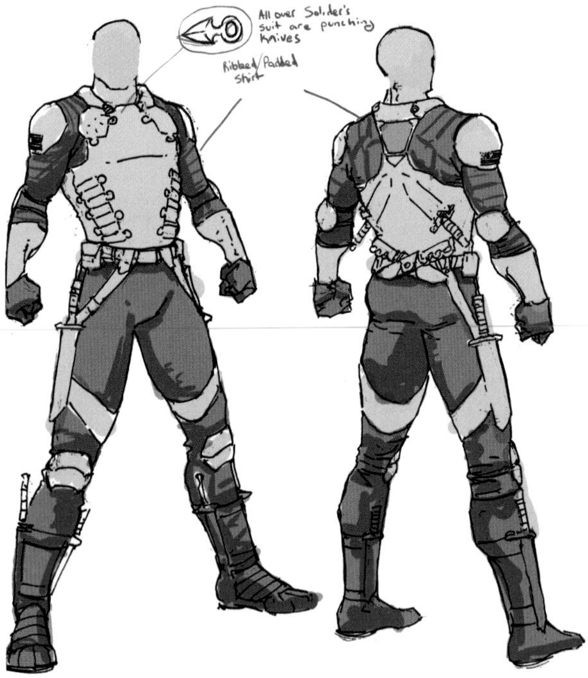
All over Solider's suit are punching knives
Ribbed/Padded Shirt

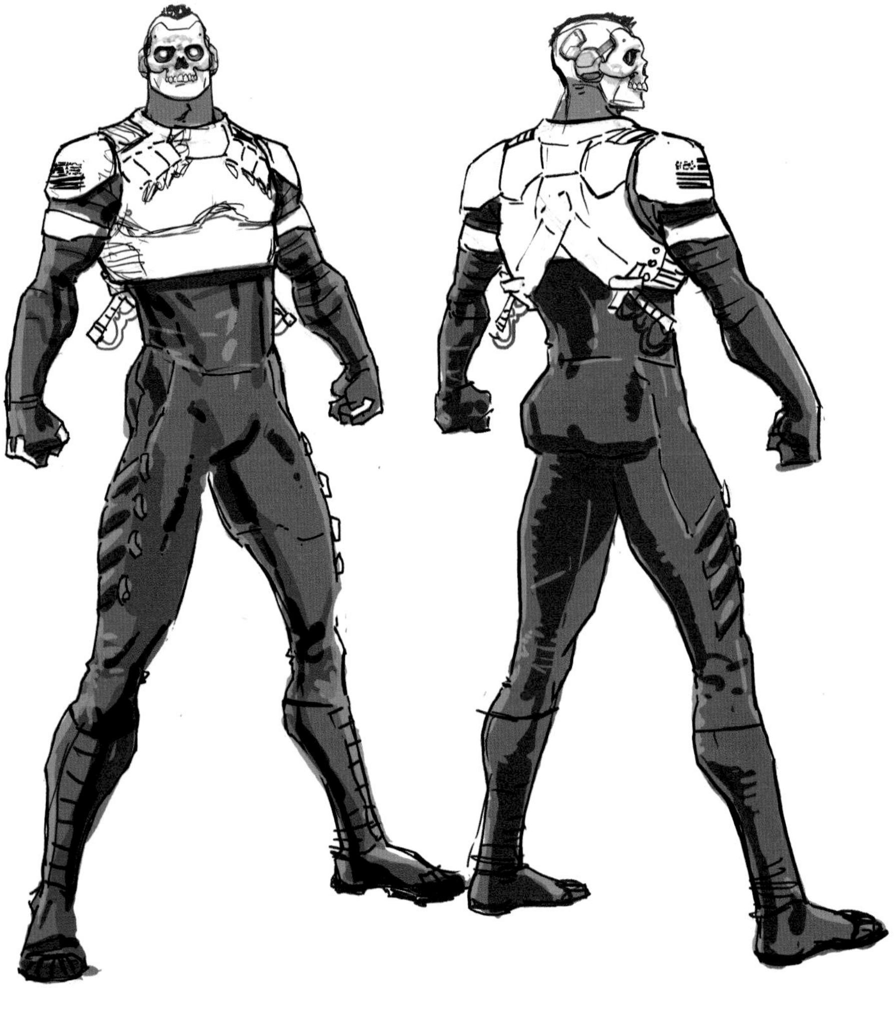

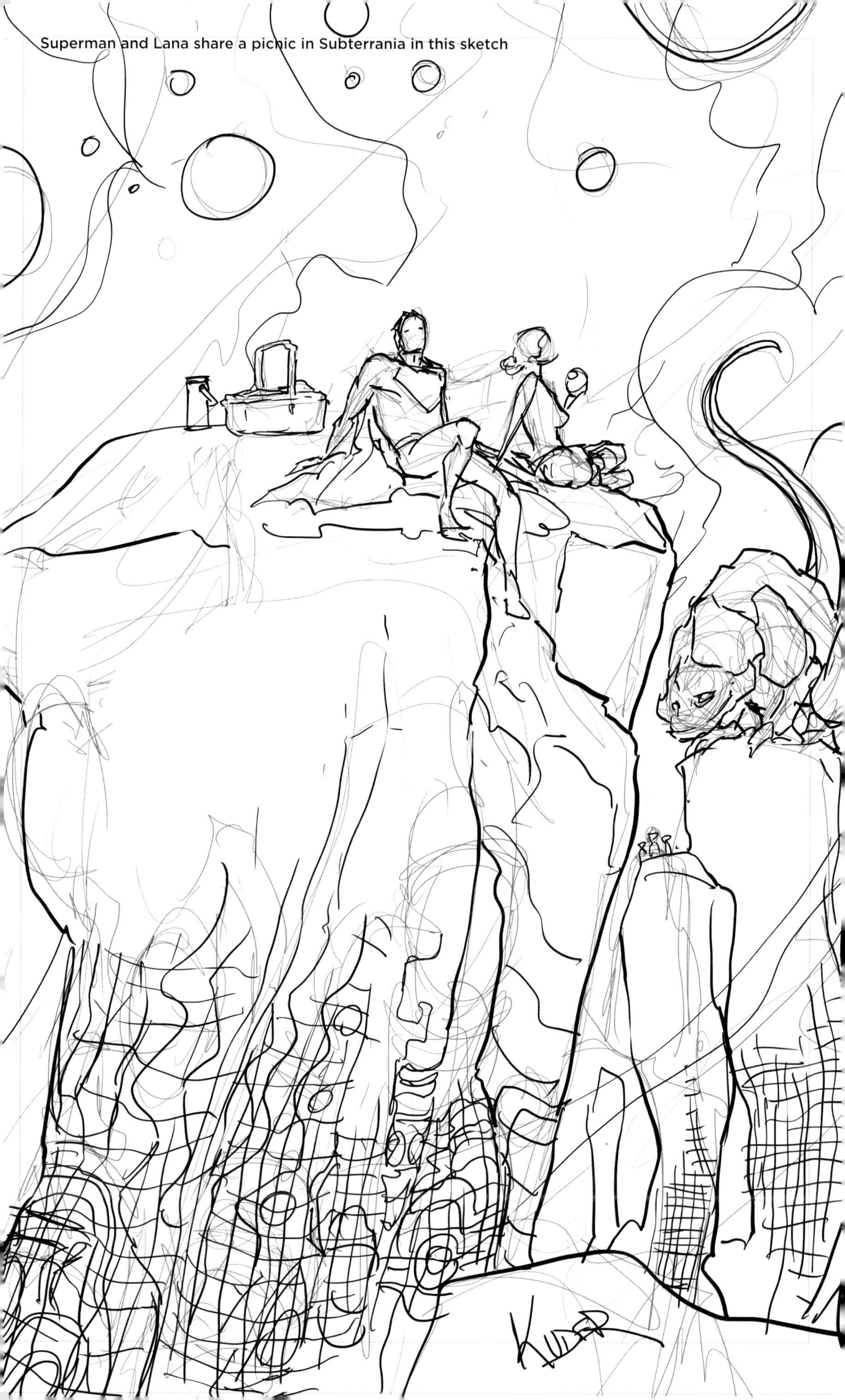

Superman and Lana share a picnic in Subterrania in this sketch

ACTION COMICS #27 page 15 rough sketches and final line art

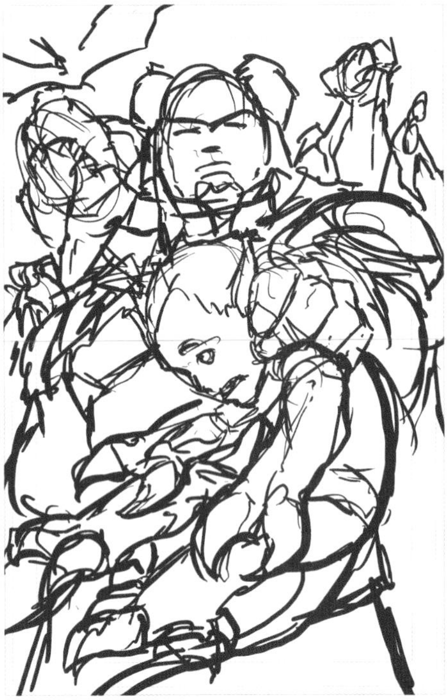

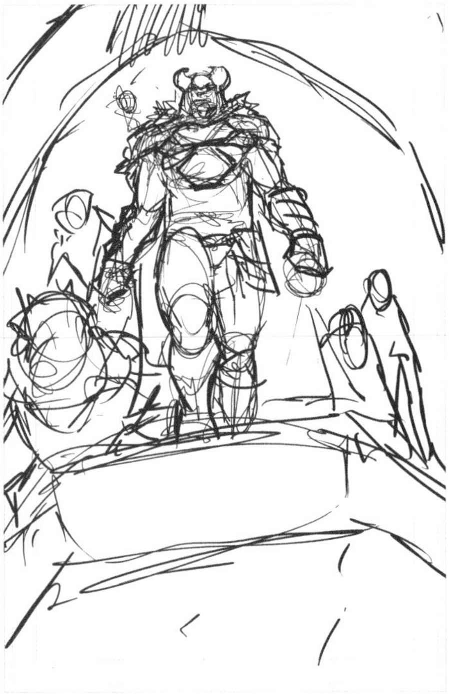

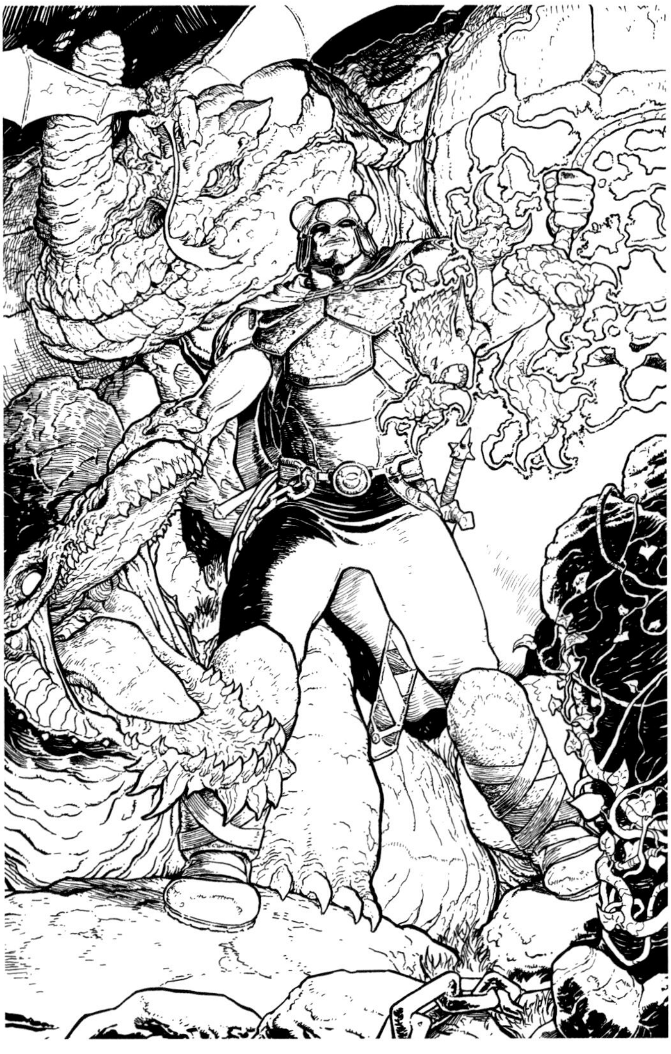

Rough artwork for ACTION COMICS #29 page 1

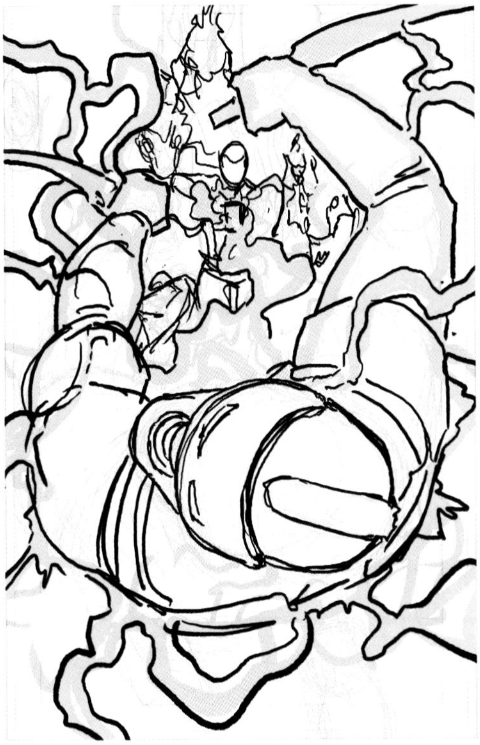

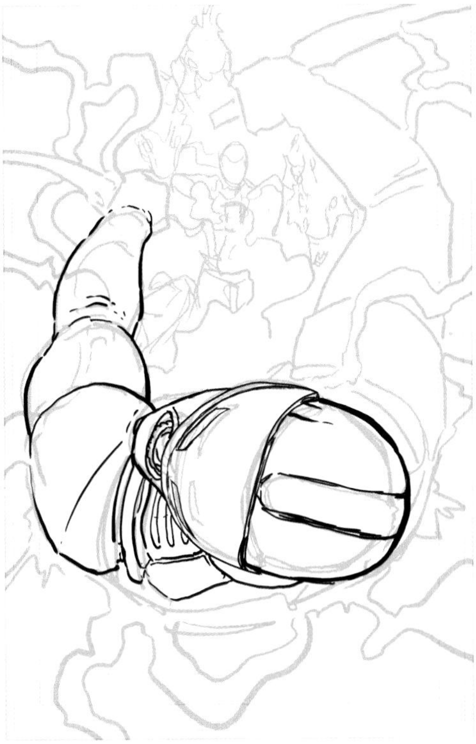

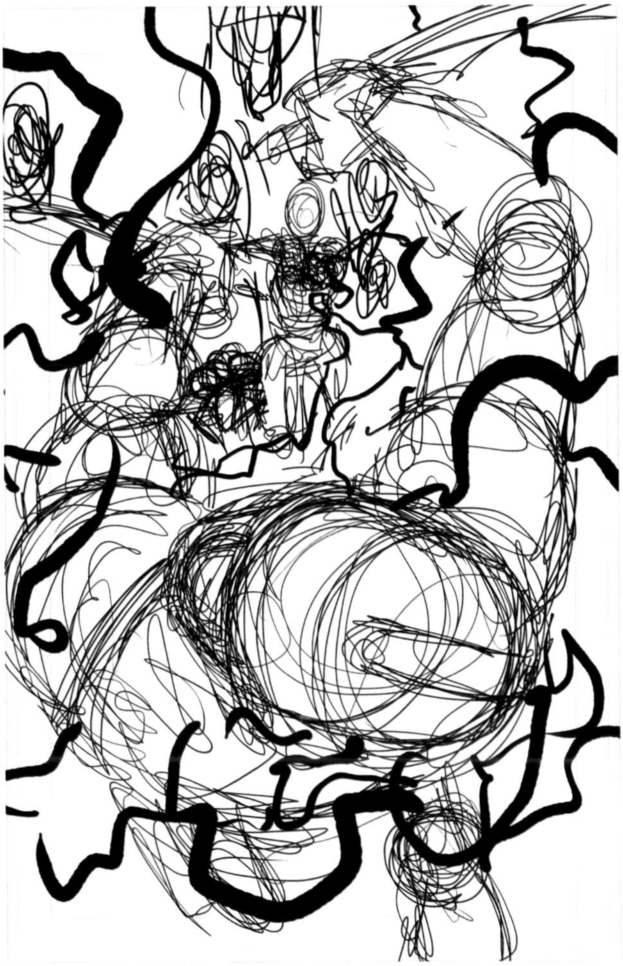

Rough artwork for ACTION COMICS #29 page 18

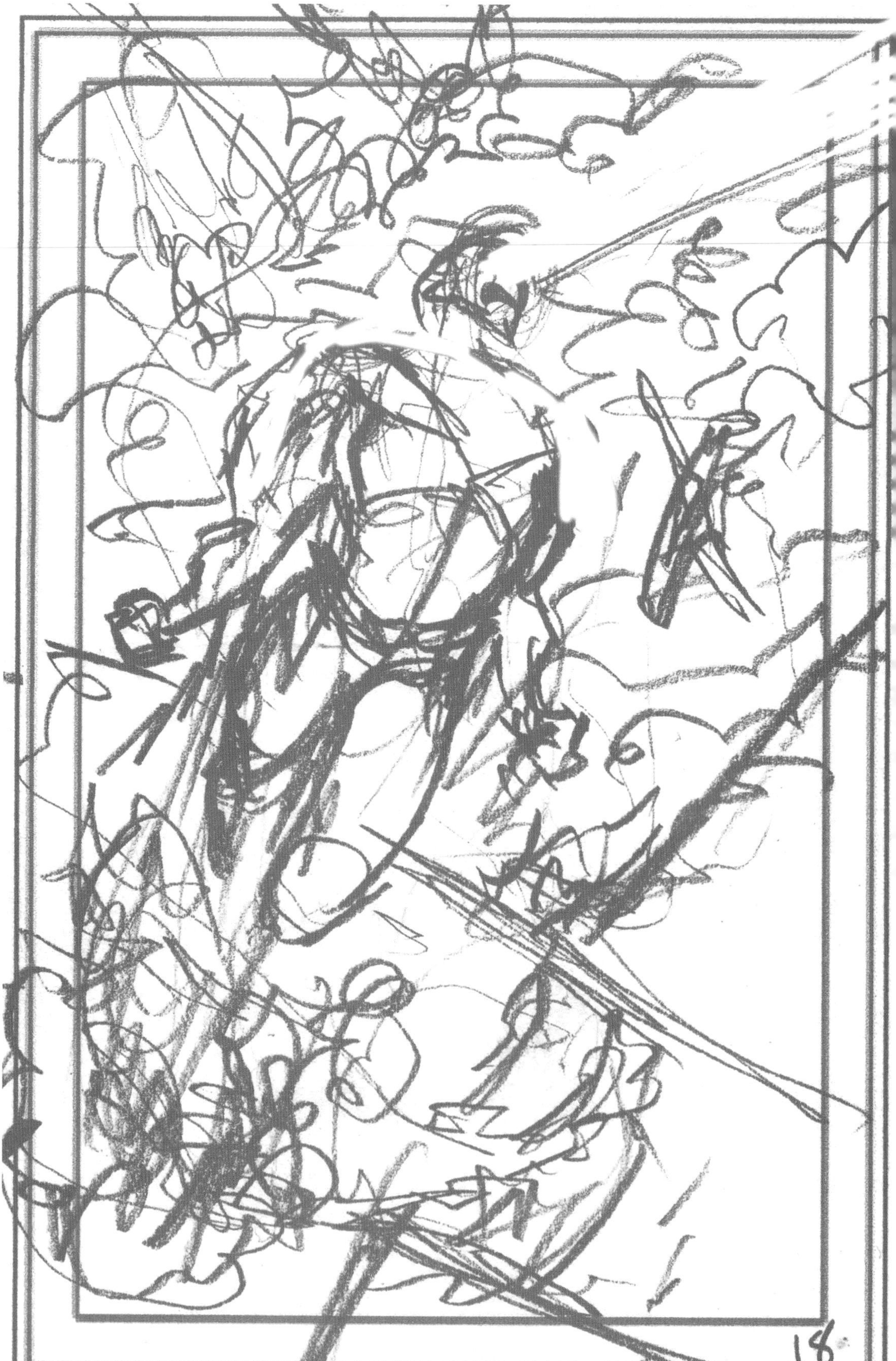
18

Cover concept for ACTION COMICS #27

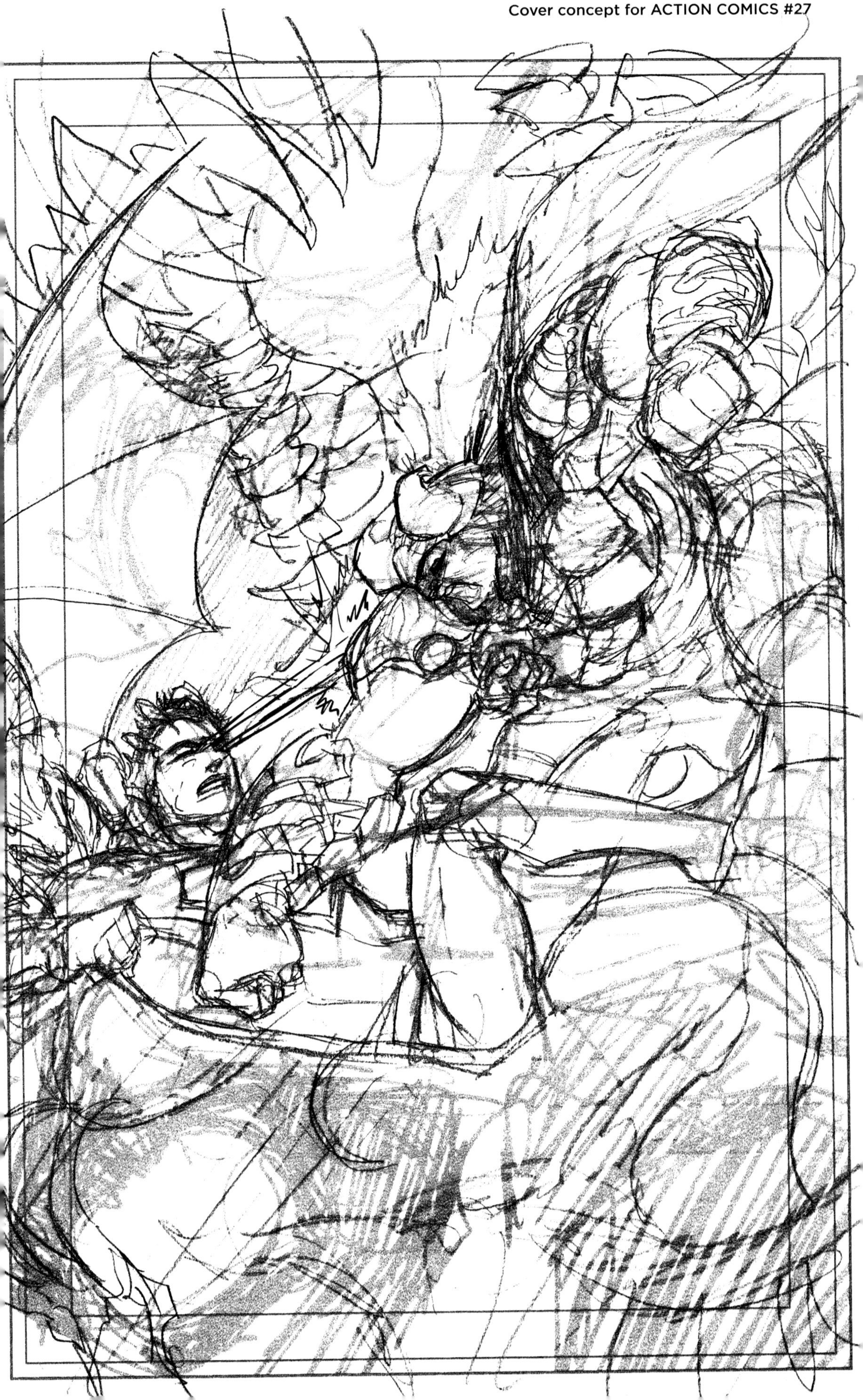

Cover concept for
ACTION COMICS #27

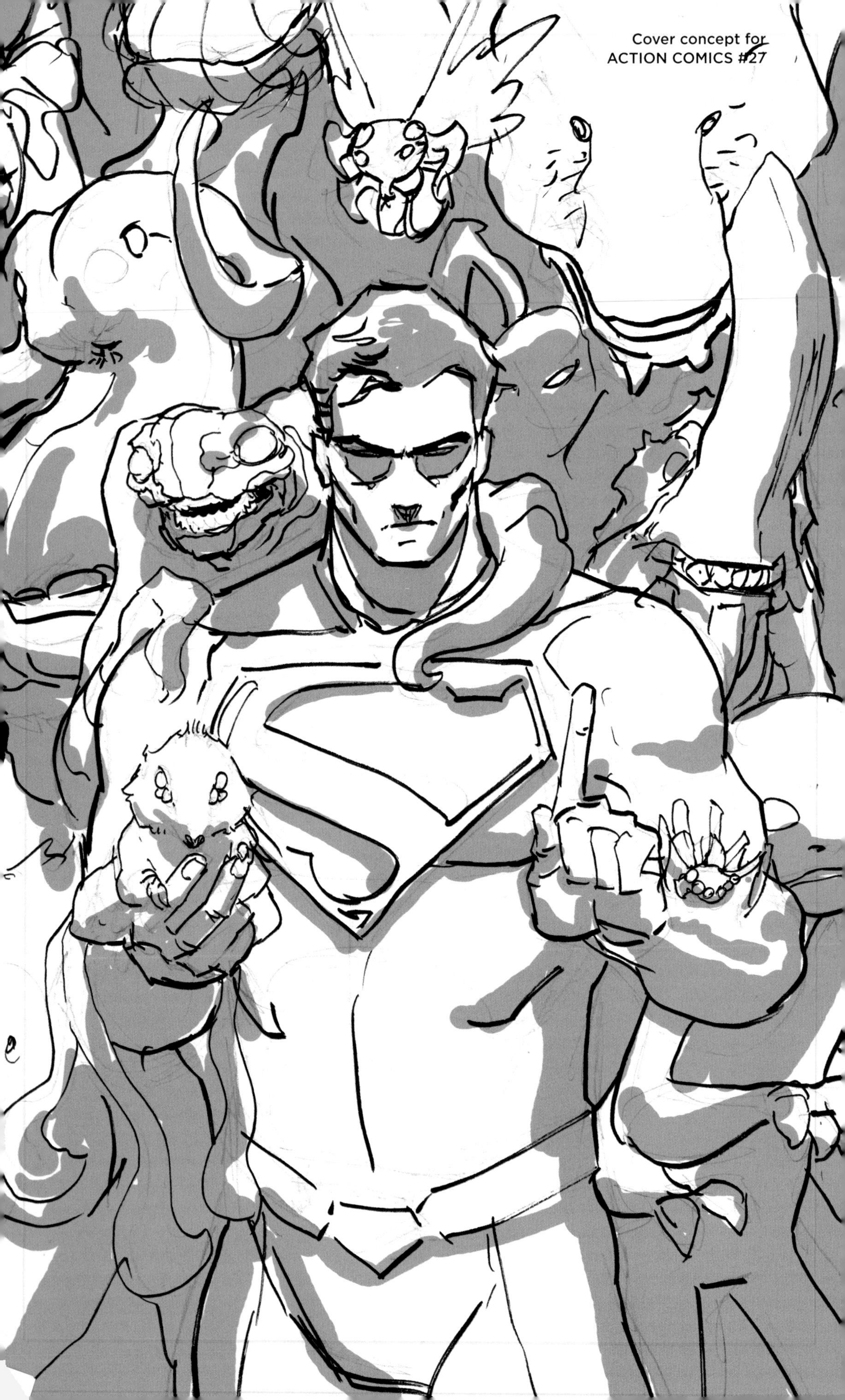

DC COMICS™

"ACTION COMICS has successfully carved its own territory and continued exploring Morrison's familiar themes about heroism and ideas."—IGN

"Casts the character in a new light, opens up fresh storytelling possibilities, and pushes it all forward with dynamic Rags Morales art. I loved it."—THE ONION/AV CLUB

START AT THE BEGINNING!

SUPERMAN: ACTION COMICS VOLUME 1: SUPERMAN AND THE MEN OF STEEL

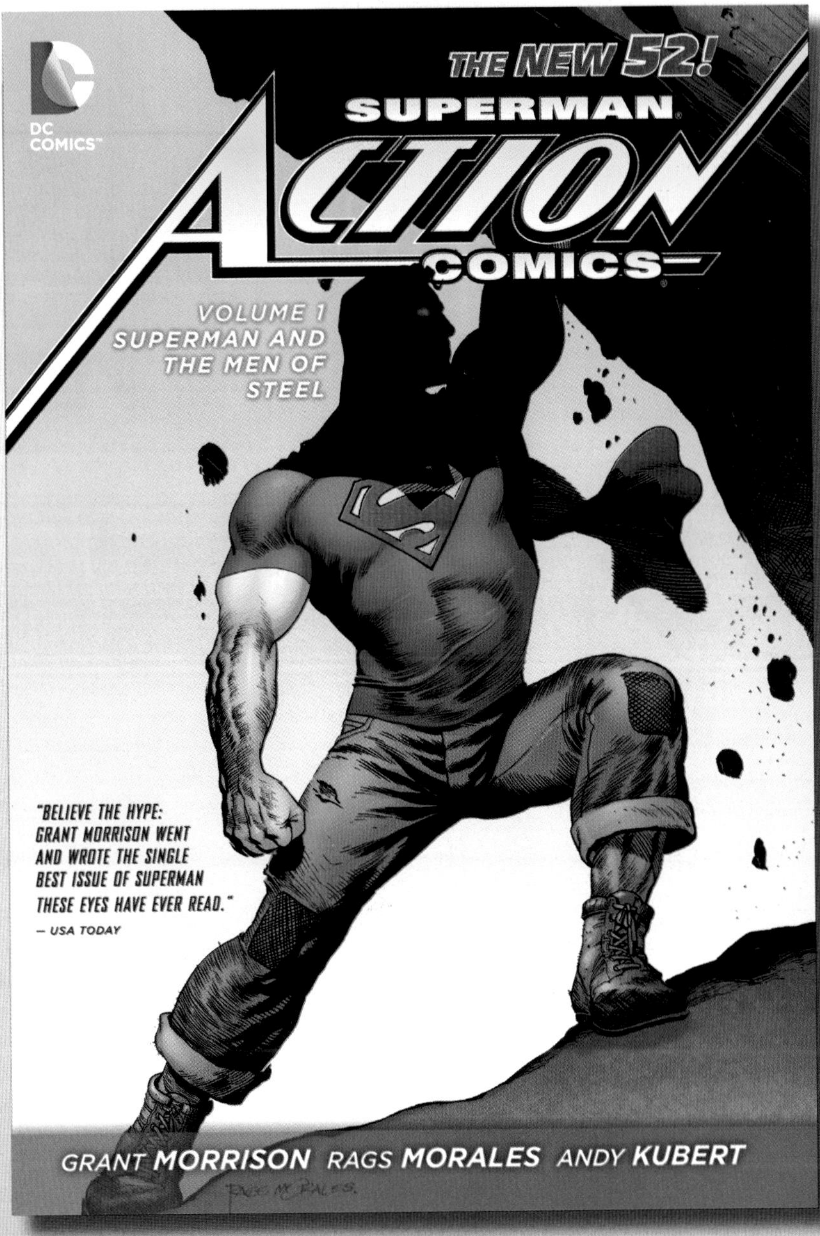

THE NEW 52!
SUPERMAN
ACTION
COMICS
VOLUME 1
SUPERMAN AND THE MEN OF STEEL
"BELIEVE THE HYPE: GRANT MORRISON WENT AND WROTE THE SINGLE BEST ISSUE OF SUPERMAN THESE EYES HAVE EVER READ."
— USA TODAY
GRANT MORRISON RAGS MORALES ANDY KUBERT

SUPERMAN: ACTION COMICS VOL. 2: BULLETPROOF

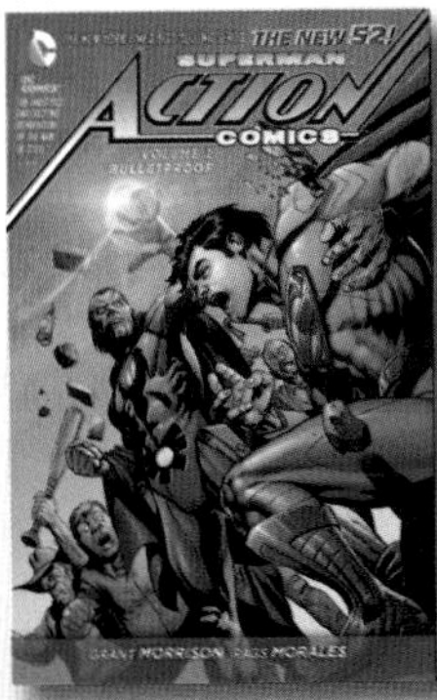

THE NEW 52!
SUPERMAN
ACTION
COMICS
GRANT MORRISON RAGS MORALES

with GRANT MORRISON and RAGS MORALES

SUPERMAN: ACTION COMICS VOL. 3: AT THE END OF DAYS

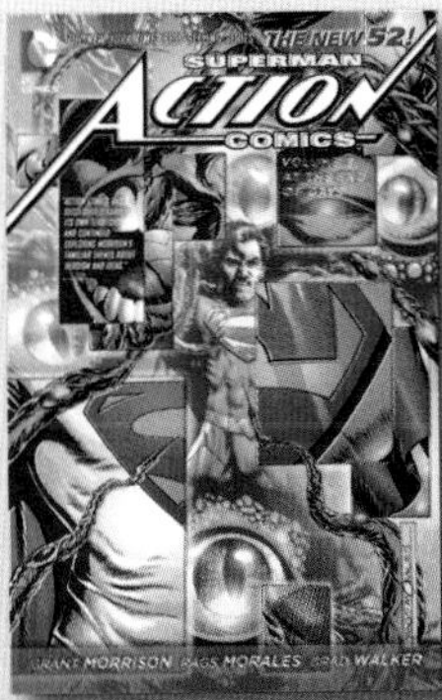

THE NEW 52!
SUPERMAN
ACTION
COMICS
GRANT MORRISON RAGS MORALES BRAD WALKER

with GRANT MORRISON and RAGS MORALES

SUPERBOY VOL. 1: INCUBATION

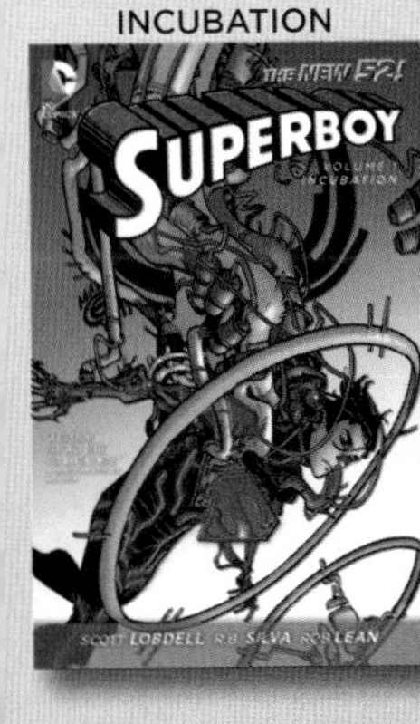

THE NEW 52!
SUPERBOY
SCOTT LOBDELL R.B. SILVA ROB LEAN

DC COMICS™

"Excellent...From its poignant domestic moments, delivered in mostly warm, fuzzy flashbacks, to its block-buster battles, Straczynski's SUPERMAN: EARTH ONE renders like a feature film just waiting for adaptation."
—WIRED

FROM *THE NEW YORK TIMES* #1 BEST-SELLING AUTHOR

J. MICHAEL STRACZYNSKI

with SHANE DAVIS

SUPERMAN EARTH ONE: VOL. 2

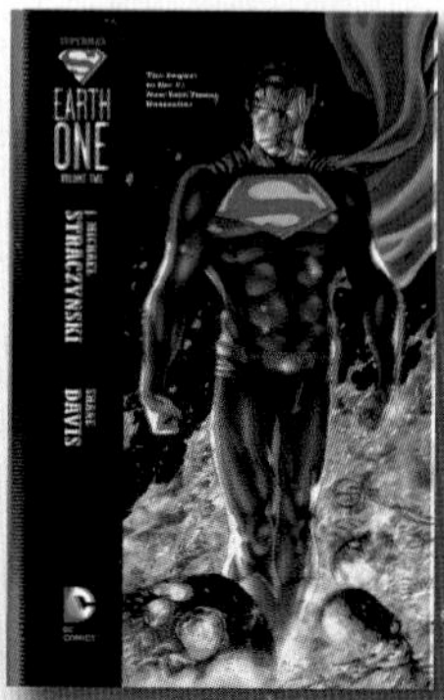
EARTH ONE
J. MICHAEL STRACZYNSKI
SHANE DAVIS

with SHANE DAVIS

SUPERMAN: GROUNDED VOLS. 1-2

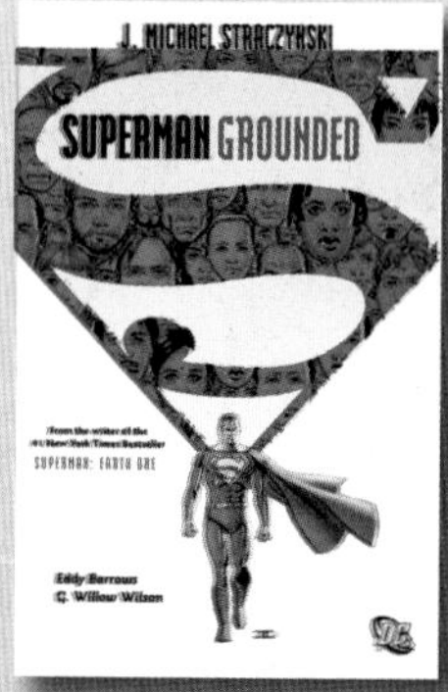
J. MICHAEL STRACZYNSKI
SUPERMAN GROUNDED

with EDDY BARROWS

WONDER WOMAN: ODYSSEY VOLS. 1-2

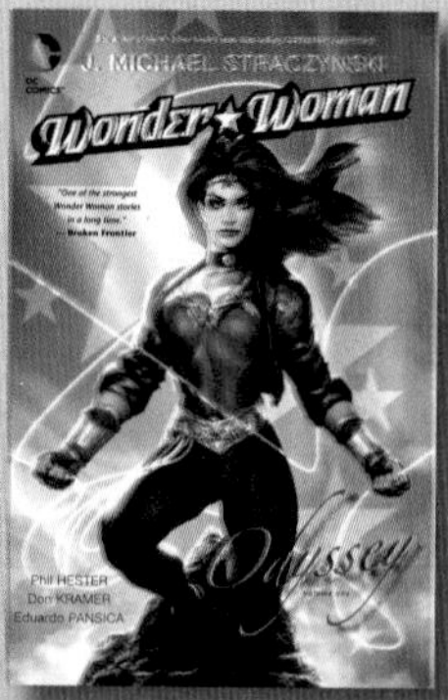
J. MICHAEL STRACZYNSKI
Wonder Woman
Odyssey

with DON KRAMER and PHIL HESTER

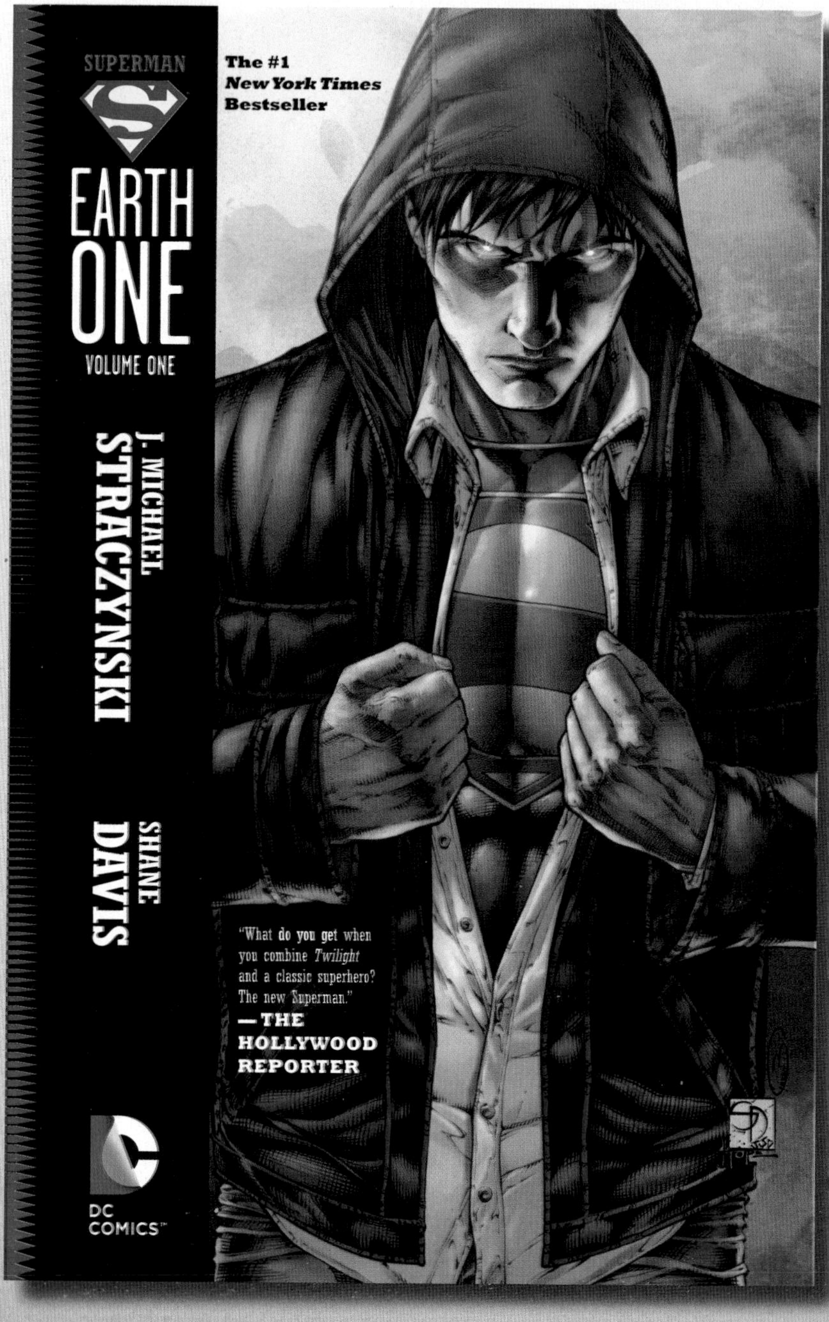
SUPERMAN
EARTH ONE
VOLUME ONE
J. MICHAEL STRACZYNSKI
SHANE DAVIS
DC COMICS™
The #1 New York Times Bestseller
"What do you get when you combine Twilight and a classic superhero? The new Superman."
—THE HOLLYWOOD REPORTER